*Law and Literature*

# LAW AND LITERATURE

## A Misunderstood Relation

RICHARD A. POSNER

HARVARD UNIVERSITY PRESS
*Cambridge, Massachusetts, and London, England*

Excerpts from "Easter 1916," "The Second Coming," "The Wild Swans at Coole," and "Leda and the Swan" by William Butler Yeats are reprinted from W. B. Yeats, *The Poems: A New Edition*, ed. Richard J. Finneran (New York: Macmillan, 1983) by permission of Macmillan Publishing Company, copyright 1919, 1924, and 1928 by Macmillan Publishing Company, renewed 1947 and 1952 by Bertha Georgie Yeats and 1956 by Georgie Yeats; and of A. P. Watt Ltd. on behalf of Michael B. Yeats and Macmillan London Ltd.

Excerpts from "The Love Song of J. Alfred Prufrock," "The Waste Land," and "Burnt Norton" by T. S. Eliot are reprinted from T. S. Eliot, *Collected Poems 1909–1962* (London: Faber & Faber, 1962) and *Four Quartets* (London: Faber & Faber, 1944) by permission of Faber and Faber Ltd. and Harcourt Brace Jovanovich, Inc.

The excerpt from *The Sweeniad* by Victor Purcell is reprinted by permission of Unwin Hyman Limited.

This book is printed on acid-free paper, and its binding materials have been chosen for strength and durability.

*Library of Congress Cataloging-in-Publication Data*

Posner, Richard A.
  Law and literature.

  Includes index.
  1. Law—Interpretation and criticism.   2. Law and
literature.   I. Title.
K290.P67   1988        340        88-11210
ISBN 0-674-51468-8 (alk. paper)

*Designed by Gwen Frankfeldt*

*For my mother, who initiated me into the pleasures of literature,
and my father, who encouraged me to go to law school*

# Contents

*Preface*

ECENT years have seen the rapid growth of the field of inquiry known as law and literature, whose practitioners seek to apply the methods of legal analysis to literary texts and the methods of literary analysis to legal texts, and in other ways to explore the interrelations between these ancient fields of learning. Literary critics are beginning to join law faculties; five books on law and literature have appeared since 1984 (they are cited in the Introduction and discussed in subsequent chapters); and the continuing spate of articles includes one by no less a public figure than the Solicitor General of the United States. See Charles Fried, "Sonnet LXV and the 'Black Ink' of the Framers' Intention," 100 *Harvard Law Review* 751 (1987), discussed in Chapter 5.

Although my own love of literature goes back to early childhood, and I am a great believer in interdisciplinary legal studies (notably, economic analysis of law, which figures in this book as well), I took no interest in the law and literature movement until one of its members used the fiction of Franz Kafka as a fulcrum for criticizing some of my academic writings. See Robin West, "Authority, Autonomy, and Choice: The Role of Consent in the Moral and Political Visions of Franz Kafka and Richard Posner," 99 *Harvard Law Review* 384 (1985). Later I realized that, like Molière's character who had spoken prose all his life without knowing it, I had contributed to the field of law and literature without knowing it. See "The Homeric Version of the Minimal State," 90 *Ethics* 27 (1979), and "Retribution and Related Concepts of Punishment," 9 *Journal of Legal Studies* 71 (1980), both reprinted in my book *The Economics of Justice* (1981), chapters 5, 8.

Not only is the field of law and literature interesting in its own right, but it illustrates an important trend in legal teaching and research. It is part of the expanding enterprise in academic law that is sometimes called "legal theory" to distinguish it from conventional law teaching and scholarship, which focus on the nuts and bolts of legal reasoning, doctrine, and practice. The main effort of legal theory is to connect law to other disciplines, such as economics and political philosophy—and now literary theory and literary criticism. Through study of the law and literature movement one can gain a better sense of the promise and pitfalls of interdisciplinary legal studies generally.

This book, the first to attempt a general survey and evaluation of the field of law and literature, seeks to organize, augment, and redirect (hence the slightly combative subtitle) scholarship in the field. The book combines theoretical discussions of such matters as the nature and survival of literature, how law gets refracted in a literary medium, the relationship between law and justice, the role of authors' intentions in the interpretation of legislative and literary texts, and the place of literary style and literary values in judicial opinions, with close and I hope to some degree fresh readings of works by Homer, Aeschylus, Sophocles, Shakespeare, Marlowe, Kleist, Dickens, Dostoevsky, Melville, Twain, Kafka, Camus, Yeats, and others, as well as of some statutes, constitutional provisions, and judicial opinions, punctuated by comparisons between my approach and approaches taken by others who have written on law and literature. The general subjects covered are literature on legal themes, analyzed both as a stimulus for jurisprudential reflection and as a possible subject for literary criticism informed by legal knowledge; the application of literary theory and practice to legislative and judicial texts and to legal advocacy; and the regulation of literature by law.

Although critical of some of the previous approaches to law and literature, and skeptical about the more extravagant claims that have been made for the movement's potential to expand our knowledge of both areas, I consider it a promising extension of traditional legal scholarship and teaching and one that deserves to have a secure place in the legal academy. And not only there. It ought to interest teachers and students of literature, as well as of law; college students trying to decide whether to go to law school, and if so what to study in college by way of preparation; practicing lawyers (including judges), whose morale and perspective might be improved through recognition of the continuity and overlap between law and literature; and indeed any person who is interested, whether as scholar or informed citizen, in the intersection of the political and cultural spheres.

I THANK the copyright holders for permission to reprint portions of three of my articles: "The Ethical Significance of Free Choice: A Reply to Professor West," 99 *Harvard Law Review* 1431 (1986), copyright 1986 by The Harvard Law Review Association; "Law and Literature: A Relation Reargued," 72 *Virginia Law Review* 1351 (1986), copyright 1986 by Virginia Law Review Association; and "From *Billy Budd* to Buchenwald," 96 *Yale Law Journal* 1173 (1987), copyright 1987 by The Yale Law Journal Co., Inc.

I wish to thank Richard Zook, Michael Keane, Laura Neebling, and Darren Fortunato for their superb research assistance. For helpful comments on previous drafts of the manuscript, I thank David Friedman, Michael Gagarin, Harrison Hayford, Stephen Holmes, John Langbein, L. H. LaRue, Saul Levmore, Richard Porter, Charlene Posner, Eric Posner, Lawrence Rosen, Cass Sunstein, Richard Weisberg, and James Boyd White.

Robin West's generosity in making extensive (and invariably constructive) comments on a work that in places registers sharp disagreement with her own contributions to the field of law and literature deserves a special acknowledgment, as do the detailed and extensive comments by Robert Ferguson and Eva Saks on the entire manuscript; I also wish to thank Michael Aronson, General Editor of Harvard University Press, for his encouragement of this project and his many helpful suggestions, and Mary Ellen Geer of Harvard Press for her meticulous editing of the manuscript.

I also wish to acknowledge specially the contributions of several literary scholars at the University of Chicago in addition to Robert Ferguson: David Bevington and Edward Rosenheim from the Department of English Language and Literature; Peter Jansen, Clayton Koelb, and Kenneth Northcott from the Department of Germanic Languages and Literatures; and James Redfield from the Department of Classical Languages and Literatures and the Committee on Social Thought. Their encouragement of this project and their generosity in reading and commenting on the work of an amateur in literature exemplify the university's unique hospitality to interdisciplinary studies.

*L*AW AND LITERATURE, the subject of this book, is a difficult field to organize. This can be seen by comparing it with law and economics, another and more established field of interdisciplinary legal studies and one that will play a role in later chapters of this book. Law and economics involves the application of economic theory to legal questions. The economic analyst of law proceeds by setting forth the relevant part of economic theory (such as the inverse relation between the price of a good and the quantity demanded, or the effect of monopoly on output) and then applying it to a legal problem, such as the regulation of accidents by means of tort law or of monopolies by means of antitrust law. The analysis may show that the spirit of legal doctrine is economic, or it may provide an argument for why some rule of law should be changed to make the law more efficient. Thus law and economics has a positive and a normative program, both derived from a single theory of human behavior.

The relation between literature and law is less tidy, because there is no central theory of literature that can be taken and applied to a body of law; because there is no central programmatic thrust, whether positive or normative, to the law and literature movement; and because the relation between the two fields does not run in just one direction, as the relation between law and economics does—from economics (theory) to law (subject). The study of law and literature seeks to use legal insights to enhance understanding of literature, not just literary insights to enhance understanding of law. The field envisages a general confrontation or comparison, for purposes of mutual illumination, of two vast bodies of texts, and of the techniques for analyzing each body. The result is a rich but confusing array of potential links between law and literature. Some may be superficial or misleading, and I begin with them.

1.  Legal writing is full of "legal fictions," a form of metaphor.[1] Some are dead metaphors, which no one notices; an example is "breaking" a contract, that is, refusing or failing to carry out a contractual obligation. Others are live metaphors—we sense that unlike things are being yoked. A drug dealer whose underlings hold and dispense the drugs is guilty of "constructive possession," which means he is punishable exactly as if *he* possessed the drugs. Language is being used figuratively: "constructive possession" literally means no possession, just as "constructive notice" literally means no notice. Much of the artificiality of legal language comes from its use of metaphor—sometimes, as in these examples, metaphor of a paradoxical sort that recalls Samuel Johnson's definition of the metaphysical poets' wit: "The most heterogeneous ideas are yoked by violence together."[2] But the resemblance to the literary use of metaphor is superficial. The legal fiction reflects the desire of judges and lawyers to create an appearance of continuity when innovating. The drug dealer who carefully avoids personal contact with the goods is punished as a possessor in recognition of the fact that his fastidiousness reflects no moral superiority, and retention of the term "possession" enforces the sense that the law is taking only a small step in extending punishment to his conduct.

If, as many lawyers believe, no one is fooled by the legal fiction, the device is harmless, but one must wonder then why they use it; it becomes a pointless circumlocution. To the extent that anyone is fooled, the legal fiction is symptomatic of legal formalism (of which more in Chapter 2) and of the euphemizing tendency in judicial prose discussed in Chapter 6. But it is not, despite its name, a literary device.

2.  The lawyer's emphasis on reasoning by analogy (as in cases holding that oil and gas are subject to the rule of capture, by analogy to more familiar examples of "fugitive" resources such as rabbits and foxes) may seem to invite comparison with the poet's use of simile, as in the opening lines of Wordsworth's Sonnet 30:

---

[1] On legal fictions see Henry Sumner Maine, *Ancient Law*, chap. 2 (1861); Lon L. Fuller, *Legal Fictions* (1967); Aviam Soifer, "Reviewing Legal Fictions," 20 *Georgia Law Review* 871 (1986). On metaphor see David E. Cooper, *Metaphor* (1986); Donald Davidson, "What Metaphors Mean," in *On Metaphor* 29 (Sheldon Sacks ed. 1979); Mark Johnson, "Introduction: Metaphor in the Philosophical Tradition," in *Philosophical Perspectives on Metaphor* 3 (Mark Johnson ed. 1981); George Lakoff and Mark Johnson, *Metaphors We Live By* (1980); John R. Searle, *Expression and Meaning: Studies in the Theory of Speech Acts*, chap. 4 (1979); Anne Sheppard, *Aesthetics: An Introduction to the Philosophy of Art* 119–129 (1987); George Whalley, *Poetic Process: An Essay in Poetics*, chap. 8 (1967).
[2] "Life of Abraham Cowley," in *Samuel Johnson: Selected Poetry and Prose* 337, 348 (Frank Brady and W. K. Wimsatt eds. 1977).

> It is a beauteous evening, calm and free,
> The holy time is quiet as a Nun
> Breathless with adoration . . .

or of T. S. Eliot's *Prufrock*:

> Let us go then, you and I,
> When the evening is spread out against the sky
> Like a patient etherised upon a table.

In poetry a simile is an analogy between what the poet is discussing (the evening) and some other thing, superficially unlike it (a praying nun, an anesthetized patient). The poet uses similes, like metaphors, to create arresting images. The essential requirement is that the things compared be dramatically unlike—shockingly so in Eliot's simile—so that an effect of vividness, novelty, and insight is produced. The lawyer's purpose is the opposite: to make things that are unlike in what might appear to be important respects—things such as oil and foxes, or possessing and not possessing illegal drugs—seem as alike as possible, so that an appearance of continuity of legal doctrine is maintained. As in the case of using legal fictions, the lawyer uses analogy to soothe the reader. Indeed, the two techniques are closely related. Reasoning by analogy is to the legal fiction as simile is to metaphor: in reasoning by analogy, as in simile, the distinction between the items compared is preserved by a semantic marker, such as "like" or "as." The poet, on the other hand, wants to jar the reader out of the conventional response to a familiar experience, such as that of evening. In *Prufrock* Eliot is trying to jar the reader out of what had become, through the efforts of Wordsworth and other Romantic poets, the conventional literary response to evening.

3. Sometimes the lawyer or judge uses figurative language in the approximate sense in which it is used in literature, and then he comes within my sights in this book. Michael Boudin, in this respect the heir of Jeremy Bentham, points out that metaphorical language in law is often a source of obfuscation.[3] A judge says, for example, that pricing is "the central nervous system of the economy,"[4] and literal-minded lawyers begin thinking about antitrust law in terms of inappropriate medical analogies. The metaphor elides the reasoning process that might indicate both the aptness and the limits of the analogy that the metaphor (a compressed analogy) conveys. Reading imaginative literature, we are

[3] "Antitrust Doctrine and the Sway of Metaphor," 75 *Georgetown Law Journal* 395 (1986). See C. K. Ogden, *Bentham's Theory of Fictions* (1932).
[4] United States v. Socony-Vacuum Oil Co., 310 U.S. 150, 226 n. 59 (1940).

on guard against taking literally what the writer says; we are protected by the expectations that we bring to such work. We are not so well prepared to discount figurative language in discursive, analytic prose.

Milner Ball, drawing on a philosophical literature that views metaphor as an inescapable method by which we give structure to our experience (see especially Lakoff and Johnson's book, *Metaphors We Live By*), argues that we should substitute for the currently dominant metaphor of law as a "bulwark of freedom" the metaphor of law as a "medium of human solidarity."[5] He works the obverse side of the same coin examined by Boudin. I explore the creative use of legal metaphors in Chapter 6.

4. Legal fictions are not the only fictions in law. In *Miles v. City Council*,[6] the owner of a talking cat named "Blackie" challenged, as a deprivation of free speech, an ordinance that required businesses to be licensed, with no exception for the commercial exhibition of talking animals. Miles testified that after much travail he had Blackie "talking real plain where you could understand him," and that he then took Blackie on tour to display the cat's gift. In ruling against Miles the court did not question the assertion that Blackie could speak. Yet it was not just being facetious in pretending to believe Blackie's owner. Miles would have had no legal leg to stand on even if Blackie had been as articulate as Demosthenes, so it was easier to treat Miles's assertions as true and go on from there.

*Melvin v. Reid*,[7] a leading case in the law of privacy, provides a subtler example of fictional facts in law. (The reader who is interested in talking animals must go to literature and not law—to such masterpieces as *Gulliver's Travels*, *Alice in Wonderland*, and Kafka's *Report to an Academy*—to satisfy his curiosity.) According to the "facts" recited by the court, the plaintiff, née Gabrielle Darley, had once been a prostitute, had been tried for murder and acquitted, and shortly afterward, in 1918, had "abandoned her life of shame and bec[o]me entirely rehabilitated." The next year she married Bernard Melvin "and commenced the duties of caring for their home, and thereafter at all times lived an exemplary, virtuous, honorable, and righteous life; . . . she assumed a place in respectable society, and made many friends who were not aware of the incidents of her earlier life." All was bliss until 1925, when the

---

[5] See Milner S. Ball, *Lying Down Together: Law, Metaphor, and Theology* (1985).
[6] 710 F.2d 1542 (11th Cir. 1983) (per curiam).
[7] 112 Cal. App. 285, 297 Pac. 91 (1931).

defendants made a lurid movie, *The Red Kimono*,[8] which was based on Gabrielle's life before her reformation and used her maiden name. From the movie her friends "learned for the first time," the opinion continues, "of the unsavory incidents of her early life. This caused them to scorn and abandon her, and exposed her to obloquy, contempt, and ridicule, causing her grievous mental and physical suffering." The court held that these facts, if proved, would establish a violation of a common-law right of privacy. Ever since, generations of law students, and (less excusably) scholars of the right of privacy, have used Gabrielle's affecting tale as Exhibit A to the case for giving people a legal right to suppress information about their past life.[9]

Yet the factual recital that I have summarized is, as far as anyone knows, fictitious. Rather than contest the facts recited in the plaintiff's complaint, the defendants had moved to dismiss the case on the ground that even if true the recital did not establish a violation of the plaintiff's legal rights. The trial court had agreed, but the appellate court reversed and sent the case back to determine the actual facts because, under that court's view of the law, *if* the facts were as alleged in the complaint Gabrielle was entitled to damages. There is no further trace of the case. The allegation that Gabrielle was completely rehabilitated within months of her acquittal is implausible; additional implausibilities are that as soon as the movie came out all her friends promptly dropped her (despite her complete rehabilitation) and that she had become so soft and refined in seven years that the exposure of her not distant past caused her "grievous mental and physical suffering." Maybe it all happened as alleged, but that was never determined. As far as anyone knows, her story as told by the California court is a charming fiction; yet somehow it has become woven into the fabric of the law of privacy.

THE MOST important connections between law and literature are the following:

1. Although in frequency as a literary subject law is dwarfed by love, the stages of life, murder, religion, war, the family, social climbing, art, and literature itself, a surprising number of literary works—some

---

[8] See "The Red Kimona" [*sic*], Feb. 3, 1926, 3 *Variety Film Reviews* 1907–1980 (1983).

[9] See, for example, William L. Prosser, "Privacy," 48 *California Law Review* 383, 392 (1960); Edward J. Bloustein, "Privacy as an Aspect of Dignity: An Answer to Dean Prosser," 39 *New York University Law Review* 962, 977 (1964); Alfred Hill, "Defamation and Privacy under the First Amendment," 76 *Columbia Law Review* 1205, 1259–60 (1976).

immensely distinguished, some much less so—are "about" legal pro-
ceedings in the sense that such a proceeding, usually a trial of some sort,
plays a central or climactic role in the work. Examples are *Eumenides,
Antigone, Wasps, Njál's Saga, The Cid, The Merchant of Venice, The White
Devil,*[10] *The Cenci, The Red and the Black, Pickwick Papers, Bleak House,
The Brothers Karamazov, Felix Holt, The Ring and the Book, Billy Budd,
Pudd'nhead Wilson, St. Joan, The Stranger, The Trial, A Passage to India,
An American Tragedy, The Just and the Unjust, Darkness at Noon, Native
Son, The Caine Mutiny,* and *To Kill a Mockingbird.*[11] An even more
distinguished body of literature is "about" general issues of justice,
notably revenge, an important stage in the transition to law as we know
it. Examples of revenge literature include both Homeric epics, many
Greek and Roman tragedies, *Hamlet* and many other Elizabethan and
Jacobean tragedies, and Heinrich von Kleist's classic novella, *Michael
Kohlhaas.*

Law provides the symbology not only of Kafka's best-known novel
but of many of his stories and fragments (including *The Judgment, In the
Penal Colony,* and *The Problem of Our Laws*). Will contests and inheri-
tance law are staples of Victorian fiction—*Bleak House* and *Felix Holt,*
again, and Balzac's *Ursule Mirouët,* plus, it seems, almost every novel by
Trollope.[12] Law and judging figure prominently in the Bible, of course,
but also in the medieval sagas, in Hesiod's *Works and Days,* and in works
(apart from those already mentioned) by Dickens, Dreiser, James
Fenimore Cooper, Melville, Mark Twain, Faulkner, Brecht, Donne,

[10] The centerpiece of another play by John Webster, *The Devil's Law-case,* a tragicomedy
written about 1618, is a lengthy trial for bastardy; and among the principal characters three are
lawyers.
[11] For many other examples, just of *novels* with legal subject matter, see Jon L. Breen, *Novel
Verdicts: A Guide to Courtroom Fiction* (1984) (with a further limitation to novels that contain
either an English or an American trial), and Karen L. Kretschman, *Legal Novels: An Annotated
Bibliography* (1979). See also Richard H. Weisberg and Karen L. Kretschman, "Wigmore's
'Legal Novels' Expanded: A Collaborative Effort," 7 *Maryland Law Forum* 94 (1977). Among
the best of the many anthologies of literary treatments of law is *Masterpieces of Legal Fiction*
(Maximilian Koessler ed. 1964). And see *The Lawyer's Alcove: Poems by the Lawyer, for the
Lawyer and about the Lawyer* (Ina Russelle Warren ed. 1900).
[12] See Fred C. Thomson, "The Legal Plot in *Felix Holt,*" 7 *Studies in English Literature
1500–1900* 691 (1967); Coral Lansbury, *The Reasonable Man: Trollope's Legal Fiction* (1981); F.
Lyman Windolph, "Trollope and the Law," in Windolph, *Reflections of the Law in Literature* 11
(1956). Balzac's fascination with law is discussed in John Marshall Gest, "The Law and
Lawyers of Balzac," 46 *American Law Review* 481 (1912), and that of the Victorian novelists in
Northrop Frye, "Literature and the Law," 4 *Law Society (of Upper Canada) Gazette* 70, 70–72
(1970). The many points of legal interest in Jane Austen's novels are discussed in G. H. Treitel,
"Jane Austen and the Law," 100 *Law Quarterly Review* 549 (1984).

and Dante[13]—and let us not forget Chaucer's *The Man of Law's Tale.*[14] *Measure for Measure* is about discretionary nonenforcement of law, and *The Merchant of Venice* and Marlowe's *Doctor Faustus* about the enforce-

[13] On the sagas (a word I am using loosely, to cover the medieval German epics as well as the Old Norse epics) see Ursula R. Mahlendorf and Frank J. Tobin, "Legality and Formality in the *Nibelungenlied,*" 66 *Monatshefte* 225 (1974); William Ian Miller, "Choosing the Avenger: Some Aspects of the Bloodfeud in Medieval Iceland and England," 1 *Law and History Review* 159 (1983); Stephen P. Schwartz, *Poetry and Law in Germanic Myth* (University of California Folklore Studies no. 27, 1973); Alan Berger, "Lawyers in the Old Icelandic Family Sagas: Heroes, Villains, and Authors," 20 *Saga-Book* 70 (1978–1979). On Dickens see, among many examples, Robert Coles, "Charles Dickens and the Law," 59 *Virginia Quarterly Review* 564 (1983); Marjorie Stone, "Dickens, Bentham, and the Fictions of the Law: A Victorian Controversy and Its Consequences," 29 *Victorian Studies* 125 (1985). On Dreiser see C. R. B. Dunlop, "Human Law and Natural Law in the Novels of Theodore Dreiser," 19 *American Journal of Jurisprudence* 61 (1974). On Cooper see Robert A. Ferguson, *Law and Letters in American Culture* 297–304 (1984); Brook Thomas, *Cross-Examinations of Law and Literature: Cooper, Hawthorne, Stowe, and Melville,* chap. 1 (1987). On Melville see, for example, id., chaps. 4, 7–10. On Mark Twain see Robin L. West, "Adjudication Is Not Interpretation: Some Reservations about the Law-as-Literature Movement," 54 *Tennessee Law Review* 203 (1987); Comment, "Mark Twain: Doctoring the Laws," 48 *Missouri Law Review* 681 (1983); D. M. McKeithan, *Court Trials in Mark Twain and Other Essays* (1958). On Faulkner see Law and Southern Literature Symposium, 4 *Mississippi College Law Review* 165 (1984). On Brecht and other modern German dramatists see F. K. Jakobsh, "The Mutable Judge: The Court Motif in Recent German Dramatic Literature," in *Crisis and Commitment: Studies in German and Russian Literature in Honour of J. W. Dyck* 108 (John Whiton and Harry Loewen eds. 1983). On Donne see Lucille Stock Cobb, "John Donne and the Common Law" (Ph.D. diss., Washington University, English Department, 1956). On Dante see Anthony K. Cassell, *Dante's Fearful Art of Justice* (1984); Allan H. Gilbert, *Dante's Conception of Justice* (1925); Judith Schenck Koffler, "Capital in Hell: Dante's Lesson on Usury," 32 *Rutgers Law Review* 608 (1979); James Williams, "Dante as a Jurist," 22 *Law Magazine and Law Review* (4th ser.) 84 (1897). And for an interesting discussion of the possible influence of a famous criminal trial on Conrad's *Lord Jim* see Allen Boyer, "Crime, Cannibalism and Joseph Conrad: The Influence of *Regina v. Dudley and Stephens* on *Lord Jim,*" 20 *Loyola of Los Angeles Law Review* 9 (1986).

[14] See Morton W. Bloomfield, "The Man of Law's Tale: A Tragedy of Victimization and a Christian Comedy," 87 *Publications of the Modern Language Association* 384 (1972); Walter Scheps, "Chaucer's Man of Law and the Tale of Constance," 89 *Publications of the Modern Language Association* 285 (1974); Betsy Seaman, "Lawyers in Chaucer's Time," 6 *American Legal Studies Association Forum* 187 (1982); W. F. Bolton, "Pinchbeck and the Chaucer Circle in the Law Reports and Records of 11–13 Richard II," 84 *Modern Philology* 401 (1987). The *Canterbury Tales* are suffused with legal allusions—see Carol Ann Breslin, "Justice and Law in Chaucer's 'Canterbury Tales' " (Ph.D. diss., Temple University, 1978)—reflecting the extensive interpenetration of law and literature during the Middle Ages; and there is the unforgettable trial, in *Gargantua and Pantagruel,* of Justice Bridlegoose for deciding cases by throwing dice. The Icelandic epic, Njál's Saga, is dense with legal maneuverings. I greatly regret that, apart from a glancing reference to *Beowulf* in the next chapter, I discuss no medieval literature in this book. There is, however, an extensive scholarly literature on the subject. See John A. Alford and Dennis P. Seniff, *Literature and Law in the Middle Ages: A Bibliography of Scholarship* (1984). Examples include John A. Alford, "Literature and Law in Medieval England," 92 *Publications of the Modern Language Association* 941 (1977); William J. Birnes, "Christ as Advocate: The Legal

ment of contracts. *King Lear* contains a mock trial.[15] So numerous are the incidental references to law in Shakespeare's plays that people have wondered whether he might not have had some legal training. Indeed, those references have helped persuade some people to attribute Shakespeare's plays to Francis Bacon, a lawyer.[16] The climax of *Alice in Wonderland* is a mock trial notable for a depiction of the jury system that critics of the system should continue to find apt.[17] The lawyer has long been a stock character in fiction. And many distinguished writers of literature were trained and some practiced as lawyers, including Ariosto, Donne, Flaubert, Kafka, Wallace Stevens, and possibly Chaucer.

2. Both legal and literary scholarship are centrally concerned with the meaning of texts. In the case of law these are constitutions, statutes, judicial and administrative rules, and judicial opinions. Interpretation is therefore a central issue in both fields. And legal scholarship, like literary scholarship, consists to a significant extent of commentary on texts temporally and culturally remote from the commentator, though the remoteness is less on average in law than in literature, for reasons explored in Chapter 2.

---

Metaphor of 'Piers Plowman,' " 16 *Annuale Mediaevale* 71 (1975); R. Howard Bloch, *Medieval French Literature and Law* (1977); Frank Jacoby, "The Conflict between Legal Concepts and Spiritual Values in the Middle High German *Reinhart Fuchs*," 1973/1 *Revue des langues vivantes* 11; Steven D. Kirby, "Legal Doctrine and Procedure as Approaches to Medieval Hispanic Literature," 8 *La Coronica* 164 (1980); W. Nicholas Knight, "Equity and Mercy in English Law and Drama (1405–1641)," 6 *Comparative Drama* 51 (1972); Frederick Carl Riedel, *Crime and Punishment in the Old French Romances* (1938); J. Wilson McCutchan, "Justice and Equity in the English Morality Play," 19 *Journal of the History of Ideas* 405 (1958).

[15] Well discussed in W. Moelwyn Merchant, "Lawyer and Actor: Process of Law in Elizabethan Drama," 3 *English Studies Today* 107 (1962).

[16] On "Baconism" see index references under Bacon in S. Schoenbaum, *Shakespeare's Lives* (1970). W. Nicholas Knight, *Shakespeare's Hidden Life: Shakespeare at the Law: 1585–1595* (1973), adds a novel twist by arguing that Shakespeare, though indeed the author of Shakespeare's plays, was himself a lawyer. On the many legal references in Shakespeare's plays see Paul S. Clarkson and Clyde T. Warren, *The Law of Property in Shakespeare and the Elizabethan Drama* (2d ed. 1968); George Greenwood, *Shakespeare's Law* (1920); O. Hood Phillips, *Shakespeare and the Lawyers* (1ᵒ72); Edw. J. White, *Commentaries on the Law in Shakespeare* (2d ed. 1913).

[17] "One of the jurors had a pencil that squeaked. This, of course, Alice could *not* stand, and she went round the court and got behind him, and very soon found an opportunity of taking it away. She did it so quickly that the poor little juror (it was Bill, the Lizard) could not make out at all what had become of it; so, after hunting all about for it, he was obliged to write with one finger for the rest of the day; and this was of very little use, as it left no mark on the slate." Lewis Carroll, *Alice's Adventures in Wonderland and Through the Looking-Glass* 108–109 (1966 ed.). American jurors usually are not allowed to take notes; so they are no better off than Bill the Lizard. Another notable literary criticism of the jury system is James Fenimore Cooper's novel *The Ways of the Hour*.

3. Many legal texts, especially judicial opinions, resemble literary texts in being highly rhetorical rather than coolly expository. Judges and other lawyers resemble literary artists in the close attention they pay to the choice of words in which to express themselves, as well as in the fondness for metaphors and similes noted earlier.

4. Literature is a traditional subject of legal regulation and literary works an occasional subject of litigation. The pertinent areas of law include copyright, obscenity, and defamation—"defamation by fiction" being a growing area of concern to authors and publishers.

5. The legal process, especially the adversary process of Anglo-American civil and criminal jury trials, has a significant theatrical dimension. This is one reason why trials are a staple of literature and why writers of fiction, such as Sybille Bedford, Truman Capote, Rebecca West, and Renata Adler, have turned their talents to the description of actual trials.[18] The more extended Continental "inquisitorial" proceeding, and the Anglo-American equity proceedings that derive from and resemble it, supply apt frameworks or metaphors in novels of protraction, torment, or obsession, such as *Bleak House*, *Crime and Punishment*, and *The Trial*.

Until recently the links between law and literature, numerous as they are, went largely unremarked and unexplored. The reasons for this lie in the sociology of academic law and academic literature. Until the 1960s, academic law was for the most part an atheoretical discipline.[19] Issues of general theory, such as justice and interpretation, which might conceivably have been illuminated by the study of literary texts and literary methods, received little attention. Legal analytic methods (which centered on the careful reading of legal texts against a background of comprehensive knowledge of legal doctrines and institutions, and

[18] The classic of this genre is Sybille Bedford, *The Faces of Justice: A Traveller's Report* (1961), but it faces a formidable challenge from Renata Adler, *Reckless Disregard: Westmoreland v. CBS et al.; Sharon v. Time* (1986), a report on the recent libel trials in New York City that pitted the Israeli general Ariel Sharon and the American general William Westmoreland against Time and CBS respectively. Other examples of writing by literary people about real as distinct from fictional law include Edmund Wilson, "Justice Oliver Wendell Holmes," in *Patriotic Gore: Studies in the Literature of the American Civil War* 743 (1962), and Wilson, "The Holmes-Laski Correspondence," in his *Eight Essays* 217 (1954).

[19] I explore this point in "The Decline of Law as an Autonomous Discipline: 1962–1987," 100 *Harvard Law Review* 761 (1987). See also Roger C. Cramton, "Demystifying Legal Scholarship," 75 *Georgetown Law Journal* 1 (1986), and references there. Of course there are exceptions to my generalization—one thinks particularly of such great early figures as Bentham, Hegel, Maine, Austin, and Holmes, and of the legal realists of the 1920s and 1930s. But theory had never been a large component of legal scholarship, at least in the Anglo-American sphere, and in the 1940s and 1950s it was very small.

heavily emphasized logical reasoning), deployed entirely on legal texts and problems, seemed adequate equipment for a law professor. The study of literature, too, was for the most part atheoretical. It is true that literary theory has a long and distinguished history, but I am speaking of central tendencies only, in the 1950s and 1960s only, and in the Anglo-American milieu only. And in that milieu, apart from that important branch of literary study, more than 2,000 years old, which seeks to establish the definitive texts of works of literature, and apart from the structuralist approach to literature that had emerged in the 1950s, most students of literature busied themselves with the elucidation and evaluation of literary works and the careful study of genres, sometimes through close reading of the text, sometimes through study of the historical or cultural context of the work or the details of its author's life, but in any case usually unhampered by overt theory. (A major exception is the essay by Beardsley and Wimsatt on intentionalism, cited in Chapter 5.) Lacking theory, the literary critic was not likely to think that his methods might be fruitfully applied to nonliterary texts. Nor was the lawyer likely to invite him to try.

Legal scholarship around 1960 and literary scholarship of the same period have something else in common: they are for the most part readable by people who have no training in either field. Being neither heavily theoretical nor highly technical, they make few demands on the reader. Indeed, lacking the power of theory, they tend to cultivate the charm of rhetoric—a substitution I shall note in Chapter 6 when I discuss some classics of judicial writing.

A sign of the times was the role that nonacademics played, and the audiences that academics cultivated, in both fields. Judges such as Holmes, Cardozo, and Learned Hand made contributions to legal thought that were as important as those of any law professor, and most law professors geared their writing to judges and practicing lawyers as well as to one another (they still do, but to a lesser extent). In literature, nonacademics such as T. S. Eliot and Edmund Wilson were among the leading critics—Eliot, indeed, was the dominant figure in criticism— while many distinguished academics, such as Cleanth Brooks, Lionel Trilling, C. S. Lewis, and Wayne Booth, wrote in a style and at a level designed to attract a lay audience as well as graduate students and professors. Even the most formidable academic critics and scholars, such as Kenneth Burke, William Empson, Northrop Frye, and William Wimsatt, were more intelligible to the laity than are their present-day successors, who bristle with the jargon of philosophy, political theory, language theory, and social science, and who thus love to use words like "hermeneutic," "deconstruction," "valorize," "foregrounding," "privileging," "problematizing," "signifier," "illocutionary," and "moment" (in the sense of a stage of conceptual development). There is a parallel tendency in legal scholarship to borrow terminology from economics, philosophy—and literary theory; words like "hermeneutic" and "deconstruction" are now encountered in law reviews as well as literary journals.

Both fields have thus become more theoretical in the last quarter-century, and because of their common concern with texts this development has opened up the possibility of convergence. Academic lawyers newly concerned with the problematics of interpreting difficult legal texts look to the study of literature for clues and find there a parallel concern with the problematics of interpretation, while literary scholars wrestling self-consciously with problems of interpretation occasionally glance across to academic law to see how such problems are being addressed there. Academic lawyers interested in the intersection between law and larger concepts of justice and obligation, and literary scholars interested in the intersection between literature and other social enterprises, find themselves with common subject matter as well as common problems of method.[20] Both fields, moreover, have been caught up in the growing politicization of intellectual life in this country. So they have something else in common: politics.

Practitioners in both fields have also become restive with the limitations of their subject matter. Neither law nor literature seems quite so glorious a subject today as a quarter of a century ago. Law has become more politicized, more commercialized, more specialized, and more bureaucratized, and is increasingly interpreted in economic terms, which distresses many law professors. The humanities have lost prestige and cultural centrality to the combined forces of natural and social science, television and movie entertainment, and technology generally and, like academic law, have experienced debilitating political, ideological, and methodological fissures. To law professors, literature offers a hope of redemption from a technocratic future.[21] To literature professors, law offers a hope of redemption from social marginality.[22]

[20] And thus one can find an article like Stanley Fish's "Anti-Professionalism," 7 *Cardozo Law Review* 645 (1986), in which a literary critic, writing in a law review, criticizes both literary and legal theory.

[21] See, for example, Peter Read Teachout, "Worlds beyond Theory: Toward the Expression of an Integrative Ethic for Self and Culture," 83 *Michigan Law Review* 849 (1985).

[22] See Geoffrey H. Hartman, "A Short History of Practical Criticism," in Hartman, *Criticism in the Wilderness: The Study of Literature Today* 284, 294, 300 (1980). The recent inroads of literary theory in nonliterary (or formerly nonliterary) fields, such as philosophy and history, have been striking. See Bruce Robbins, "Poaching off the Disciplines," *Raritan*, spring 1987, at 81. Maybe law is about to be added to the list.

The convergence of these fields is also being encouraged by a general decline in the autonomy of scholarly disciplines,[23] and, more mundanely, by the flight from humanities to law by graduate students and young faculty, who in the 1970s saw jobs and promotion opportunities drying up and salaries falling steeply in real (that is, inflation-adjusted) terms and decided to go to law school, and who today see in the field of law and literature a means of amortizing their original training. The sheer size of the academic establishments in law and in literature must also be considered. Both law and literature are inexhaustible fields, but the surface mining has been done and scholars who want to leave their mark must strike out in new directions. The field of law and literature is one such direction.

The field is not completely new. In the nineteenth century, English lawyers wrote about the depiction of the legal system by Shakespeare, Dickens, and other famous writers.[24] Wigmore thought lawyers should read the great writers to learn about human nature, and Cardozo analyzed the literary style of judicial opinions.[25] But it is only since the publication in 1973 of James Boyd White's *The Legal Imagination*, a book that audaciously claims that the study of literature should be a part of legal education, that a distinct, self-conscious field of law and literature can be said to have emerged.[26] Until then the field had been, for the

[23] See references in note 19 above; Samuel Weber, *Institution and Interpretation* x (1987) ("What is increasingly being questioned today, perhaps more than at any time since the age of the Enlightenment, is the notion of intellectual and scientific *autonomy*"); Stephen Toulmin, "From Form to Function: Philosophy and History of Science in the 1950s and Now," *Daedalus*, summer 1977, at 143.

[24] See, for example, C. K. Davis, *The Law in Shakespeare* (1883); James Fitzjames Stephen, "The License of Modern Novelists," 106 *Edinburgh Review* 128 (1857).

[25] See John H. Wigmore, "Introduction," in John Marshall Gest, *The Lawyer in Literature* ix–xii (1913); Benjamin N. Cardozo, "Law and Literature," in *Selected Writings of Benjamin Nathan Cardozo* 339 (Margaret E. Hall ed. 1947 [1925]). Other early works on law and literature are cited in subsequent chapters; see also David R. Papke, "Law and Literature: A Comment and Bibliography of Secondary Works," 73 *Law Library Journal* 421 (1980).

[26] See James B. White, *The Legal Imagination: Studies in the Nature of Legal Thought and Expression* (1973). For introductions to the contemporary field see Law and Literature: A Symposium, 29 *Rutgers Law Review* 223 (1976); Special Issue on Law and Literature, 6 *ALSA Forum* 125 (1982); Symposium: Law and Literature, 60 *Texas Law Review* 373 (1982); Law and Southern Literature Symposium, note 13 above; symposia published in 9 *University of Hartford Studies in Literature* nos. 2–3 (1977) and 5 *ALSA Forum* no. 1 (1981); William H. Page, "Review Essay: The Place of Law and Literature," 39 *Vanderbilt Law Review* 391 (1986); David Ray Papke, "Neo-Marxists, Nietzscheans, and New Critics: The Voices of the Contemporary Law and Literature Discourse," 1985 *American Bar Foundation Research Journal* 883; Richard A. Posner, "Law and Literature: A Relation Reargued," 72 *Virginia Law Review* 1351 (1986); Carl S. Smith, John P. McWilliams, Jr., and Maxwell Bloomfield, *Law and American Literature: A Collection of Essays* (1983); Richard Weisberg and Jean-Pierre Barricelli, "Literature and Law,"

most part, and with the important exception of professional Shakespearean scholarship, antiquarian and dilettantish—amounting to little more
than a series of reminders that law is a surprisingly frequent subject of
literature and that judicial opinions, and to a lesser extent other forms of
legal writing as well, sometimes have a literary character and quality.
The frequency of legal subjects in literature is, I shall argue in Chapter
2, a partly adventitious circumstance, although some literature on legal
themes is indeed relevant to jurisprudential concerns. The literary
character of judicial opinions is an important phenomenon but one that
is diminishing as more and more opinions are ghostwritten by the
judges' law clerks—recently graduated law students who are not chosen
for their ability in, encouraged in, or (with rare exceptions) capable of
literary expression.[27]

The publication since 1984 of five books on law and literature[28] attests
to the rapid growth of the field. But is it a healthy, balanced, and fruitful
growth? I have some doubts. Although some fine scholarship has
appeared, the extent to which law and literature have been mutually
illuminated is modest. Some practitioners have exaggerated the com-
monalities between the two fields, paying insufficient heed to the
profound differences between law and literature. In their hands literary
theory, or particular works of literature, are contorted to make literature
seem relevant to law, and law is contorted to make it seem continuous
with literature. At the same time, important opportunities for mutual

---

in *Interrelations of Literature* 150 (Jean-Pierre Barricelli and Joseph Gibaldi eds. 1982). For a good
recent bibliography see Richard H. Weisberg, *When Lawyers Write* 297–317 (1987). Although
from time to time I shall take issue with White, Weisberg, and some other leaders in the law
and literature movement, all deserve the credit normally accorded pioneering scholarship.

[27] See my book *The Federal Courts: Crisis and Reform* 102–119 (1985), and references there.

[28] See Robert A. Ferguson, *Law and Letters in American Culture* (1984); Richard H. Weisberg,
*The Failure of the Word: The Protagonist as Lawyer in Modern Fiction* (1984); James Boyd White,
*When Words Lose Their Meaning: Constitutions and Reconstitutions of Language, Character, and
Community* (1984); James Boyd White, *Heracles' Bow: Essays on the Rhetoric and Poetics of the Law*
(1985); Brook Thomas, *Cross-Examinations of Law and Literature: Cooper, Hawthorne, Stowe, and
Melville* (1987). Ferguson's book concerns American legal and belletristic writing, mainly
between the Revolution and the Civil War; for a parallel study of English legal and belletristic
writing see Wilfrid R. Prest, *The Rise of the Barristers: A Social History of the English Bar
1590–1640*, chap. 6 (1986) ("Lawyers and Letters"). Although Ferguson's emphasis is on
mining such writing for insights into intellectual history, he makes a number of illuminating
observations about imaginative literature on legal themes, including works by Cooper and, as
we shall see in Chapter 3, by Melville. Thomas's book covers similar ground, with a similar
objective, and includes a lengthy analysis of *Billy Budd*; I discuss that analysis in Chapter 3 as
well. I also discuss Weisberg's book in that chapter, and the two books by White in Chapters
1 and 6, though with no effort at completeness; White's books range well beyond literary and
legal texts.

illumination have been overlooked. This book attempts to strike a juster balance.


THE LAW and literature movement is interested in two types of text, the literary and the legal. They provide the subject matter respectively of Parts I and II of this book. Within each type a further division is convenient: between literary texts that are and that are not explicitly about law, and between legislative (including constitutional) texts and judicial opinions. I touch all four bases in this book and also discuss, in the single chapter of Part III, the regulation of literature by law. We shall see that the analytical issues, and even the relevant texts, cut across the divisional boundaries.

The literary texts of most obvious relevance to the law and literature movement are those that have a legal subject matter; most of the examples I gave earlier came from this category. But some practitioners of law and literature take the whole of literature as their subject, in the belief that a person with legal training and experience has a special insight into the act of reading, irrespective of subject matter. I evaluate this claim in the next chapter, which discusses the *Iliad* and *Hamlet* and, more briefly, several other works of revenge literature. Among these, *Eumenides* and *Hecuba* have substantial trial scenes, and illustrate— *Eumenides* particularly well—the transition from revenge to formal law. The other works discussed in the chapter include *The Spanish Tragedy*, *Julius Caesar*, *Michael Kohlhaas*, *Ragtime* (Doctorow), *An Odor of Verbena* (Faulkner), and Sophocles' two *Oedipus* plays.

Not only are the *Iliad* and *Hamlet* among the most celebrated works in the Western literary tradition, but they have drawn the attention respectively of two of the leaders of the law and literature movement, James White and Richard Weisberg. These works have a legal, or if one prefers a prelegal, subject matter. They are about vengeance—"wild justice" as Bacon called it, thus underscoring its relationship to law. Vengeance is either the earliest stage of law or an important part of the prehistory of law (depending on how broadly one cares to define "law"), and is therefore a fit starting point for an examination of literature on legal themes.

We can learn something about vengeance, and about legal history and anthropology, from works of literature and something about the works themselves from the scholarly literature on vengeance as ˌa social practice—we may even be able to understand better the causes of Hamlet's famous procrastination. Yet the revenge theme does not much interest White or Weisberg. The reason may be the narrowness of legal training and the limited scope of legal reasoning. The lawyer's—even the academic lawyer's—competence is confined to a narrow corner of law and justice, when these terms are broadly conceived; this is an aspect of professionalism. To make sense of revenge as a social practice we shall have to draw on economics, biology, and anthropology; we shall get little help from conventional legal scholarship.

Chapter 2 discusses a number of works that are prime candidates for inclusion in the canon of literature on legal themes. They are (in the order discussed) *The Just and the Unjust, Pudd'nhead Wilson, The Stranger, The Merchant of Venice*, (Marlowe's) *Doctor Faustus, Measure for Measure, Antigone, A Jury of Her Peers* (Susan Glaspell), *In the Penal Colony, The Trial, Darkness at Noon, Bleak House*, and *Pickwick Papers*.[29] The discussion leads to two general conclusions. The first is that the legal matter in most literature on legal themes is peripheral to the meaning and significance of the literature. Most—but not all. Important exceptions are the three Elizabethan plays (and Koestler's novel, of course, but it has only limited literary significance and I discuss it only to contrast it with *The Trial*—a much greater, yet less "legal," work). The second conclusion, which is related, is that legal knowledge is often irrelevant to the understanding and enjoyment of literature on legal themes. But again, not always; exceptions include not only the Elizabethan plays but also the Dickens novels and *The Stranger*.

The reason why literature ostensibly about law often does not engage the lawyer's professional knowledge is that, by its very nature, literature—especially great literature—deals with the permanent and general aspects of human nature and institutions. Law in a general sense is one of those aspects, but law in that sense is not lawyer's law, any more than the private justice system known as revenge is lawyer's law. Moreover, law as depicted in literature is often just a metaphor for something else that is the primary concern of author and reader.

It is no accident that literature tends to deal with basic, timeless features of human existence. The surest, maybe the only, test of literary distinction is survival over time, a process of competitive selection in the literary marketplace. The process favors works of generality, of universality. Works that are essentially local, as most works seriously about law in the lawyer's sense are bound to be, do not fare well in this competition. This idea is fundamental to Chapter 2 but also connects to many other issues discussed in this book; it figures in the analysis of

---

[29] Other works of literature on legal themes—*Billy Budd, The Brothers Karamazov, Crime and Punishment*, and Kafka's legal parables—are discussed in Chapters 3 and 4.

interpretation in Chapter 5, of moralistic literary criticism in Chapter 6, and of obscenity and copyright in Chapter 7.

Thus, not only do lawyers not have special access to literary meaning in general, even though they are trained in a certain kind of close reading and many literary works have a legal or law-related subject matter, but the legal component in literature ostensibly about law often either is metaphorical or concerns law only in a highly general sense. That sense, however, is an interesting one; and if it is more the province of legal philosophy than of legal practice, still it opens up the possibility of a significant overlap between legal and literary interests. In both Chapter 1 and Chapter 2 we shall see how a number of the monuments of Greek and Elizabethan literature stimulate reflection on issues of the highest jurisprudential importance, such as the choices between rules and standards, between law and equity, between strict liability and liability based on culpability, and between "a government of laws" and "a government of men." By the end of Part I it will be apparent that literature on legal themes composes its own distinct order of literary works. But because jurisprudence is an area of legal studies for which the ordinary professional training and experiences of a lawyer provide scant preparation, the potential contribution that lawyers can make to the study of literature on legal or prelegal themes may be a limited one.

In the teeth of the last observation, Chapters 3 and 4 explore the possibility that the lawyer's worldliness—his interest in, and experience with, social institutions—may give him a distinctive outlook on themes commonly encountered in literature. Chapter 3 evaluates Richard Weisberg's effort to relate the legalistic mentality that he finds depicted in a number of works of literature to the atrocities committed by the Nazis, and Chapter 4 evaluates Robin West's effort to find support in Kafka's fiction for the radical program of the critical legal studies movement. These attempted syntheses of law and literature are ingenious and provocative but do not convince me. They borrow the prestige of great literature for political, ideological, or ethical ends to which the literature is not germane. They make Melville and Kafka (and others) stand for a Dionysian or Romantic vision of human possibilities that law is forever thwarting; and not only is this an unrealistic vision of life and law—law is Apollonian, not Romantic—but it is not endorsed by the literary works to which Weisberg and West appeal.

Part I (Chapters 1–4) is not just concerned with exploring literature on legal themes; a continuous wrestling with problems in interpreting ambiguous texts (*Hamlet* is literature's most famous such text), it provides background to Chapter 5, which asks whether the techniques of literary interpretation can be applied fruitfully to statutory and constitutional texts, texts that are also, if less radically and less often, ambiguous. In addition, the jurisprudential issues in Part I (particularly in Chapter 2)—issues revolving around the slogan "a government of laws, not men"—recur in Chapter 5.

Part of my effort in that chapter is to protect statutes and the Constitution not so much from literary critics, only a few of whom have discussed the interpretation of legal materials, as from lawyers who have borrowed, or deplored the borrowing of, techniques of literary inter-pretation (sometimes, as in the case of deconstruction, with scant understanding of what the technique actually is) for use on statutory and constitutional texts. These borrowers include Ronald Dworkin, who has attempted to impose both a New Critical approach and a chain-novel analogy on legal interpretation, and many (not all) adherents of the critical legal studies movement, who argue that deconstruction and other reader-centered approaches to literary interpretation are applicable to legal interpretation as well.

In truth, the problems of literary and of legal interpretation have little in common except the word "interpretation." Although myself an "intentionalist" (with qualifications) in the interpretation of statutes and the Constitution, I gain no comfort from the school of intentionalist literary critics because I do not consider intentionalism a cogent theory of literary interpretation. The proposition that literary critics can point the way to solving the puzzles of statutory and constitutional interpre-tation is the falsest of the false hopes of the law and literature movement, while the antipodal proposition that deconstruction and other skeptical strains in contemporary literary criticism can demonstrate the futility, or the inescapable subjectivity, of statutory and constitutional interpreta-tion is one of the hollower battle cries of the critical legal studies movement. The social function and the conditions of composition of literary texts are so different from those of legislative texts that the best interpretive methods to use on the one type are radically different from the best methods to use on the other. And it is as important a task of law and literature scholarship to point out the differences between the fields as it is to identify the similarities.

Chapter 6 examines a more promising direction for the law and literature movement to take, namely, the application of literary insights to the writing and evaluation of judicial opinions (and, by extension, to briefs and other vehicles of legal advocacy—an extension made in the Conclusion). I compare such masterpieces of rhetoric as Antony's funeral oration in *Julius Caesar*, Yeats's poem *The Second Coming*, and Holmes's dissent in the *Lochner* case both with one other and with lesser examples of the judicial art. Although many of the points that emerge from a literary evaluation of opinions can also be made from the vantage point of language theory (but not all of the points, and not, perhaps, as pointedly), the important thing is that lawyers and judges can learn from literary criticism of judicial opinions and perhaps of other legal writing—if nothing else, can learn how important rhetoric is to law. More than rhetorical technique is involved. Also pertinent are the craft values, such as scrupulousness, that inform great literature. Judicial writing is deficient in these too. This conclusion forces me to examine the complaint that the economic analysis of law uses an impoverished vocabulary which conceals important aspects of reality and which judges should therefore eschew.

Chapter 7 (Part III) examines the regulation of literature by law. It discusses the application of copyright law, obscenity law, and defamation law to works of literature, and concludes that we might get better results in these areas if lawyers, judges, and legislators were more sensitive to literary values. (The legal profession's ignorance about the activities that law regulates is one of law's perennial problems.) The chapter expresses skepticism both about liability for defamation by fiction and about the current scope of copyright law. It also suggests that the economic concept of externalities is useful in organizing thinking about the role of law in the protection and regulation of literature. Unlike most practitioners of law and literature, I do not conceive of the field as a bulwark against further encroachments by economics and other social sciences on the autonomy of law as a discipline. That is the way of nostalgia. The social sciences have much to contribute to the understanding of law and perhaps something to contribute to the understanding of literature as well.

The Conclusion offers a brief summary of the previous chapters as well as some suggestions for better integrating the field of law and literature into university curricula. I note the variety of educational objectives that a law-school course in law and literature can serve: providing perspective by viewing law from the outside as well as from the inside (the inside perspective being the one most intensely cultivated by professional training in law); introducing the student to interdisciplinary legal studies in general and the law and literature movement in particular, along with the other fields of interdisciplinary legal inquiry that law and literature intersects—law and philosophy, law and economics, legal history, comparative law, legal anthropology, feminist jurisprudence, and critical legal studies; providing a fresh angle on topics traditionally studied in courses on jurisprudence and legal process, such as law versus equity and rule versus discretion; making students better readers and writers of legal texts; and imparting skills of advocacy.

I HAVE tried to make this book accessible to readers who are unfamiliar with some or all of the areas covered—in particular to lawyers who know little about literature and to students of literature who know little about law. (I am struck by how oblivious most academic authors are to the possibility that a nonspecialist might want to—and with just a little assistance could—read their books.) Steps to this end include the ruthless suppression of legal and of literary jargon, the plot summaries in the early chapters, and the many bibliographic references.

I have not tried to explore every corner of the law and literature field. Among the principal omissions are the following:

1. Robin West's attempt to use Northrop Frye's taxonomy of literature to classify the types of legal scholarship.[30]

2. The description by creative writers of real legal events, such as actual trials.

3. Fictional writing by lawyers, designed to illuminate real legal problems.[31]

4. Milner Ball's interesting endeavor to compare trials with plays.[32]

5. Attempts to compare the Constitution to the Bible, the latter being viewed in this comparison as a sacred rather than a literary text.[33] Very

---

[30] See Robin West, "Jurisprudence as Narrative: An Aesthetic Analysis of Modern Legal Theory," 60 *New York University Law Review* 145 (1985). Northrop Frye's masterpiece, *Anatomy of Criticism: Four Essays* (1957), is an early example of (though much different from the better-known, European versions of) "structuralist" criticism, which seeks to shift the emphasis of criticism from establishing and enforcing canons of taste to uncovering basic patterns in literature and showing their correspondence to the elemental conditions of human existence: patterns such as the structure of the human mind, or of language, or—one of Frye's emphases—the succession of the seasons. It would be surprising if legal scholarship displayed a pattern similar to the seasonal one that Frye finds helpful in classifying literature; nor do I see what is gained by forcing legal scholarship into literary categories. I raise a related issue in Chapter 6 in connection with an article by David Cole.

[31] Examples are Norval Morris, *Madness and the Criminal Law*, chaps. 1, 3 (1982), and Lon L. Fuller, "The Case of the Speluncean Explorers," 62 *Harvard Law Review* 616 (1949).

[32] See Milner S. Ball, "The Play's the Thing: An Unscientific Reflection on Courts under the Rubric of Theater," 28 *Stanford Law Review* 81 (1975). See also J. S. R. Goodlad, *A Sociology of Popular Drama* 182, 195 (1972); A. Wigfall Green, *The Inns of Court and Early English Drama*, chap. 1 (1931); John E. Simonett, "The Trial as One of the Performing Arts," 52 *American Bar Association Journal* 1145 (1966). Of particular interest from the standpoint of this book is Kathy Eden, *Poetic and Legal Fiction in the Aristotelian Tradition* (1986), which stresses the many parallels between tragic drama and court trials in ancient Athens (chap. 1), argues that the proof of facts such as intent and causation proceeds similarly in trials and dramas, and concludes with a brief discussion of *Hamlet* as an exercise in resolving factual uncertainty (for example, about the ghost's bona fides) (pp. 176–183).

[33] Discussed in Sanford Levinson, " 'The Constitution' in American Civil Religion," 1979 *Supreme Court Review* 123 (Philip B. Kurland and Gerhard Casper eds.), ingeniously comparing believers in interpretation according to the original intent of the Constitution to

occasionally I touch on the broader relationship among law, religion, and literature—a relationship that in some eras has been close—but I do not begin to give it the attention it deserves.

6. The depiction of lawyers in fiction.[34]

7. The use of literature as a source of information about specific legal institutions.[35]

8. The construction of the legal "canon." An important part of literary criticism (well illustrated by the critical writings of T. S. Eliot and F. R. Leavis, and, latterly, of feminist literary critics) is concerned with establishing the canon, or list of works that shall count as literature.[36] Lawyers, judges, and law professors face an analogous task in deciding which of the hundreds of thousands of reported cases shall be admitted to the canon of "leading" cases, the others being largely forgotten.

9. The depiction of law in detective fiction—unless the genre is defined to include such antecedents of the modern detective story as Dostoevsky's great "crime" novels, *Crime and Punishment* and *The Brothers Karamazov*—or, indeed *Oedipus Tyrannus*—all three of which are discussed in this book.[37]

---

Protestants and believers in interpretation based on precedent to Catholics; in Levinson's new book, *Constitutional Faith* (1988); and in Thomas C. Grey, "The Constitution as Scripture," 37 *Stanford Law Review* 1 (1984). See also Robert M. Cover, "The Supreme Court, 1982 Term—Foreword: *Nomos* and Narrative," 97 *Harvard Law Review* 4 (1983). On the difference between the Bible as sacred and as literary text see C. S. Lewis, "The Literary Impact of the Authorised Version," in Lewis, *Selected Literary Essays* 126 (1969).

[34] On which see E. F. J. Tucker, *Intruder into Eden: Representations of the Common Lawyer in English Literature 1350–1750* (1984); Richard H. Weisberg, "The Quest for Silence: Faulkner's Lawyer in a Comparative Setting," 4 *Mississippi College Law Review* 193 (1984). I mention such depictions briefly in Chapter 2 when discussing *The Trial* and *Bleak House*.

[35] See Ferguson, note 28 above; David Friedman, "Private Creation and Enforcement of Law: A Historical Case," 8 *Journal of Legal Studies* 399 (1979); Michael Gagarin, *Early Greek Law* (1986); David Luban, "Some Greek Trials: Order and Justice in Homer, Hesiod, Aeschylus and Plato," 54 *Tennessee Law Review* 279 (1987); William Ian Miller, "Gift, Sale, Payment, Raid: Case Studies in the Negotiation and Classification of Exchange in Medieval Iceland," 61 *Speculum* 18 (1986); Miller, note 13 above; Richard A. Posner, *The Economics of Justice*, chap. 5 (1981); Barbara Weiss, *The Hell of the English: Bankruptcy and the Victorian Novel* (1986); Hans Julius Wolff, "The Origin of Judicial Litigation among the Greeks," 4 *Traditio: Studies in Ancient and Medieval History, Thought and Religion* 31 (1946).

[36] On canon formation in literature see *Canons* (Robert von Hallberg ed. 1984); Frank Kermode, *Forms of Attention* (1985).

[37] On detective fiction as a literary genre see *Art in Crime Writing: Essays on Detective Fiction* (Bernard Benstock ed. 1983); Stephen Knight, *Form and Ideology in Crime Fiction* (1980); Dennis Porter, *The Pursuit of Crime: Art and Ideology in Detective Fiction* (1981); Tzvetan Todorov, *The Poetics of Prose*, chap. 3 (1977). For a recent example of deft legal detail (including a superb trial) in detective fiction see Scott Turow, *Presumed Innocent* (1987).

As this enumeration suggests, the field of law and literature, though still largely unknown to the legal profession, including the legal professoriat, is already too large for adequate treatment in a book of moderate length. Although some of its practitioners may claim too much for it—voices crying in the wilderness tend to be shrill—the field has promise; may this book help it to be realized.

*part i* $\mathcal{L}$ITERATURE

*on* LEGAL THEMES

# ONE

## Revenge as Legal Prototype and Literary Genre

*R*EVENGE is one of the great themes of literature. It is the theme of both Homeric epics as well as of much other epic literature, including *Beowulf*; of much of Greek, Roman, and Elizabethan and Jacobean tragedy, including the most discussed play in history (*Hamlet*); of Kleist's *Michael Kohlhaas*; of *Wuthering Heights, Moby-Dick*, and *The Count of Monte Cristo*; and of countless other plays and novels, not to mention the Old Testament. Revenge is also a traditional though nowadays infrequent subject of legal scholarship. Holmes's classic, *The Common Law*, is simply the best known of a large number of scholarly studies that argue that law grows out of revenge and that many modern legal doctrines continue to reveal traces of their origins in revenge.[1] Retribution, a concept closely related to revenge, continues to figure prominently in the theory of criminal punishment. Indeed, most of criminal law, and much of tort law besides, can be viewed as a civilized substitute for what would otherwise be the irrepressible impulse to

[1] See Oliver Wendell Holmes, Jr., *The Common Law* 2–15 (1881). See also Richard R. Cherry, *Lectures on the Growth of Criminal Law in Ancient Communities* (1890); Hans Kelsen, *Society and Nature: A Sociological Inquiry*, chaps. 3–5 (1943); L. T. Hobhouse, *Morals in Evolution: A Study in Comparative Ethics*, chap. 3 (5th ed. 1925); Roscoe Pound, *The Spirit of the Common Law* 85, 87, 139 (1921). More recent work in this vein is illustrated by Michael Dalby, "Revenge and the Law in Traditional China," 25 *American Journal of Legal History* 267 (1981); Note, "Adultery, Law, and the State: A History," 38 *Hastings Law Journal* 195 (1986); William Ian Miller, "Choosing the Avenger: Some Aspects of the Bloodfeud in Medieval Iceland and England," 1 *Law and History Review* 159 (1983). See also David Daube, *Studies in Biblical Law*, chap. 3 (1947) (retaliation and retribution in the Bible). For a wealth of information on primitive and ancient law, a focus of attention in this chapter, see A. S. Diamond, *Primitive Law: Past and Present* (1971).

The connection between law and vengeance is particularly explicit in Renaissance thought, as we shall see in discussing Elizabethan and Jacobean revenge literature. The Elizabethans distinguished among God's revenge, public revenge, and private revenge, the first two being linked in the notion that the rulers of political society are to "Smite as God Smites," wielding

avenge wrongful injuries. A correlative proposition is that if law and order break down, people will take the law into their own hands. It is no surprise, therefore, that the threat of retaliation continues to be the principal means of enforcing public international law. Finally, the Aristotelian concept of corrective justice, and perhaps its modern-day descendants (some remote in spirit from the original, to be sure),[2] grow out of revenge.

So perhaps legal training can enable one to say something fresh about revenge literature. If so, the law-trained practitioner of law and literature will have staked out an important part of the world's literature outside his normal and more limited domain of literature explicitly about law. I explore that possibility in this chapter, along with the even headier one that the literary lawyer may have privileged insights into any great literature regardless of theme. I also consider whether enlightenment might run in the other direction—from literary to legal insight—or, a third possibility, whether both the literary and the legal student of revenge can learn most about this important social practice from other disciplines.[3]

---

powers "ordained by God to fill the seat of vengeance." Lily B. Campbell, "Theories of Revenge in Renaissance England," in *Collected Papers of Lily B. Campbell* 153, 163 (1968). See also David Bevington, *Tudor Drama and Politics: A Critical Approach to Topical Meaning* 264–266 (1968); Fredson Thayer Bowers, *Elizabethan Revenge Tragedy: 1587–1642,* chap. 1 (1940); Ronald Broude, "Revenge and Revenge Tragedy in Renaissance England," 28 *Renaissance Quarterly* 38 (1975).

[2] See my article "The Concept of Corrective Justice in Recent Theories of Tort Law," 10 *Journal of Legal Studies* 187 (1981). The original concept appears in Book V, chapter 4, of the *Nicomachean Ethics.*

[3] The literature on revenge is vast but scattered. Examples of the literary and legal literature have already been cited; another example is Frederick Carl Riedel, *Crime and Punishment in the Old French Romances* 108–115 (1938). The belletristic literature ranges from Francis Bacon's wonderfully succinct two-page essay, "Of Revenge," in 6 *Works of Francis Bacon* 384 (James Spedding, Robert L. Ellis and Douglas P. Heath eds. 1858), to Susan Jacoby's fine popular work, *Wild Justice: The Evolution of Revenge* (1983). Chapter 2 of Jacoby's book discusses revenge literature, curiously omitting *Hamlet.* My own analysis of revenge draws primarily on the economic approach to the subject taken in my book *The Economics of Justice,* chap. 8 (1981) ("Retribution and Related Concepts of Punishment"); a similar approach, which draws on conflict resolution, game theory, biology, and political science and stresses the role of retaliation both in promoting and undermining cooperation, is found in Robert Axelrod, *The Evolution of Cooperation* (1984); see also Thomas C. Schelling, *The Strategy of Conflict* 35–43 (1960). There is a large philosophical literature on revenge, retribution, and retaliation (Nietzsche, Kant, Hegel, Hobbes, and many others). Illustrative modern works are Todd Glenn Buchholz, "Punishing Humans," 59 *Thought* 279, 281–285 (1984); J. P. Day, "Retributive Punishment," 87 *Mind* 498 (1978); Herbert Finagrette, "Punishment and Suffering," 50 *Proceedings of the American Philosophical Association* 499 (1977); Joel Kidder, "Requital and Criminal Justice," 15 *International Philosophical Quarterly* 255 (1975); John Kleinig, *Punishment*

## The Practice of Revenge

Imagine a society with no government and no legal system—the world community today, for example. If someone wrongs you in such a society you cannot get redress through public machinery, whether the machinery of public law (illustrated by criminal prosecution) or of private law (illustrated by tort law). Lacking the possibility of redress, which might deter an aggressor, you will be assiduous in self-protection. But self-protection can be extremely costly—indeed, impossible for one who lacks the wealth necessary to surround himself with a wall and moat, trusty guards, and so forth. The remaining possibility is retaliation against the aggressor, after he has harmed you. The problem is that if you are "rational man," you will realize that the harm is a "sunk cost"—an irretrievable bygone. No matter how much harm you do to the aggressor, the harm you have suffered will not be undone. In fact whatever dangers or other burdens you take on in order to retaliate will increase the cost to you of the initial aggression; they will be a secondary cost incurred in a futile effort to avoid the primary cost—which, having already been incurred, can no longer be prevented. Knowing that you are "rational man," the aggressor will be all the more likely to attack you. He will realize that you may well decide not to retaliate, and this realization will lower his expected costs of aggression.

*and Desert* 120–123 (1973); Jeffrie G. Murphy, "Does Kant Have a Theory of Punishment?" 87 *Columbia Law Review* 509 (1987); Robert Nozick, *Philosophical Explanations* 363–397 (1981); John Wilson, "The Purposes of Retribution," 58 *Philosophy* 521 (1983); Elizabeth H. Wolgast, "Intolerable Wrong and Punishment," 60 *Philosophy* 161 (1985). The extensive psychological literature is illustrated by Erich Fromm, *The Anatomy of Human Destructiveness* 271–274 (1973); Fritz Heider, *The Psychology of Interpersonal Relations* 265–276 (1958); Robert Hogan and Nicholas P. Emler, "Retributive Justice," in *The Justice Motive in Social Behavior: Adapting to Times of Scarcity and Change* 125 (Melvin J. Lerner and Sally C. Lerner eds. 1981) (a particularly good introduction to the literature); Elaine Walster, Ellen Berscheid, and G. William Walster, "New Directions in Equity Research," 25 *Journal of Personality and Social Psychology* 151 (1973); George A. Youngs, Jr., "Patterns of Threat and Punishment Reciprocity in a Conflict Setting," 51 *Journal of Personality and Social Psychology* 541 (1986); Dolf Zillman, *Hostility and Aggression* (1979) (see index references under "retaliatory hostility and aggression"). Sociobiology is represented by Gerald Borgia, "Human Aggression as a Biological Adaptation," in *The Evolution of Human Social Behavior* 165, 177–178 (Joan S. Lockard ed. 1980). The anthropological literature is illustrated by Robert Redfield, "Primitive Law," in *Law and Warfare: Studies in the Anthropology of Conflict* 3 (Paul Bohannan ed. 1967), and by a large number of excellent case studies, including Jacob Black-Michaud, *Cohesive Force: Feud in the Mediterranean and the Middle East* (1975); John Phillip Reid, *A Law of Blood: The Primitive Law of the Cherokee Nation*, chap. 9 (1970); J. K. Campbell, *Honour, Family and Patronage: A Study of Institutions and Moral Values in a Greek Mountain Community* 193–203 (1964); Ian Whitaker, "Tribal Structure and National Politics in Albania, 1910–1950," in *History and Social Anthropology* 253, 264–274 (I. M. Lewis ed. 1968).

Why might you retaliate anyway? One coolly rational reason would be to get something of value from the aggressor; but if this is an attractive course of action (balancing benefits against costs), it is so regardless of the aggression. Another reason would be to deter future aggression. But the aggressor may be so well protected that the costs of revenge would exceed the benefits in reducing the probability of a future aggression. To minimize aggression against yourself, you must therefore convince potential aggressors that you will retaliate even if the expected benefits of retaliation, calculated *after* the aggression has occurred, are smaller than the expected costs at that time. In other words, you must make a credible commitment to act in a way that may be irrational when the time to act comes. Yet the making of such a commitment may be rational: it may deter enough aggression to generate benefits in excess of the costs of having sometimes to honor the commitment—regardless of the costs of honoring it—by retaliating against the aggressor instead of cutting one's losses after the aggression. Legal and political analogies include the self-destructive defensive measures that corporate managers sometimes adopt to deter hostile takeovers (for example, the "poison pill," which may result in the acquirer's finding itself owning a firm that is crushed by debt), and the commitment of the United States and the Soviet Union to massive nuclear retaliation, parodied in the "Doomsday Bomb" of *Dr. Strangelove.*

In a system without legal institutions it is by definition impossible to make a legally enforceable commitment. The commitment has to come from somewhere else, from instinctive or cultural reflex reactions to aggression. One can see how, in the long prehistory of the human race, men who were endowed with an instinct to retaliate would tend to be more successful in the struggle for survival than others, and how therefore the desire to take revenge for real or imagined injuries, without calculating the net benefits of revenge at the time when it is taken, could have become a part of the human genetic makeup.[4] And societies that cultivated a sense of honor—thus adding a cultural overlay to the genetic—might, in the era before legal institutions emerged, succeed better in maintaining both internal and external security than societies that encouraged their members to turn the other cheek.[5]

---

[4] On the evolutionary advantages of an instinct for vengeance, see Jack Hirshleifer, "On the Emotions as Guarantors of Threats and Promises," in *The Latest on the Best: Essays on Evolution and Optimality* (John Dupré ed. 1988); Robert L. Trivers, "The Evolution of Reciprocal Altruism," 46 *Quarterly Review of Biology* 35, 49 (1971); Edward Westermarck, "The Essence of Revenge," 7 *Mind* (new ser.) 289, 298–299 (1898).

[5] For references, see Posner, note 3 above, chap. 8. With respect to external security this may still be true; the justice of the world community is still "wild justice."

Vengeance, however, is an extremely clumsy method of maintaining order (hence its frequent, but exaggerated, association with radical disorder and unending strife), for the following reasons:

1. It produces underspecialization of the labor force. Instead of a system where some people work full time at law enforcement, leaving the rest of the community free to specialize in other occupations, every man spends part of his time as investigator, prosecutor, judge, sheriff, and executioner.

2. By placing a premium on the sense of honor, an ethic of revenge makes large-scale cooperation more difficult. Everyone nurses his ego, knowing that the more prone to retaliate against slights he is known to be, the less likely it is that anyone will dare inflict a slight on him. And big egos have difficulty cooperating.

3. The qualification "large scale" is important. Vengeance breeds intense loyalty within small, especially within family, groups, for the victim of a wrong will often be dead, weak, or otherwise incapable of revenging himself (or herself).[6] But powerful loyalties within small groups retard the formation of larger loyalties, to the tribe, the *polis*, or the nation. Thus revenge impedes nation building. This seems to have been Plato's objection, in the *Republic*, to the portrayal of Achilles in the *Iliad*.

4. Acts of revenge tend to be too frequent and too savage,[7] both because they proceed from emotion and because the avenger, being a judge in his own cause, is likely to misjudge the balance of right and wrong in his own favor. With everyone doing this, cooperation (point 2) becomes a huge problem.

5. A related point is that revenge begets feuds, and a feud can be far more destructive than the original aggression. Aggressors become victims whose culturally sharpened instincts for revenge, activated by the revenge taken (perhaps rightfully) against them, are directed toward the original victim, or the victim's avenger. Such a response is especially likely because the aggressor may not realize that he is a wrongdoer; people are adept at rationalizing their conduct (point 4). One cause of feuds is that vengeance tends to operate against the aggressor's family as well as the aggressor himself, because one way of getting even with an

---

[6] For interesting remarks on this theme see Northrop Frye, *Fools of Time: Studies in Shakespearean Tragedy* 25–26, 28 (1967). Women in a revenge society, it should be noted, are almost completely dependent on their male relatives for protection, though literature contains many famous female revengers, two of whom—Aeschylus's Clytemnestra and Euripides' Hecuba—I shall discuss. The theme of women destroyed as a by-product of male revenge is conspicuous in works otherwise as different as *Hamlet* and *Michael Kohlhaas*.

[7] "The spirit of revenge is not economical of human life." Charles A. Hallett and Elaine S. Hallett, *The Revenger's Madness: A Study of Revenge Tragedy Motifs* 11 (1980).

aggressor is to hurt the people he loves. This increases the likelihood that the aggressor will view himself as a victim obliged to revenge the injury that has been done to him. And it further strengthens the family at the expense of the broader community.

6. Relying on revenge for justice sometimes results in too little rather than too much punishment. Because revenge depends on anger (the emotion that ensures our carrying out our genetic-cultural commitment to take revenge regardless of the present balance of costs and benefits), and because most people's anger tends to fade rapidly, revenge may not provide sufficient motivation to track down and punish—perhaps at great cost in time and danger—an aggressor who has managed to elude swift capture. A system of revenge thus places a premium on implacable anger, the harboring of grudges, and the hatred of one's enemies.[8] The passion for revenge is not a sociable emotion! This observation reinforces my earlier point that revenge is inimical to large-scale cooperation. Although vengeance is not an anarchic practice but rather a primitive method of deterring wrongdoing and hence of maintaining a modicum of public order, it depends on a cluster of emotions, such as wrath and touchiness and unforgivingness, and, above all, on refusing to behave "rationally" in the face of slights, that retard the emergence of such forms of social cooperation as the market economy. For cooperation depends on a willingness to compromise desires (the market translates our subjective valuations of goods and services into finite prices), and thus to accept limitation and commensurability as fundamental norms of social interaction.

7. The possibility of the wrongdoer's evading immediate punishment may engender *intergenerational* feuds, as descendants of the original victim pursue the original aggressor or his descendants, and vice versa. This is a further illustration of the costliness of revenge as a system of justice. Yet the blood feud may not even be usable as a law enforcement device if the crime is between family members; the father who kills his son, or the son who kills his father, is the natural avenger of the crime. (*Beowulf* contains a lament over the inadequacy of vengeance in such a situation, while *Oedipus Tyrannus* turns on an alternative "enforcement" device—the "pollution" visited on Thebes as a result of Oedipus's crimes.) Again vengeance manages to be both incomplete and terribly costly.

8. A system of justice founded on vengeance is crude from a moral standpoint once one steps outside the moral framework of the vengeance

---

[8] See C. M. Bowra, *The Greek Experience* 40–43 (1957). As we shall see in Chapter 3, the effects of vengeful feelings on the personality are a theme in Nietzsche.

system itself. The sanctions not only bear no systematic relation to the gravity of the harms inflicted, but they are imposed irrespective of fault. Lacking as it does differentiated institutions for making and applying rules of law, justice-as-vengeance has no means of distinguishing between culpable and justifiable injuries or even for developing the distinction. Liability tends therefore to be absolute. The revenger is as "guilty" as the original aggressor, because there is no concept of justification that would mitigate or eliminate the wrongful character of the injury that the revenger inflicts. This feature of a system of justice as vengeance makes the feud as logical as it is inevitable. Vengeance is a duty; and since the revenger's act is the same kind of wrong as that of the original aggressor, it imposes the same duty of revenge on the revenger's victim.

9. Finally, for the threat of revenge to be a sure deterrent and hence a dependable method of keeping rather than breaking the peace, the natural psychological tendencies of victims and aggressors have somehow to be reversed. Putative victims must have an unshakable commitment to retaliate violently for wrongs done them, regardless of cost, while putative aggressors must be prudently self-restrained by rational calculation of the costs of aggression, which include the possibility of retaliation.

Even before there is a nation or other organized community to take over from the victims of aggression, and their families, the responsibility for catching and punishing aggressors, customs emerge that alleviate some of the problems with revenge as a method for achieving justice. Among these is the idea of exact retaliation (an eye for an eye), which, rather than being bloodthirsty, prevents overreactions (your life for my eye) that are likely to spark feuds. There is also composition (in the legal sense: blood money, wergeld), whereby the victim or the victim's family is required, or at least encouraged, to accept payment in compensation for an injury caused by aggression, discharging the aggressor's liability and thereby heading off a feud. A transfer of money or goods is much less costly to society than violent retribution, and it also fosters market values and, more broadly, an ethic of cooperation.

But as soon as centralized institutions for the enforcement of law emerge, vengeance, even as mitigated by principles of exact retaliation or of composition, comes to be regarded as an archaic and destructive passion. This is partly because exact retaliation does not work well. It is not feasible for all wrongs—for defamation, for instance, or where victim and aggressor are not identically circumstanced (for example, A, who has only one eye, puts out one of B's eyes). It is not adequate in situations where the aggressor can count on avoiding retaliation much of the time, so that punishment does not equal crime when all his punishments and all his crimes are summed. And a commitment to limited retaliation is hard to stick by in the highly emotional circumstances in which revenge is administered. So vengeance falls out of favor,[9] not only in ethics but in law, where taking the law into your own hands itself becomes a crime and where practices are adopted to direct vengeful feelings into socially inexpensive channels, such as giving the victim his day in court in lieu of private vengeance. Revenge by victims and their relatives gives way to retribution by disinterested persons[10]—with advantages made transparent, as we shall see, by *Hamlet*. Yet revenge tends to break out whenever legal remedies are blocked, as when the evildoer controls the legal machinery (*Hamlet* again) or is otherwise above the law, or when public law enforcement is very lax.[11]

Intermediate stages in the evolution from revenge to public enforcement include the duel and, closely related, the trial by battle.[12] Like exact retaliation, these are devices for heading off feuds by establishing a natural terminus to a dispute. Trial by battle has the further advantage

[9] See references in note 1 above and note 12 below; also Frederic Seebohm, *Tribal Custom in Anglo-Saxon Law* (1902). But note that some coexistence of revenge with a formal legal system is possible. See Miller, note 1 above, at 161. We shall see this combination in *Hamlet* and several other works.

[10] A distinction stressed in Sidney Gendin, "A Plausible Theory of Retribution," 5 *Journal of Value Inquiry* 1 (1970).

[11] As in Elizabethan England: see Broude, note 1 above, at 52—or contemporary New York City: see Albert W. Alschuler, "Mediation with a Mugger: The Shortage of Adjudicative Services and the Need for a Two-Tier Trial System in Civil Cases," 99 *Harvard Law Review* 1808–1809 (1986) (the Bernhard Goetz affair). In commenting on Goetz's acquittal by a jury on charges of attempted murder and assault with a deadly weapon committed in circumstances more suggestive of vigilante justice than self-defense, the *New York Times* pointed out that only one in ten felonies committed in New York City is cleared by arrest and only one in fifty results in any imprisonment. *New York Times*, June 17, 1987, at 26.

[12] See Marc Bloch, *Feudal Society* 125–130 (1961); Cherry, note 1 above, lect. 6; Pound, note 1 above, at 140–142; Robert Rentoul Reed, Jr., *Crime and God's Judgment in Shakespeare*, chap. 2 (1984); J. Huizinga, *Homo Ludens: A Study in the Play-Element in Culture*, chap. 4 (1950). Cherry, at p. 68, illustrates the evolution of vengeance into law with the medieval English rule that if you are caught fighting in the king's hall the penalty is death, but if you escape and are caught later, only a money penalty is imposed. The victim will be satisfied with a less bloodthirsty revenge after his anger has cooled, and the early law imitates this pattern. The Law of the Twelve Tables (Roman, fifth century B.C.) contains a similar example of heavier punishment for a thief caught in the act than for one caught later. From the standpoint of deterrence the reverse weighting would make more sense, at least if the greater danger of error in the second case is ignored. Geoffrey MacCormack, "Revenge and Compensation in Early Law," 21 *American Journal of Comparative Law* 69 (1973), is skeptical about some aspects of the theory that law evolved out of vengeance.

of being conceived of as authoritative, and thus leads directly to the modern trial—also a form of combat but one that is less expensive (if a high value is placed on life and bodily integrity) and more likely to produce accurate results. This evolution makes transparent the origins of modern law, in its procedural as well as substantive aspects, in revenge, and shows how superficial the conventional view is, which equates law with order and vengeance with anarchy.

Notice also that law channels rather than eliminates revenge—replaces it as system but not as feeling. Vengeance through law is one of the themes of *The Merchant of Venice*, discussed in the next chapter. And notice that in the view of legal history presented here, the social contract that creates the state and formal law is not a means of overcoming the selfishness and atomistic individualism of man in nature, but virtually the opposite. Revenge is not a selfish emotion, and a revenge ethos breeds powerful family and small-group loyalties. The state creates the conditions in which selfish behavior will not endanger social order.

## Revenge Literature

The character of revenge as a substitute for law can be abundantly illustrated from literature. Consider the legend of the House of Atreus.[13] Thyestes has done various wrongs to his brother, Atreus, in revenge for wrongs done by Atreus to him. Atreus hits on an exquisite scheme of revenge. He invites Thyestes to a banquet ostensibly of reconciliation, and there feeds him the flesh of several of his sons, whom Atreus has slain for the occasion. Then Atreus shows him the sons' severed heads, and when Thyestes asks him what happened to the bodies Atreus explains that Thyestes has just eaten them. Seneca's *Thyestes*, translated into English in 1560 by Jasper Heywood, describes the banquet in excruciating detail, as when Thyestes is made to say (V.3.59–62):

> What tumult tumbleth so my guts
> and doth my bowels gnaw?
> What quakes within? With heavy peise [weight]
> I feel myself oppress'd.

Aegisthus, Thyestes' surviving son or grandson (versions of the legend differ), kills Atreus in revenge and drives away Atreus's sons, Agamemnon and Menelaus. They eventually regain power, but then go

[13] I present a truncated version. For fuller versions see Robert Graves, *Greek Myths* 125–141 (1981 ed.); Edith Hamilton, *Mythology*, chap. 17 (1969); G. S. Kirk, *The Nature of Greek Myths* 165–167 (1974).

off to fight the Trojan War. In their absence Aegisthus seduces Agamemnon's wife, Clytemnestra, who is nursing her own grievance against Agamemnon: to appease Artemis he had sacrificed their daughter Iphigenia en route to Troy. The Trojan War itself is a campaign to take revenge against the Trojans for Paris's seduction of Menelaus's wife, Helen, as well as to recover her.

On Agamemnon's return from Troy he is killed by Clytemnestra with the assistance of Aegisthus. Agamemnon's son, Orestes, then kills Clytemnestra. Pursued by supernatural furies—for Orestes himself would be the natural avenger of his mother's murder, were he not the murderer—Orestes is eventually tried and acquitted by the Court of the Areopagus in Athens, presided over by Athena, and the cycle of vengeance is broken. The story from the murder of Agamemnon to the acquittal of Orestes is the subject of Aeschylus's trilogy the *Oresteia*, of Euripides' *Orestes*, and of a little-known Elizabethan play, Pickering's *Horestes* (1567).[14] *Eumenides*, the last play of the *Oresteia*, ascribes the founding of the Court of the Areopagus, reputed to be the first formal court in the classical world, to a desire to end the cycle of vengeance— thus making transparent the relationship between vengeance and the absence of regular institutions of criminal justice.[15] The problem of

---

[14] See James E. Phillips, "A Revaluation of *Horestes* (1567)," 18 *Huntington Library Quarterly* 227 (1954–1955); David M. Bevington, *From Mankind to Marlowe: Growth of Structure in the Popular Drama of Tudor England* 179–183 (1962); Kathy Hannah Eden, "The Influence of Legal Procedure on the Development of Tragic Structure" 305–315 (Ph.D. diss., Stanford University, 1980). *Horestes* lacks a formal trial scene; other truncated versions of the Orestes story appear in the *Odyssey* and in Sophocles' *Electra*. And see Walter Kaufmann, "Nietzsche between Homer and Sartre: Five Treatments of the Orestes Story," 18 *Revue internationale de philosophie* 50 (1964).

[15] On the trial of Orestes see Michael Gagarin, *Aeschylean Drama*, chap. 3 (1976), especially pp. 74–84; David Luban, "Some Greek Trials: Order and Justice in Homer, Hesiod, Aeschylus and Plato," 54 *Tennessee Law Review* 279 (1987); Posner, note 3 above, at 226–227; Philip Vellacott, "Has Good Prevailed? A Further Study of the *Oresteia*," 81 *Harvard Studies in Classical Philology* 113 (1977). On the idea of justice in the *Oresteia* see David Cohen, "The Theodicy of Aeschylus: Justice and Tyranny in the *Oresteia*," 33 *Greece and Rome* 129 (1986); E. R. Dodds, "Morals and Politics in the *Oresteia*," in Dodds, *The Ancient Concept of Progress, and Other Essays on Greek Literature and Belief* 45 (1973); Eden, note 14 above, chap. 3; Simon Goldhill, *Reading Greek Tragedy*, chap. 1 (1986); Eric A. Havelock, *The Greek Concept of Justice: From Its Shadow in Homer to Its Substance in Plato*, chap. 16 (1978); C. W. Macleod, "Politics and the *Oresteia*," 102 *Journal of Hellenic Studies* 124 (1982); Martha Nussbaum, "Aeschylus and Practical Conflict," 95 *Ethics* 233 (1985); Thomas G. Rosenmeyer, *The Art of Aeschylus*, chap. 12 (1982); Lois Spatz, *Aeschylus*, chap. 5 (1982). Spatz points out how in *Agamemnon*, the first play in the trilogy, legal imagery is used to underscore the law-like aspect of revenge. See id. at 111–112. John Jones, *On Aristotle and Greek Tragedy* 75–79 (1962), is good on Agamemnon's dilemma about whether to sacrifice Iphigenia. For good general treatments of Greek plays discussed in this chapter see Brian Vickers, *Towards Greek Tragedy: Drama, Myth, Society* (1973); Martha C. Nussbaum, *The Fragility of Goodness: Luck and Ethics in Greek Tragedy and*

subjecting royal personages of independent city-states to those institutions is gotten around by making Athena the chief judge, but persists to this day in the international "community."

Until the trial, it is assumed that Orestes' killing of Clytemnestra, though justifiable and indeed inescapable, must itself be avenged (just as it is assumed that Agamemnon had to be killed for sacrificing his daughter, even though he had to do it to get on with the war against Troy—a war ordained by Zeus). Hence the pursuit of Orestes by the Furies. Similarly, although the *Odyssey* presents Odysseus's revenge against the suitors as eminently justifiable, it is understood that, but for Athena's intervention (see Book 24, lines 531–548), the suitors' families would have had to avenge them.

As these examples show, revenge is associated with a particularly uncompromising form of strict liability for harms inflicted however justifiably. So one is not surprised to find that early legal systems, in which the roots of law in revenge still show, rely on strict liability more heavily than modern legal systems do. The protagonist of *Oedipus Tyrannus* is guilty of parricide and incest, and must be punished terribly even though he neither knew nor had reason to know that the man he had killed was his father and the woman he had married was his mother.[16] Oedipus's punishment is an effective metaphor for the human situation. We frequently suffer as a result of acts that we do in warranted ignorance of the possible consequences; in other words, we may be

---

*Philosophy* 409–418 (1986) (*Hecuba*); R. P. Winnington-Ingram, *Sophocles: An Interpretation* (1980), especially chaps. 7–8, 11, 13. Richard Garner, *Law and Society in Classical Athens*, chap. 4 (1987), discusses the interpenetration of law and drama in ancient Athens and in particular the dependence of the tragedians on law for themes, terminology, modes of presentation, and incidental references. Finally, on the general subject of revenge in classical Greek culture see Hubert J. Treston, *Poine: A Study in Ancient Greek Blood-Vengeance* (1923) (chap. 6 is a good though dated study of law and vengeance in Greek tragedy); Margaret Visser, "Vengeance and Pollution in Classical Athens," 45 *Journal of the History of Ideas* 193 (1984); Gagarin, above, at 65–66; Posner, note 3 above, at 217–224; Winnington-Ingram, above, passim.

[16] See Cedric Watts, "King Oedipus and the Toy-vendor," in *Reconstructing Literature* 106, 117 (Laurence Lerner ed. 1983). Another example of the strictness of early law is the refusal in Homeric society to distinguish between accidental and intentional killing; they are punished with equal severity. See A. W. H. Adkins, *Merit and Responsibility: A Study in Greek Values* 52–53 (1960); Posner, note 3 above, at 199, 227. On the nature of Oedipus's guilt, see the interesting discussions in Lloyd L. Weinreb, "Law as Order," 91 *Harvard Law Review* 909, 945–946 (1978), and David Daube, "Greek Forerunners of Simenon," 68 *California Law Review* 301 (1980). And on pollution of blood as a sanction for murder within the family see Posner, note 3 above, at 217–224, and references there. Winnington-Ingram, note 15 above, chap. 11, emphasizes the vengefulness of Oedipus at Colonus, and how it will result in the death of Oedipus's nearest and dearest—Antigone. The destructiveness of revenge is a constant theme in Greek tragedy. See also id., chap. 13.

"punished" for "innocent" or, in the case of Agamemnon, justified (or at least compelled, involuntary, and hence, in modern legal systems, often excused) violations of the order of things. The implied system of liability in *Oedipus Tyrannus* as in the *Oresteia* is crude from a modern legal standpoint, yet this crudeness is bound up with its dramatic effectiveness. Absolute liability makes law a more effective metaphor of necessity—of the external world that bears down on people and ruins their dreams. This is especially true where, as in *Oedipus Tyrannus*, "nature" and "law" are not clearly distinguished.

But we must not exaggerate the legal and ethical gulf between the world of *Oedipus Tyrannus* and our world. Jocasta kills herself and Oedipus blinds himself, but these are effects of horror and remorse, rather than punishments. It is understood that Oedipus cannot remain king—but we must ask what similar revelations would do to the tenure of a modern officeholder.

By the time Sophocles came to write *Oedipus at Colonus* many years after he had written *Oedipus Tyrannus*, notions of liability may have been changing, for the later play contains an emergent sense that there is a moral difference between strict liability and liability based on personal blameworthiness. At Colonus Oedipus asserts his moral innocence, founded on lack of premeditation, or even of carelessness; and perhaps as a result, or partial result, of that innocence, his death on Athenian soil becomes a blessing to Athens rather than, as might have been expected, a curse to the city. An emergent sense of free will—the condition for distinguishing between cause and fault as grounds of liability—is also apparent in the difference between the curse that did in Oedipus in the earlier play (a curse delivered by Oedipus against the then unknown murderer of his father) and the curse delivered by Oedipus in the later play against his son Polynices. Oedipus could have done nothing to escape the consequences of his unwitting self-cursing, but Polynices could escape the consequences of Oedipus's curse just by abandoning his attack on Thebes. (The disastrous consequences of that attack are the subject of *Antigone*, discussed in the next chapter.) Polynices rejects this escape route because he would lose face if he took it, and in particular because he would be humiliated before a younger brother (Eteocles, the ruler of Thebes). So he may be said to choose his fate, and hence to be culpable in a way that Oedipus had not been.

The depiction in *Eumenides* of the trial of Orestes provides a splendid illustration of the transition from a system of absolute liability, enforced by revenge, to one of "legal" liability, based on blameworthiness. Hounded unmercifully by the Furies, Orestes takes refuge with Apollo, who had encouraged him to kill his mother. Orestes thinks it unfair that he should be punished for having done what a god ordained. Apollo agrees, and comes up with the idea of a trial ("the first trial of bloodshed," as Athena says, l. 694), to sort out blame; and the procedure at trial, apart from the presence of divine personages, is an approximation to Athenian trial procedure in the fifth century B.C. The Furies argue that if Clytemnestra's murder of her husband is punishable, which of course is the premise of Orestes' defense, so should be his murder of his mother. To this the obvious reply might seem to be that the killing of Clytemnestra was justifiable because it was punishment for her deed; an executioner is not a murderer. But Clytemnestra, with some justification, regarded her deed as punishment for Agamemnon's having killed their daughter. So Orestes would have to argue either that *that* killing, too, was justified—an unattractive argument of "the end justifies the means" variety—or, more subtly, that Clytemnestra's act, being not just murder but also usurpation, had a political resonance that made it a disproportionate punishment for Agamemnon's misconduct.

Orestes takes a different tack. He asks the Furies why *they* did not punish Clytemnestra, which would have made it unnecessary for him to shed her blood. They reply that they punish only people who kill a blood relative—a son who kills his mother but not a wife who kills her husband. This reply sets the stage for Apollo, Orestes' advocate, to deliver the crushing rebuttal that persuades Athena, and thereby assures Orestes' acquittal by an evenly divided vote of the court (which apparently consists of eleven Athenians plus Athena). Apollo says that Orestes is not really a blood relative of Clytemnestra, because a mother is merely the incubator of the father's child; the father is the only real parent. The modern reader is incredulous, and asks how the Greeks could have failed to notice the physical resemblance between mothers and children, which shows (without any need to know anything about genetics) that the mother is as much a parent as the father. Indeed, the Greeks did know this.

Yet Apollo's argument is not silly in its dramatic context. It comes right after the Furies have said that they punish only the shedding of relatives' blood. This limitation on their jurisdiction is not completely arbitrary. As I remarked in connection with *Beowulf*, murder within the family creates serious problems for a system in which revenge is a duty of family members. A supernatural agency is needed in such a system to revenge such murders, and in the *Oresteia* the Furies are that agency. (In *Oedipus Tyrannus*, also a case of crime against members of the criminal's family, the supernatural agency is the plague that Apollo sends upon

Thebes.) Other murders can be left to revenge by the victim's relatives. However, for the Furies to exclude from their jurisdiction relatives by marriage is absurd; it creates open season on such relatives. In the system of justice envisaged by the Furies, Clytemnestra can kill Agamemnon with relative impunity, knowing that the Furies will not punish her and hoping that the natural revengers (the children of her and Agamemnon) will be deterred by the knowledge that the Furies will punish *them* if they revenge him.

As we shall see in *The Merchant of Venice*, the litigant who takes his stand foursquare on technicality invites his opponent to do the same. Having asserted a distinction, arbitrary in the circumstances, between relatives by blood and by marriage, the Furies invite Apollo to make an arbitrary distinction between the male and the female parent. They are hoist by their own forensic petard. They play doubly into Apollo's hands: his belittlement of women (which the Furies invite) makes Agamamnon's wrong, the killing of Iphigenia, seem less serious. This drives an additional wedge between his wrongdoing and Clytem-nestra's, as well as distinguishing parricide from matricide.

A recurrent theme in this book is that arguments based on legal technicalities, such as Apollo's in *Eumenides* or Portia's in *The Merchant of Venice*, tend—surprising as this may seem—to be more dramatic, and hence more suitable for imaginative literature, than complex, finely balanced, well-reasoned arguments from legal principles and public policy. Technicalities dazzle and surprise, flatter the audience's expectations of what law is *really* like, and take less time to expound. (Another work of literature that turns on a legal technicality is *Felix Holt*, and there are many other examples.) *Eumenides* would be a bore as drama if Aeschylus had made the trial a serious investigation of the arguments pro and con various conceptions of justifiable or excusable homicide; and dramatic exigency is thus one reason why readers should not bring to literature too high hopes of finding legal meat.

Another fascinating literary treatment of the transition from revenge to law, again one with a trial scene though a shorter and less formal one than in *Eumenides*, is Euripides' tragedy *Hecuba*. En route back from Troy with Hecuba and other Trojan women as slaves, the Greek fleet pauses in Thrace, and there the ghost of Achilles demands, and receives, the sacrifice of Hecuba's youngest daughter, Polyxena. A further blow falls on Hecuba. Priam had sent his youngest son, Polydorus, to Thrace for safekeeping. All Hecuba's other sons are dead. Now Polydorus's corpse washes up on shore. The king of Thrace, Polymestor, has killed Polydorus for the gold that Priam had sent with him, now that Priam's fall puts Polymestor (he thinks) beyond risk of Trojan revenge. The twin blows make Hecuba mad for revenge. She asks Agamemnon, who is well disposed to her, to punish Polymestor. He refuses, on plausible political grounds—Polymestor is Greek, and the army would not understand his being punished for having killed a Trojan. Hecuba then lures Polymestor, together with his young children, to her tent. She and her female attendants set upon the visitors with knives and brooches, killing all the children and blinding Polymestor. Agamemnon comes by, drawn by the noise. Hecuba argues the justice of her revenge, while Polymestor argues that he killed Polydorus to prevent him from founding a new Troy that would seek revenge for the destruction of the old one. Hecuba convinces Agamemnon that Polymestor killed Polydorus for the gold, and Agamemnon tells Polymestor that he must bear his punishment. The play ends with Polymestor's accurately predicting the deaths of Agamemnon and Cassandra (Hecuba's only surviving child, and Agamemnon's mistress) and the transformation of Hecuba into a (literal) bitch.

Although we are doubtless meant to think that Hecuba acted excessively by punishing Polymestor's children not only for crimes of which they were innocent but also for a crime (the sacrifice of Polyxena) of which even their father was innocent, the play dramatizes a concept of justified as distinct from reflexive revenge. Justification is assessed by an impartial judge, Agamemnon, after he considers the motive for the alleged wrong (Polymestor's killing of Polydorus). However, if the objective is to domesticate revenge, an adjudication after the fact of the question whether the wrong should have been punished is not good enough. The excessiveness of punishment when left to the victim poisons the process of doing justice even if punishment is warranted. If Agamemnon had not "passed the buck" to Hecuba—if he had punished Polymestor but spared Polymestor's children—maybe Polymestor would not be calling down the wrath of the gods upon Agamemnon, with what effect we know from the *Oresteia*. And maybe it would not be necessary to crown Hecuba's sufferings with her ignominious transformation into a dog.

*Hecuba* illustrates, by the way, a frequent pattern in revenge literature. We the audience start off with great sympathy for the revenger and wish him or her complete success, only to find that as the play (or story) proceeds we cool on revenge. The vivid picture of the revenger's wrong with which we began fades and is replaced by an equally vivid picture of the horrors of the revenge itself. The audience's changing response is the literary counterpart to the cooling of an actual victim's anger, and helps us understand why revenge is infeasible in many cases and repulsive in most of the rest.

THE ELIZABETHANS were fascinated by the theme of revenge.[17] Before Shakespeare's *Hamlet* there was another *Hamlet*, which has been lost, and Kyd's *Spanish Tragedy*, which has many parallels to *Hamlet*, although the avenger in *The Spanish Tragedy*, Hieronimo, is the victim's father rather than his son.[18] The problem for Hieronimo, which will recur in slightly different form in *Hamlet*, is that even though he is a Spanish general and thus a man of power in the state, the man who killed his son and whom he wishes to kill in return—Lorenzo—is the nephew of the King of Spain. At first Hieronimo is hopeful that either God or the authorities will punish Lorenzo, but gradually he is driven to a reluctant acceptance of the fact that the burden of revenge must fall on

---

[17] The rich literature on Elizabethan revenge plays as a genre is illustrated by Philip J. Ayres, "Degrees of Heresy: Justified Revenge and Elizabethan Narratives," 69 *Studies in Philology* 461 (1972); Bowers, note 1 above; Broude, note 1 above; Richard T. Brucher, "Fantasies of Violence: *Hamlet* and *The Revenger's Tragedy*," 21 *Studies in English Literature 1500–1900* 257 (1981); Ernst de Chickera, "Divine Justice and Private Revenge in 'The Spanish Tragedy,' " 57 *Modern Language Review* 228 (1962); Charles A. Hallett and Elaine S. Hallett, note 7 above, and also Hallett and Hallett, " '*Antonio's Revenge*' and the Integrity of the Revenge Tragedy Motifs," 76 *Studies in Philology* 366 (1979); Harold Jenkins, "The Tragedy of Revenge in Shakespeare and Webster," 14 *Shakespeare Survey* 45 (1961); Mary Bonaventure Mroz, *Divine Vengeance: A Study in the Philosophical Backgrounds of the Revenge Motif As It Appears in Shakespeare's Chronicle History Plays* (1941); Reed, note 12 above; Martha Rozett, "Aristotle, the Revenger, and the Elizabethan Audience," 76 *Studies in Philology* 239 (1979); John Sibly, "The Duty of Revenge in Tudor and Stuart Drama," 8 *Review of English Literature* 46 (1967); Ashley H. Thorndike, "The Relations of *Hamlet* to Contemporary Revenge Plays," 17 *Publications of the Modern Language Association* 125 (1902). The revenge theme is ubiquitous in Elizabethan drama. Apart from the plays in which revenge is the central theme, it figures prominently in many others, such as *Romeo and Juliet*, *The Merchant of Venice*, and *Richard III*.

[18] The New Arden (1982) edition of Shakespeare's *Hamlet*, edited by Harold Jenkins, contains in its splendid 159–page introduction a thorough discussion of the antecedents of *Hamlet*, its textual and interpretive problems, and the history of literary criticism of the play. Maynard Mack, "The World of Hamlet," in *Tragic Themes in Western Literature* 30 (Cleanth Brooks ed. 1955), is a classic discussion of the play's mood and themes. A particularly good recent discussion is Alexander Welsh, "The Task of Hamlet," 69 *Yale Review* 481 (1980), while Fredson Bowers, "Hamlet as Minister and Scourge," 70 *Publications of the Modern Language Association* 740 (1955), and Catherine Belsey, "The Case of Hamlet's Conscience," 76 *Studies in Philology* 127 (1979), are good discussions of *Hamlet* as a revenge play. For some sense of the diversity of *Hamlet* criticism (in addition to examples I give later) see *Perspectives on Hamlet* (William G. Holzberger and Peter B. Waldeck eds. 1975). And for the legal buff there is Thomas Glyn Watkin, "Hamlet and the Law of Homicide," 100 *Law Quarterly Review* 282 (1984), discussing such questions as what degree of homicide was Hamlet's killing of Polonius. On *The Spanish Tragedy* see the interesting discussion in Eden, note 14 above, at 316–327.

him. He is careful about obtaining proof of the murderer's guilt, and he feigns madness in order to buy time in which to devise and carry out a suitable plan of revenge. Eventually, by staging a play in which both he and Lorenzo have parts, he is able to stab Lorenzo to death. Bellimperia, Lorenzo's sister, takes the opportunity to stab to death her oppressor, Balthazar, son of the Viceroy of Portugal, and then kills herself. In a nice Senecan touch, Hieronimo bites off his own tongue to prevent himself from giving away secrets under torture (what secrets, the play gives no hint), then kills Lorenzo's father and himself. *The Spanish Tragedy* ends with an allegorical character, Revenge himself, saying that he "shall hale" the villains killed by Hieronimo and Bellimperia "down to deepest hell, / Where none but Furies, bugs and tortures dwell, / . . . For here though death hath end their misery, / I'll there begin their endless tragedy" (IV.5.27–28, 47–48).

The death of Hieronimo is no accident; the avenger dies in virtually every Renaissance revenge play. This may reflect not only Christian ambivalence about the morality of revenge but also recognition that every act of revenge is a fresh wrong that requires punishment in turn. If the avenger were left alive, the audience would be left wondering who would be gunning for him.

*Julius Caesar* is not usually considered a revenge play, but it is one,[19] and not only because of Antony's blood-curdling vow of revenge uttered over Caesar's body (III.1.264–276):

> Domestic fury and fierce civil strife
> Shall cumber all the parts of Italy;
> Blood and destruction shall be so in use
> And dreadful objects so familiar
> That mothers shall but smile when they behold
> Their infants quartered with the hands of war,
> All pity chok'd with custom of fell deeds;

---

[19] See J. A. K. Thompson, *Shakespeare and the Classics* 202–205 (1952); Nicholas Brooke, *Shakespeare's Early Tragedies* 140–141 (1968); cf. Frye, note 6 above, at 25–26, 28. Its character as a revenge play is obscured by the fact that Caesar, the victim on whose behalf revenge is taken, does not die until the beginning of Act III. For excellent general discussions of the play see Brooke, above, at 138–162; David Daiches, *Shakespeare: Julius Caesar* (1976); Adrien Bonjour, *The Structure of Julius Caesar* (1958); John Anson, "Julius Caesar: The Politics of the Hardened Heart," 2 *Shakespeare Studies* 11 (1966); L. C. Knights, *Personality and Politics in Julius Caesar*, in Knights, *Further Explorations* 33 (1965); John Palmer, *Political Characters of Shakespeare* 1–64 (1948); Irving Ribner, "Political Issues in *Julius Caesar*," 56 *Journal of English and Germanic Philology* 10 (1957).

Throughout this book, my quotations from Shakespeare are taken from *The Complete Works of Shakespeare* (David Bevington ed., 3d ed. 1980), except in the case of *Hamlet*, where I use the New Arden edition, note 18 above.

And Caesar's spirit, ranging for revenge,
With Ate by his side come hot from hell
Shall in these confines with a monarch's voice
Cry "Havoc!" and let slip the dogs of war,
That this foul deed shall smell above the earth
With carrion men, groaning for burial.

These lines perfectly express the boundlessness of vengeful feelings. Indeed, the Renaissance sense of the infinitude of human will (so vivid in Marlowe's plays, as we shall see in the next chapter) may explain some of the attraction of the revenge theme to Elizabethan dramatists.

*Julius Caesar* establishes an opposition, typified by the attitudes of the main characters toward the duty of revenge, between two approaches to keeping order in the state. Brutus's approach is "modern," rationalistic, high-minded, and impersonal. It appeals to ideals of civic virtue, individual freedom, and self-government, and it disdains primitive emotions such as vengefulness. Caesar's and Antony's approach is personalistic. It is based on a realistic insight (exemplified by Caesar's assessment of Cassius, and by his stated preference for men who are fat and sleek-headed to those with a lean and hungry look) into the sway that personal and familial ties, emotion generally, and superstition hold over men's minds. Both Caesar and Brutus make fatal mistakes, and in both cases this is due to a failure (in Caesar's case, a failure that marks his loss of grip—his failing insight, which is making him more like Brutus) to appreciate the emotional side of human nature. Caesar fails to understand how accepting a crown, which would bring no increase in his political power, already complete, would affront the proud Senators. And he displays excessive rationalism (in the manner of Brutus) in disregarding the repeated warnings of the soothsayer, the augurs, the elements, and Calpurnia. The play, indeed, insists on linking Brutus and Caesar in small ways and large. Both have wives who want to be consulted (no other character's wife appears in the play); both are susceptible to flattery; both see themselves as occupying a higher plane than other men; both claim exemption from ordinary human weaknesses (a claim undercut in Caesar's case by his superstitiousness and his physical ailments, and in Brutus's case by his political ineptitude); both see themselves as embodiments of pure political principle—absolutism in Caesar's case, liberty in Brutus's; both suffer from hubris.

Brutus's repeated mistakes, which mark him as a political naïf, include failing to enlist Cicero in the conspiracy, sparing Antony and then letting him speak at Caesar's funeral,[20] quarreling with Cassius,

---

[20] I discuss the rhetoric of the funeral orations in Chapter 6 and the Conclusion.

and ignoring Cassius's military advice. But his overarching mistake, reflecting his ignorance of human nature, is to assume that the conspiracy must succeed because all right-thinking men will recognize that Caesar's ambition is a threat to liberty. Brutus fails to realize that the other conspirators are not actuated by high motives; that the Roman mob is not high-minded and does not care about liberty but does care about the terms of Caesar's will (which left both money and public lands to the Roman citizenry); that Antony cares nothing about either his word or the merits of Brutus's cause, but is mad for revenge out of personal loyalty to Caesar; that Antony will be able to turn the mob against Brutus, in part by stressing Brutus's ingratitude—Caesar having treated Brutus like a son; and that Caesar's ghost will hound Brutus. The ghost is the eruption of the nonrational into the political plans of this eminently rational statesman.

The abstract and impersonal conception of political justice that Brutus espouses either is too advanced for the world depicted in *Julius Caesar* or, as Shakespeare may well have believed, makes unrealistic demands on human nature; in any event, in the world depicted in the play, personal bonds trump loyalty to principles. Brutus's obtuseness to this fact is marked for us by such little things as his refusing to bind the conspirators to him by an oath and by his remark (which I imagine the audience is meant to think bizarre) that Caesar's own son, if he had had one, would have approved of the assassination once he was acquainted with the grounds and motives of the conspirators; and by such large things as his inability to comprehend what makes men like Cassius and Antony—who regards himself as Caesar's surrogate son, and who cares not a fig for the conspirators' grounds or motives—tick. Above all, Brutus cannot understand the emotional context in which he is operating, in which the assassination of Caesar must spark an unquenchable passion for revenge.

The play gives us three views of Caesar. The playwright presents him as a man past his prime. This is marked not only by the recklessness with which Caesar disregards supernatural portents but also by his indecision and inconsistency (despite his expressed disdain for superstition, his first remark in the play is a request for a magical cure for Calpurnia's sterility) and, a related point, by the bluster and hollowness of his rhetoric. Just before the assassins strike he compares himself with Mount Olympus, and shortly after having twice changed his mind about going to the Capitol he calls himself as "constant as the northern star" (III.1.60). Brutus, however, sees in Caesar not the aging, slipping tyrant but the personification of ambition. This is typical of Brutus's tendency to depersonalize political issues and deal in abstractions.

For Antony, in contrast, Caesar is simply "the noblest man / That ever lived in the tide of times" (III.1.257–258), an uncritical but unshakable view based on the personal relationship between the two men. From history and *Antony and Cleopatra* we know that if Brutus's theory of governance was premature, and would perhaps be too idealistic for any era, Antony's was becoming outmoded and would soon give way to the calculating methods of Octavius, methods more suitable for governing an empire. The powerful emotional loyalties that characterize a society in which vengeance is an organizing principle are dysfunctional in a large polity. One is reminded of Frye's comment that Shakespeare's tragedies depict a more primitive world than that of Shakespeare's own time.[21] The comment is highly apt to Julius Caesar, in which the passion for revenge dominates political life.

I SHALL leap over two centuries for my next example of revenge literature, Heinrich von Kleist's novella *Michael Kohlhaas* (1810).[22] The eponymous hero (the fictionalized version of an actual historical figure) is a prosperous horse trader in the principality of Brandenburg in sixteenth-century Germany. A Saxon nobleman extorts two beautiful black horses from Kohlhaas, mistreats them, and refuses to return them. Kohlhaas tries to sue the nobleman, but the latter is too influential and Kohlhaas gets nowhere. He decides to take the law into his own hands. With a band of armed followers he sets upon the nobleman's home and kills everyone there (except the nobleman himself, who escapes) and burns the place down. But his thirst for vengeance is unslaked; and meanwhile, as a by-product of his fruitless legal proceedings, his beloved wife has died, which further inflames him. With a growing band, Kohlhaas cuts a swath of destruction through Germany, burning down cities in his futile search for the nobleman. But now Martin Luther, the only man in all of Germany to whom Kohlhaas will listen, intervenes. Luther is furious at Kohlhaas for all the destruction he is causing, but recognizes that

---

[21] See Frye, note 6 above, at 33.

[22] For a sample of the extensive secondary literature (in English—the bulk of the literature is in German) on *Michael Kohlhaas* see John R. Cary, "A Reading of Kleist's *Michael Kohlhaas*," 85 *Publications of the Modern Language Association* 212 (1970); Linda Dietrick, *Prisons and Idylls: Studies in Heinrich von Kleist's Fictional World*, chap. 3 (1985); Denys Dyer, *The Stories of Kleist: A Critical Study*, chap. 7 (1977); John M. Ellis, *Heinrich von Kleist: Studies in the Character and Meaning of His Writings*, chap. 5 (1979); Richard Kuhns, "The Strangeness of Justice: Reading *Michael Kohlhaas*," 15 *New Literary History* 73 (1983); Charles E. Passage, "*Michael Kohlhaas*: Form Analysis," 30 *Germanic Review* 181 (1955).

Kohlhaas has been wronged and promises him an amnesty and a renewed effort at legal redress if Kohlhaas will stop the slaughter and turn himself in—which Kohlhaas does. Tangled judicial proceedings follow, but it proves impossible to recover the horses and Kohlhaas is unwilling to accept their monetary worth in damages from the nobleman, who is now terrified and contrite.

Meanwhile, because members of Kohlhaas's band are continuing to maraud, the Holy Roman Emperor decides that the terms of the Luther amnesty have been violated and that Kohlhaas must stand trial for treason. He is tried, convicted, and sentenced to death. The reader is made to understand that Kohlhaas could get his sentence commuted if only he would give the Elector of Saxony a piece of paper that had been entrusted to Kohlhaas (and that Kohlhaas now wears in a locket around his neck), on which the Elector's destiny is inscribed. But Kohlhaas, who holds the Elector responsible for having failed to bring the nobleman (a subject of the Elector) to justice, refuses. Learning that the Elector is planning to dig up his body after the execution to retrieve the paper, Kohlhaas, with an air of triumph (and a strange echo of *The Spanish Tragedy*), swallows it moments before his execution, to the horror of the Elector, who is in the audience. Kohlhaas dies a happy man.

We are meant, I believe, to understand that Kohlhaas allowed the passion for revenge to run away with him. The incident with the horses, which at the beginning of the novella makes the reader's blood boil and makes him want to egg Kohlhaas on, by the end is recognized to be disproportionate to the destruction, both of others and of self, that is set in train. This is one of the central problems of revenge. And, writing as he was shortly after the subjugation of Germany by Napoleon, Kleist also seems to be commenting on the consequences of German disunity. One reason why Kohlhaas has trouble getting justice is that his oppressor lives in a different German state from him; and the political violence and disorder to which Kohlhaas's band contributes its share are attributed to divided authority (confusingly shared by the Emperor, the Electors, and Martin Luther—the last representing a "higher law" whose principles the temporal authorities are unable to enforce) and to the absence of an effective system of justice. The ineffectuality of "public revenge," as the Elizabethans would have called it, forces Kohlhaas to assume the avenger's role. But, like Hamlet, and Achilles in the *Iliad*, he is carried too far (notably in refusing to accept damages in lieu of the lost horses—and thus symbolically in refusing to accept civil law as a substitute for revenge), becomes a kind of monster (though also hero), and is killed. His death is a curious blend of triumph and tragedy.

In one of the more unusual borrowings in literary history, E. L. Doctorow, in his novel *Ragtime* (1975), transposed the story of Michael Kohlhaas to New York at the beginning of this century. Coalhouse Walker (*Kohle* is the German word for "coal"), a black man who refuses to behave in the submissive manner prescribed for blacks at that period in our history, is the proud owner of a Model T Ford. En route to New York City in the Ford, he is stopped by a rowdy group of firemen who try to make him pay a toll for use of the public street, and when he refuses they deface his car. He tries unsuccessfully to obtain legal redress, but that route is blocked by racial prejudice. His fiancée is accidentally killed while trying to petition the President of the United States for assistance in the matter. Giving up on the law, he organizes a band of marauding black men, and they conduct a ferocious campaign of revenge that includes blowing up the firehouse (but the fire chief is away at the time) and killing firemen. The campaign is less ferocious, though, than Michael Kohlhaas's, reflecting the difference in public order between the societies depicted in the two works.

When Coalhouse Walker and his band barricade themselves in J. Pierpont Morgan's library and threaten to destroy its contents, which include a five-page letter from George Washington—the symbolic counterpart of the message that Michael Kohlhaas carried in a locket around his neck—the authorities enlist the aid of Booker T. Washington, the most famous black man of the day and the counterpart to Martin Luther in *Michael Kohlhaas*. With Washington's assistance a settlement is negotiated. The Model T is restored to its pristine state, the fire chief undergoes a public humiliation, and Coalhouse Walker surrenders—only to be shot down by the police as he leaves the Morgan library.

Doctorow is a skillful writer, and *Ragtime*—with its complex plot and large gallery of historical figures—is an undoubted tour de force, the transposition of *Michael Kohlhaas* to a most unlikely setting being accomplished with great panache. But the spirit of the original is lost. Doctorow is unable to invest the Model T Ford with the powerful symbolism of the black horses, is unable to create either a political resonance (despite the ready-at-hand theme of racism) or a supernatural one, and is unable to make credible the fear that Coalhouse Walker and his band inspire in the white community. In Doctorow's hands, *Michael Kohlhaas* becomes more a farce or fantasy than a meditation on the moral ambiguity of revenge.

## The *Iliad* and *Hamlet*

Having introduced revenge as social practice and literary type, I turn to the *Iliad* for the first of two more detailed studies of revenge literature.[23] When the poem begins, the Greeks are encamped before Troy in the tenth year of their siege. Their army, an assemblage of forces contributed by the different Greek cities (small states, really), is under the command of Agamemnon. The source of his authority is not clear. It obviously is not his intrinsic qualities of leadership, in which he is notably deficient. Apparently it comes either from Mycenae's having contributed the largest contingent to the allied army, a point stressed in the catalogue of ships in Book II, or to its having some traditional primacy among the Greek states, a speculation bolstered by the archaeological evidence from the excavation of the palace at Mycenae. By far the mightiest warrior in the Greek force is Achilles, prince of Phthia, a remote and rather minor state.

When the *Iliad* opens, Apollo has just sent a plague on the Greek camp in response to the prayers of his priest, Chryses. The Greeks had captured Chryses' daughter (Chryseis) in a raid, and in the allotment of spoils she had gone to Agamemnon. Chryses comes to the Greek camp and supplicates Agamemnon to return his daughter, offering lavish gifts and also veiled threats of vengeance. The other Greeks are eager to accept Chryses' offer but Agamemnon rudely rebuffs him, whereupon Chryses calls on Apollo for assistance and Apollo sends the plague. Achilles calls a council of the Greeks. A soothsayer to whom Achilles promptly and publicly offers his protection against any repercussions for speaking uncomfortable truths reveals the cause of the plague. The cure is obvious—return Chryseis—and Achilles, who is young, headstrong, and devoid of tact, insultingly advises Agamemnon to do just that. But in a society, like the Homeric, that lacks formal institutions of

[23] On the political organization of, and role of vengeance in, the world depicted in the *Iliad*, see "The Homeric Version of the Minimal State," in Posner, note 3 above, at 119, and references there. The secondary literature on the *Iliad* is of staggering immensity. Some good places to begin are Jasper Griffin, *Homer*, chap. 2 (1980); Martin Mueller, *The Iliad* (1984); Seth L. Schein, *The Mortal Hero: An Introduction to Homer's Iliad* (1984); James M. Redfield, *Nature and Culture in the Iliad: The Tragedy of Hector* (1975). On the Mycenaean palace culture dimly visible in the *Iliad* see John Chadwick, *The Mycenaean World* (1976); Emily Vermeule, *Greece in the Bronze Age* (1964). My quotations from the *Iliad* are from Robert Fitzgerald's translation (1974). It is an interesting commentary on social change to note how, in the more than 2,500-year span of revenge literature from the *Iliad* to *Ragtime*, the revenger descends in the social scale from a king of semidivine parentage (Achilles), to a prince or aristocrat (Hamlet or Hieronimo), to a businessman (Michael Kohlhaas), and finally to an oppressed black (Coalhouse Walker).

law and governance, this solution is problematic, as Achilles would have realized if he were more mature. The limits of Agamemnon's authority over the allied army are not well defined; nor is the legitimacy of his position established by the kind of "rule of recognition" that determines the identity of the English sovereign or the American president. If Agamemnon were a man of great personal force the ambiguities in his formal authority would not matter so much, but he is not; he is an insecure blusterer. His position being inherently unstable, he can ill afford to lose face; he must show himself ready to protect his interests. If he is to lose Chryseis he must retaliate for the resulting injury. He cannot retaliate against Apollo, so he chooses Apollo's agent, as it were, in the council—Achilles. He takes away the prize that Achilles had been allotted in the expedition that had netted Agamemnon Chryseis—Briseis. An intricate logic of retaliation is thus played out.

Of course this is a grievous error by Agamemnon; one has only to compare his action in stealing Briseis with Paris's in stealing Helen—the *casus belli*—to get the point. Moreover, since Achilles is stronger than Agamemnon and (as events will prove) even more fiercely protective of personal honor, Agamemnon's gambit is reckless, and one of many signs of his unfitness to lead the allied army. Achilles' first impulse is to kill Agamemnon on the spot, and no doubt he would have succeeded had not Athena swept down from Mount Olympus and grabbed him by the hair and told him to stay his hand, assuring him that she would arrange an even better revenge. This divine intervention creates a problem for the modern reader, who would like a more rational explanation. Perhaps it can be found in the following analysis without going beyond what is fairly implied by the text. Achilles, as he and other characters repeat again and again, has been given a choice between a long, comfortable, but inglorious life on Phthia and a short but glorious one fighting the Trojan War. Actually he has no choice, because the gods (we moderns would say, Achilles' character—yet it was Heraclitus who said, "character is destiny") have made the short, glorious life his destiny. And, although Achilles does not realize this, his choice might be undone if he killed Agamemnon. It is hard to see how the Greek alliance could survive such an astonishing blow. What would happen to the Mycenaean contingent—the army's largest? Who would take Agamemnon's place as leader of the alliance? Although Agamemnon is ill-suited for the role (just as Patroclus will later prove unsuitable in the role of Achilles), no one seems better suited—certainly not the headstrong Achilles, or the cuckolded Menelaus, or Odysseus, who comes from one of the least significant

Greek states. Athena's intervention is thus necessary to protect Achilles as well as Agamemnon.

So Achilles stays his hand, and is promised and receives a sweeter revenge, which consists of watching the Trojans make mincemeat of the Greeks in his absence, until in Book IX Agamemnon sends emissaries to Achilles' tent promising him the moon (not just Briseis back—untouched—but also Agamemnon's daughter in marriage and countless other gifts of high value) if he will rejoin the fighting. Yet acutely conscious that if he fights he will die young, and beginning to question the entire heroic ethic in which glory is considered apt compensation for dying young, Achilles does not rejoin the fighting until Hector kills Achilles' dear friend and companion, Patroclus—who wearing Achilles' armor to fool the Trojans had momentarily forgotten his own limitations and gone too near Troy. When Achilles does rejoin the fighting he pursues Hector with a savagery marked by the poet as excessive even by the standards of heroic culture. Achilles kills Hector (who—wearing Achilles' old armor, which he had stripped from the slain Patroclus—momentarily and fatally forgets his own limitations, just as Patroclus had done) and mutilates Hector's body. But in the last book of the epic Achilles surprisingly relents, and returns Hector's body, miraculously unmutilated, to Priam. We are given to understand that, by killing Hector, Achilles has sealed both Troy's fate and his own.

At one level, the level one might suppose would be most interesting to a lawyer, the *Iliad* is "about" justice, specifically revenge as a system of justice. We are given to understand that revenge works. Troy will be destroyed in revenge for Paris's having stolen Helen in violation of the norms of hospitality that are so important in primitive and ancient cultures. (Paris had been Menelaus's guest when he had stolen Helen.) But we are also made acutely conscious of the costs of this method of law enforcement, and perhaps invited to wonder whether there might not be a cheaper method of dealing with the likes of Paris. We are also made to understand that revenge ought to have some limits—that Achilles goes too far in mutilating Hector and that the return of Hector's body to Priam is necessary to prevent the Greeks from crossing the line that separates lawful revenge from barbarism.

The *Iliad* also provides a glimpse of composition—the payment of compensation for wrongs done, an early stage in the transition from revenge to law—both in Agamemnon's elaborate offer to compensate Achilles and in one of the scenes on Achilles' new shield (XVIII.466–479):

> A crowd, then, in a market place, and there
> two men at odds over satisfaction owed
> for a murder done: one claimed that all was paid,
> and publicly declared it; his opponent
> turned the reparation down, and both
> demanded a verdict from an arbiter,
> as people clamored in support of each,
> and criers restrained the crowd. The town elders
> sat in a ring, on chairs of polished stone,
> the staves of clarion criers in their hands,
> with which they sprang up, each to speak in turn,
> and in the middle were two golden measures
> to be awarded him whose argument
> would be the most straightforward.[24]

But composition is not a perfect substitute for revenge, at least not in the heroic, wartime world, in contrast to the peaceable world depicted on the shield. Or at least not for Achilles—not yet, anyway—who, in refusing Agamemnon's offer, expresses one of the recurrent problems of a revenge ethic, that of emotional excess (IX.383–386):

> Not if his gifts outnumbered the sea sands
> or all the dust grains in the world could Agamemnon
> ever appease me—not till he pays me back
> full measure, pain for pain, dishonor for dishonor.

Like Michael Kohlhaas, who refuses the nobleman's offer of damages, Achilles cannot be "bought." Until his anger runs its course or is deflected to another object (both things happen eventually), there is no possibility of a peaceful settlement with Agamemnon. Until then,

---

[24] For a good discussion of the shield scene see Michael Gagarin, *Early Greek Law*, chap. 2 (1986). For an argument that the arbiter is a public official and the proceeding a formal trial rather than, as has usually been thought, a private arbitration, see Hans Julius Wolff, "The Origin of Judicial Litigation among the Greeks," 4 *Traditio: Studies in Ancient and Medieval History, Thought and Religion* 31, 36–49 (1946). Wolff's thesis is attacked in Gagarin, above, at 28, and defended in Raphael Sealey, *The Athenian Republic: Democracy or the Rule of Law?* 78–81 (1987). Wolff's best evidence is the presence of the criers. The crier (*kerux*, usually translated "herald") is a public official (virtually the only type of public official, other than kings, in the Greek states depicted in the Homeric poems) whose job is to maintain order in assemblies. One way he does this is by handing a stave to the person whose turn it is to speak; no one else may speak until that person relinquishes the stave. The heralds and staves are present in the shield scene. But this cannot be decisive in favor of Wolff's interpretation; we would not call a rock concert an official event just because police were present to keep order. Perhaps the most sensible observation on the controversy is that the political institutions of Homeric society are too rudimentary and undifferentiated to enable a sharp distinction to be drawn between public and private methods of dispute settlement.

nothing is bad enough for Agamemnon. The *reductio ad absurdum* of this attitude is Atreus's regret that he did not make Thyestes drink his sons' blood while they were still living. We shall meet the problem again in *Hamlet*.

The *Iliad* makes us understand not only the excessive character of the passion for revenge—as epitomized by Achilles' inhuman wrath (*mēnis*, a Greek word otherwise used only of the anger of gods) and contrasted with the peaceable mode of dispute settlement depicted on Achilles' new shield—but also its fragility as a principle of social order. The vindication of the norms of hospitality through the successful completion (but at what cost!) of the siege of Troy is impeded by the vendetta between Achilles and Agamemnon. Until the last book of the *Iliad* Achilles acts entirely out of concern for his personal honor and, what is not clearly distinguished from it, his personal possessions, signally including Briseis and Patroclus. (This is his "unsociability," which troubled Plato.) It is made to seem almost an accident that at the critical moment Achilles' personal incentives to go after Hector line up with the needs of the Greek alliance, for which Achilles cares not a fig. We know he will not throw up the game and go home to Phthia but we also know that he easily could, and knowing this we are led to wonder whether a social order based on a heroic code and the violent defense of personal honor is stable; the collision between Agamemnon and Achilles in Book I suggests it is not. Not only Achilles' own questionings of the heroic code but the events of the *Iliad*, which ends before the triumph of the alliance and depicts the alliance in disarray, reinforce the suggestion. Also, beginning with the symbolic death of Achilles when Hector kills Patroclus, who is wearing Achilles' armor (and at first Hector thinks Patroclus is Achilles), images of death progressively enshroud Achilles, foreshadowing his actual death, which is to occur shortly after the close of the *Iliad*, and contributing to a sense that the heroic code is being depicted in its twilight. And we shall see in Chapter 3 that the *Odyssey* presents the heroic world more as legend than as actuality.

Against this reading can be placed the strong sense the *Iliad* conveys that death imparts dignity to life. The gods are immortal, yet no god depicted in the *Iliad* has the dignity of Achilles at his best. But when is that? Although the poet is acutely conscious of the negative side of the heroic ethic, I think he is telling us that Achilles' tragic mistake was not the refusal to yield to the entreaties of Agamemnon's emissaries in Book IX, a refusal solidly grounded in the absolutism of heroic character, but the compromise of sending Patroclus to fight in Achilles' place. The compromise has all the earmarks of modern instrumental reasoning. It is antithetical to the sacred code of honor that informs the vengeance ethic epitomized by Achilles, and it marks his doom.

James Boyd White, in a major book on law and literature, devotes one of his longest chapters to the *Iliad*, but he does not discuss the prelegal institutions that the *Iliad* depicts or the theme of justice that it develops.[25] He makes only two attempts to relate the poem to law. Concerning Achilles' statement in Book I that Agamemnon will have to wait till Troy falls before he is compensated for giving back Chryseis, White says: "The issue is stated with the directness of a modern legal case: there are apparently two accepted conceptions of what is 'fitting,' only one of which can be satisfied. It is like what happens in law when two lines of precedent, both solidly established, are seen to point opposite ways when a case that no one ever thought of comes up or when two rules of law are suddenly found to be in conflict" (p. 34). Any argument can be analogized to a legal dispute; what is significant from a lawyer's standpoint about the disputes in the *Iliad* is that the society depicted in the poem lacks public agencies for resolving disputes and must therefore fall back on custom, ritual, and the gods (as in Athena's grabbing Achilles by the hair) to minimize the costs of purely private methods of dispute settlement such as the feud. White is not interested in comparing the methods of dispute settlement in the *Iliad* to those of a society that has a public machinery of law enforcement.

White says that "the best analogue" to the language of heroic poetry "in our own experience might be the language of the law, which from some points of view may seem similarly discrete and bounded, similarly constitutive of a certain set of clear social relations and expressive of a certain set of clear values" (p. 55). It is true that both the Homeric dialect and the language of law are artificial languages, but again the analogy is too remote to illuminate either term compared. All languages are artificial, including ordinary spoken language. White's observation will not help us understand what is distinctive about either Homer or law.

As these examples (and others, discussed in Chapter 6) suggest, when White pauses to summarize, or to generalize or draw conclusions, he sometimes becomes vague, as when he says: "The *Iliad* instructs us in the reality of such a universal vision [that all human experience is at once unique and collective], while at the same time teaching us that it is imperfectly attainable by man" (p. 58). It is hard to quarrel with this but hard to get much out of it either.

[25] *When Words Lose Their Meaning: Constitutions and Reconstitutions of Language, Character, and Community*, chap. 2 (1984). In *Heracles' Bow: Essays on the Rhetoric and Poetics of the Law* 175–180, 190 (1985), White discusses the *Oresteia* briefly, again without reference to revenge.

Most of White's chapter on the *Iliad* is devoted to observations about specific features of the poem, and the observations are always intelligent. But they reveal few traces of a lawyer's skills and training. Competent literary criticism is to be valued whatever the professional background of the critic; if lawyers like Wallace Stevens and Franz Kafka can be great imaginative writers, James White can be a great critic. But so immense and distinguished is the corpus of Homeric criticism that it is hard to say much that is new about the *Iliad* without having a distinctive point of view. The fact that lawyers are sensitive to rhetoric and that the *Iliad*, like most literature, is highly rhetorical does not establish a close enough connection between the fields to give the lawyer access to such secrets as may have eluded two millennia of Homeric scholarship. If a lawyer had something fresh to say about the *Iliad* one might expect it to concern the revenge ethic displayed and (perhaps) implicitly criticized there.

I offer three conjectures on why White is not interested in that aspect of the poem. First, although revenge is the prelegal method of vindicating rights and maintaining (if erratically) the public order, it is not a subject likely to interest a lawyer. The legal literature on revenge is sparse; the analysis of revenge in the first section of this chapter drew on biology, anthropology, literary criticism, classical history, psychology, and economics. The lawyer's concern with matters of justice and order, of rights and wrongs, of claims and defenses and the machinery of enforcement, is limited to a corner of the vast domain of law and justice, the corner occupied by the formal doctrines and institutions of mature legal systems centered on courts and legislatures.

Here we should note a dilemma that faces the law and literature movement. It is a part of legal theory as defined in the Introduction and seeks to broaden the range of legal analysis, but its ability to do so is hampered by the narrowness of the lawyer's competence. When literature deals with law it tends to deal not with its technical aspects (except for their dramatic effect) but with law and justice in the large—an airy realm into which few lawyers soar. I do not mean that lawyers lack a "sense of justice"; the idea that justice and legality are opposed is a fallacy, as we shall see in subsequent chapters. But the professional training and experiences of lawyers do not give them a comparative advantage in studying nontechnical issues in law, such as the role of revenge as a principle of justice in primitive and ancient societies.

Another reason for White's lack of interest in the theme of revenge in the *Iliad* may be that this theme, although important on the narrative level, is not central to the work's significance as literature; I will explain this point after I discuss *Hamlet,* about which another literary lawyer,

Richard Weisberg, has written recently. Finally, although the revenge theme is the subject on which a lawyer seeking to say something new about the *Iliad* might be expected to concentrate, White may not care greatly about saying something new. I do not mean to sound critical. I am describing an aspect of traditional legal culture, for which White, despite his avant-garde interest in interdisciplinary legal studies, is emphatically a spokesman. As in so much legal writing, both scholarly and forensic, White's emphasis is on continuity rather than originality— this may indeed be one of the few things that mark his writing about the *Iliad* as legal rather than literary. More important, his enterprise is normative rather than scientific. A representative of the moralistic tradition in literary criticism (see Chapter 6), White believes that the function of the great texts is to make readers better people, and specifically to make lawyer-readers "better" lawyers in a sense that combines virtue and skill. He is not in quest of novel meanings.

THE STORY of *Hamlet* is familiar, but the details of its intricate plot may not be familiar to all readers of this book and are important to my analysis. Hamlet's father, the king of Denmark, has died in mysterious circumstances. The king's brother, Claudius, has ascended the throne and has married—within a month of his brother's death—the king's widow, Gertrude. The ghost of Hamlet's father appears to Hamlet and reveals that Claudius murdered him. The ghost insists that Hamlet promise to avenge the murder, and Hamlet does so with great enthusiasm. Yet, mysteriously—this is the abiding mystery of the play and the source along with the marvelous poetry of its great fascination— nothing happens. Instead of getting about his business, Hamlet feigns madness—to what end is unclear. Although *Hamlet* is an incomparably greater play than *The Spanish Tragedy*, Hamlet's motive for delay and for feigning madness is less clear than Hieronimo's. (Of course, the ambiguity and open-endedness of *Hamlet* are part of its fascination—and perhaps, as we shall see, a component of its greatness as literature.) It is plausible that Hamlet, like Hieronimo, should need time to overcome Christian scruples against private revenge, to gather proof of Claudius's guilt, and to devise a scheme to do Claudius in, and that he might want to simulate madness in order to throw Claudius off the scent in the meantime. But the play itself does not suggest that these are the causes of Hamlet's behavior, and the only effect of Hamlet's "madness" is to arouse Claudius's suspicions.

After dithering awhile and reproaching himself for his laggardness,

Hamlet takes advantage of the presence of a troop of actors to enact in Claudius's presence a thinly disguised play of his father's murder. Claudius indeed gets the point, and interrupts the performance. Hamlet, on the way to his mother's room where she has summoned him at Polonius's suggestion to explain his strange behavior (apparently Gertrude never realizes that Claudius killed her husband, although she had been carrying on with Claudius before her husband's death), sees Claudius alone, in (attempted) prayer, and draws his sword to kill him. But he changes his mind, saying to himself that if he kills Claudius at prayer Claudius will go to heaven. Hamlet proceeds to his mother's room, and there he upbraids her fiercely for her remarriage and urges sexual abstinence. In the course of the interview he stabs to death Polonius (who is hidden behind a tapestry, eavesdropping), thinking he is Claudius.

Claudius, thoroughly alarmed—which shows, by the way, what a flop the "play within the play" stratagem, like the madness stratagem, proves to be for Hamlet—dispatches Hamlet to England, a tributary state of Denmark in the medieval period in which the play is set. Hamlet's escorts, Rosencrantz and Guildenstern, carry secret orders from the king to have Hamlet put to death upon arrival. Hamlet discovers the orders, substitutes revised ones directing the English to execute the bearers on arrival, and then providentially returns to Denmark on a pirate ship. When he arrives, he discovers that Ophelia, whom he had been in love with and who had literally been driven crazy by his feigned madness and by the killing of Polonius—her father—has died in an accident. (Suicide is suspected by most of the play's characters, but the description of Ophelia's drowning suggests that it was accidental.) Hamlet also discovers that Ophelia's brother, Laertes, has come home, furious. The king, urging Laertes (with lovely irony) to take revenge against Hamlet for the deaths of Laertes' father and sister, arranges a fencing match between Laertes and Hamlet, with Laertes' foil unbated and poison-tipped, and a poisoned cup in reserve. The foils are exchanged by accident during the match, and both Laertes and Hamlet receive fatal wounds, while Gertrude drinks from the cup by mistake and dies. Realizing what is happening, Hamlet at last runs Claudius through, and for good measure makes him drink from the cup too. Then Hamlet dies from his wound.

Although the Denmark depicted in the play, unlike the society depicted in the Homeric epics, has a formal legal system, Claudius certainly, and Hamlet and the other principals probably, are effectively above the law. There is little likelihood that Hamlet might be punished for killing Polonius and trying to conceal his body (Claudius raises the issue briefly, only to reject it on the ground that Hamlet is too popular), or even for killing the king. And there is no hint that Claudius might be impeached or otherwise brought to book for murdering the rightful king and making an incestuous marriage. (The characters in the play—at least some of them—are depicted as sharing the Elizabethan view that marrying a sister-in-law is incest.) The only way for Hamlet to obtain justice against Claudius, or for Laertes to obtain justice against Hamlet, is by revenge.

Can the play be said to be a criticism of revenge? Seven people die en route to its successful consummation—Polonius, Ophelia, Rosencrantz, Guildenstern, Gertrude, Laertes, and Hamlet—and although by no means all are innocent, none deserves to die save possibly Laertes, who murders Hamlet by trick. Yet Laertes is presented as a hot-headed young fool, easily manipulated by Claudius; moreover, Hamlet did kill Laertes' father, without adequate excuse, and drive Laertes' sister crazy, with even less excuse. Laertes is provoked and manipulated, and thus more sinned against than sinning. These seven deaths mark revenge as an expensive way of doing justice.

Another problem with revenge that the play brings out is that it places responsibilities on people who are not temperamentally well suited to bear them, in contrast to a system of justice whose personnel—judges, police, prosecutors, and so forth—are volunteers (all but jurors!). When Hamlet says at the end of Act I, having just received his marching orders from the ghost, "The time is out of joint. O cursed spite, / That ever I was born to set it right" (I.5.196–198), the emphasis falls on "I." For it will soon become plain that Hamlet is not a fit instrument for the ghost's plan; only there is no one else. Hamlet kills Claudius after having given up active (and by the evidence of the earlier part of the play, bound to be bungling and ineffectual) efforts to do Claudius in. And it is only by chance that Hamlet discovers what is afoot and is able to kill Claudius before he himself dies. Moreover, his failure to check the foils before beginning the match—knowing what he knows of Claudius's previous effort to kill him and of Laertes' rage against him—is negligent in the extreme.

Claudius, implicitly commenting on Hamlet's dilatoriness in making an attempt on his life, warns Laertes that his (Laertes') anger may cool with time. Claudius is also eloquent on the theme of the "many a slip 'twixt cup and lips" problem of revenge, which again is Hamlet's problem, or one of them. But these are not Laertes' problems. Whereas Hamlet acts too slowly and cools, Laertes acts too quickly while still red hot. Laertes mistakes the object of his revenge: it should be Claudius, not Hamlet. While Hamlet wastes time building an unnecessary case against Claudius, Laertes, who as Polonius's son has the same duty of vengeance as Hamlet does toward his own father, leaps to the wrong conclusion—thus underscoring the dangers in being a judge in one's own cause.

Both Hamlet and Laertes illustrate the problem of the avenger's emotional excess. Hamlet forgoes an opportunity to kill Claudius while the latter is praying; if he had taken the opportunity, seven lives would have been spared (Hamlet does not know this, of course), but he wants to make sure that Claudius burns in hell. (Notice the parallel to *The Spanish Tragedy*.) Similarly, though characteristically more crudely, when Claudius says to Laertes, "Hamlet comes back; what would you undertake / To show yourself in deed your father's son / More than in words?" Laertes answers, "To cut his throat i'th' church." Claudius replies, "No place indeed should murder sanctuarize; / Revenge should have no bounds." (IV.7.122–127.) But of course it should; that must be one of the points the reader is meant to bring away from the play.

*Hamlet* stands to its contemporary revenge literature as the *Iliad* presumably stood to the lost heroic epics on which it built. In many Elizabethan and Jacobean revenge plays the violence and the revenger's emotional excess are so grotesque that any social or ethical observation is submerged in melodramatic effect. Consider that strange cross between *Thyestes* and *The Spanish Tragedy*, Shakespeare's early play *Titus Andronicus*. Among other horrors, Titus, the avenger (like Hieronomo a high official who cannot get justice through lawful means because the evildoers are royal personages), borrowing a leaf from Atreus, kills Queen Tamora's two sons and serves them to her in a pie, remarking to someone who asks him to fetch the boys (V.3.60–63),

> Why, there they are, both baked in this pie,
> Whereof their mother daintily hath fed,
> Eating the flesh that she herself hath bred.
> 'Tis true, 'tis true; witness my knife's sharp point

—whereupon he stabs the queen and is stabbed in turn. Or consider Cyril Tourneur's *Revenger's Tragedy*, written a few years after *Hamlet*. The pattern is familiar. The evildoer is the king; so Vindice, to avenge his wife's murder by the king, must act outside the law. Vindice has kept his wife's skull, and now he covers it with poison. He lures the king, who is a lecher, to a dark bower on pretense of supplying him with a woman. The king embraces the skull in the dark, with the desired effect.

To make the king's death still more painful, Vindice has lured the queen and her lover to the bower so that the last thing the king will see before the poison kills him is his wife in an act of adultery. When the king tries to shout, Vindice cuts his tongue out.[26]

The most dramatic rejection of the revenge ethic is found in the New Testament; and we must consider whether *Hamlet*, and perhaps the gorier revenge plays as well, are trying to remind the audience of Romans 12:19–20: "Avenge not yourselves, but rather give place unto wrath: for it is written, Vengeance is mine; I will repay, saith the Lord. Therefore if thine enemy hunger, feed him; if he thirst, give him drink: for in so doing thou shalt heap coals of fire on his head."[27] There are two ways to take this. The first (suggested by the reference to "coals of fire") is that God will straighten out all the accounts in the afterlife; the second is that God will punish the evildoer in this life. The first is not a practical formula for living. No society can maintain order just by appeals to posthumous rewards and sanctions; hence the notion mentioned at the beginning of this chapter of "public revenge" as the exercise of a power delegated to kings by God. The second interpretation, in its pure form (leave it to God to punish the wrongdoer in this life—do not even try to get the help of God's delegate, the king), is found in the fifth act of *Hamlet*. Hamlet abandons active efforts to kill Claudius, trusting in Providence to arrange time,[28] place, and manner ("There's a divinity that shapes our ends, / Rough-hew them how we will" and "The readiness is all," V.2.10–11, 218)—which obligingly it does. In Act V the ghost seems forgotten—a scary, pagan figure. The revenge ethic that the ghost embodies is made to seem primitive, pre-Christian. Christian values are more to the fore. Hamlet's death is suffused with a tragic dignity that it would have lacked had he carried out with smooth efficiency the task assigned him by his father's ghost.

Yet within the dramatic structure and implied values of the play as a

---

[26] In Webster's *White Devil*, the method of revenge against Bracchiano is to smear poison on the inside of the lower visor of his helmet, causing him hideous agonies which go on for pages; finally the avengers get impatient and strangle him.

[27] The King James Bible, from which I have quoted, was not yet in existence when Shakespeare wrote *Hamlet*. But the bibles he would have known—the *Coverdale Bible* (1535), the *Geneva Bible* (1583), and the *Bishops' Bible* (1588)—do not differ materially from the King James version in the relevant passage. Here for example is the same passage in the *Coverdale Bible*: "Avenge not yourselves, but give room unto the wrath of God. For it is written: Vengeance is mine, and I will reward, sayeth the Lord. Therefore if thine enemy be hungry, feed him. If he thirst, give him drink. For in so doing thou shalt heap coals of fire upon his head."

[28] See Frye's marvelous discussion of acting in "God's time" rather than with characteristic human impatience, note 6 above, at 89–94.

whole, quietistic resignation would not have been an adequate response by Hamlet to the ghost's urging him on to action. Although *Hamlet* portrays with consummate art the negative aspects of private revenge as a method of vindicating rights and maintaining public order—in the stupid bloodthirstiness of Laertes and the destructive ineffectuality of Hamlet's schemes of revenge—it leaves us with the abiding sense that Hamlet had no choice, despite Romans, but to try as best he could to avenge his father. When law is inoperative, private revenge becomes an inescapable duty.[29] Euripides sought to debunk the Orestes legend by situating his *Orestes* in a society with a fully operative legal system, in which—as Tyndareus, Clytemnestra's father, reminds Orestes— Orestes did not have to kill his mother; he could have turned her over to the authorities for punishment. Hamlet does not have this choice. *Hamlet* is a powerful argument for the rule of law, though of course it is much more than that.

Hamlet's biggest mistake, the standard revenger's mistake, is to get carried away. The train of unnecessary deaths is set in motion when he forgoes the opportunity to kill Claudius at prayer because he wants to make sure that Claudius's punishment is eternal. The false step of sparing Claudius has a deeper significance, however. Claudius's prayer soliloquy reveals to the audience that Hamlet is mistaken in believing that if he kills Claudius at prayer Claudius will go to heaven. Maybe the audience is even supposed to think Hamlet's mistake a stupid one. Since Hamlet never deludes himself that Claudius might voluntarily relinquish the fruits of his crimes—the kingship and the queen—he should realize that Claudius's "repentance" is false and will not save Claudius from damnation. We shall encounter a parallel example in *Doctor Faustus*, in the next chapter.

Despite appearances, I am not making the common mistake of treating characters in literature as if they were real people. There is no basis in the text of *Hamlet* for assuming that Hamlet *realizes* that Claudius will not be saved if killed at prayer, or even for the slightly more plausible assumption that Hamlet could not be so bloodthirsty as to wish to damn Claudius for eternity, and therefore the reason he gives

---

[29] For a good discussion see Belsey, note 18 above. Eleanor Prosser, *Hamlet and Revenge* (2d ed. 1971), argues that Hamlet should not have obeyed the ghost. Her argument has little support in the text and is inconsistent with the Elizabethans' ambivalence about revenge; acceptance of the argument would imply a complete absence of remedies against a bloody usurper—an unacceptable result. See the references cited in notes 1 and 17 above, and Michael Cameron Andrews, "Hamlet: Revenge and the Critical Mirror," 8 *English Literary Renaissance* 9 (1978). Also pertinent is Frye's point that Shakespeare's tragedies are set in societies depicted as more primitive than Elizabethan England.

for sparing him must be a pretext. Not only is excessive bloodthirstiness the occupational hazard of a revenger, but it is a marked characteristic of Hamlet in Act III. But what the text fairly implies is that Hamlet is a bungler at revenge and spares Claudius for an objectively foolish reason.

Pretext enters elsewhere. Hamlet's expressed concern that the ghost might be a devil, which leads him to delay his revenge so that he can stage the play within a play in order to test Claudius's guilt, seems marked as a pretext for further delay. Hamlet tumbles to the idea in the midst of reflections on his inexplicable and unpardonable tardiness in carrying out the ghost's command; and doubt about the ghost's bona fides, never before expressed by Hamlet, is a convenient rationalization for past delay and an excuse for more delay. True, one can argue from the concerns expressed by Horatio and the nightwatchmen at the beginning of the play, as well as from the general reputation of ghosts among the Elizabethans, that Hamlet had good reason to fear that the purported ghost of his father might be a devil. Jeffrey Burton Russell even argues that the ghost of Hamlet's father *is* a devil: "The specter was not the ghost of King Hamlet or of any human being."[30] All other objections to this interpretation aside, it diminishes the play by making Hamlet the puppet of demonic forces. Yet Claudius has such a civil and plausible demeanor (he is the Stanley Baldwin of Shakespearean villains) that Hamlet could well be skeptical about the ghost's uncorroborated accusation; Claudius's soliloquies are necessary to make his wickedness convincing to the audience, and Hamlet is not in the audience. So Hamlet's sudden doubt about the ghost's bona fides has some foundation and also illustrates the problem of proof that plagues a revenge system of justice (a problem also stressed in *Othello*) because there is no machinery of investigation and adjudication. Yet the doubt proceeds more from Hamlet's character than from objective circumstances; for, as late as Act V, long after the ghost's veracity has been confirmed, Hamlet is wondering whether he has enough evidence to proceed against Claudius.

A sufficient motive for delay might seem to be the possibility that Claudius might be armed, or surrounded by guards, or that someone might seek to avenge *his* killing. But these conjectures have very little basis in the text of the play (in contrast to *The Spanish Tragedy*)—and in fact no one lifts a finger when Hamlet stabs Claudius at the end of the play and then makes him drink from the poisoned cup to boot. Although the royal trappings are necessary both to elevate the characters

---

[30] *Mephistopheles: The Devil in the Modern World* 73 (1986); see id. at 69–73 for the full argument. Cf. note 29 above.

in an Elizabethan audience's esteem and to put them far enough above the law to make the duty of revenge plausible, the political overtones so prominent in Shakespeare's Roman and history plays are muted. Cassius needs to organize a conspiracy in order to assassinate Caesar, but there is little suggestion that Hamlet faces a political task in dealing with Claudius. And although the play demonstrates the tendency of revenge to miscarry, Hamlet exhibits no concern on that score except when he momentarily questions the ghost's genuineness.

It may be that an Elizabethan audience, more impressed than a modern audience with the majesty of kingship and the New Testament's injunction against vengeance, would have taken for granted that the ghost's command could not be carried out quickly and easily. The mention of the king's Swiss guards; the impression that Polonius, and later Rosencrantz and Guildenstern, have been set to watch over Hamlet; Rosencrantz's "cess of majesty" speech (III.3.15-23); and Claudius's remark to Gertrude (deeply ironic though it is), "Do not fear our person. / There's such divinity doth hedge a king / That treason can but peep to what it would, / Acts little of his will" (IV.5.123-125), may have been all the textual hints that such an audience required. Yet Hamlet himself voices no concerns along these lines. His words and deeds suggest that the basic cause of his delays and pratfalls is that he is temperamentally unsuited to play the avenger's role. He is not a Vindice, Titus, Hieronimo (who does, however, hesitate some), Kohl-haas, or Orestes.[31] As his father's ghost tells him when it returns in Act III, and as Hamlet keeps telling himself, he does not have the implacable rage, the single-minded fury, the towering wrath, that a proper avenger has. The "To be, or not to be" soliloquy is the *locus classicus* of the mind in equipoise (as well as an ingenious rationalization for inaction)—the mind that sees, perhaps too clearly for forthright action, both sides of every question. And more than a habit of mind is involved. Hamlet is labile; his strongly marked impulsiveness is the other side of his quickness to cool. When he asks the ghost to make haste to acquaint him with the details of the murder so that "with wings as swift / As meditation or the thoughts of love" he "may sweep to [his] revenge" (I.5.29-31), it is as if he realizes that unless he acts quickly he may fail to act at all—his initial anger may give way to his characteristically detached and reflective posture.

---

[31] Despite the parallels between the Hamlet and Orestes stories pointed out in Gilbert Murray, *Hamlet and Orestes: A Study in Traditional Types* (1914). Hamlet and Orestes are both princes dispossessed by the murder of a king-father by (or with the assistance of) the mother's lover, and bent on revenge.

Neither does Hamlet have that overdeveloped—and also automatic, unhesitating—sense of honor so well illustrated by the willingness of Fortinbras (another of the play's avengers) to sacrifice thousands of lives for a worthless bit of land. Hamlet lacks single-mindedness. A prey to the teeming imagination revealed in his soliloquies, Hamlet becomes distracted by what from the standpoint of vengeance is a side issue: his mother's adultery and incest. (It is a side issue because his mother is innocent of his father's murder and because his father has told him not to harm her.) Hamlet is a thinker, but not a planner like Antony. Maybe he assumes an "antic disposition" because he knows that he is no dissembler, either, again unlike Antony. Hamlet is more interested in the implications of his uncle's and mother's behavior for the human condition than in getting on with the apparently straightforward task given him by his father's ghost, as at first the task appears: for until Hamlet begins to question his fitness for the task in the "time is out of joint" couplet at the end of Act I, an audience unfamiliar with the story would think that Claudius would be killed by the end of the first scene in Act II. The only thing that "works" for Hamlet in the first four acts is the escape from the trap set for him by Claudius in the voyage to England. And because that is due to luck or Providence—a vague feeling of unease prompts Hamlet to search Rosencrantz's and Guildenstern's things for the fatal commission, and the fight with the pirates the next day enables him to get back to Denmark before Claudius discovers his couriers' fate—Hamlet is encouraged to assume a fatalistic stance in Act V.

I have said that *Hamlet* is a criticism, but not a rejection, of revenge. Should this be taken to be Shakespeare's "position" on revenge? Just to ask the question is to make three mistakes: that of projecting the implied moral values in a work of literature onto the author; that of wanting literature to be edifying or didactic; and that of trying to evaluate the morality of revenge without regard to circumstances. Shakespeare's works display a range of attitudes toward revenge, with *Hamlet* lying midway between plays like *Titus Andronicus, Julius Caesar,* and *Macbeth,* on the one hand, all of which depict it uncritically,[32] and *The Merchant of Venice* (discussed in the next chapter) and *Romeo and Juliet,* on the other, both of which reject it resoundingly. *Romeo and Juliet* is one of literature's most powerful denunciations of revenge. The "ancient grudge" between the Montagues and the Capulets is made absurd,

---

[32] Or so it seems to me; Brooke, note 19 above, at 38, makes a powerful argument that *Titus Andronicus* criticizes vengeance by showing Titus progressively brutalized by his scheme of revenge.

though not funny, by the facts that the origin of the feud has been forgotten (unlike the origin of the Jews' "ancient grudge" against the Christians in *The Merchant of Venice*) and that the feud is going on in what is depicted as a civilized, modern, and well-governed city-state; by Tybalt's motiveless malignancy; by the speed with which the feud is ended when the heads of the feuding families are finally brought to their senses by the deaths of Romeo and Juliet; and by the love between Romeo and Juliet, which makes the murderous antipathy between their families seem all the more irrational.

A particularly apt specimen of antirevenge literature is Faulkner's story *An Odor of Verbena* (the last chapter of his loosely knit novel *The Unvanquished*), because of its curious echo of *Hamlet.* The story is set in Mississippi, shortly after the Civil War. Colonel Sartoris, a violent and quarrelsome man in the tradition of the Old South,[33] has had a long-standing quarrel with a local businessman, Redmond. Sartoris's provocative behavior toward Redmond has greatly aggravated the quarrel, and a duel is inevitable. But Sartoris is "growing tired of killing men" and tells his son Bayard, a law student (and symbol of the New South that will rise on the ashes of the old), that he intends to confront Redmond unarmed. The next day Sartoris goes to Redmond's office and Redmond kills him. It turns out that Sartoris was armed with his trusty derringer. Although apparently he did not draw, Sartoris's supporters pronounce it a fair duel; yet they expect Bayard to avenge his father's killing. Bayard, however, is determined to put the revenge ethic behind him. The day after his father's death he goes to Redmond's office, unarmed. He enters and walks toward the desk where Redmond is seated. Redmond fires twice, but deliberately aims wide and misses. When Bayard reaches the desk, Redmond gets up, puts on his hat, walks bravely through the throng of the Sartoris supporters outside—his bravery lies in the fact that he knows they will think he has killed Bayard—and keeps walking straight to the train station, where he takes the next train from Mississippi (with no baggage—nothing), never to return. The Sartoris hangers-on, who serve a choral function, speaking as in a Greek tragedy the conventional wisdom, had been insistent that Colonel Sartoris's death had to be avenged; yet when they find out what Bayard has done, they are impressed by his bravery. He has made his point; Redmond has seconded it.

Colonel Sartoris had a young wife, Drusilla, who was only a few years older than Bayard, and she and Bayard had fallen in love. (It is as

[33] On which see Edward L. Ayers, *Vengeance and Justice: Crime and Punishment in the 19th-Century American South* (1984).

if Gertrude had been Hamlet's young stepmother!) Bayard had been on the verge of telling his father about his relationship with Drusilla when his father had said he was going up against Redmond the next day unarmed; Bayard kept silent. (Did he expect him to be killed? Want him to be killed?) When the colonel is killed, Drusilla is desperately eager for Bayard to avenge him. She presses him to take two immense dueling pistols, which appear to have phallic significance for her. When Bayard returns home after having spared Redmond, Drusilla has gone, apparently forever. In rejecting the revenge ethic (for the Rule of Law? Bayard is a *law* student, after all), Bayard has rejected, not entirely willingly, a whole complex of traditional southern values, in which masculinity is correlated with readiness to kill in defense of honor.

I WANT to come back to *Hamlet*. I have suggested that Hamlet's paralysis of will is due (at least on one level) to his being unsuited to play the revenger's role. Many other explanations have been offered, of course; of particular interest, given the subject of this book, are recent interpretations based on Nietzsche's conception of revenge as a manifestation of envy or resentment (see Chapter 3), on Freud's theory of the unconscious, and on deconstruction. All three types of interpretation illustrate the trend toward free interpretation discussed in subsequent chapters. Richard Weisberg, a leading figure in the law and literature movement, has put forth an interpretation of the first type. Like White in regard to the *Iliad*, Weisberg is not much interested in the theme of revenge in *Hamlet*. He attributes Hamlet's paralysis of will not to the problematics of revenge but to Hamlet's envying Claudius as a man of action who has succeeded where Hamlet has failed—namely, in a plot to kill—and to Hamlet's resentment at having to play up to Claudius in order to ensure his own succession to the throne when Claudius dies.[34] Hamlet in this analysis personifies the weak, ineffectual verbalizer confronted with the naturally strong man, the Nietzschean *Übermensch*, who is above revenge.

Hamlet is resentful, and naturally so. But the play presents Claudius

[34] See Richard Weisberg, "Hamlet and Ressentiment," 29 *American Imago* 318 (1972). Although Weisberg wrote this paper before he switched from comparative literature to law, it is of a piece with his recent book *The Failure of the Word* (which I discuss in Chapter 3), in which he reaffirms his earlier view of *Hamlet*—as he has also done, even more recently, in his "More Words on *The Failure of the Word*: A Response to Heinzelman and Levinson," 7 *Cardozo Law Review* 473, 480–481 (1986).

as a sneak, liar, tippler, mediocrity, and weakling, who dispossessed a much superior man (Hamlet senior) of position, wife, and life, and has dispossessed another superior man, young Hamlet, of his expectancy of the kingship in succession to his father (not an automatic succession as in a hereditary monarchy, but, apparently, presumptive). Claudius has a pleasant manner and is politically astute—he deftly turns aside the threats to his throne posed successively by Fortinbras and Laertes—but these are an old man's qualities that Hamlet does not admire. Hamlet could hardly envy Claudius, and the play contains no hint of such envy. Nor is it suggested that Claudius either controls the succession or has a rival candidate to Hamlet; he seems happy to let Hamlet succeed him so long as Hamlet will let him reign, and enjoy Gertrude, in peace. And Hamlet makes no efforts to ingratiate himself with Claudius—quite the opposite.

Weisberg is correct that Hamlet's reaction to the situation in which he finds himself as a result of the encounter with his father's ghost is one of "generalized negativity."[35] Hamlet becomes disgusted with women, himself, indeed all of humanity; and this disgust, rather than the task that the ghost has set him, becomes the focus of his attention until he returns to Denmark, resigned but no longer disgusted, after the aborted voyage to England. But Hamlet's generalized negativity cannot be equated with envy of Claudius; and Hamlet himself—who with all his hesitations and impetuosities is the undoubted hero of the play—is not an *Untermensch*. In any event the moral universe of *Hamlet* is not a Nietzschean one.

Just as there are affinities between Nietzsche and Freud, there are affinities between Weisberg's Nietzschean interpretation of *Hamlet* and Freud's interpretation, which attributed Hamlet's delays to the Oedipus complex.[36] By killing Hamlet's father and marrying Hamlet's mother, Claudius has done what Hamlet himself (a Freudian would say) unconsciously wanted to do. Therefore Hamlet identifies with Claudius and is made doubly uncomfortable at the thought of killing him: because it would be like killing himself and because supplanting Claudius as king would imply, in some weird symbolic sense, marrying Gertrude. There is no textual support for these conjectures,[37] and yet they (and Weis-

---

[35] "Hamlet and Ressentiment," note 34 above, at 325.

[36] The Freudian interpretation of *Hamlet*, first suggested in 1900 in *The Interpretation of Dreams*, was elaborated in Ernest Jones, *Hamlet and Oedipus* (1949).

[37] Only Shakespeare's failure to present a full explanation of Hamlet's psychology gives this approach some purchase. In contrast, *An Odor of Verbena* fairly invites a Freudian interpretation.

berg's) are tame compared to what can be found in much *Hamlet* criticism.[38] Consider the fantastic conjectures that have been built on one of the less important puzzles in the play: Claudius's failure to catch on to the play within a play when it is first performed in a dumb show (pantomime). The dumb show, as described in what apparently are Shakespeare's stage directions, clearly shows Lucianus, the villain of the dumb show, pouring poison into the king's ear—just as Claudius had done to Hamlet's father—and then successfully wooing the queen. And stage directions aside, it would be a pretty poor dumb show that omitted these details. Yet Claudius gives no sign of recognition until the scene is repeated with dialogue. The dumb show has an obvious dramatic purpose—Claudius is going to interrupt the audible play within the play, so the dumb show is necessary to make Hamlet's purpose in staging the play within the play clear to the audience—and a simple psychological explanation: it takes a repeat performance of the murder, this time with dialogue, to break Claudius. Critics have gone crazy seeking deeper explanations. One is that Claudius is not surprised by the dumb show because he had seen the play before and indeed had gotten his method of murdering Hamlet's father from it.[39] In this view the only thing that alarms Claudius is that Lucianus, the murderer in the play within the play, in the audible version turns out to be the player-king's nephew instead of brother, which implies that Hamlet may go after Claudius. The changing of the murderer from brother to nephew does pull Hamlet into the play within the play, and by thus suggesting that he is a murderer of sorts it presages his imminent murder of Polonius, which in turn will place Hamlet in the approximate relationship to Laertes that Claudius bears to Hamlet. But the idea that Claudius had seen the play before has no foundation in the text and adds nothing to the understanding or enjoyment of *Hamlet*.

One critic has said that in staging the play within the play Hamlet "is trying to recreate his infantile glimpses of his parents' coitus,"[40] another "that the manner of Claudius's crime reveals symbolically that Claudius had poisoned his brother with words, and more particularly, words that revealed to old Hamlet that he, Claudius, knew of his brother's

---

[38] Empson's fine essay on *Hamlet* conveys a vertiginous sense of the extravagances of such criticism. See William Empson, *Essays on Shakespeare*, chap. 3 (David B. Pirie ed. 1986). Examples of the extravagances themselves are Jacques Lacan, "Desire and the Interpretation of Desire in *Hamlet*," *Yale French Studies*, nos. 55/56, at ll (1977); Ned Lukacher, *Primal Scenes: Literature, Philosophy, Psychoanalysis*, chap. 6 (1986); *Shakespeare and the Question of Theory*, pt. 4 (Patricia Parker and Geoffrey H. Hartman eds. 1985).

[39] See Lukacher, note 38 above, at 231–232.

[40] Id. at 225 n. 70, summarizing a theory of Otto Rank's.

treachery in poisoning old Fortinbras" with the help of Polonius.[41] Such excesses of *Hamlet* criticism, in suggesting the degree to which some literary critics feel free to range far beyond the text—even to contradict it—in seeking to "interpret" literature, provide a foretaste of current fashions in constitutional and statutory interpretation, discussed in Chapter 5.

THERE are interesting parallels between Achilles and Hamlet. Both characters completely dominate their fictive worlds because of a natural authority sensed by the other characters and because of their unsurpassed detachment and insight. Both are young and impulsive yet seem to mature suddenly near the end of their brief lives. Both resist the tasks that character and fate have set them—fighting Trojans, in the case of Achilles, and avenging his father's death and mother's dishonor, in the case of Hamlet—and interrupt the tasks while reflecting on them. Both are inadvertently responsible for the death of their nearest and dearest plus an assortment of bystanders. And in both, the theme of revenge is incidental.

If these two great works are not really (essentially, fundamentally) about revenge, what *are* they really about? If this question is answerable at all, it is not answerable by me, and it is not answerable in a book on law and literature. Moreover, the differences between the two works, the products of vastly different cultures, may be much more important than any common elements. But I will venture the suggestion that one important thing they have in common is the theme of maturing. This commonality is relevant to the opposition that I will discuss in later chapters between a literature (and a corresponding political philosophy) of youthful values and one of mature values.

Man is the animal that can imagine a life of triumph but cannot achieve it; that can imagine eternal bliss but knows that he will die; that can imagine a better world but learns that the improvements, if any, will be modest in his lifetime; that can imagine a life of ease but lives a life of frustration. As Shakespeare's Troilus said, the will is infinite but the execution confined; the desire boundless but the act a slave to limit. It is

---

[41] Id. at 225–226, summarizing a theory of Nicolas Abraham's. There is no basis in the text for suspecting foul play in the death of old Fortinbras. He died in a fair duel—which he had provoked—with Hamlet's father. Incidentally, after being deflected from seeking revenge against the Danes, young Fortinbras will (we are led to believe at the end of the play) succeed Claudius as king of Denmark; this can be taken as another implied criticism of the ethic of revenge.

only gradually, however, that these unpleasant truths sink in. Most young people inhabit the fool's paradise of thinking that they can live their dreams and could set right all of the world's imperfections but for the fears and hesitations of the old men who run things.

At the outset of poem and play Achilles and Hamlet are distinctly young men,[42] and at once they receive a rude awakening at the hands of distinctly adult figures concerning the nature of the world—Achilles from Agamemnon, Hamlet from the overhasty and incestuous remarriage of his mother and from the encounter with the ghost. The story then concerns the process by which they adjust. Of course everything is much starker, more dramatic, and more compressed than in "real life"; but it is characteristic of literature to present familiar human situations in bizarre and arresting, and necessarily greatly telescoped, settings. The nature of these two works as literature about maturing is signaled by the global reflections to which the opening shocks provoke the protagonists. Achilles begins to think about the choice that is not a choice: although he is free from external pressure in deciding whether to have a short glorious life or a long inglorious one, his character makes the choice a foregone conclusion. In universal terms, what Achilles begins thinking about is the fact of mortality. We die after what in the scheme of things is a ridiculously short time, but as participants in a human community we can live on in a sense, in the memory of our successors.[43] The exploits of Achilles will be sung by Homer hundreds of years later, but only if the exploits are glorious, implying risk-taking and a high probability of early death. So the short glorious life is actually longer than the long inglorious life; we can cheat death only by inviting death.

---

[42] An impression reinforced by the prominence in both works of an old man—Nestor in the *Iliad* and Polonius in *Hamlet*. Lear—who despite his great age is a parallel figure not to Nestor or Polonius but to Achilles and Hamlet—is in his second childhood: his effort to divest himself of responsibility and his demand for infinite, utterly unselfish love are behaviors characteristic of a child. And it is noteworthy that the plot of *Oedipus Tyrannus* is not the Oedipus legend (just as the *Iliad* is not the story of the Trojan War); it is Oedipus's discovery, through relentless inquiry, of the horrible truth about himself. At the outset of the play Oedipus has all the confidence of triumphant youth: he solved the riddle of the Sphinx; he will solve the riddle of why a plague has been sent on Thebes. The play can from one angle be seen as an allegory of maturation into self-knowledge.

[43] Compare these lines from Walter Savage Landor, *Past Ruined Ilion*:

> Past ruined Ilion Helen lives,
>   Alcestis rises from the waves,
> Verse calls them forth, 'tis verse that gives,
>   Immortal youth to mortal maids.

But it is a more limited triumph than the young are willing to settle for.[44]

Hamlet's reflections follow a different path, his discovery being of different aspects of the human dilemma: the existence of radical evil—Claudius's deep-seated malignity and Gertrude's incredible lack of taste and of sexual propriety, reflecting the animal in man; the role of chance in human affairs; the difficulty of translating motive and desire into effective action; the ease with which we evade responsibilities and rationalize our evasions; the lack of candor in human relations (a lack displayed by Polonius, Claudius of course, Gertrude, Rosencrantz and Guildenstern, and even Ophelia). The deeply rooted nature of the vices and deficiencies exhibited is underlined by the frequent allusions to the Garden of Eden and Cain's murder of *his* brother, by the extreme plausibility of the villains—Claudius and particularly Gertrude lack the surface malignity of a Iago or an Edmund (indeed, Gertrude's love for Hamlet is extremely touching)—and by the atmosphere of drunkenness and sexual intrigue in which the play's fictive Denmark is wrapped from the beginning, an atmosphere set off by the one completely straightforward major character in the play, Horatio. The resignation that Hamlet displays in Act V reflects a hard-won understanding of the nature of the human condition and a resolution to face it with readiness (which Hamlet characteristically fails to do, however, when he accepts a foil without checking whether it is bated) rather than with elaborate plans sure to go awry, as Hamlet's plan with the players went awry and Claudius's plans with Rosencrantz and Guildenstern and later with Laertes went awry. We do not live our dreams. Those who do, like Macbeth and Faustus, find they are nightmares.

So it would be reductive in a bad sense to place the *Iliad* and *Hamlet* in a box called "revenge literature" and think we had understood these works. Nevertheless revenge literature is a coherent literary category (a "supergenre," embracing many specific genres such as Elizabethan and Jacobean revenge drama) to which these two works belong; and an understanding not only of the category, but of revenge as a radically imperfect but sometimes inescapable social practice, can help us make sense of both works. Achilles and Hamlet are more than avengers, but that is part of what they are, and a part that is important to an understanding of why they act as they do or, in Hamlet's case, why he

---

[44] Achilles' narcissistic, pre-Oedipal characteristics are emphasized in W. Thomas MacCary, *Childlike Achilles: Ontogeny and Phylogeny in the Iliad* (1982), especially pp. 30, 57–58, 70, 82, 91–93.

does not act as he is told to by the ghost. These works offer a critical perspective on revenge, though the authors were after even bigger game. And while revenge is not the modern idea of law, it is a primitive form of law, an antecedent and template of modern law, and an argument for modern law. So one might think that a lawyer would be more likely than other readers to understand the revenge motif in these works. Yet we saw that leading "literary lawyers," though greatly interested in the *Iliad* and in *Hamlet*, are not interested in them as examples—the supreme examples—of revenge literature. I do not think that this neglect can be attributed to a justified belief that revenge is no longer an interesting issue, and thus can be ignored by the modern reader. Not only is revenge still an important element in human relations, but one can hardly understand the perennial themes in literature without understanding something about the local themes; one cannot enter into the world of *Hamlet* or the *Iliad* without some understanding of the dilemmas with which the authors confronted their protagonists.

The neglect by literary lawyers of revenge as a literary theme may reflect the narrowness of legal training, which puts revenge outside the bounds of legal study and leaves to the biologist, the economist, the political scientist, the philosopher, the psychologist, the historian, and the anthropologist the task of studying a subject that has informed more great works of literature than lawyer's law has done. It is only as the study of law becomes more intellectual, more interdisciplinary (paradoxically, in directions other than the literary), that revenge literature can be brought within its reach.

# TWO

## The Reflection of Law in Literature

*L*AW IS SO frequent a subject of literature that one is tempted to infer a deep affinity between the two fields, giving the lawyer privileged access if not to the whole body of literature then at least to those works that are explicitly about law. But I shall argue that the frequency of legal subjects in literature is partly a statistical artifact and that law figures in literature more often as metaphor than as an object of interest in itself, even when the author is a lawyer (like Kafka) or a law "buff" (like Melville). But this is in general, not in every case; moreover the validity of the generalization depends on the precise sense in which the word "law" is used.

### Theoretical Considerations

The frequency with which trials and other legal phenomena crop up in literature reflects both the criteria of literary distinction and the nature and methods of literature. As is true of normative discourse generally, there is no determinate procedure for resolving differences in literary taste. Orwell (following Samuel Johnson) used to say repeatedly—and the enormous disagreements in critical discourse over the value of different authors confirm—that literature can be judged great only by a strictly Darwinian test: its ability to survive in the competition of the literary "marketplace."[1] (The quotation marks are to make clear that I

---

[1] "In reality there is no kind of evidence or argument by which one can show that Shakespeare, or any other writer, is 'good'. Nor is there any way of definitely proving that—for instance—Warwick Deeping is 'bad'. Ultimately there is no test of literary merit except survival, which is itself merely an index to majority opinion." "Lear, Tolstoy, and the Fool," in *Collected Essays, Journalism and Letters of George Orwell*, vol. 4, at 287, 290 (Sonia Orwell and Ian Angus eds. 1968).

am speaking of reputation rather than of profitability.) This is not to say that literary merit cannot be debated profitably, as a preference for blackberries over raspberries cannot be; the vast body of evaluative literary criticism, much of great distinction, shows that it can be.[2] But the debate achieves closure only with regard to very old works— suggesting that even the critics, in their hearts, accept only the verdict of time. No one is apt to question the greatness of Homer, or Dante, or Shakespeare; Tolstoy's attack on Shakespeare,[3] and T. S. Eliot's on *Hamlet* ("most certainly an artistic failure"),[4] are curiosities that do not invite emulation. The effort of some New Critics to devalue Milton along with much Romantic and Victorian literature achieved a temporary success but has now flopped; on the other hand their efforts to revalue the Metaphysical and Augustan poets upward have succeeded. Feminist literary critics are trying to boost the reputation of a number of women writers, some hitherto unknown,[5] but it is too early to say whether their efforts will succeed. That is always the case with literature and the arts; it takes many years to separate the wheat from the chaff.

The impression that so many intellectuals have of living in an age of trash reflects the fact that the winnowing effects of time have by definition not had a chance to do their work on contemporary literature. No doubt the English Renaissance produced a richer literature than has twentieth-century England, but the contrast is less stark than readers acquainted with only a handful of the best works of Shakespeare, Donne, Jonson, and a few others think. Plenty of literary trash was produced by the Elizabethans; most of it literally disappeared; what survived physically is read today only by specialists. Some of the plays discussed in the last chapter, such as *The Spanish Tragedy*, have only modest merit, and make a striking contrast to Shakespeare's mature works—as indeed does his early play *Titus Andronicus*. It may not have been until Samuel Johnson brought out his edition of Shakespeare's plays in 1765 that it was certain (as certain as these matters can be) that Shakespeare was great—that his best plays must have extraordinary qualities to be so riveting almost two centuries after their composition, despite all the intervening changes in

[2] A point forcefully made in Bernard C. Heyl, *New Bearings in Esthetics and Art Criticism: A Study in Semantics and Evaluation* 120–124 (1943).
[3] See Leo Tolstoy, *Shakespeare and the Drama* (1903), the subject of the Orwell essay cited in note 1.
[4] "Hamlet and His Problems," in Eliot, *Selected Essays* 121, 123 (new ed. 1950).
[5] See K. K. Ruthven, *Feminist Literary Studies: An Introduction* 105–128 (1984).

language, taste, and social milieu.[6] It is only today, more than sixty years after major writings by Kafka, T. S. Eliot, Joyce, and Mann, that we can say with some confidence, though more provisionally than in the case of Homer, Dante, Milton, and Shakespeare, that these men have written classics, too. And about some writers who a few years ago seemed well on the way to the status of classic writers, such as Hemingway and Gide, there are growing doubts; their work is starting to date in a way that some of their contemporaries' is not.

Orwell's view that the only test of literary greatness is the test of time rested partly on a preference for the judgment of the many over the expert few and partly on a radical skepticism about the possibility of making objective judgments of literary merit. (These are two reasons why few professional literary critics are enthusiastic about the test of time; a third, which is related to the first, is that specialists acquire a taste for obscure writers.) Orwell's skepticism paralleled that of logical positivists and other skeptical philosophers concerning the possibility of objective normative judgments, anticipated the interpretive skepticism that I shall discuss in Chapter 5, and is supported empirically by the amazing vicissitudes in literary and artistic taste.[7] Orwell's skepticism and democratic sentiments led him to suppose that aesthetic questions are and should be settled by a form of majority vote; the significance of time is that it broadens the franchise. Samuel Johnson, who was himself a skeptic in many areas and had a surprisingly egalitarian attitude toward aesthetic judgments,[8] reached the same conclusion—that the only test of artistic merit is that of time—but based it primarily on the fact that the longer the perspective in which a work of art can be evaluated, the greater is the possibility of comparison. It is from comparisons that judgments of artistic greatness, which are judgments of less and more, emerge. "Of the first building that was raised, it might be certainly determined that it was round or square, but whether it was spacious or lofty must have been referred to time."[9]

[6] On the history of Shakespeare's reputation see the interesting discussion in Harry Levin, "Critical Approaches to Shakespeare from 1660 to 1904," in *The Cambridge Companion to Shakespeare Studies* 213 (Stanley Wells ed. 1986).

[7] See, for examples, Heyl, note 2 above, at 97–102; K. K. Ruthven, *Critical Assumptions* 196 (1979); cf. William J. Baumol, "Unnatural Value: or Art Investment as Floating Crap Game," 76 *American Economic Review Papers and Proceedings* 10 (May 1986).

[8] See William K. Wimsatt, Jr., and Cleanth Brooks, *Literary Criticism: A Short History*, vol. 1, at 325, 327–328, 331–333 (1957).

[9] "Preface to the Plays of William Shakespeare," in *Samuel Johnson: Selected Poetry and Prose* 299, 300 (Frank Brady and W. K. Wimsatt eds. 1977). See also id. at 299 ("no other test can be applied

David Hume, Johnson's great contemporary, took a similar approach.[10]

If I am right that survival is the operational test of greatness in literature, we can begin to see why law is a common literary subject. For literature to survive it must deal with things that do not change much over time—must deal with the perennial concerns of human-kind and hence with the general and permanent features of the human condition.[11] Like love, death, war, and ambition, the law has been a permanent feature of human experience. Specific doctrines and procedures have changed a great deal, but the broad features of law have changed little since distinct legal institutions first emerged in Western society. The legal system of Elizabethan England and even that of Periclean Athens[12] are thoroughly accessible to modern understand-

---

than length of duration and continuance of esteem"). Notice that in arguing that the test of time is the only test used in practice, I have elided the question of whether it is a valid test—a position defended with rigor and subtlety in Anthony Savile, *The Test of Time: An Essay in Philosophical Aesthetics* (1982), and criticized in William Charlton's review of Savile's book, 58 *Philosophy* 411 (1983). For my purposes, which are pragmatic, the validity of the test is not important. What is important is that it is the operational test of greatness—the test that yields the "canon," that is, the list of great works of literature on which most critics agree at a given time. Cf. David Carrier's review of *The Test of Time* in 81 *Journal of Philosophy* 226, 228 (1984).

[10] See "Of the Standard of Taste," in David Hume, *Essays: Moral, Political, and Literary* 226, 231–233 (Eugene F. Miller ed. 1985). Discussions of the test of time by modern critics are rare; the best examples I have found are Frank Kermode, *The Classic: Literary Images of Permanence and Change* (1975), especially chap. 4, and his *Forms of Attention* (1985); Stein Haugom Olsen, *The End of Literary Theory* (1987), especially pp. 155, 186–187; David Daiches, "Literary Evaluation," in *Problems of Literary Evaluation* 163, 171–175 (Joseph Strelka ed. 1969); Ruthven, note 7 above, at 191–193. The counterpart in law to the test of time is the principle that the First Amendment to the Constitution requires the government to allow truth to be determined by the marketplace of ideas. In the words of Justice Holmes, dissenting in Abrams v. United States, 250 U.S. 616, 630 (1919), "The best test of truth is the power of the thought to get itself accepted in the competition of the market."

[11] Not surprisingly, this was Samuel Johnson's theory of Shakespeare's greatness. See his "Preface to the Plays of William Shakespeare," note 9 above, at 301. It echoes Aristotle's distinction in the *Poetics* between history (concerned with particulars) and poetry (concerned with the general features of the human condition). For good modern statements see Olsen, note 10 above, at 186–187; F. O. Matthiessen, "Tradition and the Individual Talent," in *Modern Poetry: Essays in Criticism* 176, 188 (John Hollander ed. 1968). And compare Kermode's emphasis, in *Forms of Attention*, note 10 above, on the "omnisignificance" of durable works of literature. Some legal analogies will be examined in Chapter 5; here I merely note that a contract, statute, or constitutional provision that is highly specific may not prove adaptable to unforeseen changes of circumstance and may therefore have to be modified or amended before much time has elapsed. Survivability requires generality in law as in literature.

[12] On which see, for example, Douglas M. MacDowell, *The Law in Classical Athens* (1978); Robert J. Bonner, *Lawyers and Litigants in Ancient Athens: The Genesis of the Legal Profession* (1927).

ing. Between, on the one hand, the Austro-Hungarian procedures reflected in Kafka's *Trial* or the nineteenth-century Russian criminal procedures reflected in *Crime and Punishment* and *The Brothers Karamazov*, and, on the other hand, modern Continental and even American criminal procedure, the differences, while important to lawyers, would strike most laymen as small.

So between two otherwise similar works of literature of a time remote from our own, one about law and the other about burial customs or tool making, the first is more likely to still be read in the twentieth century. But one must be careful about the meaning of "about." Literature may contain many details of vanished social customs without being "about" them, or without being just about them. The Homeric epics are in a significant sense about the heroic code, and they also contain a wealth of specific information, though much of it garbled, about Mycenaean culture. But if they were merely a depiction of vanished customs they would be read today just as historical or sociological source documents, not as literature. Moreover, few people are willing or able to immerse themselves in an alien or forgotten culture. This is another reason why, in order to be read as literature, a work must deal with aspects of culture that are universal. Law is one of them; yet it might, of course, appear in a work of literature as a metaphor for something else. Moreover, only limited aspects of law are apt to have the breadth of appeal that literature demands, and they may not be the aspects of greatest interest to lawyers, or within their special competence.

John Ellis makes the pertinent observation that the question "what is literature?" is misleading.[13] There is no set of texts that come labeled as literature—no definitional procedure for deciding whether a comic strip, or Lincoln's second inaugural address, or Pepys' diary, or Gibbon's *Decline and Fall*, is literature. According to Ellis, literature is the label we give to texts, of whatever character or provenance, that are taken to have a meaning that is independent of the specific context in which they were created. Lincoln made a political address; we who may have no interest in the political setting and purpose of the speech value it for its imagery and cadences. College courses with such titles as "The Bible as Literature" tell the whole story. It is unlikely that the authors of the Bible thought they were making literature, or that Homer thought he was making literature, or even that Shakespeare did—at least when

---

"There can be no better introduction to the study of English law than the speeches of the Attic orators." F. A. Paley and J. E. Sandys, *Select Private Orations of Demosthenes* viii (3d ed. 1898).

[13] See John M. Ellis, *The Theory of Literary Criticism: A Logical Analysis,* chap. 2 (1974).

writing plays. He seems to have made no effort to revise them for publication or to get them published.[14] He may have thought of them as strictly quotidian productions, a way of making money.

Ellis's definition must not be taken literally. If I paper my walls with pages from nineteenth-century newspapers, I have not thereby transformed the newspaper articles on those pages into literature. If I use a Babylonian sacred text as a source for a history of Babylonia, I am not making a literary use of it. But what counts as a "literary use" is an elusive question, and Ellis is right to shift our attention from the intrinsic properties of the text to the uses made of it[15] and to emphasize, as a necessary if not sufficient condition of a text's being literature, that it be read in a context different from that of its creation.

The more local or topical in its essential meaning a text is, the less likely it is to float free from its original context; the less likely it is, therefore, to survive as literature. This is a reason for expecting the aspects of law that will interest authors to be the most general ones rather than the fine mesh of historically specific and concrete legal details that constitutes lawyer's law. The greater the generality of the legal theme or references, the less likely they are to engage the expert knowledge of the lawyer.

We must therefore distinguish between concrete legal problems, which lawyers are expert in solving, and broader issues of legality, governance, and justice that are grist for moral, political—and literary—examination rather than for technical legal analysis. Every society has machinery for resolving serious disputes in accordance with rules or customs deemed authoritative, in some sense official. And every such

---

[14] See David Bevington, "General Introduction," in *The Complete Works of Shakespeare* 2, 79 (David Bevington ed., 3d ed. 1980); S. Schoenbaum, *William Shakespeare: A Compact Documentary Life* 159, 188, 220 (1977). Shakespeare retired to Stratford several years before his death, a comparatively wealthy man, and could have taken steps to see to the preservation or publication of his plays, but apparently took none. However, absence of copyright protection, discussed in Chapter 7, may have been a factor. And Shakespeare's sonnets, which were published in his lifetime, contain expressions—though possibly ironic ones—of a desire for the immortality of print. See the discussion of his Sonnet 65 at the end of Chapter 5.

[15] Or to how people acquire their sense of what literature is: "The general education of well-trained readers tends to develop a sense of what literature is by teaching them to read a set of canonical texts—Homer, Vergil, Shakespeare, selected works of lyric poetry and representative novels. These texts develop two basic expectations—that we should be able to sympathize with the conditions, actions, feelings, and thoughts of the principal characters and that we should be able to reflect upon the potential general significance of their actions, feelings, etc., by considering the rhetorical and structural patterns informing the text." Charles Altieri, "A Procedural Definition of Literature," in *What Is Literature?* 62, 72 (Paul Hernadi ed. 1978). See also Olsen, note 10 above, stressing that literature is the class of writings that repays a certain kind of attention.

machinery runs into problems of "fit" between formal rules and application. These problems include the difficulty of ascertaining the facts that are the predicate for applying a rule and the tendency of a rule to take a dichotomous cut at a continuous problem: classifying a person as disabled or not disabled, literate or illiterate; distinguishing between a business gift and a personal gift; distinguishing "speech" from "action"—in short, drawing clear lines where there are no lines. Related problems are the inflexibility of rules, which creates an irresistible demand for principles of "equity" designed to reduce the rigidity of purely "legal" rules; the problem of discretion that arises if rules cannot be bent and have to be changed (who shall be authorized to change them, and on what grounds?), or if it is infeasible or undesirable to enforce a rule in all cases to which the rule applies; and, similar to the problem of inflexibility, the gap between the ethical or political principles that underlie and animate a rule and the rule itself, which for purposes of admininistrability is likely to be much cruder than the principle. Thus from the principle that there ought to be an end to disputes the legal system may derive a rule that a specified type of claim is extinguished forever unless sued on within two years, no matter how meritorious the claim is or how trivial would be the inroads on the principle if a particular late suit (late by just a day, maybe) were allowed.

The frequent discontinuity between the spirit and letter of the law, or between its general aim and its concrete application, is one reason why law so often strikes laymen as arbitrary. And law's apparently arbitrary and undeniably coercive character, combined with the inevitable errors of fact and law and the resulting miscarriages of justice and with law's "otherness" (law, like language, the state, and the market economy, is a human institution frequently—by some theorists of natural law, literally—perceived as external to man, like a natural phenomenon), makes law a superb metaphor for the random, coercive, and "unfair" light in which the human condition—"life"—appears to us in some moods. We shall see literary artists make good use of this metaphor.

Mediating the governance of human behavior by rules may be the quintessential legal art; but the fundamental problems which I have just described that arise from reflecting on that art are better described as problems of justice than of law. They not only cut across legal systems but raise issues that, because of their universality and generality, do not require legal training to understand. When written by and for lawyers or other specialists, the literature on jurisprudence and the legal process tends to focus on issues more technical and topical than are likely to find their way into a work of imaginative literature.[16] The growing interest of legal professionals in legal theory reflects in part a desire to bring the broader problems of justice more securely within the compass of legal education and scholarship. The field of law and literature may provide an angle of approach.

A final reason for the frequency of law as a subject of literature has to do with literary technique. Literature is characteristically (though not always) dramatic, and thus traffics in conflict. As a system for managing conflict, law provides a rich stock of metaphors for writers to use. It also provides, in the trial—especially the Anglo-American trial, which is more adversary, more theatrical, than its Continental counterpart—a ready-made dramatic technique.[17] Whether historically the trial is modeled on the theater and offers the litigants and society (the audience) the type of catharsis that the theater does, or vice versa, or whether both the trial and the drama have a common origin in religious rituals—issues not discussed in this book—few social practices are so readily transferable to a literary setting as the trial or so well suited to the literary depiction of conflict. And notice the parallel between the trial in literature and the play within the play (for example, in *Hamlet*): both are techniques for creating an audience within the work of literature (the tribunal and spectators, in the case of the trial;

---

[16] Examples are Henry M. Hart, Jr., and Albert Sacks, *The Legal Process: Basic Problems in the Making and Application of Law* (tentative ed. 1958); H. L. A. Hart, *The Concept of Law* (1961); David Lyons, *Ethics and the Rule of Law* (1984); Neil MacCormick, *Legal Reasoning and Legal Theory* (1978); William Twining and David Miers, *How to Do Things with Rules: A Primer of Interpretation* (2d ed. 1982); Vilhelm Aubert, *In Search of Law: Sociological Approaches to Law* (1983). Useful compendia are Ruggero J. Aldisert, *The Judicial Process: Readings, Materials and Cases* (1976); George C. Christie, *Jurisprudence: Text and Readings on the Philosophy of Law* (1973); Joel Feinberg and Hyman Gross, *Philosophy of Law* (3d ed. 1986); Philip Shuchman, *Cohen and Cohen's Readings in Jurisprudence and Legal Philosophy* (2d ed. 1979). For good introductions to jurisprudence see Jeffrie G. Murphy and Jules L. Coleman, *The Philosophy of Law: An Introduction to Jurisprudence* (1984); Martin P. Golding, "Jurisprudence and Legal Philosophy in Twentieth-Century America—Major Themes and Developments," 36 *Journal of Legal Education* 441 (1986).

[17] See references in the Introduction, note 32; and observe that the ancient Greek trial is more like the Anglo-American trial than the Continental European trial (the roots of which are Roman): more a private contest, a struggle, a drama, than an official inquiry. It is no accident that English and American popular literature, but not that of the Continent, is full of trials and other legal incidents. Popular literature, especially, tends to be dramatic, and law in the Anglo-American system is more dramatic than law in the Continental system—though we shall encounter some Continental trials that are much like Anglo-American trials. The definition of literature that I use in this book automatically excludes most "popular" literature from my purview because most such literature is ephemeral; it flunks the test of time. Yet some of that literature contains insights into law.

the playgoers in the internal play) to play off against the audience for the work itself.

But it does not follow that what is transferred must retain its legal character. Consider the adultery trial of Vittoria in Webster's *The White Devil*. The trial begins with the prosecuting lawyer mumbling incomprehensible legal jargon. The Cardinal, who is presiding, quickly shoos him off the stage and takes over the prosecutor's role. There is no more law talk in the trial. An analogy can be drawn to "academic" novels by such writers as Mary McCarthy, Bernard Malamud, C. P. Snow, and David Lodge. Despite these writers' first-hand familiarity with academic life, their academic novels convey little sense of what academics do that is different from what other people do. The focus—understandably, since the novelist is reaching out to an audience composed primarily of nonacademics—is on personal rivalries, foibles of character, comic predicaments, sexual adventures, and other aspects of conduct and character that academics share with other people, rather than on the things that set them apart.

And while the legal trial may have a dramatic structure, and some celebrated trials (for example, the Scopes trial) may have performed a cathartic role comparable to that which Aristotle assigned to tragedy, the essential spirit of the law is not dramatic. Law's aim is to mediate, often to diffuse, but rarely if ever to aggravate, conflict. Most statutes represent compromises. The vast majority of legal disputes are settled out of court. Judges in their decisions seek to reduce rather than increase social tensions. The resemblance between drama and trial may be superficial, making it all the more likely that any borrowing by the first from the second will be metaphoric.

Here is a reason why we should not expect law to be as securely a theme of literature as revenge is; this may help to explain why there is more great revenge literature than great "law" literature. Revenge is a practice, and therefore has a form that can be imitated (in Aristotle's sense) by literature; law is a complex of rules and institutions, from which a writer can borrow but which does not lend itself to being imitated.

## "Legal" Novels by Cozzens, Twain, and Camus

To illustrate these points I begin in low key with a work that after more than forty years seems on its way to being recognized as a minor classic—James Gould Cozzens's novel *The Just and the Unjust*, a work so pervasively and accurately "about" law that one might think the author an experienced lawyer (he had no legal training).[18] Yet this is an illusion; the book is not about law in any interesting sense.

The setting is a small town in an unimportant rural county, circa 1940. The ostensible subject is a murder trial that begins at the start of the novel and concludes at the end. The protagonist is the county's assistant district attorney, Abner Coates—young, able, but rather priggish—who tries the case for the prosecution along with the district attorney. The D.A. is in charge but Coates takes an active role, making the opening statement to the jury and examining several important witnesses. The trial reveals that the defendants—repulsive hoods named Howell and Basso—had, along with a third man, Bailey, kidnapped a drug dealer named Zollicoffer. After the ransom was paid, Bailey decided it would be unsafe to return Zollicoffer alive. On the way to the spot where the kidnappers were to drop Zollicoffer off, Bailey shot him, and Howell and Basso helped Bailey weight Zollicoffer down with leg irons and dump him into a river. Bailey later died fleeing the police. Although Howell and Basso do not deny having taken an active part in the kidnapping, it never becomes clear whether they authorized, knew about in advance, or participated in the murder. As Coates, the D.A., and the judge all emphasize to the jury in urging a verdict of first-degree murder (which would mean the electric chair), the defendants' lack of participation in the actual murder affects their guilt not a whit. Provided they participated in the kidnapping, as unquestionably they did, they are guilty of first-degree murder because Zollicoffer was killed in the course of a felony in which they participated. However, to the disgust of Coates, the D.A., and the judge (who dresses down the jury afterward), the jury convicts Howell and Basso only of second-degree murder. The author leads us to understand, through one of the wise old codgers who people the novel, that the jury has exercised its prerogative of nullifying a law that

[18] The book is dedicated to Edward Biester, a prosecutor whom Cozzens consulted extensively in writing the novel. Cozzens modeled the trial in the novel on a real murder trial; he even took some dialogue verbatim from the trial transcript. See Morris H. Wolff, "The Legal Background of Cozzens's *The Just and the Unjust*," 7 *Journal of Modern Literature* 505 (1979). The distinguished (and very literate) Harvard Law School Professor Zechariah Chafee, Jr., called Cozzens's novel "one of the best legal novels the reviewer has ever read," and "the best account I know of the daily life of ordinary lawyers." Book Review, 56 *Harvard Law Review* 833 (1943). For other discussions see Pierre Michel, *James Gould Cozzens* 70–85 (1974); John P. McWilliams, "Innocent Crime or Criminal Innocence: The Trial in American Fiction," in Carl S. Smith, John P. McWilliams, Jr., and Maxwell Bloomfield, *Law and American Literature: A Collection of Essays* 45, 107–114 (1983); John William Ward, "James Gould Cozzens: The Condition of Modern Man," in *James Gould Cozzens: New Acquist of True Experience* 15 (Matthew J. Bruccoli ed. 1979).

it considers unjust—the felony-murder rule, a legal fiction that punishes a felon who is not a murderer as if he were one.[19]

While the trial is wending its way to its surprising conclusion—for the reader is given no clue that the jury might fail to convict the defendants of first-degree murder—Coates is both getting engaged to be married and agreeing to run for D.A. (the incumbent is leaving for another job). It is understood that Coates cannot lose the election; he is a Republican, and Republicans always win in this county. But to agree to run he must overcome his aversion to the local Republican boss, who Coates fears will interfere in the D.A.'s office, though in fact the boss is pretty straight. The suspense in the novel is focused not on the trial, which seems a foregone conclusion but is not, but on whether Coates will overcome what are plainly priggish scruples to marrying his utterly charming childhood sweetheart and accepting the tremendous career opportunity opened up by the D.A.'s impending departure.

From this brief summary it should be plain that *The Just and the Unjust* is not really about trial strategy, the legal profession, the felony-murder rule, or the power of juries to acquit lawlessly, and thus that critics miss the point when they accuse Cozzens of "belligerent legalistic conservatism."[20] This is a rite of passage novel, a *Bildungsroman*. The hero is a prissy kid at the beginning and a man at the end, having assumed family responsibilities and learned the difference between pure forms (of law, of career advancement) and sordid realities (law may diverge from the lay sense of justice, politics influences promotions), as well as the need to compromise, to moderate demands, to scale down ideals, to trim absolutes, to empathize—with the Republican boss, and above all with his sweetheart, to whose feelings Coates is remarkably insensitive at the beginning of the novel. The work has none of the resonance of *Hamlet* or the *Iliad* but is recognizably part of the same broad category of works, in which youthful idealism becomes tempered with realism through a series of crises.

That the law is rather a detail in all this, as revenge is rather a detail (though an essential one) in the other works, can be made clearer by a comparison with another and finer Cozzens novel, *Guard of Honor,* perhaps the best American novel about World War II. Set in Florida, it

---

[19] On the felony-murder rule, which has long been controversial, see Rollin M. Perkins and Ronald N. Boyce, *Criminal Law* 136–137 (3d ed. 1982). Note that the rule imposes a form of strict liability—and strict liability is one of the things that makes lay persons think of law as something inexorable and nonrational, like the tides. But this aspect is not stressed in Cozzens's novel.
[20] McWilliams, note 18 above, at 114.

recounts a brief period in the administration of an air base by a young major general. He is champing at the bit to be sent overseas to do more fighting (he had held a major command in the North African campaign). But we soon understand that his command of the base, which involves dealing with domestic crises that have no martial dimension (race relations, a training accident), is an important preparation for the major combat command that he is slated to assume next—and that, with nice irony, is the command of fighter cover for the invasion of Japan, which of course never took place. Again it is a rite of passage novel, with the professional setting, in this case military, again incidental. The hero, at first insufficiently worldly-wise to handle senior administrative responsibilities, like Coates matures in the course of the novel by meeting the challenges of everyday life.

If either novel were about the *professional* challenges of its protagonists—if either one showed lawyers correcting their legal errors or generals correcting their military errors—they would not have much appeal, even to members of these professions. A novelist with neither legal nor military training is unlikely to have significant insights to impart at the level of actual practice, though some exceptions to this rule will be discussed in the Conclusion.

THE JUST AND THE UNJUST is one of a large number of American "legal" novels[21] (the large number reflecting Americans' traditional preoccupation with law). I discuss another, *Billy Budd*, in the next chapter, but I am conscious of not doing justice to this interesting genre,[22] which includes such other well-known works as *Native Son*, *The Caine Mutiny*, and *Intruder in the Dust*. By way of partial amends I shall discuss another American legal novel here, Mark Twain's *Pudd'nhead Wilson*. I choose it because it is one of the most distinguished representatives of the genre—yet may actually have little to do with law—and because it is discussed in an interesting essay by Robin West, a talented and energetic contributor to law and literature scholarship.[23]

---

[21] See the Kretschman bibliography cited in the Introduction, note 11.

[22] On which see, for example, McWilliams, note 18 above.

[23] See "Adjudication Is Not Interpretation: Some Reservations about the Law-as-Literature Movement," 54 *Tennessee Law Review* 203, 219–244 (1987). An interpretation somewhat like West's appears in Earl F. Briden, "Idiots First, Then Juries: Legal Metaphors in Mark Twain's *Pudd'nhead Wilson*," 20 *Texas Studies in Literature and Language* 169 (1978), especially p. 177; see also James E. Caron, "Pudd'nhead Wilson's Calendar: Tall Tales and a Tragic Figure," 36 *Nineteenth-Century Fiction* 452 (1982); Michael L. Ross, "Mark Twain's *Pudd'nhead Wilson*," 6 *Novel* 244 (1973). A work of considerable ambiguity (like so many of the works discussed in

The novel, written toward the end of the nineteenth century, is set in Dawson's Landing, a sleepy Missouri town on the Mississippi River. The title character moves to the town as a young man in 1830, hoping to practice law, but his hopes are dashed by a joke he makes. A dog is annoying people with its barking; Wilson says that he would like to buy half the dog, and kill his half. The townspeople (who throughout the book are portrayed as extremely gullible hicks) think Wilson is serious, pronounce him a "pudd'nhead," and refuse to give him any legal business. He bides his time, doing some surveying and accounting, and pursuing his hobby of fingerprinting (a novelty, obviously, in 1830).

At about the time Wilson had arrived in Dawson's Landing, Roxana, a slave in the household of the town's leading citizen, had given birth to a son. Roxana is fifteen parts white and one part black, while the child's father (another leading citizen) is all white; so the son, Chambers, is only one thirty-second black. The wife of Roxana's master had given birth at the same time as Roxana, and Roxana must take full care of both children, since the mother of the "white" child, Tom, dies a week after giving birth. Fearful that her child might one day be "sold down the river" (that is, to owners of cotton plantations, who we are given to understand treat their slaves much worse than the slaveholders in Missouri), Roxana switches the babies. Her inattentive master does not notice. Roxana brings up her Chambers as "Tom," and the real Tom as "Chambers." "Chambers" turns out to be a sweet and noble character, "Tom" a devil. His principal vice is gambling, and it leads him to theft—and worse. Roxana's master has meanwhile died in debt, and "Tom" has been adopted by his (supposed) uncle, a wealthy man. Roxana's master had freed her in his will, yet "Tom," with terrible,

---

this book), *Pudd'nhead Wilson* is the subject of a large secondary literature. A few more examples are Robert Rowlette, *Twain's Pudd'nhead Wilson: The Development and Design* (1971); George E. Toles, "Mark Twain and Pudd'nhead Wilson: A House Divided," 16 *Novel* 55 (1982); John C. Gerber, "*Pudd'nhead Wilson* as Fabulation," 2 *Studies in American Humor* 21 (1975); James W. Gargano, "Pudd'nhead Wilson: Mark Twain as Genial Satan," 74 *South Atlantic Quarterly* 365 (1975); Stanley Brodwin, "Blackness and the Adamic Myth in Mark Twain's *Pudd'nhead Wilson*," 15 *Texas Studies in Literature and Language* 167 (1973); Marvin Fisher and Michael Elliott, "*Pudd'nhead Wilson*: Half a Dog Is Worse Than None," 8 *Southern Review* 533 (1972). For a good general discussion see Malcolm Bradbury, "Introduction," in *Mark Twain: Pudd'nhead Wilson and Those Extraordinary Twins* 9 (Malcolm Bradbury ed. 1969). On the subtheme of revenge in *Pudd'nhead Wilson* (another illustration of the ubiquity of revenge in literature) see Rowlette, above, at 113. Finally, like many other works discussed in this book (including *Hamlet*, *The Trial*, and *Billy Budd*), the text of *Pudd'nhead Wilson* is in poor shape (the result of Mark Twain's careless revising). Hershel Parker, *Flawed Texts and Verbal Icons: Literary Authority in American Fiction* 139–143 (1984), questions whether it can sensibly be approached as a thematic unity.

unconscious irony (considering why Roxana had switched the babies in the first place), sells her down the river. "Tom"'s career of crime reaches its culmination when he kills the uncle with a stolen knife during a botched attempt to steal his money.

Meanwhile the town has recently become home to—of all things— twin Italian counts. Bad blood has arisen between them and "Tom"'s uncle, and they have the misfortune to be passing by the uncle's house when he is murdered. They hear his screams and rush in, and are still there when the neighbors arrive. And it turns out that the murder weapon, which "Tom" has discarded in his flight, had been stolen from one of the twins. They are suspected of the murder, and put on trial. Wilson defends them—it is his first big case. As chance would have it, on the evening before Wilson is to put on what we are led to expect will be a hopeless defense, "Tom" is visiting him and happens to place his thumb on a glass slide from Wilson's fingerprint collection, leaving a print that Wilson immediately recognizes as the same one he had taken from "Tom" when "Tom" was seven months old. Wilson discovers the baby switch by examining the set of prints he had taken of Tom and Chambers when they were a few weeks old—for in that set Chambers has the same print as "Tom" and Tom the same print as "Chambers."

The next day in court, Wilson presents blowups of the fingerprints. The twins are immediately released, and "Tom" (who was in the audience) is arrested. He is convicted of murder and sentenced to life imprisonment, but the uncle's creditors (the uncle, too, had died poor) insist that he is their property and should be sold, and he is—down the river. "Chambers" is restored to his status as a white man, but since his accent, gait, and manners are irrevocably those of a slave, he cannot adjust happily to his new lot. Roxana, who had regained her freedom and was in the courtroom when "Tom" was exposed as a slave and a murderer, is broken-hearted.

Although written a half-century before *The Just and the Unjust*, Mark Twain's novel seems more modern because of its irony, surrealism, and open-textured quality; it has a resonance (perhaps the serendipitous result of its author's careless revising!), and a fascination, that Cozzens's novel lacks. The presence not only of the twin Italian counts but of Wilson himself in a southern backwater town is entirely incongruous; the townspeople are comically absurd; the treatment of white people as Negro slaves (first Roxana and Chambers, then Tom) as if it were the most natural thing in the world—no one in the novel remarks on the oddness of treating a person who to all appearances is white as if he or she were black—is sinisterly absurd. Yet there is no overt criticism of slavery or racism; and maybe the reader is being invited to agree with Roxana that the false Tom's one thirty-second part Negro ancestry is responsible for his villainous behavior. (On the other hand, it may be his spoiled "white" upbringing that is responsible.) There is not only irony, but a mordant commentary on bigotry, in the fact that environment makes "Chambers" (who is white) more Negro than "Tom" (who is black). Furthermore, Roxana is the most impressive character in the novel, while the white people, except for Wilson, are basically ridiculous. Still, I wonder whether the book is essentially about slavery or racism, let alone about law, rather than about the debate—very lively in the late nineteenth century—over Nature versus Nurture (or genetics versus environment); about how easily people are taken in by appearances; and maybe even about the triumph of science and rationality, in the person of Wilson, over rural ignorance and complacency.

Robin West believes that the novel contains an implicit criticism of legalism. She points out that Wilson proves not only that the Italians are innocent (because the fingerprint on the murder weapon is "Tom"'s) but also that the murderer is a slave. She argues that by exposing "Tom," Wilson goes further than necessary to save his clients, and does so because, like most lawyers, he accepts uncritically the legal system, which happens to classify some people as slaves. How persuasive is this?

In light of what "Tom" had done to his mother, his being sold down the river is poetic justice; it is also a lighter punishment than he could have expected. Wilson does not know that this will be "Tom"'s punishment. On the contrary, he believes that "Tom" will be hanged for the murder—he says so at the climax of the trial. In that event, however, it is plainly better that "Tom" should be exposed, so that "Chambers" can be freed rather than being condemned to a lifetime of slavery, as he will be if the secret of the baby switching is buried with "Tom." Furthermore, in order to clinch the case for his clients, Wilson must produce not just a discrepant fingerprint but the real murderer— and "Tom," as the slave who usurped the real Tom's place, is a more plausible candidate than if "Tom" were believed to be the victim's real nephew. The novel, moreover, places no emphasis on Wilson's legal skills, or his acculturation as a lawyer; he owes his great success in the Italians' trial to his scientific hobby. He is the American as garage tinkerer, not as lawyer. Perhaps the reader is meant to look askance at Wilson for having become so well assimilated (at long last) into the hick society of Dawson's Landing that he has come to internalize its dubious values of chivalry, slavery, and racism, but there is no indication that we are meant to infer that his legal education and scarcely employed legal skills are responsible.

WRITTEN at about the same time as *The Just and the Unjust*, and also revolving about a murder case, Camus's *The Stranger*[24] reflects an entirely different outlook. The novella is narrated by its protagonist, Meursault, a Frenchman living in Algiers before World War II, when Algeria was still a French possession. The novella opens with the death of Meursault's mother. Through his reaction to her death we learn that he does not think about past or future, does not form deep emotional attachments, lacks ambition, piety, or pretension—or indeed conscience—and above all is honest about his feelings, or rather lack of them. One could describe him as a pagan sensualist except that this would make him sound fun-loving, which he is not. His passive, anesthetized manner is inconsistent with *joie de vivre*; he lacks "affect."

The day after his mother's funeral Meursault begins sleeping with a new girlfriend, Marie. He later accepts her proposal of marriage, while admitting to her that he does not love her and would probably have accepted the same proposal from any number of other women. Before they get around to marrying, Meursault and some pals get into a fight with a group of Arabs as a result of some disreputable business in which a friend of Meursault's had been involved—with his help. Afterwards Meursault finds himself walking alone on the beach, still carrying a pal's revolver lent him during the fight (no shots had been fired, though). He sees one of the Arabs lying on the beach. The sun is beating down mercilessly. Meursault continues walking toward the Arab, without knowing why he is doing this. The Arab draws a knife but makes no threatening gesture with it, and there is no suggestion that Meursault feels endangered. Nevertheless he shoots the Arab, once—and, after a pause, four more times.

He is arrested and questioned. The questioning brings out what the examining magistrate considers Meursault's disgusting callousness, as shown by his lack of remorse at either his mother's death or the Arab's,

---

[24] An unsatisfactory translation of *L'Etranger*, which is closer to "The Foreigner" or "The Outsider"—the latter being Camus's meaning. For a good treatment of the legal theme in *L'Etranger* and in several other works by Camus see Marilyn K. Yalom, "Albert Camus and the Myth of the Trial," 25 *Modern Language Quarterly* 434 (1964); see also A. D. Nuttall, "Did Meursault Mean to Kill the Arab?—The Intentional Fallacy Fallacy," 10 Critical Quarterly 95, 102–104 (1968). For splendid general criticism see René Girard, *"To Double Business Bound": Essays on Literature, Mimesis, and Anthropology*, chap. 2 (1978) ("Camus's Stranger Retried"); also very good is Conor Cruise O'Brien, *Albert Camus of Europe and Africa* 20–28 (1970).

his beginning his affair with Marie the day after his mother's funeral, and his rejection of Christianity. At Meursault's trial the prosecutor harps skillfully on these features of Meursault's character. The jury brings in a verdict of first-degree murder (as we would call it), and Meursault is sentenced to be guillotined. The end of the novella depicts his fierce rejection of the efforts of the prison chaplain to convert him to Christianity and his reaffirmation of the pagan values that he has lived by. He has lost his earlier inarticulateness.

The contrast with Cozzens's novel is striking. Camus tells his story through the eyes of the criminal and makes the trial a sinister farce in which the defendant is condemned not for having murdered the Arab but for rejecting bourgeois values. The victim is nameless and faceless, and the impending execution of Meursault—the only fully realized character in the novella—is made to seem a far worse crime than the murder, which indeed is made to seem an unimportant incident on a par with Meursault's having forgotten how old his mother was when she died.

What will strike an American lawyer as particularly odd is how evidence of Meursault's "bad" character (bad in a conventional sense rejected by the novella) is allowed into the trial and indeed becomes the decisive factor in his condemnation. Although the author plainly disapproves of the verdict, this is not because of any procedural irregularity. He accepts the legal relevance of Meursault's character; he merely rejects the ethical system which pronounces that character bad. Possibly the novella can be read as a criticism of capital punishment, yet if Meursault had instead been condemned to spend his youth in prison this might have seemed, in the author's implied ethical universe, an even crueler punishment.

In an American trial the character evidence so damaging to Meursault's chances would not have been let in: character evidence is not admissible to show that the defendant probably acted in conformity with the character shown by that evidence in the incident for which he is being prosecuted.[25] It is admissible to show motive, knowledge, and

[25] See, for example, Rule 404 of the Federal Rules of Criminal Procedure and the accompanying Notes of Advisory Committee to Proposed Rules; also *McCormick on Evidence* § 190, p. 557 (Edward W. Cleary ed., 3d ed. 1984). There is no comparable rule limiting evidence of bad character in a French criminal trial. See Roger Merle and André Vitu, *Traité de droit criminel*, vol. 2, at 155, 165–166 (3d ed. 1979). On the contrary, Article 331 of the French Code of Criminal Procedure, added in 1960, provides: "Witnesses shall testify only either on the facts charged against the accused *or on his character and morals.*" *The French Code of Criminal Procedure* 116 (Gerald L. Kock trans. 1964) (emphasis added). At the time Camus wrote *L'Etranger*, the code did not contain even this tepid restriction on the scope of a witness's testimony. See *Code*

so forth, but Meursault's behavior toward his mother and his rejection of Christianity are far too remote from the crime to be allowed into evidence for any of these purposes. We may therefore be tempted to find in the novella reasons for preferring the Anglo-American adversary procedure to the Continental system, though it does not seem to have been Camus's purpose to criticize the only type of criminal procedure he knew anything about. He had a larger fish to fry—the bourgeois Christian world view.

The refusal to exclude evidence of Meursault's character from his trial was probably not a violation of French criminal procedure. Therefore the novella does provide a reason, however inadvertent on Camus's part, for preferring the Anglo-American system. And in doing so it illustrates the possibility that the law and literature movement can contribute to the study of comparative law. But it is a limited possibility. If one wanted to make a comparative evaluation of American and French criminal procedure, one would not do so on the basis of novelistic depictions; one would study actual trials. Besides, the trial of Meursault is, in at least one respect, profoundly unrealistic—not in the admission of but in the weight given to the character evidence. A colonial French court would not have been so eager to convict and sentence to death a Frenchman accused of murdering a "native."

And even in an American criminal court, Meursault might have been

---

*d'Instruction Criminelle* art. 317 (1932). Furthermore, consistent with the inquisitorial tradition of Continental procedure, a French criminal trial begins with the interrogation of the defendant by the presiding judge, and apparently no details of the defendant's personal history (many of which will be in a dossier compiled during the investigation of the crime) are out of bounds. See Merle and Vitu, above, vol. 2, at 165; A. V. Sheehan, *Criminal Procedure in Scotland and France: A Comparative Study, with Particular Emphasis on the Role of the Public Prosecutor* 27 n. 14, 28–29, 48–49, 73 (1975); cf. Fernand Chapar, *Manuel de la Cour d'Assises* 140–141 (1961). As best I can determine, the type of character evidence introduced in Meursault's trial would be admissible even today in a French criminal trial. A striking example is recorded in a recent article in *Le Monde*. See Maurice Peyrot, "Aux assises de Paris: Un accusé qui s'affirme non-violent répond d'une tentative de viol," *Le Monde*, Sept. 12, 1987, at 11. (I am indebted to James Beardsley for bringing this article to my attention.) The article describes a trial in the Cour d'Assises (the French felony court) for attempted rape, before a tribunal of three professional judges and nine lay judges (that is, jurors) sitting together; a majority vote of the lay judges is required for conviction. The defendant was convicted. There was extensive testimony about his character and personality—that he was nervous, sensitive, nonviolent, accommodating, suggestible, impulsive, and emotional. The *pièce de résistance* was the testimony of a popular singer, who had never met the defendant, but who, having been informed that the defendant was one of his fans, testified as follows: "I am opposed to all forms of violence. Those who care for me do so because this is my philosophy. What strikes me about the accused is his concern over being accused of an act of which he totally disapproves. If I am present today, it is because I am absolutely convinced that he is innocent."

convicted of first-degree murder. Although the Arab displays a knife, Meursault appears not to be in fear of death or serious bodily injury when he shoots him, so there would be no basis for acquittal on grounds of self-defense. Moreover, while an actual but unreasonable fear of death or serious bodily injury would mitigate his guilt, Meursault has no fear. And those four shots fired after a pause are highly indicative of premeditation. Actually, it seems that Meursault shot the Arab in a sort of trance brought on by the fierce sun beating down on the beach, and did not intend to kill him; and the absence of premeditation would reduce his offense to second-degree murder. But who knows whether the jury would believe this, or indeed even know about it? Meursault testified at his trial but was unable to give a coherent account of the circumstances of the killing, and there were no eyewitnesses.

The fact that Meursault was guilty of a very serious crime, even if not first-degree murder, emphasizes the moral gulf between Camus and Cozzens. One cannot imagine Cozzens, who is very definitely a spokesman for the conventional values of Protestant New England, sympathizing with a Meursault. All else to one side, Meursault is incapable of remorse for his action. Indeed, a case can be made that he is a psychopath, utterly self-absorbed and incapable of any feeling for his fellow human beings, whether his mother, his lover, or the Arab. So at least it would seem to Cozzens.

It is possible to transpose *The Stranger* to a more symbolic key, where what from one angle is Meursault's psychopathic personality is seen from another as merely the isolation of the self from others; or to emphasize Meursault's growth in self-awareness (certainly in articulateness) under the stress of his interrogation, trial, and sentencing.[26] It may be possible to regard the work as a commentary on the inherent shortcomings of conceptualization—reason's inability to comprehend passion; for we never do learn *why* Meursault pulled the trigger. But it is difficult to shake off the impression that Camus is inviting the reader to take Meursault's part despite his crime and lack of remorse, by depicting him as victim rather than killer and by depersonalizing the real victim (the Arab). The ambiguous circumstances of the murder operate to preserve the reader's sympathies for Meursault without making his punishment completely implausible. As René Girard explains,

> Meursault had to commit some truly reprehensible action, but in order to retain the sympathy of the readers, he had to remain innocent. His crime had to be involuntary, therefore, but not so involuntary that the essential Meursault, the man who does not cry at his mother's funeral, would

[26] See Germaine Brée, *Camus* 114–115 (1961); Yalom, note 24 above, at 436–437.

remain untouched by the sentence. All the events leading to the actual scene of the shooting, including that scene itself, with its first involuntary shot followed by four voluntary ones, are so devised that they appear to fulfill these two incompatible exigencies. Meursault will die an innocent, and yet his death sentence will be more significant than a mere judicial error.[27]

No reader would believe that Meursault would be sentenced to death for not crying at his mother's funeral, so he must commit a capital offense, but in circumstances that preserve his essential innocence so that the reader will believe that Meursault's failing to cry at his mother's funeral, and his other defiances of bourgeois pieties, were the real reasons for the conviction and sentence. This analysis shows how little *The Stranger* has really to do with law and how much it has to do with a form of neoromanticism in which criminals are made heroes.

Behind Meursault stands an even less lovely amoralist, Gide's Lafcadio (*Les Caves du Vatican*), who shoves an inoffensive pilgrim to his death from a railroad carriage, just for the heck of it; and Dostoevsky's Raskolnikov (*Crime and Punishment*), who murders and robs a pawnbroker, partly at least to demonstrate his superiority to conventional morality. The difference between Camus and Gide, on the one hand, and Dostoevsky and Cozzens, on the other, is that the first two appear to take the side of the criminals and the last two do not (though Raskolnikov is portrayed much more sympathetically than the criminals in *The Just and the Unjust*). A lawyer is not likely to approve the hostility to law expressed by Camus and Gide; yet, surprisingly, in the next chapter we shall see Richard Weisberg doing just that. For now it is enough to note that law appears to interest Camus not in itself but as a symbol of the entire complex of conventional civilized values. On whether a lawyer has anything to say in defense of those values—or in support of the attack on them—the reader should reserve judgment until the next chapter.

## Dilemmas of Jurisprudence in Shakespeare, Marlowe, and Sophocles

I turn now to a group of literary works both greater and more substantially engaged with law than the works discussed so far in this chapter. I start with the two "legal" plays of Shakespeare (*The Merchant*

---

[27] Girard, note 24 above, at 17. Girard summarizes the connection between Meursault's passivity and Camus's effort to preserve the reader's sympathy for him in this deft rhetorical question: "How could Meursault premeditate murder, since he cannot premeditate a successful career in Paris or marriage with his mistress?" Id. at 14.

*of Venice* and *Measure for Measure*)[28] and, sandwiched in between for reasons to be explained, Christopher Marlowe's *Doctor Faustus*.

The legal issue in *The Merchant of Venice* has its root in the fact that Bassanio, a Venetian aristocrat, needs money to woo Portia in proper style but is a spendthrift and has no assets to pledge as security for a loan. His friend Antonio, the merchant of the title, is wealthy and generous but at the moment has no liquid assets. He agrees, however, to give his bond in guaranty of a loan to Bassanio, and the pair approach Shylock for the loan. As it happens, there is no love lost between Antonio and Shylock. Antonio lends money but refuses to charge interest, thus competing unfairly (as it seems to Shylock) with the Jewish money lenders.[29] And Antonio has made no secret of his contempt for Jews— has indeed kicked and spat on Shylock. Shylock hates Antonio both as a Christian and because of the specific wrongs, commercial and personal, that Antonio has done to him. Nevertheless he agrees to lend the money that Bassanio wants and to charge no interest, provided Antonio will pledge a pound of his flesh should there be a default. It is possible, though extremely unlikely, that Shylock intends the bond as a joke[30]—even that he is trying to display generosity toward the Chris-

---

[28] For good discussions of the treatment of law in Shakespeare's plays see George W. Keeton, *Shakespeare's Legal and Political Background* (1967); W. Moelwyn Merchant, "Lawyer and Actor: Process of Law in Elizabethan Drama," 3 *English Studies Today* 107 (1962), which also discusses Shakespeare's contemporaries; Note, "Shakespeare and the Legal Process: Four Essays," 61 *Virginia Law Review* 390 (1975). Cf. Bertil Johansson, "Law and Lawyers in Elizabethan England, As Evidenced in the Plays of Ben Jonson and Thomas Middleton," 18 *Stockholm Studies in English* (1967). Law crops up in other Shakespeare plays besides *The Merchant of Venice* and *Measure for Measure*, as I noted in the Introduction. See, for example, Jack Benoit Gohn, "Richard II: Shakespeare's Legal Brief on the Royal Prerogative and the Succession to the Throne," 70 *Georgetown Law Journal* 943 (1982).

[29] There is no suggestion in the play that lending at interest is illegal, as distinct from controversial and, probably, ethically dubious. That was the situation in Shakespeare's England. Though not respectable, and hedged about with many restrictions—the vestiges of which are found in modern "usury" laws, which impose ceilings on interest rates—lending at interest was no longer flatly forbidden, as it had been (to Christians) during the Middle Ages. See P. S. Atiyah, *The Rise and Fall of Freedom of Contract* 66 (corrected ed. 1985).

[30] He says (I.3.140–148):

> This kindness [an interest-free loan] will I show.
> Go with me to a notary, seal me there
> Your single bond; and, in a merry sport,
> If you repay me not on such a day,
> In such a place, such sum or sums as are
> Express'd in the condition, let the forfeit
> Be nominated for an equal [exact] pound
> Of your fair flesh, to be cut off and taken
> In what part of your body pleaseth me.

tians who despise him, but if so he is motivated by a desire to reproach them for their mistreatment of him (as he deems it), rather than by any genuine magnanimity. Probably he is hoping that Antonio will default and is "buying" this chance by forgoing interest. In any event, soon after the deal is made, Shylock, inexplicably abandoning his rule of never having social intercourse with Christians, goes to dinner at Bassanio's house. While he is there, his daughter, Jessica, runs off with her Christian lover, taking the family jewels with her. (She later marries him and converts to Christianity.) This incident makes Shylock desperate for revenge, and by a happy coincidence the ships carrying Antonio's goods are just then lost at sea and as a result the loan goes into default. Shylock insists on his pound of flesh and makes clear that he is going to take it from the region of Antonio's heart, killing him.

Although not doubting the legality of Shylock's demand, Antonio asks him for mercy (not forcefully, however—he is, as Keats would have put it, "half in love with easeful death"). Shylock refuses. The Duke of Venice also urges mercy unsuccessfully. Bassanio has succeeded in marrying Portia and as a result has enough money to repay the loan with generous interest, and he offers to do so, but Shylock refuses to discharge the bond on this basis. It looks as though Antonio is a goner, when all of a sudden Portia appears, disguised as a (male) doctor of laws. At first she pretends to be a legal stickler and wins Shylock's praise. This interlude serves two purposes: it puts Shylock on record as accepting her as an authoritative exponent of the law, and it hardens his resolve not to accept Bassanio's offer—which Portia had funded—of double Shylock's principal back.

Then she turns on him. She points out that the bond refers to flesh, not blood, and she says that if Shylock sheds a drop of Antonio's blood while executing the bond he will not be protected by the bond and therefore will be guilty of murder. And this means that Shylock is already guilty of a capital crime—in plotting to kill Antonio by execution of the bond—and should be executed! Everyone is astonished by Portia's legal sagacity, and no one offers a counterargument. However, to show that Christians are more charitable than Jews, the Duke offers to release Shylock if he will surrender all his wealth and convert to Christianity. He protests, and either half or maybe the whole forfeiture is then remitted,[31] except that he must leave all his wealth at

---

[31] Half is returned to Shylock outright, half is to be held by Antonio in "use" (trust) for Jessica upon Shylock's death. If Shylock is to be the beneficiary of the trust during his life, then the whole forfeiture has been remitted subject only to Jessica's rights on Shylock's death. If the income of the trust is to accumulate for Jessica, only half of the forfeiture has been remitted. It is as difficult as it is unimportant to determine which interpretation is correct.

his death to Jessica, whom he had disinherited when she ran away. He accepts the modified offer, and departs.

The legal aspects of *The Merchant of Venice* (which are the subject of an extensive literature)[32] are on one level absurd; and the trial, with its imposture (by Portia) and its technicalities, could almost be a satire on law and lawyers, except that it does not have the feel of satire. No reason is given for the pound-of-flesh bond—for example, that it is intended to incite Antonio to greater than usual efforts to safeguard his assets so that he does not default. The bond recalls and is no doubt meant to remind the audience that Jews were thought to eat the flesh of Christians at Passover; and the reminder is apropos, since Shylock seems to be motivated by the long-shot chance of eliminating his hated Christian competitor. But no civilized sixteenth-century legal system (and Venice is presented as a civilized state) would enforce a penalty bond of this character; by the end of the sixteenth century the English court of equity was relieving debtors against merely pecuniary penalties in bonds.[33] Enforcement would be especially odd if the borrower had managed to come up with enough money to repay the loan in full, and offered to pay generous interest to boot even though the loan was interest-free. Since the loan was only for three months, Bassanio's offer to double Shylock's principal implies interest at an annual rate of 400 percent. Shylock's refusal is a further indication that the bond is not a commercial guarantee at all, but a gamble, with Antonio's life as the stakes. (Shylock never argues that he must enforce the bond in order to protect his standing with future borrowers.) Although the law does not enforce gambling

[32] See, for example, Alice N. Benston, "Portia, the Law, and the Tripartite Structure of *The Merchant of Venice*," 30 *Shakespeare Quarterly* 367 (1979); "On Christian and Jew: *The Merchant of Venice*," in Allan Bloom (with Harry V. Jaffa), *Shakespeare's Politics* 13 (1964); William Chester Jordan, "Approaches to the Court Scene in the Bond Story: Equity and Mercy or Reason and Nature," 33 *Shakespeare Quarterly* 49 (1982); Keeton, note 28 above, chap. 9; W. Moelwyn Merchant, "Introduction," in William Shakespeare, *The Merchant of Venice* 20–32 (New Penguin ed. 1967); O. Hood Phillips, *Shakespeare and the Lawyers*, chap. 8 (1972); Frederick Pollock, "A Note on *Shylock v. Antonio*," 30 *Law Quarterly Review* 175 (1914); Barbara Tovey, "The Golden Casket: An Interpretation of *The Merchant of Venice*," in *Shakespeare as Political Thinker* 215 (John Alvis and Thomas G. West eds. 1981); E. F. J. Tucker, "The Letter of the Law in 'The Merchant of Venice,' " 29 *Shakespeare Survey* 93 (1976). Cf. W. Nicholas Knight, "Equity and Mercy in English Law and Drama (1405–1641)," 6 *Comparative Drama* 51 (1972). For exemplary general criticism see René Girard, " 'To Entrap the Wisest': A Reading of *The Merchant of Venice*," in *Literature and Society* 100 (Edward W. Said ed. 1980); Norman Rabkin, *Shakespeare and the Problem of Meaning*, chap. 1 (1981).

[33] See A. W. B. Simpson, "The Penal Bond with Conditional Defeasance," 82 *Law Quarterly Review* 392, 416 (1966); A. W. B. Simpson, *A History of the Common Law of Contract: The Rise of the Action of Assumpsit* 118–119 (1975). The Roman Law of the Twelve Tables allowed creditors to cut up a defaulting debtor into as many pieces as there were creditors—but that law dates from the fifth century B.C.

contracts, no one in the play doubts the legality of Shylock's demand for the pound of flesh until Portia comes up with her hypertechnical argument—which Shylock does not attempt to rebut by pointing out that the bond must implicitly have authorized him to shed Antonio's blood since otherwise he could not get his pound of flesh.

The absence of explicit reference to equity jurisprudence or to any other basis for the amelioration of penalties and forfeitures in contracts is unrealistic, but a literary imperative: the audience must take seriously the possibility that Antonio will be killed, and it would not do so if the law of Venice as depicted in the play refused to enforce penalty clauses. The additional rabbit that Portia pulls out of her hat—the law making it a capital offense to plot to kill a Venetian—somewhat undermines that possibility: why didn't Antonio, Shylock, and the others know about the law when the bond was signed, or when the trial began? But there are plenty of obscure laws; and, realistic or not, the invocation of this law is dramatically necessary in order to complete Shylock's defeat. If he merely could not enforce the bond he would be disappointed but would have his wealth intact (except maybe for the money loaned Bassanio) and would not have to convert to Christianity. Here as elsewhere Shakespeare sacrifices plausibility to dramatic effect.[34]

The lack of realism in the play's treatment of law extends to the procedures as well as the substance of law. Portia not only is an imposter but has an undisclosed interest in the outcome of the trial; the parties have no lawyers; Venice has no professional judges; a civil case ends in a criminal conviction.[35] And yet the play is about law in a more profound sense than any other work considered thus far.

The character of Shylock manages an unlikely but suggestive combination of three dispositions: the commercial ethic (Shylock as "economic man"); vengefulness; and legal formalism in its lay sense of using the letter of the law to accomplish an unjust end. Shylock is at once the Jew stereotyped as modern, commercial man and, somewhat inconsistently, the Jew stereotyped as Old Testament avenger ("an eye for an eye") who rejects the New Testament's command to turn the other cheek. He

[34] Another example in *The Merchant of Venice* is the simultaneous loss at sea of all the ships carrying Antonio's cargoes, and their miraculous reappearance. Moreover, no one asks why Antonio did not protect himself from default by insuring his cargoes, as he could have done. See C. F. Trenerry, *The Origin and Early History of Insurance, Including the Contract of Bottomry*, chap. 25 (1926); William D. Winter, *A Short Sketch of the History and Principles of Marine Insurance* 9 (Ins. Soc'y of N.Y. 1925).

[35] The fact that the Duke of Venice has to send to Padua to find an expert on the law of Venice may seem another unrealistic aspect of the law in the play, but is not; Padua was both a center of legal studies and a possession of Venice—though Shakespeare does not bother to tell the audience either of these things.

actually prefers taking lethal revenge on Antonio to receiving extravagant interest on his loan.[36] Not without reason, Shylock hates Christians, although his hatred also reflects, in his words, the "ancient grudge" between Jews and Christians (I.3.44) and thus puts us in mind of the feud between the Montagues and the Capulets in *Romeo and Juliet*. When the Christians "steal" his daughter—and really do steal his jewels—he is wrought to a furious pitch of vengefulness. But unlike Achilles or Hamlet, Shylock is subject to law and tries to use his legal rights as the agency for revenge. Michael Kohlhaas tried too, and only after failing turned to private revenge. We are made to see how law is a substitute for revenge and could in principle provide a basis for obtaining revenge in as gruesome a form as the avenger might desire.

Shylock's opposite in many respects is Antonio. A melancholy bachelor and foe of money lenders, generous to the point of improvidence, heedless of danger, and altogether willing to die to save Bassanio ("I am a tainted wether of the flock, / Meetest for death. The weakest kind of fruit / Drops earliest to the ground, and so let me," IV.1.114–116), Antonio is an echo of Jesus Christ, though one distorted by his profession as a merchant and his ugly treatment of Shylock as Jew—not just as usurer. In his debate with Shylock over the question of whether there is biblical authority for lending at interest, we may sense the temptation of Christ by Satan; Antonio even complains about the devil quoting scripture. In rejecting Old Testament vengefulness and Judaic preoccupation with formal, law-like observances, Antonio rejects Shylock's dominant characteristics. Had Shylock gotten his pound of flesh, this would have been the reenactment of the crucifixion of Jesus at the behest of the Jewish priestly establishment.

If I am reading Antonio aright, the providential appearance of Portia casts a remarkable light on Shakespeare's own values, at least as reflected or implied in this play (always an important qualification when dealing with Shakespeare or any other author of imaginative literature). Portia represents the *via media* between Shylock and Antonio. Worldly—even

---

[36] This may seem to put Shylock's commercial incentives at war with his vengeful ones; but actually Shylock is moved by avarice as well as vengeance. He says (III.1.119–121): "I will have the heart of him if he forfeit, for were he out of Venice I can make what merchandise I will." Antonio explains Shylock's desire to enforce the bond in similar terms (III.3.21–24): "He seeks my life. His reason well I know: / I oft deliver'd from his forfeitures / Many that have at times made moan to me; / Therefore he hates me." As we shall see in Chapter 4, the play seems to equate exacting repayment of a commercial obligation with taking revenge—both belonging to a system of strict reciprocity that is inconsistent, in the implied values of the play, not only with Christian mercy but even with secular, pragmatic equity—and to criticize market values, which were emerging in the Elizabethan period.

sensual, in comparison with the frugal, chaste, and self-denying natures of both Shylock and Antonio—she is not above using legal technicalities, and even ethically dubious tricks, to save a life, just as she is not above bending the terms of her father's will to increase the likelihood that the debonair and easygoing Bassanio will win her hand in competition with the other suitors, and just as she is not above tricking Shylock out of settling his dispute with Antonio for double his principal back, which would have come out of her fortune. (The ring trick in Act V provides still another example of Portia's fluent manipulation of contracts.) Whatever the law might say, the enforcement of the bond would be absurd and Portia does what is necessary to prevent it. Yet she is explicitly concerned to accomplish this without establishing a bad precedent or damaging Venice's commercial standing, which, as Shylock repeatedly points out, requires that an alien (a Jew could not be a Venetian citizen in the sixteenth century) receive the same justice as a citizen.

In legal terms one might say that Portia personifies the spirit of equity[37]—the prudent recognition that strict rules of law, however necessary to a well-ordered society, must be applied with sensitivity and tact so that the spirit of the law is not sacrificed unnecessarily to the letter. One is reminded that in the evolution of a legal system the first stage after revenge is law in the sense of fixed rules, formally or as one might say technically interpreted; strict liability, of which Shylock is an exponent, looms large at this stage, as we saw in Chapter 1. The next stage is equity, where the rules are tempered in application in order to bring them into closer harmony with their underlying principles, or, to put the same point differently, in order to make a better fit between the rules and the conduct sought to be regulated by them.[38]

---

[37] See, for example, Merchant, note 32 above, at 20n, 23; W. Nicholas Knight, "Equity in Shakespeare and His Contemporaries," 56 *Iowa State Journal of Research* 67, 71 (1981). There is a debate over the degree to which equitable principles as actually enforced by the court of chancery in the sixteenth century inform the trial scene in *The Merchant of Venice* (see sources cited in note 32 above), but it is sterile. The concept of equity—as a more flexible, moralistic system of jurisprudence than rule-bound "law"—is not tied to a specific court system, and indeed in *The Merchant of Venice* is extralegal. For a fascinating though highly speculative argument that *The Merchant of Venice* may have influenced English equity jurisprudence, see W. Nicholas Knight, "Equity, 'The Merchant of Venice' and William Lambarde," 27 *Shakespeare Survey* 93 (1974). On the Aristotelian roots of English equity jurisprudence see Stephen W. DeVine, "The Concept of *Epieikeia* in the Chancellor of England's Enforcement of the Feoffment to Uses before 1535," 21 *University of British Columbia Law Review* 323 (1987).

[38] See Henry Sumner Maine, *Ancient Law* (1864), and my book *The Economics of Justice*, chap. 7 (1981); but see Sally F. Moore, "Legal Liability and Evolutionary Interpretation: Some Aspects of Strict Liability, Self-Help, and Collective Responsibility," in *Allocation of Responsibility* 51 (M. Gluckman ed. 1972). Thus the member of a primitive legal culture might

The "spirit" of equity in the play, it must be emphasized, is just that—spirit, not legal substance. No equitable principles actually inform the law of Venice as it is presented in the play. Portia's great "quality of mercy" speech (IV.1.182–203) is cast as an appeal to Shylock's faculty of mercy (he has none), not as a legal argument. When that appeal is turned down, Portia is forced to argue in the legalistic terms that are the only ones available in the legal culture depicted in the play. Within those terms her argument is stronger than it first appears. To rebut it by pointing out that the bond must have authorized whatever acts were necessary to execute it, and therefore the shedding of Antonio's blood, Shylock would have had to appeal to the spirit rather than the letter of the bond; for the bond is silent on the matter of shedding blood. But once he had done that he would have found it hard to maintain his legal position. The spirit of the bond is to make sure that Shylock is repaid in full, and Bassanio has offered to repay him double, or even more if Shylock insists—but Shylock suffers from the avenger's standard vice of immoderateness.

In recognition of the subtlety and generosity, by sixteenth-century standards, of Shakespeare's characterization of the Jew, it should be noted that Shylock's insistence on the principle of literal interpretation need not be viewed merely as the product of a primitive and vengeful spirit. As an unpopular alien (a point that Shylock harps on and the Christians do not deny), naturally he would mistrust a jurisprudence that gave judges a broad discretion to mitigate the rigors of legal rules, for he could expect any discretion to be exercised against him. A punctilious legalism is the pariah's protection. But he who lives by the letter of the law may perish by it, too.

The play takes the side of equity against law in law's narrow sense of

---

side with Shylock—as did, indeed, a Somali tribesman, Farah, to whom Isak Dinesen told the story of *The Merchant of Venice*:

"Did the Jew give up his claim? He should not have done that. The flesh was due to him, it was little enough for him to get for all that money."

"But what else could he do," I asked, "when he must not take one drop of blood?"

"Memsahib," said Farah, "he could have used a red-hot knife. That brings out no blood."

"But," I said, "he was not allowed to take either more or less than one pound of flesh."

"And who," said Farah, "would have been frightened by that, exactly a Jew? He might have taken little bits at a time, with a small scale at hand to weight it on, till he had got just one pound. Had the Jew no friends to give him advice? . . . He could have done that man a lot of harm, even a long time before he had got that one pound of his flesh."

I said: "But in the story the Jew gave it up."

"Yes, that was a great pity, Memsahib," said Farah.

*Out of Africa and Shadows on the Grass* 269–270 (1985).

a set of mechanically, inflexibly, unimaginatively enforced rules, but also against the transcendental values personified by Antonio, whom Portia cheats of martyrdom. Apparently Shakespeare was not the kind of Christian who thinks it possible to manage society using the Sermon on the Mount as one's blueprint of social engineering (not that the Sermon on the Mount was intended to be used for that purpose). The evidence is not solely internal to the plays: we know that Shakespeare was a canny, successful businessman, that he was careful to keep clear of political controversy, that he gave the theatergoing public what they wanted, that he was married and had children, that he retired from the theater young to become a country gentleman, that he was charming and companionable, and that he was litigious.[39] He was, in short, a man of the world rather than a saint or a fanatic.[40] There is much in the plays and sonnets to suggest great turmoil beneath the placid surface of Shakespeare's personality, but nothing to indicate that he was alienated from his society, or was a rebel, or a marginal figure like many Romantic and modern poets. He aspired to be, and eventually became, an "establishment" figure, and his plays seem for the most part (though with many qualifications and undertones) to approve establishment values. This is not the key to their greatness; I do not think it is even relevant to their greatness. The key is found in their brilliant plots and dramatic devices, in their poetry, and in the largeness of spirit which enabled Shakespeare to breathe humanity into the most incredible monsters—as Othello the black miscegenator, Shylock the Jewish usurer, the senile Lear, Brutus the priggish regicide, and Macbeth and his wife all would have struck the average Elizabethan theatergoer.[41] But all I want to argue here is that Shakespeare celebrates mature values, as does Homer and in his minor way Cozzens, but not the Camus of *The Stranger,* and that those values imply a view of law in which the primitive impulse of revenge and the earliest, formalistic

[39] See Bevington, note 14 above, at 41–70, for a lucid sketch of Shakespeare's life; Schoenbaum, note 14 above, especially chap. 13 and pp. 255–259; S. Schoenbaum, "The Life of Shakespeare," in *The Cambridge Companion to Shakespeare Studies,* note 6 above, at 1. On the perils of biographical criticism of Shakespeare's plays, C. J. Sisson, "The Mythical Sorrows of Shakespeare," 20 *Proceedings of the British Academy* 45 (1934), is particularly good.

[40] See Orwell, note 1 above, at 298–300, for a characteristically vivid statement of this point. Further evidence is the treatment of Brutus in *Julius Caesar,* discussed in Chapter 1, and of Angelo in *Measure for Measure,* discussed later in this chapter.

[41] To understand the generosity with which Shylock is depicted, one has only to look at his grotesque counterpart, Barabas, the protagonist of *The Jew of Malta*; and Marlowe was not only a great dramatist but a great iconoclast. On the depiction of Barabas see Wilbur Sanders, *The Dramatist and the Received Idea: Studies in the Plays of Marlowe and Shakespeare* 41–50 (1968); and on the Elizabethan conception of the Jew see id. at 339–351.

stage of law are rejected in favor of a more flexible or equitable jurisprudence, but without embracing the illusion that society can replace positive law with transcendental values. Shakespeare gives Shylock some pretty good lines against Antonio; one is not likely to forget the comparison of Antonio to a "fawning publican" (I.3.38). There is something not altogether wholesome about Antonio—and he did, after all, sign the bond. We are meant, I think, to sense an affinity between him and Shylock despite the many points of opposition between them.

BEFORE resuming the theme of equity in Shakespeare, I want to examine another depiction of contract in Elizabethan drama, Faustus's pact with the devil.[42] Faustus conjures Mephostophilis, and after brief negotiations signs (in blood) a deed conveying his soul to Mephostophilis's master in exchange for various undertakings. The document states in full (I.5.95–114):

On these conditions following:
   First, that Faustus may be a spirit in form and substance.
   Secondly, that Mephostophilis shall be his servant, and be by him commanded.
   Thirdly, that Mephostophilis shall do for him, and bring him whatsoever.
   Fourthly, that he shall be in his chamber or house invisible.
   Lastly, that he shall appear to the said John Faustus at all times, in what shape and form soever he please.
   I, John Faustus of Wittenberg Doctor, by these presents, do give both body and soul to Lucifer, Prince of the East, and his minister Mephostophilis, and furthermore grant unto them that four and twenty years being expired, and these articles above written being inviolate, full power to fetch or carry the said John Faustus, body and soul, flesh, blood or goods, into their habitation wheresoever.
   By me, John Faustus.

[42] For relevant discussions see Cleanth Brooks, "The Unity of Marlowe's *Doctor Faustus*," in Brooks, *A Shaping Joy: Studies in the Writer's Craft* 367 (1971); John P. Cutts, *The Left Hand of God: A Critical Interpretation of the Plays of Christopher Marlowe*, chap. 4 (1973); Sara Munson Deats, "*Doctor Faustus*: From Chapbook to Tragedy," 3 *Essays in Literature* 3 (1976); Wolfgang S. Seiferth, "The Concept of the Devil and the Myth of the Pact in Literature Prior to Goethe," in *Lives of Doctor Faust* 209, 221–224 (Eric Bockstael ed. 1976); *Christopher Marlowe: Dr. Faustus: The A-Text* xliii–iv (David Ormerud and Christopher Wortham eds. 1985).
   All my quotations from Marlowe in this book are from Christopher Marlowe, *The Complete Plays* (J. B. Steane ed. 1969).

At the end of the play the twenty-four years are up and a posse of devils appears and carries Faustus off to hell.

As the maker of an immoral contract Faustus might seem a parallel figure to Shylock. There is indeed a diabolical aspect to Shylock's bond,[43] but the two characters have little in common except that both are damned (unless Shylock is saved by his conversion). Shylock is primitive, vengeful man; Faustus is modern, individualistic man. In contrast to the orthodox Christian view that the soul belongs to God, Faustus thinks he owns his soul and therefore can transfer it for appropriate consideration to the devil. And being a man of honor and in his own way a hero, he makes no effort to break the contract when the time comes to fulfill his obligations under it.[44] He substitutes the sanctity of contract for the sanctity of God; this shows his modernity. His adherence to the contract is all the more striking because Mephostophilis has broken *his* side of the bargain, and the contract expressly conditions Faustus's grant of body and soul to Lucifer on "these articles above written being inviolate." Shortly after signing and delivering the contract Faustus had asked Mephostophilis for a wife, and Mephostophilis had temporized, then produced "*a* DEVIL *dressed like a woman, with fireworks,*" whom Faustus spurns: "A plague on her for a hot whore." Mephostophilis comments, "Tut, Faustus, marriage is but a ceremonial toy. / If thou lovest me, think no more of it." (I.5.149–156.) The matter is dropped.

But it would be too simple to dismiss the pact as a mere pretext for Faustus's refusal to repent. The lawyer's distinction between an executory and a half-executed contract helps show why. An executory contract is one in which neither party has begun to perform his contractual undertaking; it is a bare exchange of promises. If the contract is illegal, the law will not enforce it. But what if after one party has performed his side of the bargain, the other party asks to be excused from having to perform, because the contract is illegal? Maybe party A has, as agreed, built a house for B, and now it is time for B to pay, and B refuses. The court may be less sympathetic to a defense of illegality in such a case.[45] And that is Faustus's case. His part of the bargain was not

---

[43] Harold Fisch, "The Pact With the Devil," 69 *Yale Review* 520, 525 (1980).

[44] As stressed by Brooks, note 42 above, at 378, quoting one of Faustus's replies to an old man who begs him to repent: "Hell claims his right, and with a roaring voice / Says 'Faustus, come, thine hour is almost come' / And Faustus now will come to do thee right" (V.1.55–57).

[45] See, for example, Kelly v. Kosuga, 358 U.S. 516 (1959); E. Allan Farnsworth, Contracts 328 (1982). And even if the court holds the contract unenforceable, it may require the party who broke the contract to make restitution to the other party of the value of the latter's

to be performed until the devil had finished performing *his* part. For Faustus to be allowed to repudiate the contract after having enjoyed its benefits for twenty-four years—benefits less ample than he bargained for but considerable nevertheless—would be to let him off scot-free after all those years of grossly immoral behavior. In these circumstances a sincere repentance, though feared by Mephostophilis, who keeps trying to intimidate Faustus into keeping his side of the bargain, is hard to visualize.

The legal aspect of the play is not the most important, however. The pact signed in blood serves mainly to symbolize the irrevocability of Faustus's choice. With eyes wide open he chooses a course of conduct that leads inevitably to his damnation; contract is a metaphor for commitment.

I SHALL revisit *Doctor Faustus* in later chapters—Marlowe's works have a surprising pertinence to the law and literature field. But now I return to Shakespeare and take up the legal themes in *Measure for Measure*.[46] Vienna, where the play is set, has very strict laws, including the death penalty for fornication, but the laws are not enforced. Although the Duke of Vienna is unhappy with this situation—prostitution, adultery, and fornication are flourishing—he is unwilling to crack down in person (I.3.19–36):

performance. See, for example, American Law Institute, *Restatement of Contracts (Second)* §§ 197 (and comment b), 198 (1979). But how could Faustus have restored to Mephostophilis the value (with interest!) of the goods and services that Mephostophilis had provided over the twenty-four years that the pact was in force? Penance would be of no benefit to Mephostophilis—quite the opposite. Of course, despite these nice legal points, no court would enforce a pact with the devil, in any circumstances; and it would detract from Faustus's grandeur—and blasphemy—if he were *legally* bound to the contract with Mephostophilis. All that my analysis suggests is that it was not unjust in a legal sense to hold Faustus to his bargain.

[46] Discussions of the play that stress its legal aspects include Darryl J. Gless, *Measure for Measure, the Law, and the Convent* (1979), especially pp. 35–51; Harold Skulsky, "Pain, Law, and Conscience in *Measure for Measure*," 25 *Journal of the History of Ideas* 147 (1964); John W. Dickinson, "Renaissance Equity and *Measure for Measure*," 13 *Shakespeare Quarterly* 287 (1962); Ronald Berman, "Shakespeare and the Law," 18 *Shakespeare Quarterly* 141 (1967); Margaret Scott, " 'Our City's Institutions': Some Further Reflections on the Marriage Contracts in *Measure for Measure*," 49 *ELH* 790 (1982); Ernest Schanzer, *The Problem Plays of Shakespeare: A Study of Julius Caesar, Measure for Measure, Antony and Cleopatra*, chap. 2 (1963), especially pp. 114–120; William T. Braithwaite, "Poetry and the Criminal Law: The Idea of Punishment in Shakespeare's *Measure for Measure*," 13 *Loyola University of Chicago Law Journal* 791 (1982). For general criticism see William Empson, "Sense in Measure for Measure," in Empson, *The Structure of Complex Words* 270 (1951); Arthur H. Scouten, "An Historical Approach to *Measure for Measure*," 54 *Philological Quarterly* 68 (1975).

We have strict statutes and most biting laws,
The needful bits and curbs to headstrong weeds,
Which for this fourteen years we have let slip;
. . . . .
· · · So our decrees,
Dead to infliction, to themselves are dead,
And liberty plucks justice by the nose;
. . . . .
Sith 'twas my fault to give the people scope,
'Twould be my tyranny to strike and gall them.

Instead the Duke arranges to take a leave of absence, leaving his strict and ascetic deputy, Angelo, in charge. Though he pretends to leave town, the Duke actually stays, disguised as a friar, so that he can see how Angelo handles things.

True to character, Angelo promptly sentences Claudio—a young gentleman who has impregnated his fiancée, Julietta—to death for fornication. Lucio, an acquaintance of Claudio, implores Claudio's sister, Isabella, who is a novitiate in a nunnery, to plead with Angelo for her brother's life. She does so, and Angelo becomes smitten with her and offers to spare her brother—if she will have intercourse with him. She indignantly refuses. When she reports all this to Claudio, to her astonishment he urges her to accept Angelo's offer. She is dismayed by her brother's thinking his life more important than her immortal soul, whose salvation might be jeopardized by sex with Angelo. Why it would be is not made clear. Would not fornication, the least deadly of the deadly sins (as Claudio points out to her), be excused if it were necessary to save an innocent life? Maybe the point is that since Claudio in fact is guilty of fornication, and death is a legal punishment for his crime, Isabella would not be sacrificing her chastity to save an innocent man; indeed, she would be guilty of bribery as well as fornication. Fortunately, the Duke, who is lurking about in his guise as a friar, comes up with a solution for their problems. He instructs Isabella to tell Angelo that she accepts his offer but to insist that their sexual encounter be brief and in the dark. The friar will substitute in her place Mariana, Angelo's former fiancée, whom Angelo had jilted because her dowry had been lost in a shipwreck.

All is done as arranged, but to compound his perfidy Angelo decides to execute Claudio anyway lest Claudio seek revenge when he finds out what Angelo has done to his sister. (This is another example of the ubiquity of the revenge motif in Elizabethan drama.) Angelo orders Claudio's head sent to him, but the Duke-friar arranges the substitution of the head of a prisoner who has just died of natural causes. The Duke now sends word that he is returning to Vienna and will want an accounting of Angelo's stewardship. When the Duke and Angelo meet outside the city's gates Isabella steps forward and accuses Angelo, who denies everything. His position begins to crumble when Mariana also steps forward and gives her evidence. The Duke, having left momentarily, reappears in the guise of the friar; and the jig is up when Lucio, who has spent the play slandering the Duke to the friar, pulls off the friar's cowl to reveal—to everyone's surprise—the Duke. Showing mercy like his counterpart in Venice, the Duke pardons Angelo after making him marry Mariana. Claudio is freed and marries Julietta. The Duke (we are given to understand) is going to marry Isabella.

There are many parallels to *The Merchant of Venice*. Like Shylock, Angelo is at once austere, a stickler for law, and (beneath his cold exterior) prey to a lawless, violent passion which drives him to attempt on Isabella the very crime that he has sentenced Claudio to die for. He misuses his legal authority in much the same way that Shylock misuses the law of contracts. The great difference between them is that Shylock has always been evil, whereas Angelo is awakened to evil—is tempted, and falls. Less obvious is the affinity within *Measure for Measure* between Angelo and Isabella. It is poetic justice for Angelo that Isabella is the first woman to awaken his sensuality, for they are alike in both being moral fanatics.[47] Probably we are meant to think capital punishment for fornication absurd and to laugh at Isabella's indignant refusal to sacrifice her virginity for her brother's life.[48] Poetic justice for her is being made an accomplice in the Duke's scheme of arranging a sexual encounter between Angelo and Mariana and being snatched from the jaws of the nunnery to become the Duke's wife.

The Duke plays a role similar to that of Portia in *The Merchant of Venice*—arranging things to come out right through a series of none-too-creditable stratagems. The initial departure from Vienna,

---

[47] Gless, note 46 above, chap. 2 and p. 97, places Shakespeare's portrayal of Isabella's "spiritual overreaching" in the context of Elizabethan antimonasticism. There are other parallels. Both Angelo, in his austere bachelorhood, and Isabella, in her decision to renounce the world for the nunnery, display an aversion to close human relationships. Both also share the same conception of law, as we are about to see; but this point must be qualified by the observation that Isabella's plea to Angelo for mercy parallels that of Portia in *The Merchant of Venice*.

[48] After all, the Duke incites Mariana to commit the same crime for which Claudio is supposed to be executed; and Shakespeare's first child was conceived before he married the mother. See Empson, note 46 above, at 282; Scouten, note 46 above, at 70–71. The Duke's pardoning Angelo on condition that he marry Mariana reflects what apparently in Elizabethan England, as until recently in this country, was the standard "punishment" for fornication. See Gless, note 46 above, at 108. On contemporary practice on the Continent see Guido Ruggiero, *The Boundaries of Eros: Sex Crime and Sexuality in Renaissance Venice*, chap. 2 (1985); id. at 20 (table 1). Although the Puritans made adultery a capital crime, as it is also under Islamic law, I have never heard of a legal system that made fornication a capital crime.

leaving Angelo to enforce the laws strictly, to take the blame, and to get humiliated on the Duke's return, recalls Machiavelli's *The Prince*.[49] The Duke puts a terrible scare into Claudio (by repeatedly telling him, when disguised as the friar, that he is going to be executed), scares Isabella by telling her that Claudio has been executed and by ordering her to be arrested for slandering Angelo, arranges an apparently illicit sexual encounter (between Angelo and Mariana), and seems bent on luring a nun aspirant into marriage. But it all works. Angelo's reign of terror succeeds, we are led to believe, in curtailing prostitution without impairing the Duke's popularity. Angelo is taught a lesson. Mariana obtains justice at long last. Moderate officials, like Escalus (Angelo's deputy) and the keeper of the jail, are vindicated. And Isabella, a cold and priggish young lady, becomes a woman fit for a glorious marriage.

Though a much greater work than *The Just and the Unjust*, Shakespeare's play resembles Cozzens's novel in celebrating the practical virtues and in scoffing at the angelic aspirations—the striving for a more than human purity—of Angelo and Isabella. Angelo on the one hand, and the bawds who provide comic relief in this not very funny comedy on the other hand, represent at the opening of the play the extremes— angel and animal—between which man, in the medieval and Elizabethan world view, is intermediate;[50] and the angel turns out to be an animal after all. Extremes of particular interest to the law-trained reader are the law that is never enforced and the law that is enforced too strictly. We are made to understand that attempting to outlaw fornication would be as quixotic in the culture of the play as it would be in our own culture. We are also made to understand that both extremes are serious failures of statecraft and that the Duke achieves the prudent mean—law enforced in moderation, which apparently means that the "punishment" for fornication is marriage and that prostitution is no longer flaunted even if not completely suppressed. Moderate ends, which give due recognition to the realities of human nature (and in particular the sexuality that Angelo and Isabella at first deny), achieved by worldly means—this is also the lesson of *The Merchant of Venice* and *The Just and the Unjust*.

Angelo's insistence on enforcing law to the hilt reflects a conception

[49] See Skulsky, note 46 above, at 163–164; Norman N. Holland, "*Measure for Measure*: The Duke and the Prince," 11 *Comparative Literature* 16 (1959); Harry V. Jaffa, "Chastity as a Political Principle: An Interpretation of Shakespeare's *Measure for Measure*," in *Shakespeare as Political Thinker*, note 32 above, at 181, 188–189.

[50] See John Erskine Hankins, *Backgrounds of Shakespeare's Thought*, chap. 7 (1978); E. M. W. Tillyard, *The Elizabethan World Picture* 25 (1943). On the complex relation between Shakespeare's thought and that of his age see W. R. Elton, "Shakespeare and the Thought of His Age," in *The Cambridge Companion to Shakespeare Studies* 17 (Stanley Wells ed. 1986).

of law that he shares not only with Shylock but also with Isabella—and, of special interest in light of the concerns of this book, with many lawyers, judges, and students of law to this day. That is the conception of law as something existing apart from man, a conception that is congenial to people who lack warmth in human relationships, as Shylock, Angelo, and Isabella do. Angelo cannot understand acting leniently toward Claudio just because there are extenuating circumstances (Julietta was Claudio's fiancée, and the law against fornication had not been enforced for many years); to him that would imply tampering with the law, because to him law is a set of rigid rules inflexibly applied. When Isabella pleads for her brother's life, Angelo replies, "It is the law, not I, condemn your brother. / Were he my kinsman, brother, or my son, / It should be thus with him" (II.2.84–86). The image of a judge condemning his own son expresses the sharpest possible cleavage between law and human feeling; Angelo is glancing ahead to Robert Louis Stevenson's *Weir of Hermiston: An Unfinished Romance* (1896), the climax of which was to be a judge's condemning his own son to death. Angelo's "angelism" is the unattainable and unnatural divorce of body from spirit—the same thing attempted by Caesar and Brutus. Isabella shares Angelo's conception of law as a thing apart from man. The ground on which she pleads for Angelo's life at the end of the play (before she discovers that Claudio is alive) is that since her brother was, after all, guilty, his execution was not wrongful despite the judge's corruption. Evidently Shakespeare did not think that law and government could be abstracted from human feeling in this way; Escalus is much closer to Shakespeare's idea of a proper judge than Angelo.

In both *The Merchant of Venice* and *Measure for Measure* Shakespeare is wrestling with the fundamental problem of law, which is how to control human behavior effectively by means of rules. The nature of the problem is brought into sharp focus by a recent analysis of the law in these plays. The literary critic Terry Eagleton believes that Shylock clearly has the law on his side: "It is Shylock who has respect for the spirit of law and Portia who does not. Shylock's bond does not actually state in writing that he is allowed to take some of Antonio's blood along with a pound of his flesh, but this is a reasonable inference from the text, as any real court would recognize . . . Portia's ingenious quibbling would be ruled out of order in a modern court, and Shylock (given that his bond were legal in the first place) would win his case."[51]

---

[51] *William Shakespeare* 36–37 (1986). The full discussion of the two plays occupies pages 35–58 of Eagleton's book.

This discussion overlooks three points. The first (perhaps hinted at in the remark "given that his bond were legal in the first place") is that no real court would have enforced Shylock's bond. The principle of freedom of contract would not have been pressed so far in the sixteenth century, let alone by a "modern court." That such bizarre bargains must be enforced is not, as Eagleton supposes, entailed by commitment to the rule of law.[52] Second, as I noted earlier, any attempt by Shylock to appeal to the spirit of the law would be inconsistent with his refusal to accept repayment of his loan, which is the spirit of the bond. By committing himself to literal interpretation Shylock provides the fulcrum for Portia to hurl literalism back in his face by pointing out that the bond nowhere mentions blood. Third, equity has been a part of law since ancient times; Aristotle emphasized it in the *Nicomachean Ethics* (see note 37). The law does not consist just of unbendable rules that must be enforced to the hilt regardless of consequences; meliorative doctrines are a part of law too.

An oversight similar to the third undermines Eagleton's analysis of *Measure for Measure*. He argues that not punishing Claudio to the maximum extent authorized by law fatally undermined the law's generality (pp. 55–57), and that justice can never be tempered by mercy because "how is mercy to break the vicious circle of prosecutions when it must somehow spring from inside that circle, from a humble solidarity with vice?" (p. 57). But it is not true that the concept of legality entails always imposing the maximum punishment. The very existence of a maximum implies that lawful punishment is a range, not a point. Anglo-American law has always both given law enforcement officials discretion not to prosecute every offense, and, within each category of offenses (for example, fornication), allowed the judge to vary the punishment according to the severity and mitigating circumstances of the individual defendant's conduct. It is because judges traditionally have great discretion in sentencing that writers who want to criticize judges often focus on the sentence, a neglected example being Galsworthy's fine play *Justice* (1910).

There are solid utilitarian reasons, independent of any "solidarity with vice" felt by judges, for the mixture of rule and discretion in criminal justice. Because the legislature lacks information about the particular

---

[52] Eagleton might but does not argue that any compromise with freedom of contract, as in refusing to enforce a bond agreed to by consenting adults in full possession of their faculties and all relevant information, undermines the premises of a capitalist system. Such an argument, which I shall examine in Chapter 4, should be congenial to Marxist literary criticism, of which Eagleton is a distinguished practitioner.

circumstances in which its laws might be violated, it fixes only the outer limits of punishment and leaves to the prosecuting, judicial, and sometimes correctional authorities the task of fitting the punishment to the conduct and circumstances of each criminal. This is a rational division of labor, and does not contradict the idea of law.

Most important, Eagleton's suggestion that "for law to be law its decrees must be general and impartial, quite independent of and indifferent to any concrete situation" (p. 36) exaggerates the "ruledness" of law. He thinks that law, to be law within the framework of assumptions that has shaped Western notions of law and society since the end of the Middle Ages, must be an inhuman abstraction—the sort of thing a Shylock, an Angelo, or an Isabella regards as law. Since law so conceived is intolerable, self-contradictory, and quickly abandoned, he believes that the capitalist (or "liberal") pretense to govern society by the "rule of law" is a fake.

This widely accepted radical view of legality[53] rests on a misunderstanding that *The Merchant of Venice* and *Measure for Measure* can help dispel. It is not true that Shylock, Angelo, Isabella, and Eagleton represent law, and Portia and the Duke of Vienna not-law. What is true is that the first four represent one end of the spectrum of conceptions of law while the last two are over toward the other end. The distinction between law (in an incomplete sense) and equity is one of several paired opposites that can be used to locate a person along the spectrum. The accompanying table presents a fuller list. The left-hand column lists a number of different terms—jurisprudential, philosophical, psychological—with which to represent law as an abstraction, a thing apart from the people charged with responsibility for enforcing the law and adjudicating disputes. The terms suggest ways of minimizing the human factor, minimizing discretion, and maximizing "ruledness" or "legalism." The emphasis is on professionalism, logic, strict rules, sharp distinctions, positive law, and "hard" cases (meaning, not as it has come to mean, cases that are difficult, but cases that reach harsh results, showing that head and heart are firmly separated); on abstracting from the specific circumstances of a case, from the tug of emotion, and from the personalities of the disputants.

[53] See, for example, Roberto Mangabeira Unger, *Knowledge and Politics*, chap. 2 (1975), and his *The Critical Legal Studies Movement* 64 (1986) (discussing *The Merchant of Venice*). For criticism see Charles Fried, *Contract as Promise: A Theory of Contractual Obligation* 90–91 (1981). Unger is a leading figure in the critical legal studies movement. Another and fuller examination of Shakespeare from the standpoint of critical legal studies is John Danvir, "William Shakespeare and the Jurisprudence of Comedy," 39 *Stanford Law Review* 825 (1987). See id. at 827–832 (*Merchant of Venice*), 832–835 (*Measure for Measure*).

Table of Opposed Conceptions of Law

| Held by Shylock, Angelo, Isabella—and Terry Eagleton | Held by Portia, Duke of Vienna, and Escalus |
| --- | --- |
| government of laws | government of men |
| formalism | realism |
| law | politics |
| law | equity |
| law | mercy |
| law | justice |
| rule | discretion |
| rule | standard |
| rule | principle (for example, equity maxim) |
| logic | policy |
| rigid | flexible |
| right answers | good answers |
| positive law | natural law |
| decision by precedent | arbitration |
| judge | Qadi, jury |
| strict liability | negligence (unreasonableness) |
| objective theory of contracts | subjective theory |
| objectivity | subjectivity |
| impersonality | personalism (nepotism, "clout") |
| principled (neutral principles) | result-oriented |
| rights | needs |
| statute law | common law |
| statute law | constitutional law |
| interpretivism | noninterpretivism |
| strict construction | flexible or loose construction |
| letter | spirit |
| judge finds law | judge makes law |

Some feminists believe that this congeries of attributes reflects a distinctively male style of thinking.[54] Portia's "quality of mercy" speech can be cited in support. Yet, in tension with the feminist view, notice that the Shakespearean men who embrace the "male" conception of law with the most ardor, Shylock and Angelo, are weak rather than strong figures. Shylock is a pariah; and we have seen how a legalistic conception of law

[54] See, for example, Carol Gilligan, *In a Different Voice: Psychological Theory and Women's Development* 105 (1982) (discussing *The Merchant of Venice*); Robin West, "Jurisprudence and Gender," 55 *University of Chicago Law Review* 1 (1988); K. C. Worden, "Overshooting the Target: A Feminist Deconstruction of Legal Education," 34 *American University Law Review* 1141 (1985). Gilligan's book develops a contrast between an "ethic of rights" and an "ethic of care" (see index references under "care" and "rights"), corresponding roughly to the left-hand and right-hand columns in my table. Literary pairings of a male embodiment of

can be a protection for pariahs. Angelo is presented to the reader as a natural Number 2 man. When the Duke tells him he's in charge now, Angelo protests that he isn't ready. Rather than take responsibility for his decisions, he retreats behind the law; the law becomes his master in lieu of the absent Duke. His legalism is connected with his being a natural underling, as well as with his effort to transcend the body and become all spirit. It comes as no surprise that excessive legalism has been associated with immature, weak, and father-fixated personalities.[55]

No society has ever embraced the legalistic conception in its full rigor, though many lawyers and judges have given it lip service and nineteenth-century American legal formalism made it the official legal ideology. Every society softens the rigors of strict legalism by some or all of the means listed in the right-hand column of my table. There is no inconsistency in this. It is false that law is not law unless it banishes every human, mitigating, discretionary, or "feminine" characteristic. The choice between rule and standard—even the choice of whether to make the administration of law a little more political by having an elected rather than an appointed judiciary—is a choice within law rather than a choice between law and not-law.[56] It is because the strict enforcement of rules is intolerable ("working to rule" is a familiar device by which workers disrupt their employer's operations) that law is the *art* of governance by rules, not just an automated machinery of enforcement.

---

"masculine" jurisprudence and a female embodiment of "feminine" jurisprudence include not only Shylock-Portia but also Creon-Antigone and Orestes-Clytemnestra. Orestes took revenge in order to punish a political as well as a personal wrong (regicide), while Clytemnestra had taken revenge to punish a purely personal wrong—the sacrifice of her daughter for political ends. See Simon Goldhill, *Reading Greek Tragedy* 91–96, 152–153 (1986).

[55] This is the burden of Jerome Frank's famous denunciation of legal formalism, *Law and the Modern Mind* (1930). On the child's tendency to embrace a formalistic conception of justice see Jean Piaget, *The Moral Judgment of the Child* (1948); Nancy Eisenberg Berg and Paul Mussen, "The Origins and Development of Concepts of Justice," 31 *Journal of Social Issues*, no. 3, at 183 (1975).

[56] On the choice between more and less "ruledness," see Isaac Ehrlich and Richard A. Posner, "An Economic Analysis of Legal Rulemaking," 3 *Journal of Legal Studies* 257 (1974); Colin S. Diver, "The Optimal Precision of Administrative Rules," 93 *Yale Law Journal* 65 (1983); Pierre Schlag, "Rules and Standards," 33 *UCLA Law Review* 379 (1985); Twining and Miers, note 16 above, at 184–185. Continental jurisprudence distinguishes between *Gesellschaft* (society) and *Gemeinschaft* (community) as polar conceptions of legal order; the distinction is similar to that between the two columns in my table. See, for example, Eugene Kamenka and Alice E.-S. Tay, "The Traditions of Justice," 5 *Law and Philosophy* 281, 288–292 (1986). The former is more characteristic of large and complex societies, the latter of small and simple ones. But in all except the simplest both conceptions play a role. Thus, formalism plays an important role in primitive and ancient law (see Posner, note 38 above, at 178, 185, 200–202) even though primitive and ancient societies tend to be small and simple.

An equally important point, however, is that if one goes too far in making the administration of law flexible—"unruly"—one ends up with anarchy, tyranny, or both: with some form of "people's justice." A huge problem with Athenian justice, it is illustrated by the trial of Socrates, and Aristophanes lampooned it in *Wasps* and *Clouds*.[57] There is a hint of the anarchic in the way the Duke of Vienna conducts state affairs in *Measure for Measure*. The broader point is that the inhuman formalism of an Angelo is the abuse of a good thing rather than the essence of a bad. We recall that impersonality is one of the features that distinguishes law from revenge, and that the confusion of the victim's and the law enforcer's role in a revenge system is one of the terrible weaknesses of such a system. The emotional detachment of law enforcers—more broadly, the objectivity of law—is a good idea, though like most good ideas it can be pushed too far and become absurd and even vicious. The Shakespearean characters whom I have placed in the right-hand column of the Table of Opposed Conceptions of Law do not go all the way to the opposite and equally untenable extreme of wholly discretionary, personalistic law, which is no law. Portia is concerned not to create a bad precedent, and she also knows that a measure of impersonality in the administration of the laws—and thus a willingness to provide justice to aliens—is necessary to preserve Venice's commercial position. Even the Duke of Vienna is concerned with the breakdown of law and order in his state, although he is not scrupulous about the means of restoring them.

Although the concept of law is not exhausted by the left-hand column in the table, it is noteworthy that Portia distinguishes mercy from law rather than regarding it as a part of law; for her as for Shylock, law is the domain of strict rules, strictly enforced. This is the usual way in which law is presented in literature, partly because it is the layman's view of law and partly because the harsh, legalistic, rule-dominated side of law is the side that produces surprise, abrupt reversals of fortune, and cruel destinies—and all these are the stuff of literature. Consider the legend of the Sibyl of Cumae as told by Ovid in the *Metamorphoses*. Apollo wants

---

[57] And Plato in *Gorgias* implicitly compares the trial of Socrates to the trial of a physician before a jury of children on the accusation of a cook. See Plato, *Gorgias* 100–101 (W. C. Helmbold trans. 1952). On the manifold deficiencies of Athenian popular justice, in which criminal (including capital) as well as civil cases were brought by private denouncers and tried before huge juries with no jury deliberation, no judges, and no appeal, see Robert J. Bonner and Gertrude Smith, *The Administration of Justice from Homer to Aristotle*, vol. 2 (1938); Robin Osborne, "Law in Action in Classical Athens," 105 *Journal of Hellenic Studies* 40 (1985). A sunnier view of Athenian justice is presented in Raphael Sealey, *The Athenian Republic: Democracy or Rule of Law?* (1987).

to make love to the Sibyl, and to soften her up offers her a gift—anything she wants. She asks for as many extra years of life as there are granules in a nearby pile of soil, and Apollo grants her wish. But she has forgotten to ask for eternal youth to go with eternal life. Apollo tells her that he will throw that in, too—if she will sleep with him. She refuses. Later she realizes that age will wither her until there is nothing left but a voice. A modern court (or, indeed, a Roman court of Ovid's time) would say that the gift of eternal youth was implicit in the gift of eternal life, since without it the latter gift would be worth little (might even have negative value); or that the Sibyl should be allowed to reject the gift once she has learned its full conditions; or that it was unconscionable for Apollo to try to coerce her into having sex with him by refusing to complete the gift if she did not consent. But if Apollo were not allowed to spring his trap all the drama would drain out of the story—and likewise if Oedipus could have pleaded mistake of fact as a defense in *Oedipus Tyrannus*. Literary exigencies constrain the literary depiction of law.

As a further illustration of the polar conceptions of law, consider Sophocles' *Antigone*. The play is set in Thebes, now ruled by Creon after the fall of Oedipus. Polynices, who we recall is one of Oedipus's sons, revolts and attacks the city. The other son, Eteocles, defends the city. Both are killed in the fighting. Creon orders an honorable burial for Eteocles but orders that Polynices shall remain unburied—a hideous punishment in the theology of the ancient Greeks and a recurrent motif in Greek literature (for example, the *Iliad*, *Hecuba*). Antigone defies the order and buries her brother. She is caught, and in a brief trial scene—in which she asserts the primacy of divine law and Creon the inviolability of his decrees—is condemned by Creon to death. Horrible things ensue, including the deaths of Creon's son (who is betrothed to Antigone and decides to die with her) and wife, and we are made to understand that Creon has acted with dreadful impiety and must be terribly punished.

It would be a mistake, however, to think Creon a monster who gets his just deserts, though this is a common view. There is a case to be made for him. Polynices, the traitor, and Eteocles, the hero, were both killed in the revolt; to give them both honorable burial would, by blurring the moral distinction between them, encourage future revolts. Having therefore decreed that Polynices shall remain unburied—a decree with all the presumptive legitimacy of a modern statute or court order—and having further decreed the death penalty for anyone who violates the burial decree, Creon is confronted by a blunt challenge to his authority, and the authority of law, in Antigone's actions. It does not help any that Antigone is a woman, that she is the daughter of the former ruler and the sister of the rebel, and that she states her position with uncompromising self-righteousness rather than asking for mercy— she gives Creon no way to avoid condemning her without a severe loss of face. (Notice the parallel to the confrontation between Achilles and Agamemnon in Book I of the *Iliad*.) It is a "no win" situation for him, and he is punished terribly; the play is his tragedy as well as Antigone's.[58]

The natural law that Antigone sets up in opposition to Creon's positive law is not only, and perhaps not primarily, a decree from on high commanding proper burial even for traitors. The natural law most emphasized in the play is the tie of blood between sister and brother. Like Clytemnestra and the Furies in *Eumenides*, Antigone places blood relationships above the political relationship (loyalty to Thebes, to the *polis*) that Creon's decrees are intended to cement. The conflict is not just higher law versus human law but nature with its elemental bonds versus society with its more abstract bonds, emotion versus rationality, and (to Sophocles as to Carol Gilligan) female versus male.[59]

The harshness of Antigone's challenge to Creon—the irreconcilability of their competing visions of justice—may reflect, as Winnington-Ingram argues, the persistence of the revenge ethic in the rudimentary city-state political culture depicted in the play. We saw in the last chapter how that ethic encourages the formation of tightly knit family units and discourages loyalty to impersonal social groups. Modern people balance loyalty to family and to state; Antigone is incapable of that.

Let us turn from works written by men that present a feminine conception of justice to a work of that character written by a woman. In Susan Glaspell's short story *A Jury of Her Peers* (1917), a farmer is found dead in his bedroom, strangled by a rope. There is no indication of forced entry or of suicide, so the widow is strongly suspected, and she is arrested and taken off to jail. Peters, the sheriff, returns to the scene of the crime to investigate further. He is accompanied by the county

[58] For good general discussions of the play see Charles Segal, *Tragedy and Civilization: An Interpretation of Sophocles*, chap. 6 (1981); R. P. Winnington-Ingram, *Sophocles: An Interpretation* (1980), especially chap. 6. And for good discussions of the legal-political dimension see Bernard M. W. Knox, *The Heroic Temper: Studies in Sophoclean Tragedy* 75–90 (1964); Martha C. Nussbaum, *The Fragility of Goodness: Luck and Ethics in Greek Tragedy and Philosophy*, chap. 3 (1986); Lloyd L. Weinreb, *Natural Law and Justice* 21–24 (1987).

[59] Cf. Segal, note 58 above, at 184, 186. Knox, note 58 above, at 77–78, usefully compares Antigone with the Furies, and emphasizes that the "natural law" she expounds is a religious obligation to obtain a proper burial of her brother rather than any general, impersonal, or, in a word, modern concept of justice.

attorney and by Hale, the man who had discovered the body. Peters and Hale bring their wives, who remain downstairs while the men investigate in the bedroom. Poking about in the kitchen (the quintessential "woman's room," which the men had not thought to search carefully), the women discover irrefutable proof of the wife's guilt: the body of her pet bird, its neck broken. Mrs. Hale understands in a flash that the bird had been the only bright spot in the bleak life of this lonely, childless farm woman; that the husband—a cold, hard man—had killed the bird; and that his deed had driven her to kill him. Mrs. Hale decides that the men must not be told about her find. The sheriff's wife has qualms about withholding evidence, but goes along.

The men are smug and patronizing; it would never occur to them that the women might have discovered something that they had overlooked. That is the irony in the story. There may also be a point about law. Obviously the breaking of the bird's neck is not the sort of provocation that excuses a murder in the eyes of the law. But those are not the eyes the women train on the matter. More sensitive (we are made to understand) than men would be to the full particulars—the total context—of the crime, less committed to the "legalistic" view that guilt should be determined in accordance with rules that necessarily abstract from those particulars (which may be considered only at the sentencing stage of the criminal proceeding), the women are prepared to become accessories after the fact to the murder by withholding what they know is vital evidence. Whether the implied difference between male and female conceptions of justice is real (it could just be an artifact of the women's sympathy for the farmer's wife), and if so whether it is rooted in inherent differences between men and women or is purely cultural and likely to change as the social role of women changes, are profound and unanswered questions in feminist jurisprudence.

A final point to note on the theme of rule versus discretion in law is the parallel tension in literature. A writer is subject to all sorts of rules—of grammar, of pronunciation (which determines rhyme), of meter, of genre (for example, a sonnet must have fourteen lines—though some sonnets have more). But he has some freedom to break them, just as a judge has some freedom to depart from precedent. "How much" is the unanswerable question in both cases. The reader may have noticed a literary "violation" of the laws of grammar in the Introduction, where I quoted the first lines of Eliot's *Prufrock*: "Let us go then, you and I, / When the evening is spread out against the sky . . ." The grammatically correct form would be "you and me," but it would spoil the rhyme.

I WANT to tie up a loose end concerning the law in *Measure for Measure*. By speaking of Julietta and Mariana as "fiancées" of Claudio and Angelo, I bypassed the most discussed legal question in the play—the status of the two marriage contracts.[60] Claudio calls Julietta his "wife" in Act I, and under the law in force in Elizabethan England a marriage contract probably created a valid, though irregular and perhaps sinful, marriage even if it was not solemnized, although the legal picture is very obscure. Yet no one in the play doubts that Claudio is guilty of fornication, including Claudio. On the other hand, the Duke tells Isabella that it would be fitting, in light of the marriage contract with Mariana that Angelo had broken, to substitute Mariana for Isabella in the sexual encounter with Angelo. This might seem to imply that the law of Vienna is the same in this respect as English law—but if so, why does the Duke and everyone else in the play insist that Claudio is guilty of fornication? In her excellent study of the marriage-contract issue, Scott (see note 46) points out that the Council of Trent had outlawed informal marriage in 1563, and she notes that the play represents Vienna as an emphatically Roman Catholic state, in this respect wholly unlike England. So what exactly is going on?

Scott's eminently sensible suggestion is that the legal world of the play is not to be identified with any real-life legal regime, whether English or Continental. Since fornication is a capital crime in the world of the play but apparently nowhere else, there should be no difficulty in accepting that informal or clandestine marriages are illegal in the play regardless of the legal position outside. We are dealing after all with a comedy, even if a "dark" one, rather than a documentary. The required suspension of disbelief is less here than in imagining that Shylock's bond would have been enforceable if only it had been drafted more carefully, for example to provide for death by strangulation so that no blood would have to be shed. Yet that is the "law" of *The Merchant of Venice*. Shakespeare is not concerned with depicting law realistically in either its substantive or its procedural aspects. Angelo points out that a jury verdict is not invalid just because one of the jurors is a thief; but there are no juries in the legal world depicted in *Measure for Measure*, where Angelo is attorney general, judge, jury, and court of appeals all in one.

Scott's point does not solve the problem of the Duke's treating the two contracts inconsistently. But that problem is superficial. The Duke

---

[60] See Scott, note 46 above, for an up-to-date discussion with many references to the previous literature; also Braithwaite, note 46 above, at 800 n. 12; Schanzer, note 46 above, at 75–79. A parallel problem in Chaucer is discussed in Karl P. Wentersdorf, "Some Observations on the Concept of Clandestine Marriage in *Troilus and Criseyde*," 15 *Chaucer Review* 101 (1981).

does not deny that Angelo and Mariana will be committing fornication; the idea rather is that turnabout is fair play. The Duke must know that he is going to pardon both couples, and the fact that fornication is a deadly sin never seems to worry him. What might be thought a more serious inconsistency is Isabella's failing to raise any objection to the Duke's scheme. She does not say, "Hold on—Mariana's immortal soul will be jeopardized, just as mine would have been." Instead her reaction is, what a nifty idea ("the image of it gives me content already," III.1.257). Of course the fact that the idea comes from a friar, as she thinks the Duke is, may alleviate any theological concerns that might occur to her. But we may also be meant to treat her reaction as further evidence that she is priggish rather than principled, or as evidence that she is beginning to share the Duke's pragmatic outlook. Perhaps the best explanation is that Isabella would be likely to think that Mariana's marriage contract, although illegal under the law of Vienna (as presented in the play), will mitigate Mariana's deed in heaven's eye; this ties in with the apparent clerical sponsorship of the deed. Isabella could raise no such "defense" if she yielded her body to Angelo. So Mariana can save Claudio with less jeopardy to her soul than Isabella's to her own. The law, whether of Shakespeare's England or Catholic Austria, has little to do with any of this; the play's jurisprudential interest is not trivial, but it lies elsewhere.

## Kafka and Dickens

No author of imaginative literature has seemed to have more to say about law than Kafka, himself a lawyer, whose great novel *The Trial* opens with the arrest of the protagonist, Joseph K., and ends with K.'s execution one year later, and whose short stories and fragments frequently have law for their theme. In Chapter 4 I shall both evaluate Robin West's claim that Kafka's fiction is a criticism of the economic model of human behavior that lies at the heart of the influential school of legal studies known as law and economics, and discuss three of Kafka's legal parables. Here I discuss *The Trial* and *In the Penal Colony*, a short story that Kafka interrupted work on *The Trial* to write in 1914.

In the story an explorer (as the German word *Reisende* is usually rendered in translations of the story, although it just means traveler) has been invited to the penal colony of a colonial European power to witness an execution that is to be conducted in the manner traditional in the colony, and to report his impressions to the newly appointed commandant of the colony. A soldier on guard duty had fallen asleep and an officer had struck him with his riding whip to wake him up; as he awoke, the soldier had grabbed the officer by the legs and threatened to devour him. For this misconduct the soldier has been sentenced to death. The officer in charge of the execution, who is the unnamed protagonist of Kafka's story (there are no proper names in the story), explains to the explorer in loving detail the manner of execution, which had been devised by the former commandant of revered memory (revered by the officer, in any event). It works as follows. The condemned is stripped naked and placed on a table-like surface in a kind of giant sewing machine. The moving part of the machine, suggestively nicknamed "harrow," inscribes the judgment (which in the case of this condemned is "Honor your superiors"), with many curlicues and flourishes, by means of moving needles that jab deeper and deeper while the bed of the machine rotates the body and sops up the blood with cotton. The turning point in the execution comes in the sixth hour, when (as the officer explains to the explorer) the condemned, who has not been told what the judgment is, comes to understand it in his body through the repeated jabbing of the needles. In the twelfth hour, having had six hours to reflect on the judgment, the condemned dies and the machine tosses him into a pit dug next to it.

The explorer expresses surprise that the condemned is not told the judgment or given any opportunity to defend himself against the charge. But the officer explains that since he (the officer) is prosecutor, judge, and executioner all in one, the problem of error that plagues complex justice systems is avoided; to give the accused a chance to speak in his own defense would merely precipitate a stream of lies. The officer pours his heart out to the explorer, for he knows that the new commandant, disliking the traditional mode of execution, hopes the explorer will make a negative report on it. The officer is particularly distressed by the decline of public interest in executions—the whole population of the colony, including children, used to attend them, all solemnly awaiting the climactic moment when the condemned would comprehend the judgment—and by the diminution in appropriations for them.

In the most disgusting incident in the story, the condemned man, after being laid on the machine, vomits, because standing orders not to feed the condemned too near to the time for execution have been disobeyed and because lack of funds has forced the officer to use the same gag over and over again. This incident, which results in soiling the machine, in combination with the explorer's refusal to join in a zany scheme by which the officer hopes to recapture public support for the traditional mode of execution, is the last straw for the officer. He sets the condemned man free, changes the judgment in the machine to read "Be just," undresses, climbs on the machine, and takes the filthy gag in his mouth. Although he does not press the start lever, the machine begins to operate—at first smoothly, but after a while it goes crazy. Instead of just tattooing the judgment on the officer's body, it stabs him through the forehead with a single spike, killing him instantly and denying him his moment of illumination, and the back of the machine opens up and spills out hundreds of gears. After stopping briefly at the cafe where the old commandant is buried under a table in the patio, the explorer takes the first ship departing from the colony; for with the death of the officer and the disintegration of the machine, there is no need to make his report to the commandant.

A summary cannot adequately convey the extreme strangeness of the story. Many people think of Kafka as an oracular figure, like George Orwell, and regard *In the Penal Colony* as a prophecy of the Nazi concentration camps or an allegory of World War I, and *The Trial* as a prophecy of the state terrorism practiced by Hitler and Stalin.[61] A lawyer might be tempted to read *In the Penal Colony* as a commentary on due process and cruel and unusual punishment. My view is that Kafka is not a political commentator (though he had some political interests—in Zionism for example), and that the legal and political details in his fiction are metaphoric. The style of justice embodied in the old commandant, his acolyte, and the torture machine is even less realistic than the trial in *The Merchant of Venice*. More important, no point is being made about law, equity, or even justice. Rather, the point of the story (if it is ever possible to speak of the point of a Kafka story) seems to lie in the juxtaposition of the absurdity of the whole procedure with the utter seriousness with which the officer expounds

[61] Illustrative is J. P. Stern's remark that "*The Trial* is a prophetic—or rather an anticipatory—fictional account of both the concepts underlying national socialist legislation and the practice of its law courts." "The Law of *The Trial*," in *On Kafka: Semi-Centenary Perspectives* 22, 30 (Franz Kuna ed. 1976). See also George Steiner, "K," in *Language and Silence: Essays on Language, Literature, and the Inhuman* 118, 121 (1974). For sensible comments on the "prophetic" qualities of *The Trial* see Ritchie Robertson, *Kafka: Judaism, Politics, and Literature* 96–98 (1985). There is, of course, a literature genuinely about totalitarian law; an example is Koestler's *Darkness at Noon*. And see Richard Weisberg, "Solzhenitsyn's View of Soviet Law in *The First Circle*," 41 *University of Chicago Law Review* 417 (1974).

its virtues. The officer's problem—a recurrent theme in Kafka's work—is his inability to get anybody to pay the slightest attention to what he believes to be the most important thing in the world. Hence his fascination with the machine, which "communicates" legal judgments more effectively than words can. The condemned man is depicted as an imbecile (or worse—remember the nature of his threat) who could not possibly understand what was going on. For him there would have been no ray of insight at the sixth or any other hour; he does not understand the language spoken by the officer and would not understand the machine's "body language" either. The soldier who guards the condemned is also a clod. The only other observer is the explorer, who affects a glacial detachment modulating into polite distaste but eventually makes clear his utter lack of sympathy with the officer's obsession. With the spatial clarity that is so striking a feature of Kafka's work, we are made to feel the officer's total isolation in the grim desert setting—the pathos of the obsession that has cut him off from all human contact. We come to feel sorry for this monster, sensing in him the pathological extreme of what is after all the ordinary human inability to get others to share our plans and passions. Despite the overt theme of justice perverted, the heart of the story is further from law than the Elizabethan plays that I discussed earlier.

I thus am not persuaded by a recent effort to present *In the Penal Colony* as an allegory of law, with the torture machine symbolizing the "machinery of justice" and its destruction the impossibility of a "mechanical" jurisprudence, a jurisprudence from which all discretion has been banished—in other words, the very jurisprudence that Terry Eagleton might think entailed by the concept of law.[62] This interpretation cannot account for the major elements of the story—in particular that the machine does not formulate rules, find facts, render judgments, or do anything else that a justice system does except announce and administer the sentence. Nor can the interpretation explain the personality or pathos of the sadomasochistic protagonist.

---

[62] See Lida Kirchberger, *Franz Kafka's Use of Law in Fiction: A New Interpretation of In der Strafkolonie, Der Prozess, and Das Schloss*, chap. 2 (1986). Although I do not find Kirchberger's interpretation of *In the Penal Colony* persuasive, I am not so reckless as to suggest that mine is the only possible interpretation; the quest for definitive interpretations of Kafka is surely chimerical. For examples of interesting approaches quite different from mine but, like mine, finding the heart of the story elsewhere than in law or punishment, see Clayton Koelb, " 'In der Strafkolonie': Kafka and the Scene of Reading," 55 *German Quarterly* 511 (1982); Roy Pascal, *Kafka's Narrators: A Study of His Stories and Sketches*, chap. 3 (1982); Arnold Weinstein, "Kafka's Writing Machine: Metamorphosis in the Penal Colony," 7 *Studies in Twentieth-Century Literature* 21 (1982–1983).

THE TRIAL is a remarkable work, and full of legal detail from start to finish,[63] yet again its heart seems to lie elsewhere than with law. Joseph K., a successful bank executive and also a fussy and self-important bachelor, is arrested on the morning of his thirtieth birthday, at the boarding house where he lives, by two plainclothesmen and an inspector. They produce no identification and give no hint of what agency they work for or what the charge against K. is; and since he has committed no offense and is a respectable member of the middle class, naturally he is indignant. "Who could these men be? What were they talking about? What authority could they represent? K. lived in a country with a legal constitution, there was universal peace, all the laws were in force; who dared seize him in his own dwelling?" (p.7). He asks the inspector, " 'Who accuses me? What authority is conducting these proceedings? Are you officers of the law? None of you has a uniform, unless your suit'—here he turned to Franz [one of the arresting officers]—'is to be considered a uniform, but it's more like a tourist's outfit' " (p.16). But they say nothing to the point.

From my description thus far the novel might seem to be about the denial of due process of law. But the comment about the tourist's outfit is a clue that something is off-key. From the beginning K. had been fascinated by Franz's outfit. He had noticed that Franz "wore a closely fitting black suit, which was furnished with all sorts of pleats, pockets, buckles, and buttons, as well as a belt, like a tourist's outfit, and in consequence looked eminently practical, though one could not quite tell what actual purpose it served" (p.4). One begins to get the impression that K. is preoccupied, rightly or wrongly, with aspects of his predic-

---

[63] Kafka was a lawyer, and *The Trial* faithfully reproduces many details of Austro-Hungarian criminal procedure. See Martha S. Robinson, "The Law of the State in Kafka's *The Trial*," 6 *ALSA Forum* 127 (1982). For examples of literary criticism of *The Trial* see Wilhelm Emrich, *Franz Kafka: A Critical Study of His Writings*, chap. 6 (1968); Ronald Gray, *Franz Kafka*, chap. 7 (1973); Simon O. Lesser, "The Source of Guilt and the Sense of Guilt—Kafka's *The Trial*," 8 *Modern Fiction Studies* 44 (1962); Joan Mellen, "Joseph K. and the Law," 12 *Texas Studies in Literature and Language* 295 (1970); Robertson, note 61 above, chap. 3; Solomon J. Spiro, "Verdict—Guilty! A Study of *The Trial*," 17 *Twentieth Century Literature* 169 (1971); *Twentieth Century Interpretations of The Trial: A Collection of Critical Essays* (James Rolleston ed. 1976). My quotations will be from Franz Kafka, *The Trial* (Willa and Edwin Muir trans., definitive ed. 1960). Good as the Muirs' translation is, it does in places alter Kafka's meaning, sometimes, as we shall see, significantly. See Ronald Gray, "But Kafka Wrote in German," in *The Kafka Debate: New Perspectives for Our Time* 242 (Angel Flores ed. 1977); Irmgard Hobson, "The Kafka Problem Compounded: *Trial* and *Judgment* in English," 23 *Modern Fiction Studies* 511 (1977–1978). A more recent English translation of *The Trial*—not as vivid as the Muirs', not in print in the United States, but more faithful to the original—is Franz Kafka, *The Trial* (Douglas Scott and Chris Waller trans. 1977).

ament that are unrelated to due process. Meanwhile the arresting officers have taken K.'s underwear, allegedly for safekeeping, and are busy wolfing down his breakfast, while through the open window of his room people living across the alleyway are staring at the goings-on in the room "with truly senile inquisitiveness" (p. 5). K. asks the inspector whether he can call his friend the public prosecutor (*Staatsanwalt*— mistranslated by the Muirs as "lawyer"), and the inspector says, certainly, but it's pointless. K. becomes furious, and petulantly announces that he will not call the prosecutor after all, as if by this refusal he is scoring a point against the inspector.

The atmosphere of the book is dream-like, but until the last chapter not nightmarish. Having arrested K., the mysterious trio informs him that he is free to go about his business—the court will get in touch with him in due course—and they depart. K. is not "booked" and does not have to post bond. There is next a mysterious interlude in which K. makes advances to Fräulein Bürstner, who thereafter disappears from the book; later we are made to understand that K. is mistakenly seeking the aid of women in dealing with the court.

Next (the book was left in an unfinished state when Kafka died, and is choppy and episodic—more like a series of short stories than a novel) K. is summoned for his first interrogation by the examining magistrate of the court (never named) that directed his arrest. The court turns out to occupy a rabbit warren of musty rooms in a tenement building. When K. finally penetrates to the courtroom—there are no signs or other trappings of an offical enterprise—the scene is like a cross between the Court of Chancery in *Bleak House* and a circle of hell in the *Divine Comedy*. We come to understand that no one obtains justice from this court; one just attends until broken by old age. Needless to say, there is no interrogation. When K. returns the next week (unbidden, but he is trying to expedite his case—at least find out what the charge is), the place is deserted. He rummages through the books on the judges' bench, but they are not law books—they are dirty novels. He has a brief flirtation with a woman washing clothes and a run-in with a law student. (I discuss that scene in Chapter 4.) Next comes a scene reeking of sadomasochism: K. opens a storage room at the bank where he works—and finds the two officers who had arrested him being whipped for having stolen his underwear.

K.'s uncle, who has heard about the mysterious judicial proceeding against his nephew, appears at the bank and advises K. to consult an eminent lawyer, Huld (German for "grace"), which K. does. Huld turns out to be the Austro-Hungarian counterpart of a "Washington lawyer."

He lets it be known that he has inside knowledge about the workings of the mysterious court, knows the judges, has heard about K.'s case, has clout, finesse—just leave everything to him. "The most important thing was counsel's personal connection with officials of the Court; in that lay the chief value of the Defense" (p. 146). Of course nothing happens. K. becomes distracted by Huld's maid, Leni, and has a flirtation with her similar to the one with Fräulein Bürstner earlier.

K. is becoming mesmerized by the case. Not that anyone from the court is bothering him; after that first, abortive summons to an interrogation the court has made no effort to get in touch with him. But K. is distracted at work and fears that his principal rival at the bank, the deputy director, is gaining on him, though there is no suggestion that the arrest and ensuing proceeding have stigmatized K. A client of K.'s puts him in touch with a painter, Titorelli, who it turns out is the court's official portraitist. After escaping a clutch of faintly sinister teenage girls, K. finds Titorelli's tenement apartment. Naturally it is in the court's building; all roads lead (Joseph K.) to the court. Titorelli explains that, assuming K. is innocent, there are three possibilities: real acquittal (which is out of the question), ostensible acquittal (where the accused is liable to rearrest and reprosecution at any time—a concept that is one of Kafka's uncanny foreshadowings of totalitarian practices), and indefinite postponement. The impression conveyed is that K. will never get free from the clutches of the court. It is as if Titorelli had told him that he had a chronic, incurable disease which if carefully managed might not shorten his life.

Feeling that he is making no progress with his case, K. decides to fire Huld, who all this time has been working laboriously (or so he says—doubtless lying) on a draft of K.'s first plea. The question of how the plea can be made when neither K. nor Huld has the faintest idea of what the charge is does not faze Huld in the least, and is one of the many jokes in this unexpectedly funny book. It happens that Huld has another client, Block, whose case is now five years old and who is utterly devoured by it, more even than K. (but K.'s case is still less than a year old). Block has actually moved into Huld's house, and Leni has taken to locking him into her room during the day to keep him out of her hair. In an effort to dissuade K. from firing him, Huld gives one of the finest fictional renditions extant of the lawyer's trick of intimidating a client by making the law seem wholly beyond lay comprehension. With K. looking on, Huld (in bed, where he spends most of the time—he is old, and pretends to be sick) reports a conversation he had had recently with a judge of the court about Block. Huld says, quoting the judge,

> " 'Block is merely cunning . . . But his ignorance is even greater than his
> cunning. What do you think he would say if he discovered that his case had
> actually not begun yet, if he were to be told that the bell marking the start
> of the proceedings hadn't even been rung?' "—"Quiet there, Block," said
> the lawyer, for Block was just rising up on trembling legs, obviously to
> implore an explanation. (p. 244)

One can imagine how poor Block feels—he has blown all his money on
the case only to discover that the case has not even begun. The time is
ripe for Huld to assert his mastery:

> "That remark of the Judge's has no possible significance for you . . . Don't
> get into a panic at every word. If you do it again I'll never tell you anything
> . . . All that I said was to report a remark by a Judge. You know quite well
> that in these matters opinions differ so much that the confusion is
> impenetrable. This judge, for instance, assumes that the proceedings begin
> at one point, and I assume that they begin at another point. A difference of
> opinion, nothing more. At a certain stage of the proceedings there is an old
> tradition that a bell must be rung. According to the Judge, that marks the
> beginning of the case, I can't tell you now all the arguments against him,
> you wouldn't understand them, let it be sufficient for you that there are
> many arguments against his view." In embarrassment Block sat plucking
> at the hair of the skin rug lying before the bed . . . "Block," said Leni in
> a tone of warning, catching him by the collar and jerking him upward a
> little. "Leave the rug alone and listen to the lawyer." (pp. 245–246)

Another marvelous chapter follows. K. is supposed to show an Italian
client of the bank the sights of the city, and they are to meet at the
cathedral. K. goes there, but the client does not show up. It is dark, still,
almost empty in the cathedral. A priest mounts the pulpit. K. does not
want to hear a sermon, and begins sidling out. All at once "he heard the
priest lifting up his voice. A resonant, well-trained voice. How it rolled
through the expectant Cathedral! But it was no congregation the priest
was addressing, the words were unambiguous and inescapable, he was
calling out: 'Joseph K.!' " (p. 262). The priest turns out to be another
functionary of the court—the prison chaplain. He tells K. a parable
(separately published by Kafka as *Before the Law*). Before the law stands
a doorkeeper. A man from the country comes and asks to be admitted.
The doorkeeper says it is impossible. The man sits down on a stool
provided by the doorkeeper, to wait. He waits for years, continually
imploring the doorkeeper for admittance. Finally he is an old man,
dying, and he says to the doorkeeper,

> "Everyone strives to attain the Law . . . How does it come about, then,
> that in all these years no one has come seeking admittance but me?" The

doorkeeper perceives that the man is nearing his end and his hearing is failing, so he bellows in his ear: "No one but you could gain admittance through this door, since this door was intended for you. I am now going to shut it." (p. 269)

The chaplain and K. engage in an inconclusive debate over the meaning of the parable. As K. is about to leave, he asks the chaplain, "Don't you want anything more from me?" The chaplain answers, "I belong to the Court . . . So why should I want anything from you? The Court wants nothing from you. It receives you when you come and it dismisses you when you go" (p. 278).

Nevertheless, in the next and last chapter, K. is executed. (Apparently Kafka intended to write additional chapters between it and the cathedral chapter.) Like the prisoner in *In the Penal Colony*, he is not told the sentence. On the evening before K.'s thirty-first birthday, "two men came to his lodging . . . in frock coats, pallid and plump, with top hats that were apparently irremovable" (p. 279). They escort him on foot to the country, and when they get to an isolated spot they place him against a boulder, and take out a knife. He understands (without anything being said) that he is expected to plunge the knife into his own chest, but

he could not completely rise to the occasion, he could not relieve the officials of all their tasks; the responsibility for this last failure of his lay with him who had not left him the remnant of strength necessary for the deed. His glance fell on the top story of the house adjoining the quarry. With a flicker as of a light going up, the casements of a window there suddenly flew open; a human figure, faint and insubstantial at that distance and that height, leaned abruptly far forward and stretched both arms still farther. Who was it? A friend? A good man? Someone who sympathized? Someone who wanted to help? Was it one person only? Or was it mankind? Was help at hand? Were there arguments in his favor that had been overlooked? Of course there must be. Logic is doubtless unshakable, but it cannot withstand a man who wants to go on living. Where was the Judge whom he had never seen? Where was the High Court, to which he had never penetrated? He raised his hands and spread out all his fingers.

But the hands of one of the partners were already at K.'s throat, while the other thrust the knife deep into his heart and turned it there twice. With failing eyes K. could still see the two of them immediately before him, cheek leaning against cheek, watching the final act. "Like a dog!" he said; it was as if the shame of it must outlive him. (pp. 285–286)

And so this remarkable book ends. To believe it a book centrally or essentially about due process of law is possible only for someone who brings to it unshakable preconceptions. Granted, the "trial" itself—

*Prozess*, better translated as "case" or "proceeding" because what is depicted in parodic form is the stretched-out, nonadversarial Continental criminal proceeding, which progresses through a series of interrogations—is full of authentic details of Austro-Hungarian criminal procedure (most of the novel was written just before World War I). But the point is not to show how awful it is to be arrested and charged with an unspecified offense by a secret court whose proceedings drag on interminably (except for those defendants such as K. who are unfortunate enough to be executed early on). The legal proceeding that provides the novel's framework is a huge, typically Kafkaesque "sick joke" on the protagonist, akin to the transformation of Gregor Samsa into a giant bug in the opening sentence of *The Metamorphosis*. Imagine waking up one morning and finding that you have been turned into a giant bug; imagine waking up one morning to be arrested on unspecified charges and it is impossible to find out what the charges are—and anyway you have done nothing that violates any law.[64] In each case something incomprehensible happens to the protagonist, and we watch him struggle absurdly and pathetically and finally go down to ignominious defeat. At the same time we are made to feel (as with the torturer in *In the Penal Colony*) that the protagonist's grotesque dilemma is somehow emblematic of the human condition.

I said in the last chapter that strict liability can be a symbol of life's unfairness; but this metaphoric use of "law" is not employed in *The Trial*. Strict liability means being made legally responsible for the consequences of conduct that may not be blameworthy—indeed may be completely unavoidable. Joseph K. is not punished for anything he does, whether blameworthy or not. He has *done* nothing. That is the joke on him. He inhabits a world in which not only desert and consequence but action and consequence have been severed.

*The Trial* is not without legal interest. By focusing more than most readers do on the chapters in which Huld appears, one can experience the novel as a layman's nightmare of being a party to a lawsuit yet unable to figure out what is going on because of the legal mumbo-jumbo. One can even think of the novel as the elaboration in literature of a theme announced by Judge Learned Hand: "After some

---

[64] The mirror image in Kafka's writings of the defendant who does not know the charges against him (Joseph K. in *The Trial*) is the eponymous hero of *The Stoker* (the first chapter of Kafka's novel *Amerika*, but also published separately). The stoker has a grievance against his superior that he is unable to articulate in the hilarious "trial" scene that forms the centerpiece of the story. (Compare the failure of communication of the officer in *In the Penal Colony*.) The mob of witnesses whom his antagonist summons to confute the stoker's mindless babble is wonderfully comic overkill. Inability to explain himself is one of Joseph K.'s problems, too.

dozen years of experience I must say that as a litigant I should dread a lawsuit beyond almost anything else short of sickness and death."[65] For Joseph K. it *is* sickness and death. Or one can notice that the "law" under which Joseph K. is tried is discretionary justice gone crazy. More fancifully, one may feel that both Joseph K. and the man from the country are seeking eternal principles of law—are seeking natural law (symbolized, perhaps, by the glow from behind the door in *Before the Law*). But this theme appears with greater clarity in some of Kafka's shorter works, as we shall see in Chapter 4.

The heart of *The Trial* lies, I believe, elsewhere, in K.'s futile efforts to find a human meaning in a universe (symbolized by the court) that, not having been created to be accommodating or intelligible to man, is arbitrary, impersonal, cruel, deceiving, and elusive—like the doorkeeper in *Before the Law*, who not only thwarts the effort of the man from the country to reach the source of the "radiance that streams inextinguishably from the door of the Law" (p. 269) but makes the man's effort ridiculous and pathetic. K. inhabits a post-Nietzschean ("God is dead") universe whose reigning deities have descended from the starry heavens to tenement attics. The situation in this universe is one of unintelligibility, dislocatedness, alienation, total human isolation. All of K.'s moves are wrong, but we sense there is nothing he could have done that would have changed the outcome. Not only is K. unable to understand the logic of the events and circumstances that disrupt his normal life and lead to his humiliating death, but, like the officer in *In the Penal Colony*, he is unable to explain himself. He cannot get anybody to listen to his "defense"—his *apologia pro vita sua*.

The novel also invites psychiatric interpretation; it is so like a long anxiety dream, full of guilt, obsession, sexual dysfunction, sadism, and masochism. It is to neurosis what *Macbeth* is to ambition. The legal proceeding might almost be a figment of K.'s imagination; for, like the man from the country in the parable, he can walk away from the whole business whenever he wants to; the chaplain as much as tells him so, after recounting the parable. Only obsession prevents K. from opting out of the case. But maybe it would be more accurate to say that *The Trial* stubbornly resists interpretation—and indeed owes some of its prestige and fascination to the resistance that it (like *Hamlet*) puts up to interpretive efforts.

To treat *The Trial* as a prophetic critique of totalitarian "justice" also seems wide of the mark, though there are parallels between the legal

---

[65] "The Deficiencies of Trials to Reach the Heart of the Matter," 3 *Lectures on Legal Topics 1921–1922* 89, 105 (Association of the Bar of the City of New York, 1926).

process depicted in *The Trial* and the legal process used by Hitler's Germany, Stalin's U.S.S.R., and other totalitarian regimes in dealing with political crimes. I mentioned the absence of definitive acquittal—how no accused is given a clean bill of health, but if released is subject to rearrest and reprosecution at any time, and thus to double jeopardy. The stricture against placing a person in double jeopardy is central to the rule of law—the idea, which is wholly opposed to the premises of totalitarianism, that the state is bound by law as well as private citizens.[66] By placing the accused beyond the power of the state to reprosecute, definitive acquittal would undermine the totalitarian state's pretensions to infallibility and omnipotence. Then there is the secrecy of the court in *The Trial*, its labyrinthine bureaucracy, its existence distinct from but parallel to the public organs of the state, its punishing of nonexistent offenses—all premonitions of totalitarian "justice" as well as echoes of the medieval church militant and therefore aspects of the novel's theological symbolism.

But the essential features of a totalitarian system are missing. This can be seen by comparing *The Trial* with a novel truly about totalitarian justice, Arthur Koestler's *Darkness at Noon*. The novel deals with the Soviet purge trials of the 1930s. The protagonist, Rubashov, is an "old Bolshevik" who, though he is not in fact plotting against Stalin ("No. 1" in the novel), arouses Stalin's paranoid fears. Rubashov is arrested in the middle of the night, hauled off to Lubyanka prison, and interrogated with the aid of a variety of subtle psychological pressures (there is no physical torture) until he signs a confession to having plotted the death of No. 1. He comes to realize that this confession is his last act for the Bolshevik cause, and at his show trial he repeats it with complete sincerity (though knowing it is false), after which he is hauled away and executed by a shot behind the ear in the cellars of Lubyanka.

The novel is altogether chilling, and though in fact many of the confessions used in the purge trials were extracted by less fancy means—for example, by threats to kill the defendants' families—it conveys an authentic if incomplete impression of totalitarian justice, Soviet style.[67]

---

[66] It is thus no surprise that Athens had a rule against double jeopardy and Sparta did not. See Douglas M. MacDowell, *Spartan Law* 143–144 (1986).

[67] See Robert Conquest, *The Great Terror: Stalin's Purge of the Thirties* 189–191 (rev. ed. 1973). Rubashov apparently is a composite of Bukharin, Trotsky, and Radek. See id. at 190n. On other methods used by the Soviets to extract confessions see id., chap. 5; Nathan Leites and Elsa Bernaut, *Ritual of Liquidation: The Case of the Moscow Trials* (1954); F. Beck and W. Godin, *Russian Purge and the Extraction of Confession*, chap. 4 (1951). Leites and Bernaut stress the undertone of resistance and the covert messages of defiance in the confessions at the Moscow trials; apparently the brainwashing of the defendants was less complete than Koestler's novel implies.

The novel might even interest people professionally concerned with interrogation (as might Porfiry's interrogations of Raskolnikov in *Crime and Punishment*). But it bears no resemblance to *The Trial*, whose protagonist is also executed for nonexistent criminal activity, if for anything. A superior piece of political and legal journalism, *Darkness at Noon* belongs to the genre of 1930s and 1940s documentary novels that includes works by Malraux, Orwell, and other fine writers. *The Trial*, despite its authentic legal details and its apparent theme of denial of due process, does not have the "feel" of a documentary novel. It is closer in spirit to such works as *Pudd'nhead Wilson*, where law is brought into fiction for distinctly ulterior ends, than to works of "serious" social and political commentary such as *Darkness at Noon*. So the law-trained reader runs the risk of missing the point.

More than "feel" is involved; the essential difference between *The Trial* and a "real" exposé of totalitarian police methods is the lack of any political point to *The Trial*. Far from being a subversive, Joseph K. is completely apolitical. And the court has no political mission, is not concerned (so far as one can tell) with political crimes, and is not part of some official system of intimidation. The proceeding against K. is not intended to and does not cow any of the other characters in the novel. The court is no more part of an apparatus of political repression than is the English Court of Chancery as depicted in *Bleak House*—from which, indeed, Kafka apparently borrowed in depicting the court in *The Trial* (see note 70).

For related reasons, I am not convinced by the efforts of some critics to link *The Trial* with *Michael Kohlhaas*.[68] It is true that Kafka was greatly interested in Kleist's writings and may have borrowed details from them. Joseph K.'s interview with the prison chaplain may echo Kohlhaas's interview with Martin Luther, while the "shadowy establishment network"[69] against which Kohlhaas struggles in his vain quest for justice resembles the "attic court" with which Joseph K. struggles. Everywhere Kohlhaas turns he finds connections with the nobleman who wronged him; everywhere K. turns he finds connections with the court (as in his encounters with Titorelli and the prison chaplain). The character of the two works, however, is different. Kohlhaas is a

[68] See J. M. Lindsay, "Kohlhaas and K.: Two Men in Search of Justice," 13 *German Life and Letters* 190 (1959); Eric Marson, "Justice and the Obsessed Character in Michael Kohlhaas, Der Prozess and L'Etranger," 2 *Seminar (A Journal of Germanic Studies)* 21 (fall 1966); F. G. Peters, "Kafka and Kleist: A Literary Relationship," 1 *Oxford German Studies* 114 (1966).

[69] John M. Ellis, *Heinrich von Kleist: Studies in the Character and Meaning of His Writings* 74 (1979). Compare Charles Bernheimer, "Crossing Over: Kafka's Metatextual Parable," 95 *Modern Language Notes* 1254, 1263 (1980).

traditional revenger, with the revenger's standard problem of going too far, and Kleist wants to make a point about the breakdown of justice in a divided Germany. Joseph K. is a fly caught in a spiderweb largely of his own spinning, who reacts to his predicament not with the revenger's implacable fury but with futile, comical gestures.

WRITTEN in 1851 by a keen and experienced observer of the legal scene, *Bleak House* revolves around the fictional case of *Jarndyce v. Jarndyce*, a will dispute that has been going on for many years in the Court of Chancery. By the end of the novel the case has petered out because the entire estate has been consumed in legal fees and other costs of suit. Dickens's symbol for the court is fog; and the impenetrable mystery and futility of its proceedings resemble nothing so much as those of the court in *The Trial*—which is no surprise, since Kafka greatly admired Dickens[70] and since equity procedure, with its leisurely course, its emphasis on documentary evidence, and its somewhat "inquisitorial" tone, is closer to Continental procedure than the procedure of the classic Anglo-American trial is. It may not be an accident that the centerpiece of Dickens's other and much sunnier law novel, *Pickwick Papers*—the trial in the breach of promise case of *Bardell v. Pickwick*—is a case at law rather than in equity, though equity takes some knocks in *Pickwick Papers* too.

The judicial proceedings themselves are mainly in the background in *Bleak House*. The courtroom drama of a *Bardell v. Pickwick* is missing; indeed, the legal variety of *Pickwick Papers*, a novel which touches on bankruptcy and estate law as well as on breach of promise and whose gallery of lawyers includes the sympathetic figure of the solicitor Perker, is not to be found in *Bleak House*. But Bleak House is particularly rich in unforgettable portraits of unattractive lawyer types—particularly Tulkinghorn and Guppy—and also of those unfortunates, the crazy court buffs who follow litigation, their own or others', with paranoid intensity (for example, Miss Flite), as well as of the soberer sorts who nevertheless become obsessed and eventually ruined by the hope of

---

[70] See, for example, George H. Ford, *Dickens and His Readers* 254–256 (1965); Gray, note 59 above, at 72; Ernst Pawel, *The Nightmare of Reason: A Life of Franz Kafka* 159 (1984). Specific parallels between *Bleak House* and *The Trial* are discussed in Mark Spilka, *Dickens and Kafka: A Mutual Interpretation*, chap. 10 (1963), and in Deborah Heller Roazen, "A Peculiar Attraction: *Bleak House, Der Prozess*, and the Law," 5 *Essays in Literature* 251 (1978). See also Murray Krieger, *The Tragic Vision* 138–140 (1960). Spilka, above, at 291 n. 10, also points out some parallels between *Pickwick Papers* and *The Trial*.

scoring big in litigation, such as Richard Carstone. (Recall the tradesman Block in *The Trial*.)

Although there is exaggeration and even fantasy in *Bleak House*, and although the chancery court is not merely a target of criticism but also a metaphor for broader problems of human selfishness and indifference that preoccupied Dickens,[71] the novel unquestionably was intended to be a serious, and is on the whole an informed if slightly unfair, criticism of a particular legal procedure, that of chancery.[72] This can be said of no other work discussed thus far in this chapter, though it is emphatically true of *Pickwick Papers*. The centerpiece of that novel is Mrs. Bardell's groundless suit against Pickwick for breach of a marriage promise (which he had never made), and her futile efforts to collect the large judgment that the jury awards her. The proceeding is likely to strike a modern reader—even, or perhaps especially, one with legal training—as a farce, and this for two reasons besides Dickens's fondness for farce. First, neither Mrs. Bardell nor Mr. Pickwick testifies in the trial, and thus the best evidence of whether there was a promise of marriage is withheld from the jury. Second, no procedure exists for levying execution of the judgment against Pickwick's considerable assets—all that Mrs. Bardell can do is have him imprisoned for contempt of court when he refuses to pay it. But all this is fact, not farce. At the time Dickens wrote *Pickwick Papers*, parties to lawsuits were not permitted to testify; and securities—the form in which Pickwick's wealth was held—could not be levied against to satisfy a judgment.[73] Thus the novel is among other things a pointed criticism of the legal procedure of the time.

The problem with chancery proceedings as in *Bleak House* was not that they were encrusted with the kind of legal barnacles that *Bardell v. Pickwick* scraped up against—equity, as we know already, is more flex-

[71] See, for example, Trevor Blount, "Chancery as Evil and Challenge in *Bleak House*," 1 *Dickens Studies* 112 (1965); Joseph L. Fradin, "Will and Society in *Bleak House*," 81 *Publications of the Modern Language Association* 95 (1966); D. A. Miller, "Discipline in Different Voices: Bureaucracy, Police, Family, and *Bleak House*," 1 *Representations* 1 (1983). For good general discussions of *Bleak House* see *Twentieth Century Interpretations of Bleak House: A Collection of Critical Essays* (Jacob Korg ed. 1968), especially Robert A. Donovan, "Structure and Idea in Bleak House," in id. at 31; Edmund Wilson, "Dickens: The Two Scrooges," in Wilson, *The Wound and the Bow: Seven Studies in Literature* 1, 35–43 (1947); Q. D. Leavis, " 'Bleak House': A Chancery World," in F. R. Leavis and Q. D. Leavis, *Dickens the Novelist* 118 (1970). A linkage between *Bleak House* and *The Merchant of Venice* is argued in R. D. Drexler, "Note on *Bleak House* and *The Merchant of Venice*," 82 *Dickensian* 149 (1986).

[72] See, for example, W. P. Woolliams, "Of and Concerning '*Jarndyce v. Jarndyce*,' " 41 *Dickensian* 26 (1944); John Butt, " 'Bleak House' in the Context of 1851," 10 *Nineteenth-Century Fiction* 1 (1955); Frank A. Gibson, "Hard on the Lawyers?" 59 *Dickensian* 160 (1963); Trevor Blount, "The Documentary Symbolism of Chancery in *Bleak House*," 62 *Dickensian* 47 (1966).

[73] See William S. Holdsworth, *Charles Dickens as a Legal Historian*, chap. 4 (1929).

ible, less hidebound (and rule-bound) than law—but that they were very slow and costly.[74] The chancery court had a monopoly of important classes of litigation, notably those involving trusts and guardianships (hence the expression "a ward in Chancery"), as well as those seeking equitable relief—an injunction, a receivership, a complex accounting, or the specific performance of a contract—rather than the standard "legal" remedy, which was (and is) damages. The chancery court made greater use of written evidence than the regular law courts, and this slowed down proceedings. Another thing that slowed them down was that the Lord Chancellor personally reviewed virtually all cases.[75] The sluggishness of chancery was particularly conspicuous because trials in the regular English courts had traditionally been very swift (they still are); few lasted more than a day. Chancery was expensive, too; judges were compensated out of the court fees paid by the litigants, and the fees in chancery were very high, in part because the classes of litigation that the court monopolized were lucrative ones. The Lord Chancellor had one of the highest incomes in England.

Thus *Bleak House* can fairly be described as a satirical denunciation of a real, and seriously flawed, legal institution. But this is far from being the most interesting thing about the book. Someone who wants to learn about the nineteenth-century English chancery court is not likely to spend much time on *Bleak House*, because there are fuller and soberer sources of data;[76] it is not like the Homeric epics or the Old Norse sagas, which are the main sources of our knowledge of their societies' legal institutions. Viewed merely as description and critique of the Court of Chancery, *Bleak House* is a 135-year-old piece of journalism—albeit of incomparable vividness.

Another limitation of *Bleak House* when viewed as social commentary rather than imaginative literature is that Dickens, for all his keen sense of injustice, was not a practical reformer.[77] He was acutely conscious of the evil in the world but, without being in the least quietistic or resigned, had no suggestions for getting rid of it. Although greatly

[74] See id., chap. 3; John P. Dawson, *A History of Lay Judges* 170–172 (1960); G. W. Keeton, *An Introduction to Equity* 18–20, 35 (6th ed. 1965); D. M. Kerly, *An Historical Sketch of the Equitable Jurisdiction of the Court of Chancery*, chap. 13 (1890).

[75] See John H. Langbein, "Fact Finding in the English Court of Chancery: A Rebuttal," 83 *Yale Law Journal* 1620, 1629 (1974). This had changed, however, by 1851. See, for example, George W. Keeton and L. A. Sheridan, *Equity* 73–74 (1969). The element of unfairness of Dickens's portrait of the chancery court lies in the fact that some of the worst abuses that he pilloried had already been corrected—which he neglected to mention.

[76] Such as those cited in the two preceding notes.

[77] See, for example, George Orwell, "Charles Dickens," in *Collected Essays, Journalism and Letters of George Orwell*, note 1 above, vol. 1, at 413; Robert A. Donovan, "Structure and Idea in *Bleak House*," 29 *Journal of English Literary Theory* 175 (1962).

distressed by the delays and expense of chancery, he seems to have accepted these things as part of the natural order, and he is rather warning the reader to avoid falling into the clutches of the court than trying to make those clutches less fell; it is like telling people in tornado country to build better storm cellars.

The most interesting aspect of *Bleak House* from a legal viewpoint is the contrast between the picture of equity that it presents and the picture that we find in *The Merchant of Venice* and *Measure for Measure*. The jurisdiction of the Lord Chancellor—the original equity jurisdiction in England—had arisen in the Middle Ages, in response to the rigidity and hypertechnicality of the law courts, which were unable to render simple justice in a large class of cases: they would enforce a contract even if it had been procured by fraud; they could not protect the legal rights of children and the insane; they had no procedures by which litigants could obtain pretrial discovery of essential facts; they could not enjoin a litigant who filed a torrent of redundant suits in order to wear out his opponent. *Bardell v. Pickwick* illustrates the persistence of the quirky deficiencies of common-law procedure well into the nineteenth century.

The Lord Chancellors, originally clerics (such as Thomas à Becket and Cardinal Wolsey), dispensed justice according to conscience rather than strict legal forms. Later the rules and remedies of equity jurisprudence, as the jurisprudence developed by the Lord Chancellors came to be known, were institutionalized in the Court of Chancery. It is the spirit of equity that Portia symbolizes. The irony so effectively exploited by Dickens in *Bleak House* is that the court of conscience had become the nation's worst example of legal abuses. This made it the perfect target for a moralist who believed (very much in the spirit of the Romantic movement) that institutions pervert the inborn goodness of people. A lawyer might want to point out, however, that equity had the weakness of its strengths, just as law had the strength of its own weaknesses. It is the old dilemma of rule versus discretion. Equity started out as a truly discretionary jurisdiction. This proved intolerable, and *rules* of equity emerged; nevertheless equity procedure remained relatively formless, and the result eventually was tremendous delays and uncertainty. Proceedings at law were full of crotchets and traps but at least moved along at a smart pace. The underlying dilemma may be inescapable.

# THREE

## The Literary Indictment
## of Legal Injustice

*T*HIS CHAPTER continues the inquiry into whether the study of
literature on legal themes can illuminate issues of justice, but with
a shift of emphasis to two works of literature not discussed in previous
chapters, *Billy Budd* and *The Brothers Karamazov*, and to the surprising
issue of legal Romanticism. My jumping-off point is Richard Weisberg's book *The Failure of the Word*,[1] an ambitious examination of fiction
about law. Using the methods of both literary criticism and legal
reasoning, Weisberg—a professor of law who was once a professor of
literature—tries to show how a lawyer's knowledge can enrich our
understanding of such fiction and how a critic's knowledge of such
fiction can enrich our understanding of law. His book is both a good
example of the promise and pitfalls of the law and literature movement
and a good framework for the discussion in this chapter.

### Law and Ressentiment

Weisberg's central theme is that of "ressentiment." A word whose
currency is due primarily to Nietzsche,[2] it means the rancorous envy of
the naturally weak toward the naturally strong. Weak men overcome

---

[1] Richard H. Weisberg, *The Failure of the Word: The Protagonist as Lawyer in Modern Fiction*
(1984). Unless otherwise indicated, page references in this chapter are to Weisberg's book.
[2] See, for example, Friedrich Nietzsche, *On the Genealogy of Morals* 73–75 (II.11), 121–129
(III.14–16) (Walter Kaufmann and R. J. Hollingdale trans. 1969); Gilles Deleuze, *Nietzsche and
Philosophy*, chap. 4 (1983); Walter Kaufmann, *Nietzsche: Philosopher, Psychologist, Antichrist*,
371–378 (4th ed. 1974); Max Scheler, "Ressentiment," in *Nietzsche: A Collection of Critical
Essays* 243 (Robert C. Solomon ed. 1973); John Burt Foster, Jr., *Heirs to Dionysus: A
Nietzschean Current in Literary Modernism* 68–75 (1981); cf. René Girard, *Deceit, Desire, and the
Novel: Self and Other in Literary Structure* 11–14 (1965). Note that I give part (or essay) and
section (or paragraph, or aphorism) references in parentheses after page references to

strong ones—the strong man being highly vulnerable to certain forms of attack because he is open, trusting, nonverbal, unsubtle, indeed unreflective—by spinning conceptual webs. The three most important are Christianity, legalism, and the translation of experience into words, which falsifies the experience.[3] The last two are Weisberg's own variations on Nietzsche's theme, but it is worth pausing to notice how Nietzsche himself had related ressentiment to law. As often, Nietzsche is on both sides of the question. One side, the side most congenial to Weisberg's own approach, is summarized in a sentence in *Thus Spoke Zarathustra*: "And when they say, 'I am just,' it always sounds like 'I am just—revenged.' "[4] Ressentiment, the bitter mood in which the weak and defeated nurse grievances and plot revenge, is in the realm of psychology what revenge itself is in the realm of action; and the person who seeks to vindicate his legal rights, like the revenger, is deformed by ressentiment. Shylock exemplifies ressentiment. (Cassius is another Shakespearean exemplar of ressentiment.) The *Übermensch* is above envy, takes no notice of slights, and therefore has no use for revenge or indeed for law. As we saw in Chapter 1, Weisberg considers Hamlet to personify ressentiment (a claim repeated in *The Failure of the Word*; see pp. 8–9, 27). This is the only case in which Weisberg ascribes ressentiment to a revenger; the resentment that concerns Weisberg is otherwise closer to envy of people happier than oneself than to the indignation that a wrongful injury provokes.

Weisberg believes that the ressentiment felt by the European intelligentsia was one of the causes of the extermination of European Jewry by the Nazis. He defends this thesis with a brief article (excerpted and

Nietzsche's works; this is to make it easier for the reader to find the cited passage in other editions. Where sections are numbered consecutively throughout the entire work, I give only the section number (preceded by "§") in parentheses.

[3] "Word" in Weisberg's title is an ironic echo of the Christian "Word" in the gospel according to St. John. On Weisberg's equation of law and religion see p. 116 of his book.

[4] Friedrich Nietzsche, *Thus Spoke Zarathustra: A Book for All and None* 95 (II.5) (Walter Kaufmann trans. 1966). The translation is a confusing attempt to render a pun. The German is: "Und wenn sie sagen: 'ich bin gerecht,' so klingt es immer gleich wie: 'ich bin gerächt.' " *Recht* is the German word for justice, *Rache* for revenge. On Nietzsche's views on revenge, see also David Cartwright, "Revenge, Punishment, and Mercy: The Self-Overcoming of Justice," 17 *International Studies in Philosophy* 17, 22–23 (no. 2, 1985); cf. Joan Stambaugh, "Thoughts on Pity and Revenge," 1 *Nietzsche-Studien* 27 (1972).

In *On the Genealogy of Morals*, however, Nietzsche describes law as an effort to overcome ressentiment—indeed, as a substitute for ressentiment, for vengeful feelings, and even for conscience (a faculty that Nietzsche despised)—rather than as an expression of ressentiment. See Nietzsche, note 2 above, at 73–76 (II.11); Richard H. Weisberg, "Text into Theory: A Literary Approach to the Constitution," 20 *Georgia Law Review* 939, 972–976 (1986).

translated on pp. 181–182 of the book) by a French lawyer, published in 1943, on when a person of mixed Jewish and non-Jewish "blood" should be classified as a gentile, and with discussions of works by Dostoevsky (*Crime and Punishment* and *The Brothers Karamazov*), Flaubert (*Salammbô* and *Sentimental Education*), and Camus (*The Stranger* and *The Fall*); and, at greater length, *Billy Budd*. Each of these works, Weisberg argues, depicts characters consumed by ressentiment; in several, such characters overcome naturally strong men. Legal inquiries or proceedings figure prominently in the two novels by Dostoevsky, as well as in *Billy Budd* and *The Stranger*, while the central characters in both *Sentimental Education* and *The Fall* are lawyers, and Raskolnikov, the murderer in *Crime and Punishment*, is a former law student.

In discussing these works, Weisberg usefully emphasizes differences between Anglo-American and Continental criminal procedure that an American reader of such works as *Crime and Punishment*, *The Stranger*, and especially *The Trial* might miss. The examining or investigating magistrate in Continental law plays a role that places him in a different relationship to a suspect or accused from that of any official in Anglo-American criminal justice systems—a relationship more intimate, more paternalistic, more invasive of privacy, less structured, less adversary.[5] As Weisberg explains, this relationship provides a convenient vehicle for the exploration of character. But he does not pursue the implications of this insight. In particular, he does not consider the possibility that the purpose of the criminal investigation in a Continental novel may be to reveal character rather than to criticize law.

The only other emphatic intervention of Weisberg the lawyer comes in the discussion of *Billy Budd*. He asserts that the drumhead court-martial and execution of Billy Budd are marred by serious

---

[5] On Continental criminal procedure generally, see John Henry Merryman, *The Civil Law Tradition: An Introduction to the Legal Systems of Western Europe and Latin America*, chap. 17 (2d ed. 1985); John H. Langbein and Lloyd L. Weinreb, "Continental Criminal Procedure: 'Myth' and Reality," 87 *Yale Law Journal* 1549 (1978); and note 25 in Chapter 2. The reader should be aware that the examining magistrate is of declining importance today in France. See Edward A. Tomlinson, "Nonadversarial Justice: The French Experience," 42 *Maryland Law Review* 131, 150–155 (1983). Nor is he an important figure in modern German criminal procedure. See generally John H. Langbein, *Comparative Criminal Procedure: Germany* (1977), and "Land without Plea Bargaining: How the Germans Do It," 78 *Michigan Law Review* 204 (1979); Gerald L. Kock, "Criminal Proceedings in France," 9 *American Journal of Comparative Law* 253 (1960). The contrast between English and Continental criminal procedure is vividly depicted in Sybille Bedford, *The Faces of Justice: A Traveller's Report* (1961), but should not be overdrawn: the legal proceedings in *The Brothers Karamazov* resemble a modern English or American trial, while, as noted in the last chapter, English equity procedure resembles the Continental system.

procedural and substantive errors. They could not be Melville's errors, he says, because Melville, though not himself a lawyer, was well versed in the law of the sea. Yet if there are legal errors in *Billy Budd* (a question I take up later), it is far from certain that Melville would have been aware of them. Although he had served on an American warship for fourteen months beginning in 1842 and had a long-standing interest in naval discipline, he may have known little about eighteenth-century British law; and *Billy Budd*, though written between 1888 and 1891, is set in the British navy of 1797. Moreover, since Melville was writing a novella rather than a law review article, he may have changed the law for literary reasons. Nothing in the text of *Billy Budd* would alert a lay reader to the possibility of legal errors, and not even a lawyer reading it (and it was not written mainly for lawyers) would find any such clues unless he happened to be an antiquarian. Weisberg has gone outside the proper frame of reference.[6]

This is also what he did when he ascribed to Hamlet envy of Claudius; in neither case is there an adequate basis in the text for the interpretation. Yet more than a personal idiosyncrasy is involved. Literary critics have become freer in their interpretations in recent years, to the point where some critics no longer view their role as interpretive in an understandable sense. This tendency[7] reflects many things: the decline of authority and consensus in modern societies; the rise of cultural relativism; Freud's theory of the unconscious; and the open-ended character of so much modern literature, illustrated by the French *nouveau roman* and by *Finnegans Wake*, and also by Kafka's unfinished novels and by such other modern classics as *Ulysses* and *Four Quartets*. But there are much older examples of open-ended literature, including some of Shakespeare's plays and even works written in the twelfth century[8] and, for that matter, much earlier (parts of the Bible, for example). Works of literature in which the

---

[6] As noted in Merton M. Sealts, Jr., "Innocence and Infamy: *Billy Budd, Sailor*," in *A Companion to Melville Studies* 407, 418 (John Bryant ed. 1986); L. H. LaRue, "The Portrayal of Law in Literature: Weisberg's *Failure of the Word*," 1986 *American Bar Foundation Research Journal* 313, 318. Melville often took great liberties with the facts, for his artistic purposes. See, for example, the editors' "Explanatory Notes" in Herman Melville, *Omoo: A Narrative of Adventures in the South Seas* 341–438 (Harrison Hayford and Walter Blair eds. 1969).

[7] Usually traced to some remarks by Nietzsche on interpretation, see Allan Megill, *Prophets of Extremity: Nietzsche, Heidegger, Foucault, Derrida* 84–92 (1985); Samuel Weber, *Institution and Interpretation* 4–6, 38 (1987), although Nietzsche was critical of free interpretation of texts. See Hendrik Birus, "Nietzsche's Concept of Interpretation," 3 *Texte: Revue de critique et de théorie littéraire* 87 (1984); Weisberg, note 4 above, at 962–976.

[8] See Frank Kermode, *The Art of Telling: Essays on Fiction* 128–129 (1983); Eugène Vinaver, *The Rise of Romance* (1971), especially chaps. 1–3.

author seems unwilling or unable to achieve closure invite the reader to become a collaborator in the creation of meaning.

It may be that most literature shares this characteristic to a greater or lesser degree. Literature must be general to survive the immediate occasion of its creation—to be literature—and this may imply, in many though not all cases (I shall discuss an exception at the end of Chapter 5), that it must to some extent be open-ended. But when pushed to the point where every work of literature becomes a Rorschach test, emphasis on the indeterminacy of literary works turns literary criticism into navel-gazing. And by doing so it undermines rather than supports efforts to relate literature to law. Suppose *Billy Budd* really is so plastic that a mind such as Weisberg's imbued with the tragedy of the Holocaust can find premonitions of it in the novella. Does it not follow that Weisberg is merely pulling out of *Billy Budd* what he himself put in it? If so, should he not cut out the middleman and make his points directly, without dragging in Melville?

Other than in the specific respects I have indicated, Weisberg's book is about law and lawyers mainly in the sense, familiar from the last chapter, in which a certain conception of law—Shylock's in *The Merchant of Venice* or Angelo's in *Measure for Measure*—might be thought to foster injustice. Shylock, brimming over with ressentiment, would be a perfect symbol of legalism as injustice, but it is one that Weisberg, understandably, avoids; it would blur the connection that he is trying to make between ressentiment and anti-Semitism.

The legalistic cast of mind can indeed be exasperating and lead to, or more commonly blind one to, injustice, but is it the important source of atrocities and genocide that Weisberg believes it to be? The suggestion is sufficiently *outré* to require evidence, but little is forthcoming, and the opposite thesis could be argued from Weisberg's own analysis of *Billy Budd*: if he is right about eighteenth-century British naval law, Billy Budd would not have been executed (not so soon, anyway) had Captain Vere been a stickler for legal niceties. And recall what I said in the last chapter about legalism being the pariah's protection. Furthermore, the insinuating style of the European examining magistrate illustrates not the operation of legal technicalities but the power of informal, discretionary procedures. A system of criminal justice like the American one, which throws greater protections (many highly legalistic) around the criminal suspect, would have made it harder for the examining magistrate in *Crime and Punishment* to push Raskolnikov toward confessing or for the jury in *The Stranger* to convict Meursault (a pariah, like Shylock—the primary meanings of *étranger* being "foreigner," "alien," and "outsider" rather than "stranger").

I shall return to *Billy Budd*, but first I must show how Weisberg uses the deeply Romantic concept of ressentiment to turn conventional social values upside down and present prosecutors as villains and criminals as heroes. Only then will the stage be set for understanding his unorthodox reading of *Billy Budd* and his equally unorthodox reading of *The Brothers Karamazov*.

## Romantic Values in Literature and Law

Behind the concept of ressentiment lies an opposition between two human types—"natural" man, and "social" or "civilized" man (for Nietzsche, resentful man). The first type, whose original representatives in Western literature are Achilles in the *Iliad* and Prometheus in *Prometheus Bound*, is the individualist par excellence, whose boundless ego and devotion to honor place him on a collision course with the herd of ordinary men, with their supine conformity to social norms. Although even Achilles is presented as something of an overreacher, the claims of society in the *Iliad* are weak; Achilles' placing his own honor entirely above the welfare of the Greek cause in the Trojan War is shown as admirable rather than treasonable.[9] The Greek and Elizabethan tragedies temper admiration for individualism with a sharp awareness of the competing claims of society (*Prometheus Bound* and *Tamburlaine the Great* may be exceptions), and often present the great protagonists as evil (Macbeth), greatly deluded (Oedipus, Lear, Brutus, Othello), or initially immature (Hamlet). (Among lesser figures in the tragedies, the excesses of individualism are especially vivid in Gloucester's "natural" son in *King Lear*, the villainous Edmund.) In explicitly Christian literature, such as the *Divine Comedy* and *Paradise Lost*, the great individuals are consigned to Hell and the social virtues (what Nietzsche would call the herd instinct or slave morality)—order, restraint, hierarchy, obedience—receive their most powerful literary celebration.[10]

Marlowe's greatest plays provide a particularly sharp contrast be-

[9] On Homeric values see, besides references in Chapter 1, A. W. H. Adkins, *Merit and Responsibility: A Study in Greek Values*, chap. 3 (1960), and his "Values, Goals, and Emotions in the *Iliad*," 77 *Classical Philology* 292 (1982); Michael Gagarin, "Morality in Homer," 82 *Classical Philology* 285 (1987). On Achilles as Nietzsche's "blond beast" see W. Thomas MacCary, *Childlike Achilles: Ontogeny and Phylogeny in the Iliad* 249 (1982).

[10] See the forceful argument of this point in C. S. Lewis, *A Preface to Paradise Lost*, chap. 11 (1942). On Milton's Satan as an inversion of the epic hero see John M. Steadman, *Milton and the Renaissance Hero* (1967), and on Renaissance ambivalence about the heroic (illustrated by Marlowe's plays) see *Concepts of the Hero in the Middle Ages and the Renaissance* (Norman T. Burns and Christopher J. Reagan eds. 1975).

tween the celebration of individualistic and of social virtues—or, as a Christian might say, between rebellion and obedience. *The First Part of Tamburlaine the Great* depicts the triumph of an indomitable will, which carries a Scythian shepherd to the heights of worldly power.[11] Tamburlaine explains his philosophy to the Persian king whom he has just overcome in battle (II.7.12–29):

> The thirst of reign and sweetness of a crown,
> That caus'd the eldest son of heavenly Ops
> To thrust his doting father from his chair,
> And place himself in the imperial heaven,
> Mov'd me to manage arms against thy state.
> What better precedent than mighty Jove?
> Nature, that fram'd us of four elements
> Warring within our breasts for regiment,
> Doth teach us all to have aspiring minds.
> Our souls, whose faculties can comprehend
> The wondrous architecture of the world,
> And measure every wandering planet's course,
> Still climbing after knowledge infinite,
> And always moving as the restless spheres,
> Wills us to wear ourselves and never rest,
> Until we reach the ripest fruit of all,
> That perfect bliss and sole felicity,
> The sweet fruition of an earthly crown.

Tamburlaine's "precedent" is successful rebellion, and his goal—blasphemous from a Christian standpoint—is the possession of an earthly, not a heavenly, crown. Notice how he ties pride and worldly ambition to scientific curiosity and growth of scientific knowledge. The vision is of the individual's taking control of his destiny instead of accepting his place in a hierarchical universe. This is a subversive as well as a blasphemous vision; the suggestion that "all of us" can aspire to an earthly crown is a frontal thrust at the divine right of kings. Tamburlaine is the political counterpart of Hamlet, who in Northrop Frye's words is "aware of the infinite possibilities inherent, at least in theory, in being human and conscious . . . A naive consciousness would say that, although bounded in a nutshell, it was also king of infinite space,

---

[11] For good discussions see Johannes H. Birringer, "Marlowe's Violent Stage: 'Mirrors' of Honor in *Tamburlaine*," 51 *English Literary History* 219 (1984); *Christopher Marlowe's Tamburlaine Part One and Part Two: Text and Major Criticism* 133–352 (Irving Ribner ed. 1974); Richard A. Martin, "Marlowe's *Tamburlaine* and the Language of Romance," 93 *Publications of the Modern Language Association* 248 (1978); Harry Levin, *The Overreacher: A Study of Christopher Marlowe*, chap. 2 (1952), especially pp. 38–39.

but Hamlet's consciousness is not naive, and it dreams."[12] Tamburlaine's is naive. Not even on his deathbed, in *The Second Part of Tamburlaine the Great*, does he display awareness of the finitude of human potentiality.

The hero of *Doctor Faustus* is at first as self-confident and aspiring as Tamburlaine, but receives a dramatic comeuppance when he is dragged away to Hell twenty-four years after signing the pact with the devil. Like Macbeth, but unlike Tamburlaine, Faustus dies a wiser man, having discovered the resistance that reality puts up to the transformative efforts of the human imagination. Both Macbeth, with the assistance of the weird sisters, and Faustus, with the assistance of Mephostophilis, get most of what they ask for, but it turns out not to be what they want. They differ, for us, mainly in that Faustus's aspirations for sexual freedom, scientific knowledge, and control of his environment make him a more distinctively modern figure than the usurper-murderer Macbeth.

Whether the audience of *Doctor Faustus* was intended to take an orthodox Christian view of the pact with the devil or to identify with Faustus's Promethean aspirations is a much debated issue.[13] The best capsule summary of Faustus may be Potter's: "magnificent villainy."[14] By the pact with the devil Faustus seeks to annul the limitations that God imposes on human aspiration, and when made forcibly aware of those limitations he refuses to yield to them even at the price of damnation. Even the Christian reader admires his courage, while deploring his blasphemy.

The writers of the Romantic period exalted the "aspiring mind" as never before or since. One has only to compare Goethe's *Faust* with Marlowe's before him and Thomas Mann's after him.[15] Tamburlaine's

---

[12] *Northrop Frye on Shakespeare* 98–99 (Robert Sandler ed. 1986).

[13] See Chapter 5; and, for fuller discussions, Max Bluestone, "*Libido Speculandi*: Doctrine and Dramaturgy in Contemporary Interpretations of Marlowe's *Doctor Faustus*," in *Reinterpretations of Elizabethan Drama* 33 (Norman Rabkin ed. 1969); Lily B. Campbell, "*Doctor Faustus*: A Case of Conscience," 67 *Publications of the Modern Language Association* 219 (1952); Robert Ornstein, "Marlowe and God: The Tragic Theology of *Doctor Faustus*," 83 *Publications of the Modern Language Association* 1378 (1968); Robert Potter, *The English Morality Play: Origins, History and Influence of a Dramatic Tradition* 125–129 (1975); Wilbur Sanders, *The Dramatist and the Received Idea: Studies in the Plays of Marlowe and Shakespeare*, chap. 11 (1968). Particularly interesting is George Santayana's argument, in *Three Philosophical Poets: Lucretius, Dante, and Goethe* 133–135 (1910), that Marlowe's play marks the beginning of the rehabilitation of the Faust figure's image.

[14] Potter, note 13 above, at 128.

[15] On Mann's conception see Marguerite De Huszar Allen, *The Faust Legend: Popular Formula and Modern Novel*, chap. 5 (1985); Erich Heller, "Parody, Tragic and Comic: Mann's *Doctor Faustus* and *Felix Krull*," 66 *Sewanee Review* 519, 533 (1958). On the improvement of Faust's "image" between the medieval and Romantic periods see Santayana, note 13 above, at 132–178; J. W. Smeed, *Faust in Literature* 3–10 (1975).

"aspiring minds" speech could serve as a manifesto of the Romanticism of William Blake,[16] except that the Romantics lacked the Renaissance enthusiasm for science. Blake, who thought Satan the real hero of *Paradise Lost*, like Tamburlaine engineered an explicit inversion of conventional values. Natural man is good, society is repressive and evil, as Blake explains in *The Garden of Love*:

> I went to the Garden of Love,
> And saw what I never had seen:
> A Chapel was built in the midst,
> Where I used to play on the green.
>
> And the gates of the Chapel were shut,
> And "Thou shalt not" writ over the door;
> So I turn'd to the Garden of Love
> That so many sweet flowers bore;
> And I saw it was filled with graves,
> And tomb-stones where flowers should be;
> And Priests in black gowns were walking their rounds,
> And binding with briars my joys and desires.

One finds traces of this attitude in *Bleak House*, and it receives much play in twentieth-century literature as well, *The Stranger* being only one example.

Although the word "Romanticism," if it is to be used with any precision, should be reserved for a cluster of particular (and actually quite diverse) movements in the social, political, and artistic thought of the late eighteenth and early nineteeth centuries,[17] the "Romantic" temperament is one of humankind's fundamental moods, reflecting the boundless egoism of early childhood and the sense of loss that accom-

---

[16] On which see Northrop Frye, *Fearful Symmetry: A Study of William Blake* (1947); Frye, "Blake's Treatment of the Archetype," in *English Romantic Poets: Modern Essays in Criticism* 55 (M. H. Abrams ed., 2d ed. 1975).

[17] See Arthur O. Lovejoy, "On the Discrimination of Romanticisms," in *English Romantic Poets*, note 16 above, at 3. On Romantic literature and thought, see, besides Abrams's fine collection of essays on the English romantic poets, note 16 above, Walter Jackson Bate, *From Classic to Romantic: Premises of Taste in Eighteenth-Century England*, chap. 6 (1946); Carl Woodring, *Politics in English Romantic Poetry*, chap. 2 (1970); Northrop Frye, *A Study of English Romanticism* (1968); *Romanticism and Contemporary Criticism* (Morris Eaves and Michael Fischer eds. 1986); Jerome J. McGann, *The Romantic Ideology: A Critical Investigation* (1983); Harold Bloom, *The Ringers in the Tower: Studies in Romantic Tradition*, chap. 20 (1971); Géza von Molnár, *Romantic Vision, Ethical Context: Novalis and Artistic Autonomy* (1987). The continuity with twentieth-century "neoromantic" poets, notably Yeats, is well discussed in George Bornstein, *Transformations of Romanticism in Yeats, Eliot, and Stevens* (1976), especially chaps. 1 and 2, and Denis Donoghue, *The Ordinary Universe: Soundings in Modern Literature* (1968).

panies growing up.[18] An ancient example of the turn from Romance to maturity is the false tale of his life that Odysseus tells his swineherd Eumaeus in Book 14 of the *Odyssey* (lines 199–359). Odysseus has just returned to Ithaca, after twenty years of war and wandering, disguised as a beggar. He tells Eumaeus the following tale. He was born in Crete, the bastard son of a wealthy man who had many legitimate sons. The father honored him equally with his brothers, but when the father died, the legitimate sons, who were arrogant, divided his property by lots, assigning only a small holding to the narrator. Nevertheless, he was able to get a wife from a wealthy family because of his prowess—he was good at the ambush, loved to charge the fleeing foe, and so forth. (Here he interrupts to remark that if Eumaeus will look closely at him, he will be able to see the shadow of the man he once was.) Such was he in battle, but farming and domestic management were not for him. His world was that of ships and battles and the like, things other people dreaded. Before the Trojan War he led nine sea raids against foreigners, won a lot of booty, and was feared and respected by his fellow Cretans.

Then Zeus decreed that awful journey—as the narrator calls the Trojan War—which killed many men. The people kept urging the narrator and Idomeneus, who in the *Iliad* is the leader of the Cretan contingent in the allied Greek force, to lead the ships to Troy. There was no way to get out of it, so harsh would the verdict of public opinion have been. After Troy fell, the narrator managed to reach home; but he remained there for only a month before his spirit moved him to sail to the Nile. He anchored and sent some men out as scouts. The rest he

---

[18] See Northrop Frye, *Fools of Time: Studies in Shakespearean Tragedy* 5 (1967); Girard, note 2 above, especially chap. 1; T. E. Hulme, "Romanticism and Classicism," in *Criticism: The Major Texts* 564 (Walter Jackson Bate ed., 1970 enlarged edition); Howard Felperin, "Romance and Romanticism," 6 *Critical Inquiry* 691 (1980); cf. Thomas Sowell, *A Conflict of Visions: Ideological Origins of Political Struggles* (1987), especially chap. 2 (conflict between "constrained" and "unconstrained" visions, the latter reflecting the Romantic temperament). On the roots of the Romantic temperament in the psychology of infants see Jean Piaget, *The Child's Conception of the World* (1929). And for an interesting stab at a genetic explanation see Charles S. Peirce, *Essays in the Philosophy of Science* 7–8 (Vincent Tomas ed. 1957) (footnotes omitted): "Most of us . . . are naturally more sanguine and hopeful than logic would justify. We seem to be so constituted that in the absence of any facts to go upon we are happy and self-satisfied; so that the effect of experience is continually to contract our hopes and aspirations. Yet a lifetime of the application of this corrective does not usually eradicate our sanguine disposition. Where hope is unchecked by any experience, it is likely that our optimism is extravagant. Logicality in regard to practical matters . . . is the most useful quality an animal can possess, and might, therefore, result from the action of natural selection; but outside of these it is probably of more advantage to the animal to have his mind filled with pleasing and encouraging visions, independently of their truth; and thus, upon unpractical subjects, natural selection might occasion a fallacious tendency of thought."

ordered to stay by the ships, but they were cocky, and trusting to their strength ravaged the Egyptians' fields. The Egyptians sallied forth from their town and routed the Cretans, sparing only the narrator (who interrupts the story at this point to say, "Would that I had died there in Egypt!"). He clasped and kissed the Egyptian king's knees in supplication, and the king pitied him and shielded him from the angry populace.

The narrator spent seven years in Egypt, gathering wealth, but in the eighth year a deceitful merchant persuaded the narrator to accompany him to Phoenicia. The narrator remained there for a year. Then the merchant sent him with a cargo to Libya, ostensibly to trade, but actually intending to sell him into slavery when the ship arrived. The ship was wrecked in a storm, and after floating for ten days clinging to the mast the narrator was washed ashore in the land of the Thesprotians. The son of Pheidon, the ruler of the Thesprotians, found the narrator, exhausted from his ordeal, and led him to his home and clothed him. Pheidon asked the crew of a Thesprotian ship that was sailing in the direction of Crete to take the narrator with them. As soon as they were out of sight of land they took away his good clothes and gave him beggar's clothes. When the ship stopped that evening at Ithaca, the crew bound him and put him in the hold while they went ashore to eat, but he slipped his bonds and swam to shore.

The extensive commentary on the false tale[19] overlooks what may be its main artistic purpose: not as one might think to glorify Odysseus by contrasting his career with that of the narrator, but rather to bring the story and character of Odysseus down to earth by retelling his life, and reinterpreting his character, in terms appropriate to the comparatively realistic setting and events of the poem's dénouement. While the *Odyssey* has many Romantic elements—the tale of Odysseus's adventures at Troy and of his wanderings before he lands in Ithaca is shot through with them—the direction of the poem is anti-Romantic. The significance of

[19] See, for example, W. J. Woodhouse, *The Composition of Homer's Odyssey* 132 (1930); G. S. Kirk, *The Songs of Homer* 42, 162, 260 (1962); Charles Rowan Beye, *The Iliad, the Odyssey, and the Epic Tradition* 185–186 (1966); Howard W. Clarke, *The Art of the Odyssey* 65, 72–73 (1967); Bernard Fenik, *Studies in the Odyssey* 167–171 (1974); G. S. Kirk, *Homer and the Oral Tradition* 66 (1976); C. R. Trahman, "Odysseus' Lies (*Odyssey,* Books 13–19)," 6 *Phoenix,* no. 2, 31 (1952); Reynold Z. Burrows, "Deception as a Comic Device in the *Odyssey,*" 59 *Classical World* 33, 36 (1965); Julia Haig Gaisser, "A Structural Analysis of the Digressions in the *Iliad* and the *Odyssey,*" 73 *Harvard Studies in Classical Philology* 1, 27–31 (1969); James Redfield, "The Making of the Odyssey," in *Parnassus Revisited: Modern Critical Essays on the Epic Tradition* 141, 149–150 (Anthony C. Yu ed. 1973); P. Walcot, "Odysseus and the Art of Lying," 8 *Ancient Society* 1, 12–15 (1977); Chris Emlyn-Jones, "True and Lying Tales in the *Odyssey,*" 33 *Greece and Rome* 1 (1986). Many critics regard the false tale as one of the *longueurs* of the *Odyssey.*

Odysseus's rejection at the beginning of the poem of Calypso's offer of a sensual and luxurious immortality on the island of Ogygia in favor of his minor kingship, mortal span of years, grown son, and middle-aged wife is underscored by the fact that the Ogygian idyll was for Odysseus the culmination of a career of near-superhuman achievement at Troy and adventures of mythic proportion thereafter (with the Cyclops, Circe, and so on). Ogygia is a kind of Valhalla, and thus a fitting climax one might suppose to Odysseus's doings at Troy—which have already passed into legend and song—and his subsequent wanderings. Nevertheless, Odysseus leaves Ogygia; and the end of the poem presents him as a hero on a human rather than superhuman scale. He has been outwitted by his wife and has suffered intolerable indignities at the hands of the suitors. He has finished the suitors off neatly—but they are a poor match for his fabulous adversaries in the first half of the poem—to come into his own as the restored king of his small realm, husband, son, and father. We are made to understand that reintegration into human society is both a desirable and a realizable goal of a heroic career: a lesson reinforced by the frequent references to the fate of Agamemnon and of other heroes of the Trojan War.

The parallels between the "true" story of Odysseus's life before he returns home from Troy and the narrator's tale are numerous, though the latter is of an average, restless, disappointed, and unlucky man—a minor, and now rather soured, adventurer. The narrator's service at Troy was apparently without distinction, and his subsequent wanderings certainly so. Instead of being rescued like Odysseus by a beautiful princess (Nausicaa of Scheria) who promptly falls in love with him, he is rescued by a prince (the son of Pheidon of Thesprotia). Instead of returning to Ithaca on a ship that rows itself, supplied by the king of a magic kingdom (Scheria), he is conveyed by a bunch of thugs who rob him, and he has to scramble furtively ashore and hide in a thicket. And he is not really home; he lives in Crete, not Ithaca. He is stranded far from home, a beggar.

The false tale thus accentuates a basic movement in the *Odyssey*, which is to make Odysseus more distinct and, correlatively, more recognizably human. At first he is a vague offstage presence, and although we know he is alive, many of the characters in the poem do not. When he first appears he is only quasi-human, eating ambrosia in Calypso's cave; and then we see the fabulous hero of the Trojan War and the wanderings. Reborn in Ithaca, dealing with the members of his household, attending to domestic chores, recalling his life before the

Trojan War, he is a more fully realized human character, and the Odysseus of the earlier books becomes a memory.[20]

An intersecting movement in the poem, crossing from below the demythologizing of Odysseus, is the maturing of his son, Telemachus. At the beginning of the poem father and son are worlds apart, and their physical separation symbolizes the emotional gulf between the shallow youth of Book 2 and the hero of the Trojan War. The rapid maturing of Telemachus through a series of adventures constituting, much like the false tale told to Eumaeus, a scaled-down version of Odysseus's career, coupled with the redefinition of Odysseus as a human hero, enables father and son to join as approximate equals in the three-generation tableau that ends the poem. Family continuity is presented as an alternative way of achieving immortality to that of fame (Achilles' way in the *Iliad*), or of personal immortality, which Odysseus rejects in leaving Ogygia.

In contrast to the critical perspective on attempts to transcend the human condition that a work such as the *Odyssey* offers, Romantic literature is forever lamenting the loss of the child's sense of boundless potential. Wordsworth's *Ode: Intimations of Immortality from Recollections of Early Childhood* tells us that

> Our birth is but a sleep and a forgetting:
> The Soul that rises with us, our life's Star,
>     Hath had elsewhere its setting,
>         And cometh from afar:
>     Not in entire forgetfulness,
>     And not in utter nakedness,
> But trailing clouds of glory do we come
>         From God, who is our home:
> Heaven lies about us in our infancy!

---

[20] Cf. George E. Dimock, Jr., "The Name of Odysseus," in *Homer: A Collection of Critical Essays* 106 (George Steiner and Robert Fagles eds. 1962). It is always important to distinguish between the foreground and background stories in a work of literature. In a sense the *Odyssey* is the story of Odysseus's career, just as in a sense the *Iliad* is the story of the Trojan War and *Oedipus Tyrannus* the story of the Oedipus legend. But in all three cases the foreground story is more limited. In the *Odyssey* it is the story of Odysseus's return not from Troy but from Ogygia. He moves from West to East, from immortality to mortality, from a life of ease to a life of struggle, and does so through a liquid medium (the sea) and is symbolically reborn from a cave in Ithaca. He chooses life over death, reality over imagination. See Pierre Vidal-Naquet, "Land and Sacrifice in the Odyssey: A Study of Religious and Mythical Meanings," in *Myth, Religion and Society: Structuralist Essays* 80, 83 (R. L. Gordon ed. 1981) (discussing Odysseus's "return to normality . . . [and] his deliberate acceptance of the human condition"); Charles Paul Segal, "The Phaeacians and the Symbolism of Odysseus' Return," 1 *Arion* 17, 25, 29 n. 13 (winter 1962).

Shades of the prison-house begin to close
　　Upon the growing Boy
. . . . .

Thou [six-year-old], whose exterior semblance doth belie
　　Thy Soul's immensity;
Thou best Philosopher, who yet dost keep
Thy heritage, thou Eye among the blind,
. . . . .

　　Mighty Prophet! Seer blest!
　　On whom those truths do rest,
Which we are toiling all our lives to find.

This is magnificent poetry, although the surface meaning is absurd; six-year-olds do not have the knowledge that we spend our whole lives trying to recapture. What is true is that well-treated and well-beloved children, and young people generally, have a tremendous sense of vitality, of infinite horizons, of unlimited power to do good, which aging and experience gradually rub off, leaving in some people a sense of profound loss: "The sunshine is a glorious birth; / But yet I know, where'er I go, / That there hath past away a glory from the earth."

The Romantic poets' cult of the child, like Rousseau's parallel celebration of the noble savage, leads directly to the rejection of institutional Christianity (illustrated by Blake's *Garden of Love* and even more strikingly by his *Marriage of Heaven and Hell*) with its doctrine of original sin.[21] It also leads to the rejection of science, because of its realism, and economics, because of its emphasis on constraints. Romanticism transfers the attributes of divinity from God to man, and by doing so holds out the promise that man (like God) can create his own reality by an act of unconstrained imagination, if only society will let him. Romanticism teaches that natural man is good but becomes corrupted by institutions—the domain of the adult, the experienced, the cynical, the worldly.

The Romantic outlook has a tendency to encourage radicalism,

---

[21] On the Romantic cult of the child see Laurence Goldstein, *Ruins and Empire: The Evolution of a Theme in Augustan and Romantic Literature*, chap. 11 (1977) ("The Wordsworthian Child"). On Rousseau see Jean-Jacques Rousseau, "Discourse on the Origins and the Foundations of Inequality among Men, Part One," in Jean-Jacques Rousseau, *The First and Second Discourses* 141 (Victor Gourevitch trans. 1986); Ronald Grimsley, *The Philosophy of Rousseau*, chap. 4 (1973); James Miller, *Rousseau: Dreamer of Democracy* 173–181 (1984). The English Rousseau, William Godwin, was an important influence on the English Romantic poets. On Godwin and Romanticism see, for example, Richard Bellamy, "Godwin and the Development of 'The New Man of Feeling,' " 6 *History of Political Thought* 411 (1985). Godwin's novel *Caleb Williams* (1794), a savage attack on English law, deserves consideration (which to my knowledge it has not yet received) as a "legal novel."

whether of the left or of the right. This tendency is illustrated by Blake's poems of social and political protest, such as *London* and his poems on the French and American revolutions, and by a number of Shelley's poems, such as *The Mask of Anarchy*, which is about the Peterloo Massacre.[22] To most Romantics the political, legal, and religious restraints that have evolved to tame the beast in man and create peace and prosperity are a fraud, their actual purpose and effect being to promote selfishness and exploitation, to thwart community, to poison mankind's natural goodness.

Nietzsche, although hostile to Romanticism as he understood it, is Romantic in the generic sense.[23] He believed that man creates his own reality and that man's natural vitality, health, and flourishing have been drained by institutions that express the will to power of inferior men, the herd. Especially pertinent to this chapter is the twist that Nietzsche imparts to the Romantic hostility to institutions by attacking Christianity, and the Jews as its inventors. The importance that *The Failure of the Word* assigns to Nietzsche in the creation of the *übermenschlich* values that Weisberg sets up in opposition to Nazi anti-Semitism makes it pertinent to recall Nietzsche's view of the Jewish role in the overthrow of those values and the rise of ressentiment in their stead:

> The priests are the *most evil enemies* [of, in Nietzsche's words, powerful physicality, a flourishing, abundant, even overflowing health, together with that which serves to preserve it: war, adventure, hunting, dancing, war games, and in general all that involves vigorous, free, joyful activity]—but why? Because they are the most impotent. It is because of their impotence that in them hatred grows to monstrous and uncanny proportions, to the most spiritual and poisonous kind of hatred [compare

---

[22] See Thomas R. Edwards, *Imagination and Power: A Study of Poetry on Public Themes*, chap. 4 (1971); Woodring, note 17 above, at 265–268. On Blake's politics see id. at 59–65 and Renée Winegarten, *Writers and Revolution: The Fatal Lure of Action*, chap. 1 (1974).

[23] On Nietzsche's Romanticism see Megill, note 7 above, introduction and chap. 1. On Nietzsche's thought generally, Alexander Nehamas, *Nietzsche: Life as Literature* (1985), and J. P. Stern, *A Study of Nietzsche* (1979), are particularly good. Stern's summary of Nietzsche's position on individual versus society deserves quotation: "The category of the single and individual prevails in every argument, even where it seems irrelevant. Both 'life' and 'the will to power' . . . were seen as principles relating to the being and morality of individual persons only—on the occasions when the ethos of groups is considered, it is seen as wholly at the mercy of the charismatic leader. Nietzsche's consistent preference is clear: he is always for the single man against the herd, for genius against justice, for grace against deserts; he favours inspiration against the rule of rules and professional competence, and the heroic in every form against all that is 'human, all too human'. The catastrophic—non-gradual—perception, the unpremeditated insight and sudden conviction, the flash-like inspiration—these, for Nietzsche, are the authentic modes of knowledge-and-experience." Id. at 127.

Blake's *Garden of Love*]. The truly great haters in world history have always been priests . . . All that has been done on earth against "the noble," "the powerful," "the masters," "the rulers," fades into nothing compared with what the *Jews* have done against them; the Jews, that priestly people, who in opposing their enemies and conquerors were ultimately satisfied with nothing less than a radical revaluation of their enemies' values, that is to say, an act of the *most spiritual revenge* . . . With the Jews there begins the *slave revolt in morality*; that revolt which has a history of two thousand years behind it and which we no longer see because it—has been victorious.[24]

This passage does not give a complete picture of Nietzsche's attitude toward the Jews, for alongside it must be placed passages of lyrical philo-Semitism[25] together with diatribes against anti-Semitism and German nationalism (indeed, against Germans, period). Although Nietzsche gave currency to (though he did not coin) the word *Übermensch*, which was to play so large a role in Nazi racial doctrine, he did not use it in a racial sense (that is, he did not believe that there was a race of *Übermenschen*) and only rarely—but the qualification should be

---

[24] Nietzsche, note 2 above, at 33–34 (I.7) (emphasis in original—as is true throughout this book except where otherwise indicated). See also id. at 35 (I.8).

[25] For some examples, see Friedrich Nietzsche, *Beyond Good and Evil: Prelude to a Philosophy of the Future* 185–189 (§§ 250, 251) (Walter Kaufmann trans. 1966); *Daybreak: Thoughts on the Prejudices of Morality* 124–125 (§ 205) (R. J. Hollingdale trans. 1982); *Human, All Too Human: A Book for Free Spirits* 228–229 (§ 475) (Marion Faber trans. 1984); *Joyful Wisdom* 288–289 (§ 348) (Thomas Common trans. 1960). Yet in *Beyond Good and Evil* (§ 195) Nietzsche again speaks of the Jews as "a people 'born for slavery' " (quoting Tacitus approvingly) and again says "they mark the beginning of the slave rebellion in morals" (p. 108). And in *Daybreak* he says (§ 377), "The command 'love your enemies' had to be invented by the Jews, the best haters there have ever been" (p. 170). About such passages Danto remarks judiciously that "it is hard not to suppose that he [Nietzsche] meant to imply that the Jews were really natural inferiors and enemies of life if the slave morality itself is life contrary—which he often enough says it is. It would have exacted a measure of subtlety utterly unreasonable to demand from his readers that they see in this anything but ascription of blame to the Jews for the evils of the modern world. If he was not an anti-Semite, his language is misleading to a point of irresponsibility." Arthur C. Danto, *Nietzsche as Philosopher* 166 (1965). See also Werner J. Dannhauser, *Nietzsche's View of Socrates* 31 (1974). Even in the middle of praising Jews in *Human, All Too Human*, Nietzsche pauses to remark (§ 475): "Perhaps the youthful Jew of the stock exchange is the most repugnant invention of the whole human race" (p. 229). And see his remarks on Jewish "megalomania," and on the smelliness of Polish Jews, in sections 43 and 46 of *The Anti-Christ*. Friedrich Nietzsche, *Twilight of the Idols and The Anti-Christ* 159, 161 (R. J. Hollingdale trans. 1968). For similarly offensive remarks about the Jews see Friedrich Nietzsche, *The Will to Power* 112 (§ 186), 117 (§ 199) (Walter Kaufmann and R. J. Hollingdale trans. 1967) (published posthumously). On the complexity of Nietzsche's attitudes toward the Jews see also *Studies in Nietzsche and the Judaeo-Christian Tradition* (James C. O'Flaherty, Timothy F. Sellner, and Robert M. Helm eds. 1985), especially the essays by Neumann and Gilman.

noted—did he speak approvingly of slavery or of racial purity.[26] Much, maybe most, of what appears to be vicious in Nietzsche's writings can be interpreted figuratively, as designed to promote "positive thinking": he is trying to get people to "say 'Yes' to life" by encouraging them to break out of the shackles of custom and habit, to stop being craven and weak, to cultivate a healthy ego, to learn from experience, to ignore slights, to take responsibility for their lives—in short, to be individuals. Nietzsche admired much in the Old Testament and criticized the Jews chiefly for having invented Christianity. Yet he repeatedly asserts that the Jews are ultimately responsible (though perhaps not culpably so) for virtually everything that is bad in the modern world, and he continuously advocates pagan values in opposition to the gentler Christian ones.[27] Nietzsche considered both anti-Semites *and* Jews to be consumed by ressentiment. The Nazis ignored the first part of this condemnation; Weisberg ignores the second.

One thing is clear: with friends like Nietzsche, the Jews do not need enemies. Consider this passage from *Daybreak* (see note 25):

> Among the spectacles to which the coming century invites us is the decision as to the destiny of the Jews of Europe. That their die is cast, that they have crossed their Rubicon, is now palpably obvious: all that is left for them is either to become the masters of Europe or to lose Europe as they once a long time ago lost Egypt . . . The psychological and spiritual resources of the Jews today are extraordinary . . . The way in which they honour their fathers and their children, the rationality of their marriages and marriage customs, distinguish them among all Europeans. In addition to all this, they have known how to create for themselves a feeling of power and of eternal revenge out of the very occupations left to them (or to which they were left); one has to say in extenuation even of their usury that without this occasional pleasant and useful torturing of those who despised them it would have been difficult for them to have preserved their own self-respect for so long . . . Their demeanor still reveals that their souls

---

[26] See Kaufmann, note 2 above, chaps. 10–11; Richard Schacht, *Nietzsche*, chap. 7 (1983). Yet we read in *Daybreak*, note 25 above, at 149 (§ 272): "Crossed races always mean at the same time crossed cultures, crossed moralities; they are usually more evil, crueller, more restless . . . Races that have become pure have always also become *stronger* and more *beautiful*." And in *Human, All Too Human*, note 25 above, at 211 (§ 439): "A higher culture can come into being only where are two castes of society: the working caste and the idle caste, capable of true leisure; or, to express it more emphatically, the caste of forced labor and the caste of free labor." For other examples of Nietzsche's flirtations with racism, exploitation, and genocide see Ofelia Schutte, *Beyond Nihilism: Nietzsche without Masks*, chap. 7 (1984) ("Nietzsche's Politics").

[27] As in: "You say it is the good cause that hallows even war? I say unto you: it is the good war that hallows any cause." Nietzsche, note 4 above, at 47 (I.10).

have never known chivalrous noble sentiments nor their bodies handsome armour: a certain importunity mingles with an often charming but almost always painful submissiveness . . . They themselves know that a conquest of Europe, or any kind of act of violence, on their part is not to be thought of: but they also know that at some future time Europe may fall into their hands like a ripe fruit if they would only just extend them. To bring that about they need, in the meantime, to distinguish themselves in every domain of European distinction and to stand everywhere in the first rank: until they have reached the point at which they themselves determine what is distinguishing . . . Then, when the Jews can exhibit as their work such jewels and golden vessels as the European nations of a briefer and less profound experience could not and cannot produce, when Israel will have transformed its eternal vengeance into an eternal blessing for Europe: then there will again arrive that seventh day on which the ancient Jewish God may *rejoice* in himself, his creation and his chosen people—and let us all, all of us, rejoice with him! (pp. 124–125, § 205)

This passage supports the view that Nietzsche was not an anti-Semite; its spirit is remote from the passages on the Jews in *Mein Kampf*, in Marx's *On the Jewish Question*, or in Ezra Pound's wartime broadcasts from Rome. Yet in it an anti-Semite would find his worst fears about the Jews confirmed. And while I do not want to turn Weisberg completely on his head by blaming Nietzsche for the rise of Hitler, the affinity between some of Nietzsche's most strongly asserted ideas and fascist ideology is unmistakable. Indeed, it would not be difficult to stitch together much of the Nazi program out of passages from Nietzsche's abundant and frequently irresponsible writings.[28] Nazism—

---

[28] See Crane Brinton, *Nietzsche*, chap. 8 (1941); George L. Mosse, *The Crisis of German Ideology: Intellectual Origins of the Third Reich* 205–208 (1964); Stern, note 23 above, passim; and, above all, Thomas Mann's great novel of Nietzsche and Nazism, *Doctor Faustus* (1947). Consider three examples of proto-Nazi sentiment in Nietzsche, the first from *Human, All Too Human*, note 25 above, at 230–231 (§ 477): "*War essential.* It is vain rhapsodizing and sentimentality to continue to expect much (even more, to expect a very great deal) from mankind, once it has learned not to wage war . . . Such a highly cultivated, and therefore necessarily weary humanity as that of present-day Europe, needs not only wars but the greatest and most terrible wars (that is, occasional relapses into barbarism) in order not to forfeit to the means of culture its culture and its very existence." The second example is from *The Anti-Christ*, note 25 above, at 116 (§ 2): "What is good?—All that heightens the feeling of power, the will to power, power itself in man. What is bad?—All that proceeds from weakness . . . The weak and ill-constituted shall perish: first principle of *our* philanthropy. And one shall help them to do so. What is more harmful than any vice?—Active sympathy for the ill-constituted and weak—Christianity." The third example is from *Joyful Wisdom*, note 25 above, at 250 (§ 325): "Who can attain to anything great if he does not feel in himself the force and will *to inflict* great pain? . . . Not to perish from internal distress and doubt when one inflicts great suffering and hears the cry of it—that is great, that belongs to greatness."

the triumph of Dionysian over Apollonian values—drew on currents in Romantic thinking that are particularly pronounced in those writings. The German *Volk* united in the person of Adolf Hitler, the triumph of the will over material circumstances, the glorification of war, the replacement of bourgeois by barbarian values, the creation of a master race of the strong and the beautiful, the release of Satanic energies—all this not only is Romantic but is the distinctive Romanticism, strongly flavored with Darwinism, of Nietzsche (though Nietzsche considered himself an enemy of Darwin as well as of the Romantics). It links Nietzsche with fascism, and with those neoromantic modern poets who flirted with fascism (notably Yeats, who was much taken with Nietzsche), at a deeper level than anti-Semitism.[29]

I am suggesting an affinity, not a cause. Romanticism no more causes fascism than classical, neoclassical, or Enlightenment values cause capitalism. Each system of thought is so broad (or so vague) that it can encourage diverse and indeed opposed political movements. One strain in Romantic thinking—the emphasis on organic unities—supports not only the radical communitarianism of the Marxists but also the conservative communitarianism of Edmund Burke.[30] T. S. Eliot's classicism led him in the direction of fascism, while Benthamite utilitarianism, which is anathema to Romantics, can be used to argue both for socialism and for laissez-faire capitalism.[31] As these examples show, even the relation between individualism and Romanticism is ambiguous. Although in one sense the extreme of individualism, in another sense—illustrated not only by fascism but by the Dionysian outlook depicted in Nietzsche's *Birth of Tragedy*; by some applications of utilitarianism, as we shall see shortly; and by the communitarian legal scholarship that we shall get a glimpse of in the next chapter—Romanticism is the annihilation of the boundaries

---

[29] On the affinities between the Romantic movement and fascist (particularly Nazi) ideology see John R. Harrison, *The Reactionaries* 20, 23–24 (1966); Woodring, note 17 above, at 40–41; Fritz Stern, *The Politics of Cultural Despair: A Study in the Rise of the Germanic Ideology* 277–280, 292n, 294 (1961); Ronald Gray, *The German Tradition in Literature 1871–1945* 72–77 (1965); Rohan D'Olier Butler, *The Roots of National Socialism*, chaps. 2, 7 (1942); Mosse, note 28 above, chaps. 1 and 3 and pp. 283, 306; Peter Viereck, *Metapolitics: From the Romantics to Hitler* (1941). On Nietzsche's influence on Yeats see Denis Donoghue, *William Butler Yeats* 52–61 (1971); Otto Bohlmann, *Yeats and Nietzsche: An Exploration of Major Nietzschean Echoes in the Writings of William Butler Yeats* (1982); Frances Nesbitt Oppel, *Mask and Tragedy: Yeats and Nietzsche, 1902–10* (1987).

[30] See James K. Chandler, *Wordsworth's Second Nature: A Study of the Poetry and Politics* (1984); Woodring, note 17 above, at 327.

[31] See William M. Chace, *The Political Identities of Ezra Pound and T. S. Eliot*, pt. 2 (1973); Richard A. Posner, *The Economics of Justice* 33–59 (1981).

between individuals. But I am merely questioning whether Nietzsche (and more broadly the Romantic movement that may be said to have culminated in him) is the antidote to fascism that Weisberg believes him to be.

ANYONE who, having swallowed Romanticism whole, wants to turn the moral order upside down might begin by questioning the taboo against murder. Macbeth can be viewed in this light—as a man risking his immortal soul to challenge the most fundamental norm of conventional morality—though the reader is meant to be appalled rather than (as well as?) thrilled by the challenge. The Romantic cult of spontaneity, epitomized by Blake's aphorism in *The Marriage of Heaven and Hell*, "Sooner murder an infant in its cradle than nurse unacted desires," invites a dismissive attitude toward the murder taboo as toward the other supports of the social order. Such an attitude is found in twentieth-century neoromantic novels by Gide, Genet, Camus, and others. And Nietzsche's celebration of war is consistent with it, although he did not go so far as to approve murder; nor did Blake. Nietzsche's complaint about Christian values is not that they repress homicidal impulses but that they are "anti-life." To see his point one need only compare Odysseus's rejection of immortality in a reasonable facsimile of paradise on Ogygia with the traditional Christian view that our life on earth is merely an unpleasant way station to eternity.

Weisberg interprets several of the novels discussed in *The Failure of the Word* as taking Nietzsche a step further and depicting, with profound disapproval, rancorous *Untermenschen* engaged in the repression of noble, inarticulate—though homicidal—*Übermenschen*. Raskolnikov, an aspiring *Übermensch*, commits two murders, one of which would be first-degree murder in our system, to express *übermenschlich* defiance of conventional morality. Meursault kills an Arab basically because it is a hot day: second-degree murder. Billy Budd strikes a petty officer, killing him, but without intent to kill: manslaughter (at least in civilian law—an essential qualification, as we shall see). Weisberg seems to approve of the inversion of values that he thinks these works bring about, for in a number of passages he expresses sympathy for the criminal act and antipathy toward the people who bring criminals to justice—those people are consumed by ressentiment. Thus he says that "the perception of the criminal act as a declaration of freedom from ressentiment is a fundamental contribution of modern literature," that "the criminal is not prone to ressentiment," and that "almost diametrically opposed to the case of the criminal is that of the intellectual" (pp. 27–28). Meursault rebels against "an arbitrary value system" because he has "his own system of what are, on balance, positive values. Meursault stands, as an individual, for the total rejection of verbal sentimentality. As such, he partakes of the free flow of human existence with honesty, if not perfect Cartesian rationality" (pp. 119–120). The witnesses at Meursault's trial "fail to convey the benignity of the defendant's moral system" (p. 120). Criticized for "willfully ignoring" what Meursault has actually done, Weisberg replies inconsequently that among a group of fictional characters who include both Meursault and one character falsely accused of murder (Dmitri Karamazov) "none, taken alone, is meant to be a sterling moral paradigm."[32] In discussing how the examining magistrate in *Crime and Punishment* uses lawyer's wiles in an effort to entrap Raskolnikov into confessing, Weisberg compares Raskolnikov's plight to that of Joseph K. in *The Trial*, overlooking the fact that Raskolnikov has murdered two people while Joseph K. never even discovers what crime he is accused of. And in calling Billy Budd "an innocent man" and a "joyful innocent" (pp. 155, 162), Weisberg makes light of the fact that Billy Budd struck a lethal blow to a superior officer at sea in wartime; after doing that, Billy was innocent no longer. To Weisberg the notion of innocence is not a legal notion. The legally guilty and the legally innocent are both innocent in his eyes; the law and its agents, being repressive, are guilty.

Yet a lawyer should be the first to realize that law is not merely, or mainly, repressive. Much law is enabling (one might even say liberating) rather than prohibitory[33]—for example, contract law, which enables people to make binding commitments, and property law and corporate law, which encourage investment. Form facilitates; it does not just constrain. (The best example is the rules of language; they are the precondition, rather than an impediment, to communication.) The attack on form is the Dionysian impulse described and applauded by

[32] See Susan Sage Heinzelman and Sanford Levinson, "Words and Wordiness: Reflections on Richard Weisberg's *The Failure of the Word*," 7 *Cardozo Law Review* 453, 465 (1986); Richard H. Weisberg, "More Words on *The Failure of the Word*: A Response to Heinzelman and Levinson," 7 *Cardozo Law Review* 473, 483 (1986).

[33] A point made, with reference to the Constitution, in Steven Holmes, "Precommitment and Self-Rule," in *Constitutionalism and Democracy* (Jon Elster and Rune Slagstad eds. 1988), and discussed further in the next chapter. The corresponding mistake in literary criticism would be to regard the sonnet form as constraining rather than enabling.

Nietzsche. It is a worrisome characteristic of Romantic and neoromantic thought.

Even the repressive part of law serves human liberty, most of the time anyway. A society in which there is no security against the depredations of thieves, rapists, and murderers is a society with little freedom. Dostoevsky and Melville are more sensitive to this point than Weisberg.[34] The reader of *Crime and Punishment* is meant to be horrified by Raskolnikov's conduct[35]—and not because he fails to live up to his self-billing as *Übermensch*. As for Porfiry, the examining magistrate— exaggeratedly described by Weisberg as "coercing Raskolnikov into confession and moral conformity" (p. xii; see also p. 54)—his efforts to catch Raskolnikov off guard are standard, albeit dramatized, interrogative tactics; they are likely and apparently intended to be accepted as such by the readers of *Crime and Punishment*.[36]

Weisberg owes it to his readers to confront forthrightly the question of whether they should condone the killings depicted in the works he discusses. Even if all the killers were approved within their fictional universes, which they are not, it would not follow that we should approve them. His concluding apologetic for Meursault lays Weisberg open to the accusation of not taking crime seriously:

[34] Camus, as should be plain from the discussion in Chapter 2, is another matter: Meursault is in the Gallic tradition of immoral protagonists apparently approved by their creators. See also Albert Camus, "Preface to the American University Edition of *L'Etranger*," in *Albert Camus: A Study of His Work, Lyrical and Critical* 251 (Philip Thody ed. 1967); Germaine Brée, *Camus* 112–117 (1961); René Girard, *"To Double Business Bound": Essays on Literature, Mimesis, and Anthropology*, chap. 2 (1978); Girard, note 2 above, at 257–271. The contrast between Gide and Dostoevsky is well discussed in Carl Niemeyer, "Raskolnikov and Lafcadio," 4 *Modern Fiction Studies* 253 (1958).

[35] See Roger L. Cox, *Between Earth and Heaven: Shakespeare, Dostoevsky, and the Meaning of Christian Tragedy*, chap. 7 (1969); Gary Rosenshield, *Crime and Punishment: The Techniques of the Omniscient Author* 99–121 (1978); Derek Offord, "The Causes of Crime and the Meaning of Law: *Crime and Punishment* and Contemporary Radical Thought," in *New Essays on Dostoyevsky* 41 (Malcolm V. Jones and Garth M. Terry eds. 1983); Avrahm Yarmolinsky, *Dostoevsky: Works and Days* 213–222 (1971); *Crime and Punishment, And the Critics* (Edward Wasiolek ed. 1961).

[36] See Leonid Petrovich Grossman, *Dostoevsky: A Biography* 365 (Mary Mackler trans. 1975); Ernest J. Simmons, *Dostoevsky: The Making of a Novelist* 143–144 (1950). See generally *Twentieth Century Interpretations of Crime and Punishment: A Collection of Critical Essays* (Robert Louis Jackson ed. 1974). And, contrary to Weisberg's assertion, Porfiry cannot be said to have coerced Raskolnikov into confessing. Apart from the absence of coercion in any accepted sense of the word, it is by no means clear that Raskolnikov's confession is due to Porfiry's interrogation. Raskolnikov confesses—and to another official, not to Porfiry—after Porfiry has given up on trying to pin the crime on Raskolnikov.

> When the defendant declares that "the sun" produced the homicide, we know that within a system based on openness to sensual experience, the natural environment on the day of the murder—coupled with the slight drunkenness from the luncheon wine, a condition never revealed by the legal ratiocination—did in effect rob him of free will. Indeed, in an American court, Meursault's lack of real premeditation would have formed the basis of a viable defense; with the "personality" issue virtually inadmissible there as well, Meursault might have received a relatively light sentence for manslaughter. (pp. 121–122; citations omitted)

The unedifying message is obscured by evasive locutions ("in effect," "real," "viable," "relatively") and by the omission to mention that Meursault shot his (unnamed, un-French, depersonalized) victim five times and never expressed the slightest regret or remorse for the murder.

As this example suggests, the danger of inhuman abstraction in legal reasoning is not limited to defendants, such as Antonio and Claudio, but is as great when the victim of a wrong is dehumanized but the wrongdoer is portrayed as richly human.[37] Although a consistent commitment to legalism might have saved Meursault, a consistent commitment to viewing his case in its full human dimensions—and thus with due regard for the Arab's humanity as well as for Meursault's— might have condemned him. Weisberg overlooks both possibilities, together with a third: if "justice" depends on the type of person the victim and the injurer are, then the popular man will get justice and the unpopular one will not. If the nonconformist is by virtue of the fact likely to end up an outlaw (one interpretation of the trial and condemnation of Socrates under the Athenian system of popular justice), the pressure on people to conform to community norms will be intensified. Romantic self-assertion can lead to the deadliest conformity; the association made in the Western liberal tradition between legalism and individualism is not arbitrary.

I do not belong to the school that believes that literature must be

---

[37] See Conor Cruise O'Brien, *Albert Camus of Europe and Africa* 25–26 (1970). A modern example is the murder of a female student at Yale by a Hispanic from a poor home who not only received great sympathy from the Catholic Church but was given only a short prison sentence for his crime. See Willard Gaylin, *The Killing of Bonnie Garland: A Question of Justice* (1982); Peter Meyer, *The Yale Murder* (1982). See generally Lynne N. Henderson, "Legality and Empathy," 85 *Michigan Law Review* 1574 (1987). Might not the charge of lack of empathy for victims of crime be leveled against *A Jury of Her Peers* (Chapter 2)? Could not that story, too, have been told from the victim's standpoint? Maybe he was jealous of his wife's bird, like Harry in John Steinbeck's short story *The White Quail*, who kills, apparently out of jealousy, the bird that his wife loves.

morally uplifting to be great.[38] Great writers have a remarkable ability to make the reader suspend ethical judgment while reading. Nor do I think that immoral literature causes immoral behavior. (I shall have more to say about these matters in Chapters 6 and 7.) But when a "literary lawyer" places literature in the service of justice, he makes the ethical content of literature relevant. Weisberg has allowed his admiration for Camus as a writer to cause him to find ethical uplift in an immoral work of fiction. Law, a bastion of Apollonian values, is problematic for anyone whose outlook is Dionysian. Weisberg has not faced up to the implications of transposing such an outlook from literature to law.

## Billy Budd and The Brothers Karamazov

Weisberg's *pièce de résistance* is an unorthodox reading of *Billy Budd*. The eponymous hero of Melville's novella is a young seaman impressed onto a British man-of-war during the war between Britain and the French Directory (the interregnum between the Revolutionary regime and Napoleon). The British navy has recently experienced a serious mutiny and everyone is on the lookout for a recurrence, especially among impressed seamen. John Claggart, the petty officer in charge of security on the ship, decides to frame Billy, and he therefore tells Captain Vere that Billy is a mutineer. Vere does not believe Claggart, and summons Billy to confront his accuser in the captain's cabin. Billy, who suffers from a speech impediment, is unable to respond to Claggart's accusations. Vere puts his arm on Billy's shoulder in a fatherly way and tells him that there is no hurry about speaking; the speechless and enraged Billy reacts by striking Claggart dead with a single punch. Vere convenes a drumhead (that is, summary) court-martial, the members of which are inclined to leniency until Vere reminds them that striking one's superior in wartime is a capital offense and that any leniency might encourage mutiny. They reluctantly sentence Billy to death and he is hanged the next morning—his last words being, "God save Captain Vere." Vere, fatally wounded in a battle shortly afterward, dies whispering "Billy Budd."

In Weisberg's interpretation, Billy is Rousseau's noble savage, Nietzsche's *Übermensch*, Wordsworth's Seer blest; Vere as well as

---

[38] A school illustrated by Edmund Fuller, *Man in Modern Fiction: Some Minority Opinions on Contemporary American Writing* (1958) (see id. at 12 for Fuller's opinion of Meursault), and by John Gardner, *On Moral Fiction* (1978).

Claggart is consumed by ressentiment; the execution of Billy is a gross injustice. Although capturing some elements in an ambivalent narrative, this interpretation fails to explain some of its most important features: that Melville portrays Billy Budd not as (or not just as) a pagan, but as a stand-in for Christ; that Vere is presented as a man of wisdom, humanity, and moral courage; that Billy is depicted as having been lawfully found guilty of a capital offense; and that leniency might spark a mutiny, given the recent mutinies in the British navy and Claggart's position as the ship's security officer.[39]

Weisberg argues that the court-martial was irregular. But his tone is one of special pleading—for example, in the contention that Claggart was not "in the execution of his office" when Billy struck him (pp. 154–155). (He was; ferreting out mutiny was his foremost task as the ship's security officer.) Weisberg's argument that the death penalty is excessive for Billy Budd's offense misreads the historical record: a seaman in the eighteenth-century British navy who struck and killed a superior officer was quite likely to be executed. Illustrative is the case of seaman John Cumming, tried in 1784 for striking the boatswain of his ship and sentenced to be hanged at the fore-yardarm, with no recommendation for mercy, even though he apparently did not kill the boatswain.[40] Most of the supposed procedural irregularities that Weisberg has brought to light reflect merely the difference between the fairly elaborate procedures required in a regular court-martial and the informality of a drumhead court-martial. Weisberg, it is true, argues that under English law Vere should have waited until the ship rejoined the fleet before proceeding against Billy and should then have asked the admiral commanding the fleet to convene a regular court-martial; the drumhead court-martial was proper only if Billy's striking Claggart could be construed as mutinous. But there is authority that striking a superior officer in wartime was considered mutinous per se.[41] And we must not read modern compunctions about capital punishment into a story written a century ago about events a century before that. Life was cheap on an eighteenth-century British warship.

Even if Weisberg were correct about eighteenth-century law and

[39] L. H. LaRue, in his review of *The Failure of the Word* (see note 6 above, at 318–320), and the student author of a book review in 84 *Michigan Law Review* 974 (1986), also criticize Weisberg's interpretation.
[40] See John MacArthur, *Principles and Practices of Naval and Military Courts Martial*, vol. 2, at 437 (4th ed. 1813); see id., vol. 2, at 419–451, for a detailed survey of cases.
[41] See Thomas Simmons, *The Constitution and Practice of Courts Martial* 79 (7th ed. 1875).

practice, his interpretation would be refuted by the absence of any suggestion in the text of *Billy Budd*—nor could the reader be assumed to know from other sources—that the court-martial and execution of Billy are illegal. Harsh, maybe horrible, maybe even precipitate (the ship's surgeon, a member of the court-martial, thought that so unusual a case should have been referred to the admiral)—yes. But illegal—no. Not Vere but the narrator tells the reader that the drumhead court-martial was proper in the circumstances.[42] Nor does Melville scatter clues that the narrator himself might be unreliable or that the reader would be well advised to conduct research into eighteenth-century British law.

It is, moreover, a novelistic imperative that Billy Budd should be tried on the ship. A delay to rejoin the fleet, followed by a shift of the action to a court-martial in which Vere would play no role, would have blurred the plot and delayed the dénouement, to no artistic purpose. And to have given Billy a punishment clearly lawful for a drumhead court-martial—a lashing, say—would have robbed the novella of its tragic overtones. A further point relates to the combination of law functions in the person of Vere, a combination that would be highly questionable in any setting other than that of a drumhead court-martial. Essentially Vere is prosecutor, jury, and judge all in one; the nominal members of the court-martial are foils. This streamlining of legal procedure is necessary, however, to maintain the brisk pace of the narrative. In literature, art trumps due process. The liberties Melville takes with the law for artistic purposes recall Shakespeare's strategy in *The Merchant of Venice* and *Measure for Measure*. We begin to see how an understanding of literature on legal themes as a coherent literary genre can help prevent misunderstandings about the literary significance of departures from legal regularity.

Although the officers of the drumhead court-martial exhibit misgivings—the surgeon even questions Vere's sanity—they do so not because of legal reservations but because Billy Budd is such an attractive person and because the provocation (in a layman's, not a lawyer's, sense) for striking Claggart was so great. The opposition portrayed is between the sympathies of subordinate officers of narrow outlook and limited understanding and the responsibilities that rest on the captain's shoulders alone. (This is another reason for the combination in Vere of legal

---

[42] "In wartime on the field or in the fleet, a mortal punishment decreed by a drumhead court— on the field sometimes decreed by but a nod from the general—follows without delay on the heel of convicting, without appeal." Herman Melville, *Billy Budd, Sailor (An Inside Narrative)* 114 (Harrison Hayford and Merton M. Sealts, Jr., eds. 1962). My page references to *Billy Budd* are to this edition.

functions that in the real world normally are separated.) Vere is isolated by his intelligence. There is no one with whom he might take counsel or share responsibility for dealing with the consequences of Billy's outburst. The surgeon's speculation that Vere might be crazy should not be taken at face value; rather, it is a commentary on the surgeon's inability to understand a greatly superior person.

Assuming the role of devil's advocate in almost a literal sense, Weisberg argues that Billy Budd is Nietzsche's "blond beast" and Claggart is Jesus Christ: "Claggart-Christ," Weisberg calls him (p. 174). Billy does have the qualities of natural man according to Nietzsche, as elaborated by Weisberg—robust health and high animal spirits, primal rage but no rancor or vengefulness, heedlessness for the future (he does not worry about being impressed onto a warship in wartime), guilelessness, and inarticulateness (symbolized by the speech impediment that conveniently silences him at the critical moment), a trait he shares with Meursault in *The Stranger*.[43] But Billy is also associated in the novella with Adam before the fall (Christ is frequently referred to in Christian literature as "the second Adam") and with the Lamb of God; there are heavenly portents attending his execution; and he forgives Vere. The novella also emphasizes that Vere has a fatherly attitude toward Billy, thus putting us in mind of the fact that, in Christian theology, God sacrificed his Son to save mankind. Claggart, in contrast, is repeatedly likened to a serpent. A monster from the deep, he is a symbol of Satan, not of Jesus Christ. True, he has the same initials as Christ and dies at about the same age when Christ died; but even a rabid anti-Christian—even a Nietzsche—could not find any similarity in character or deeds between Christ and Claggart.[44]

The other inversion that Weisberg performs on Melville's fictive world is to make Vere a villain. Weisberg is not the only critic who

[43] A curiosity of Nietzschean psychology is that the *Übermensch* tends to lack a mind. Empathy, sensitivity, forward planning, and other characteristic human mental operations are in Nietzsche's view devices by which the *Untermensch* seeks to overcome his weakness and express his will to power. "He who possesses strength divests himself of mind." *Twilight of the Idols: or How to Philosophize with a Hammer*, note 25 above, at 76 ("Expeditions of an Untimely Man," 14). See also *Daybreak*, note 25 above, at 90 (§ 142).

[44] Like Weisberg, Nietzsche believed that Christianity had destroyed the Roman Empire (others might think it extended the Empire's life). But unlike Weisberg he distinguished between Jesus Christ, whom he thought admirable and even "pagan," and institutional Christianity, founded by Paul, whom Nietzsche loathed. See *The Anti-Christ*, note 25 above, at 139–153, 180–183 (§§ 27–40, 58–59). It was Nietzsche, after all, who said, "In reality there has been only one Christian, and he died on the Cross." Id. at 151 (§ 39). There is no evidence that Melville outdid Nietzsche in hostility to Christ and Christianity. See generally Rowland A. Sherrill, "Melville and Religion," in *A Companion to Melville Studies*, note 6 above, at 481.

believes that Melville intended readers to condemn Vere's conduct.[45] Most liberals in the contemporary sense of the word (and most literary critics are liberals in this sense) are uncomfortable with authority, including military authority, and hate capital punishment. They do not find Vere a sympathetic figure, and some of them project their lack of sympathy onto Melville. But Weisberg goes them one better by accusing Vere not only of having acted with undue harshness but also of having violated military law to obtain a death sentence against Billy Budd—and of having done so out of rancorous envy of Admiral Nelson. Weisberg's thesis is that Vere, though a competent officer, is no Nelson (which is true); that Vere resents the comparison (which is false); and that because Nelson and Billy Budd share the quality of perfectly uniting thought and action, Vere identifies one with the other[46] and condemns Billy out of envy of Nelson (which is preposterous). It is almost a detail that Weisberg makes aesthetic hash out of *Billy Budd* by breaking the novella into two unrelated stories: a struggle between paganism and Christianity that ends with the death of Claggart (which dooms Billy—that is, Rome), and the acting out of Vere's envy of Nelson, which begins with Claggart's death and ends with Vere's death.

Melville provides no textual clue that Vere might envy Nelson, let alone that such envy might have impelled Vere to condemn Billy Budd. (Remember that until Billy assaults Claggart, Vere, far from trying to entrap Billy, is trying to protect him from Claggart.) The novella presents Vere to the reader with high accolades: "a sailor of distinction even in a time prolific of renowned seamen . . . Vere had seen much service, been in various engagements, always acquitting himself as an officer mindful of the welfare of his men, but never tolerating an infraction of discipline; thoroughly versed in the science of his profes-

---

[45] Weisberg summarizes the views of these critics on pp. 141–145; see also Brook Thomas, *Cross-Examinations of Law and Literature: Cooper, Hawthorne, Stowe, and Melville*, pt. 3 (1987). The contrary view is well argued in Milton R. Stern, "Introduction," in *Billy Budd, Sailor (An Inside Narrative)* vii (Milton R. Stern ed. 1975).

[46] The identification is far-fetched. Weak and sickly to begin with, only 5 feet 2 inches tall, Nelson lost both an eye and an arm in combat. And, far from being a free spirit, he apotheosized duty, as in the famous signal to the fleet before Trafalgar: "England expects every man to do his duty." Physically unimpressive, indeed crippled, yet eloquent and a man of authority, he is the opposite of Billy Budd. And he talks just like Vere. "Our country has the first demand for our services; and private convenience or happiness must ever give way to the public good. Duty is the great business of a sea officer: all private considerations must give way to it, however painful." Quoted in Robert Southey, *The Life of Nelson*, vol. 1, at 69 (1813). Nelson once wrote a letter congratulating an admiral for hanging four seamen on a Sunday and said he would have approved hanging them on Christmas. *Dispatches and Letters of Vice Admiral Lord Viscount Nelson*, vol. 2, at 408–410 (1845).

sion, and intrepid to the verge of temerity, though never injudiciously so" (p. 60). To take Vere down a peg Weisberg quotes the following from the same page: "Ashore, in the garb of a civilian, scarce any one would have taken him for a sailor." But Weisberg omits the words that immediately follow: ". . . more especially that he never garnished unprofessional talk with nautical terms, and grave in his bearing, evinced little appreciation of mere humor . . . But in fact this unobtrusiveness of demeanor may have proceeded from a certain unaffected modesty of manhood sometimes accompanying a resolute nature" (p. 60). It is true that Vere is no Nelson, but neither was Nelson in 1797, for that was before the battles of the Nile, Copenhagen, and Trafalgar—the victories for which he is mainly remembered.

Neither the apostrophe to Nelson in chapter 4 of *Billy Budd*, nor the reference in chapter 5 to Nelson's having prevented a possible mutiny on the *Theseus* by his mere presence, is intended to pull Vere down. There is no mention of any acts of violence on the *Theseus*, and we can be sure that, if there had been violence, Nelson would have responded with the utmost firmness. The purpose of the references to Nelson is to lend verisimilitude to the novella (as with the insertion of Martin Luther into *Michael Kohlhass*) and maybe even to suggest what Vere might have become had he not fallen in action shortly after the trial and execution of Billy Budd. For someone remarks of Vere, "'Spite the gazettes, Sir Horatio [Nelson] . . . is at bottom scarce a better seaman or fighter" than Vere, albeit Vere is "pedantic" (p. 63). Maybe, then, Vere dies to leave open the possibility that he would have had a glorious career. Or maybe he dies because he committed an impious deed—maybe you do not kill Christ and live. Maybe he dies so that Melville can show us through Vere's dying words the impact on a sensitive person of doing one's duty.

Weisberg is right to see in Billy and Vere the contrast between natural and civilized man, a contrast underscored by Billy's stammer and lack of education and by Vere's bookishness; Vere is no rough-and-tumble old salt. But it is unlikely that Melville would have evaluated the contrast as Nietzsche might have done. And Weisberg overlooks the narrative functions both of Billy's stammer and of Vere's bookishness. The stammer is needed to prevent Billy from putting up a defense against Claggart's accusations. If he could defend himself verbally, his action in striking Claggart would be unintelligible, or at least out of character for Billy; and the striking of Claggart is necessary to the unfolding of the story. Vere's bookishness makes plausible the elaborate argumentation by which he seeks to persuade the court-martial that it must convict

Billy and sentence him to death; places him on a higher intellectual plane than the officers of the court-martial; and, most important, by depicting him as an introspective man rather than merely a tough military commander, imparts tragic overtones to his decision to condemn Billy Budd and to his whispering Billy's name on his own deathbed. To the historical Nelson the trial and hanging of Billy would have been all in a day's work and quickly forgotten.

The most important point that Weisberg overlooks is that Vere is in sole command of a major warship in a major war. This is an awesome responsibility. When the most popular sailor on board kills the most hated petty officer in circumstances of provocation that do not, however, extenuate the capital nature of his offense under the Articles of War, Vere, a sensitive man and not a martinet, finds himself torn between private feeling and public responsibility. He chooses the latter. We are not meant to think that he had no choice, but no more are we meant to think that he was acting illegally or out of envy. His bookishness, his "pedantry," are intended to make us realize that Vere *knew* he faced a tough choice.

If Melville in *Billy Budd* "is wondering whether youth, feeling, and love can survive into the drabness of a civilization dominated by material and organizational values," still Vere is presented as "a very superior and very human man," "faced with an awful choice," as Charles Reich, whom I am quoting, acknowledges.[47] Robert Ferguson points out that the choice is between obedience to positive and to natural law, and emphasizes the affinity between Vere's style of legal reasoning and the approach of the legal positivists—notably Holmes—which was making headway when Melville was writing *Billy Budd*.[48] Vere refuses

---

[47] Charles A. Reich, "The Tragedy of Justice in *Billy Budd*," 56 *Yale Review* 368, 379, 381, 388–389 (1967).

[48] See Robert A. Ferguson, *Law and Letters in American Culture* 288–290 (1984). Holmes's classic of legal positivism, *The Common Law*, had appeared in 1881; what better antidote to natural-law conceptions of justice than to stress, as *The Common Law* had done, that law originates in vengeance? See my book review of Kellogg, *The Formative Essays of Justice Holmes* and Pohlman, *Justice Oliver Wendell Holmes and Utilitarian Jurisprudence*, in 53 *George Washington Law Review* 870, 874 (1985). Helpful discussions of *Billy Budd*, besides Reich's and Ferguson's, include William Domnarski, "Law-Literature Criticism: Charting a Desirable Course with *Billy Budd*," 34 *Journal of Legal Education* 702 (1984); Thomas J. Scorza, *In the Time before Steamships: Billy Budd, the Limits of Politics and Modernity* (1979), especially chap. 6; Sealts, note 6 above; Christopher W. Sten, "Vere's Use of the 'Forms': Means and Ends in *Billy Budd*," 47 *American Literature* 37 (1975); Stern, note 45 above; Thomas, note 45 above, pt. 3; John P. McWilliams, Jr., "Innocent Criminal or Criminal Innocence: The Trial in American Fiction," in Carl S. Smith, John P. McWilliams, Jr., and Maxwell Bloomfield, *Law and American Literature* 45, 71–80 (1983); Barbara Johnson, "Melville's Fist: The Execution of *Billy*

to allow the positive law governing naval discipline to be trumped by appeal to the "higher law" under which Claggart's death was well deserved. In the trial scene Vere says: "Before a court less arbitrary and more merciful than a martial one, that plea [that Billy Budd intended neither mutiny nor homicide] would largely extenuate. At the Last Assizes it shall acquit. But how here? We proceed under the law of the Mutiny Act" (p. 111). In terms of the Table of Opposed Conceptions of Law (see Chapter 2), Vere is (so far) firmly in the left-hand column—a problematic location, as we saw. There is a touch of Angelo when he says, "Would it be so much ourselves that would condemn as it would be martial law operating through us? For that law and the rigor of it, we are not responsible" (pp. 110–111). He says that "the heart . . . sometimes the feminine in man . . . must be ruled out" (p. 111). There is a touch of Brutus when he says that "did he [Billy] know our hearts, I take him to be of that generous nature that he would feel even for us on whom in this military necessity so heavy a compulsion is laid" (p. 113).

Vere does not just invoke the letter of the law, however; he argues policy, as a lawyer would say—the danger of mutiny. This is the most unsettling part of Vere's argument, even though it has nothing to do with legalism or ressentiment—even though it is, indeed, the rejection of legalism. Vere's emphasis on Billy Budd's moral innocence, as when he says, "How can we adjudge to summary and shameful death a fellow creature innocent before God, and whom we feel to be so?" (p. 110), puts the reader in mind of the most disturbing feature of utilitarian ethics: it countenances the sacrifice of an innocent person for the sake of the general good. This type of utilitarian "balancing" owes nothing to legal formalism—to which Bentham, the greatest of the utilitarians, was resolutely opposed. Utilitarianism treats the whole society as a single individual, and this equation makes it as natural to kill one person for the greater good of society as it would be to remove a cancerous organ. This is *Gemeinschaft* rather than *Gesellschaft* thinking. But before accusing Vere of a particularly nasty form of utilitarian thinking, one must

---

Budd," in Johnson, *The Critical Difference: Essays in the Contemporary Rhetoric of Reading* 79 (1980); *Twentieth Century Interpretations of Billy Budd: A Collection of Critical Essays* (Howard P. Vincent ed. 1971). Of course one could believe both that the novella approves of Vere and that it is wrong to do so. This is the tack taken by an article that treats *Billy Budd* as a paean to authoritarian values: Stephen Vizinczey, "Engineers of a Sham: How Literature Lies about Power," *Harper's*, June 1986, at 69, 71–73. Sealts, note 6 above, at 418, offers (without endorsing) a fascinating biographical interpretation of *Billy Budd*, in which Vere is Melville and Billy is a composite of Melville's sons, with whom he had a troubled relationship.

remember that in the eyes of the law Billy was guilty of a capital crime; he would be guilty of a serious (though not capital) crime under modern military law as well.

In his *Cross-Examinations of Law and Literature* (see note 45), Brook Thomas gives an interesting twist to criticism of Vere. He is unimpressed by Weisberg's procedural criticisms, which he thinks reflect a Vere-like "legalistic point of view that focuses on technicalities" (pp. 211–212). For he is persuaded that the same result would have been reached—Billy's execution—even if every legal formality had been observed. Moreover, Weisberg's emphasis on procedural irregularity detracts from what Thomas considers the central message of the novella—that law, which in Thomas's view is a means by which the upper classes oppress the lower, is such a beguiling ideology that it persuades even its victims that it is just: "Captain Vere projects such an image of fairness that not even Billy himself protests the call for his execution" (p. 219). But if Captain Vere's ideology is really so beguiling, it is difficult to argue, at least from the text, that Melville is not himself beguiled by it; and indeed Thomas assumes rather than argues that the reader is meant to pierce the image of fairness to the underlying reality of oppression. Moreover, like Weisberg and other detractors of Vere, Thomas does not acknowledge the practical reasons for Vere to let the law (the law as Melville presents it to the reader, whatever the eighteenth-century reality may have been) take its harsh course.

Once it is acknowledged that Vere faces a difficult choice, it becomes an open question whether readers are meant to think he made the right one. In support of an affirmative answer there is first the fact that Claggart had a cabal of informers on the ship; what will they think and say if Billy Budd receives lenient treatment for killing their boss? Also, Vere explains to the court-martial that to the unsophisticated crew Billy's deed,

> however it be worded in the announcement, will be plain homicide committed in a flagrant act of mutiny. What penalty for that should follow, they know. But it does not follow. *Why?* They will ruminate. You know what sailors are. Will they not revert to the recent outbreak at the Nore? Aye. They know the well-founded alarm—the panic it struck throughout England. Your clement sentence they would account pusillanimous. They would think that we flinch, that we are afraid of them—afraid of practicing a lawful rigor singularly demanded at this juncture, lest it should provoke new troubles. (pp. 112–113)

Chapter 29 of *Billy Budd* provides corroboration for Vere's concerns. A newspaper widely circulated throughout the fleet is quoted as having given an inaccurate and sensational account of how Billy, the "ring-leader" of a sinister plot (p. 130), had stabbed Claggart to death while being arraigned by him before the captain.

Melville, like Shakespeare, seems not to have believed that the affairs of a fallen world could be regulated by exclusive reference to higher law. The execution of Billy Budd is presented as a justifiable act within the implied if distinctly earthbound moral universe of the novella. The book is sufficiently ambiguous to enable the reader to shade its meaning according to whether he sympathizes more with Nature, personified by Billy Budd, or Culture and Society, personified by Captain Vere, but it does not support a reading in which Vere's behavior is lawless and resentful.

To disregard Vere's reasons for condemning Billy is like disregarding Creon's reasons for condemning Antigone—but worse, because Vere has better reasons than Creon. In neither case, however, is it just a matter of upholding "the law," come what may (*ruat caelum ut fiat iustitia*). Although that is an important consideration to both Vere and Creon, neither is a prisoner of the impoverished jurisprudence that regards the law as impervious to the equity of the facts, to mercy, and to justice. Both think they have justice (granted, human rather than divine justice) on their side, and both have some basis for thinking this. Robert Cover's attempt to equate Vere (and Creon) to the judges—including Melville's father-in-law, Chief Justice Lemuel Shaw of the Massachusetts Supreme Judicial Court—who before the Civil War enforced the slave laws because they were "the law" is unconvincing;[49] the law enforced by Vere was harsh but, in the desperate circumstances in which it was invoked, not vicious.

We can pursue the affinity between Vere's mode of thinking and that of Oliver Wendell Holmes by considering Holmes's opinion in *Buck v. Bell*, the opinion that contains his famous aphorism "three generations of imbeciles are enough."[50] A Virginia statute authorized the compulsory sterilization of inmates of certain state institutions if the inmate had a hereditary form of insanity or imbecility. The opinion describes Carrie

---

[49] See Robert M. Cover, *Justice Accused: Antislavery and the Judicial Process* 1–6 (1975). Cover properly emphasizes the use of formalistic techniques to mask the character of the slave laws being enforced. See id. at 229–238; cf. Bruce McLeod, "Rules and Rhetoric," 23 *Osgoode Hall Law Journal* 305, 318–319 (1985). It is only his attempt to analogize the judges to Vere and Creon that I criticize.

[50] 274 U.S. 200, 207 (1927). See Chapter 6 for further discussion of this opinion; and note that, in all probability, none of the "three generations" involved in the case was in fact feebleminded. See Paul A. Lombardo, "Three Generations, No Imbeciles: New Light on *Buck v. Bell*," 60 *New York University Law Review* 30 (1985).

Buck, an inmate of a state institution for the "feebleminded," as the feebleminded daughter of another feebleminded inmate of the institution, and the mother of an illegitimate feebleminded child. In holding that neither the equal protection nor the due process clause of the Fourteenth Amendment forbade the state to sterilize Carrie Buck, Holmes wrote: "We have seen more than once that the public welfare may call upon the best citizens for their lives. It would be strange if it could not call upon those who already sap the strength of the State for these lesser sacrifices, often not felt to be such by those concerned, in order to prevent our being swamped with incompetence" (p. 207). This passage mixes nationalism (in the allusion to conscription, used by this country not only in World War I but also in the Civil War, in which Holmes had been wounded three times), Darwinism, and utilitarianism—all three of which "isms" share the quality of being concerned with aggregates rather than individuals (nation, species, society)—in a brew congenial to Captain Vere, as to much nineteenth-century thought, but distasteful to most modern students of law as well as of literature. It might have been distasteful to Melville as well, but would he not have thought that the Virginia authorities, like Captain Vere, had made a *permissible* choice?

The examples of both Vere and Holmes show the perils of trying to hold the two sides of the Table of Opposed Conceptions of Law separate. We saw how Vere worked both sides. Holmes, in his emphasis on objective standards of liability and therefore on the justice of sometimes sacrificing innocents, and in his positivism, was very much a man of the left-hand column (rule, formalism, and so forth); but in his rejection of any general principle of strict liability and in his insistence that the life of the law had been experience rather than logic, he was very much a man of the right-hand column. Indeed, he is the father of legal realism.[51] Vere embodies the same duality. These examples are further evidence that the concept of law is not exhausted by its conventional association with rules and objectivity. The fact that literature can help us see this is one of the fruits of the law and literature movement.

---

[51] The classics of Holmes's jurisprudence are *The Common Law* (1881), and "The Path of the Law," 10 *Harvard Law Review* 457 (1897). Thomas, note 45 above, at 232–236, in arguing that Holmes's jurisprudence undercuts Vere's position, overlooks the "hard" side of that jurisprudence—the separation of law and morals, the emphasis on sacrifice, the Social Darwinism, the disdain for natural law. Although it would be a gross oversimplification to regard Holmes as the reincarnation of Thrasymachus (see Book I of Plato's *Republic*), there is that element in Holmes.

AMONG the least plausible features in Weisberg's account of *Billy Budd* is his equation of Claggart with Christ. The hostility to Christianity that this equation implies is not surprising given Weisberg's belief that Christianity, along with legalism, was a principal cause of the destruction of European Jewry by the Nazis. Nor, given his reading of *Billy Budd*, is one surprised that Weisberg should find in *The Brothers Karamazov* an implied rejection, rather than a celebration, as most readers have thought, of Christianity. Let us see whether the text supports Weisberg's interpretation.

*The Brothers Karamazov* (1880) is, among other things, a "legal" novel, about one-fifth of it being devoted to the interrogation and trial of Dmitri Karamazov (the legal component in *Crime and Punishment* is smaller). Thought by many the greatest novel ever written, it demands consideration in a book on law and literature quite apart from the role it plays in *The Failure of the Word*.[52]

The novel is really two novels, skillfully interwoven. The first is the action–packed love–and–detective story of the rivalry between Dmitri and his father, Fyodor, for the beautiful Grushenka; Fyodor's murder by his valet, Smerdyakov, who probably is also his illegitimate son; and the arrest, interrogation, erroneous conviction, and sentencing of Dmitri for the crime. The second is a philosophical novel (the genre exemplified by *The Magic Mountain*) about religion. The principals in this novel are Ivan and Alyosha, Fyodor's other (legitimate) sons; Alyosha's mentor, Father Zossima; the boy Ilusha; and Ivan's fictional creation, the Grand Inquisitor. The philosophical novel is not only more interesting and resonant but, paradoxically, more vivid than the (comparatively) realistic novel, though it could not exist without the latter, which provides the essential narrative scaffold. The dependence is mutual. Ivan's atheism, and its corollary principle that "everything is lawful," operating on the warped intellect of Smerdyakov, makes the murder possible; while Dmitri's assault on Ilusha's father—one of the causes of Ilusha's

---

[52] For compendious background and commentary see Victor Terras, *A Karamazov Companion: Commentary on the Genesis, Language, and Style of Dostoevsky's Novel* (1981), and also Fyodor Dostoevsky, *The Brothers Karamazov* (Constance Garnett and Ralph E. Matlaw trans., Matlaw ed. 1976) (text plus commentary). For good brief discussions see Maximilian Braun, "*The Brothers Karamazov* as an Expository Novel," 6 *Canadian-American Slavic Studies* 199 (1972); A. Boyce Gibson, *The Religion of Dostoevsky*, chap. 7 (1973). On Dostoevsky's life and work see, besides works cited in notes 35 and 36 above, Konstantin Mochulsky, *Dostoevsky: His Life and Work* (1967), chaps. 22 and 23 of which deal with *The Brothers Karamazov*; and Edward Wasiolek, *Dostoevsky: The Major Fiction* (1964). On the characteristics of Russian legal procedure in Dostoevsky's time—including the use of juries (a Western import) at a time when they were fast disappearing from the rest of the Continent—see Samuel Kucherov, *Courts, Lawyers, and Trials under the Last Three Tsars* (1953), especially pp. 74–86, 168–179.

tragic death—suggests that the conviction of Dmitri, though a judicial error, is consistent with a higher justice, is part of the divine plan, and indeed is the condition of Dmitri's redemption.

The philosophical novel revolves around the question, how can the existence of God be reconciled with the prevalence of suffering in the world, and in particular the suffering of children, that is, of innocents? Ivan's inability to answer the question to his own satisfaction drives him to atheism, then madness. The suffering of children is rendered with great vividness, culminating in the story of Ilusha; and many other challenges are offered to religious belief—ranging from the premature decay of Father Zossima's corpse to the powerful arguments of the Grand Inquisitor. But all the challenges are overcome by the end. We come to understand that the suffering, the baseness, the horrors, and the scandals of the human condition are both redeemable and redemptive. They are a necessary condition of a religious faith that is chosen rather than imposed, and hence of salvation through resurrection. For example, the premature decay of Zossima's corpse, by shaking Alyosha's faith, enables him to rebuild it on a foundation of free choice rather than supernatural coercion.

The legal scenes belong to the "realistic novel"—yet not entirely. Dmitri is innocent of his father's murder in a legal sense, but both he and Ivan are guilty in a moral sense: Dmitri for wanting to kill his father and for being, in fact, quite capable of doing so in the right circumstances, and, more profoundly, for being—as he frequently and truthfully confesses—a scoundrel; Ivan for having inspired, if unwittingly, Smerdyakov to commit the actual crime. Moreover, Dmitri's conviction and sentencing are presented as stations on the way to his salvation.

Another connection between the legal scenes and the philosophical novel is the idea expressed by several of the characters that if God does not exist, anything goes. To the possible response that law by itself can deter crime, making supernatural sanctions unnecessary, the trial and conviction of Dmitri provide rebuttal. The wrong man is convicted, while the murderer escapes through suicide. Smerdyakov hangs himself on the eve of Dmitri's trial; since he does not believe in God or an afterlife and his life is a miserable one, suicide provides a costless escape. It also seals Dmitri's fate, by making it impossible for the real murderer ever to confess (as had happened, in the real-life murder case on which Dostoevsky modeled Dmitri's case, ten years after the conviction of the innocent defendant). We are made to feel the inadequacies of secular justice.

There is also the contrast between the rational, but futile, procedures of the legal system and the spiritual intensity not only of Alyosha and Father Zossima but even of Dmitri. Amidst the cruelty, the passions, and the tears that saturate the rest of the novel, the legal scenes stand out as islands of humane rationality. The atmosphere of these scenes is entirely different from that of the legal scenes in *The Stranger*. It is true that the authorities, and even Dmitri's own lawyer, the brilliant Fetyukovitch, do not understand Dmitri.[53] And we are led to understand that the members of the jury are hostile to Dmitri because of his outrageous behavior on many occasions during his sojourn in the town where his father lived and the events of the novel take place. Yet in point of solicitude for the rights of the accused and for finding the truth, both the preliminary interrogation in the hotel where Dmitri is arrested and the trial can stand comparison with modern American procedure. The basic reason for Dmitri's conviction is not that the jury is prejudiced against him because of his wild behavior (though it is), but that the evidence of his guilt is overwhelming; Smerdyakov framed him brilliantly, and is dead. Not only is the trial basically fair, but Dmitri's sentence (twenty years of penal servitude in Siberia) is lenient for the time, place, and circumstances, which the judges and jury believe to be parricide in the course of theft.

The parallels between nineteenth-century Russian and twentieth-century American criminal procedure are underscored by the following contrast between Dostoevsky's two great legal novels, *Crime and Punishment* and *The Brothers Karamazov*: the first emphasizes inquisitorial procedure, the second adversary procedure. Oddly, considering all the suffering that is depicted in *The Brothers Karamazov*, it is a sunnier, more exhilarating novel. This impression may be connected with the freer give-and-take, and the greater drama, of adversary procedure. The inquisitorial method of Continental and chancery proceedings lends itself to novels of protraction and obsession, which *Crime and Punishment* (like *The Trial* and *Bleak House*) is but which *The Brothers Karamazov*,

---

[53] The same problem occurs in a modern "legal" story, Katherine Anne Porter's *Noon Wine*, perceptively discussed in James Boyd White, *Heracles' Bow: Essays on the Rhetoric and Poetics of the Law* 181–191 (1985). Pursuing this theme, one might suggest that Vere's commitment to rational methods of inquiry (suggested by, among other things, his name, with its echo of "veritas" and "verity") prevents him from truly understanding, though sympathizing deeply with, Billy Budd. Melville's short story *Benito Cereno* has a similar theme. One begins to see how seemingly disparate works of literature on legal themes compose an order of literature, repaying study together.

like *Pickwick Papers* (another novel in which a jury renders an erroneous verdict), is not.

*The Brothers Karamazov* contains implied criticism of law, but the criticism has less to do with the particulars of Russian criminal justice circa 1880 (with the possible exception of the use of juries) than with the very idea of secular justice. Not only does the legal system get the facts wrong, but the elaborate reconstructions of Dmitri's character, which dominate the great closing arguments of the prosecutor and Fetyukovitch, miss the essential dimensions of that character. This failure connects with the novel's religious theme at a deep level. To Dostoevsky, reconciliation of the goodness of God with the fact of human suffering lies neither in authority (the miracles, expected but not forthcoming, at Zossima's death) nor in reason (where Ivan searches futilely), but in faith, deepened by that very suffering and affording insight into the divine plan. *Credo quia absurdum est.* The idea that law, despite or maybe because of its commitment to reason, misunderstands life is one that *The Brothers Karamazov* shares with *The Stranger*; but in the earlier and greater novel it is seen to reflect the inherent limitations of human reason and to argue for religious values, while in the later one it is equated with the persecution of nonconformists by a nasty bourgeoisie.

Weisberg approaches *The Brothers Karamazov* with preconceptions that prevent him from doing justice to either the legal aspects of the novel or its much more important religious aspects (see pp. 54–81 of his book). For him not only Dmitri but also Alyosha are noble pagans brought down by resentful, wordy, legalistic Christians. This picture is unconvincing even with regard to Dmitri, the victim of a miscarriage of justice. To call him innocent and leave it at that, as Weisberg essentially does, is to oversimplify. As Dmitri says of himself many times, and with solid grounds, he is a scoundrel—a man of unbridled, frequently vicious passions, a spendthrift and sponge, who treats women dishonorably, assaults his father, and nearly kills his father's faithful servant (Grigory), as well as causing great suffering by dragging Ilusha's father by his beard through the streets of the town, right in front of Ilusha. Far from being inarticulate, Dmitri quotes great swatches of Schiller; far from being natural man, he appears at his trial dressed like a dandy. Although he is the victim of a judicial error, his conviction and sentencing may be just in a larger sense. Dostoevsky does not regard him simply as a victim of persecution, as Camus appears to regard Meursault.

Weisberg is not the first student of Dostoevsky to believe that *The Brothers Karamazov*, although intended by its deeply religious author to be a religious work,[54] is actually antireligious. The fact that Dostoevsky would be shocked to see the novel read so is not decisive against the interpretation, for reasons that will become clearer in Chapter 5. What is important is that the text does not support the interpretation.[55] Although I am no more predisposed than Weisberg to find Christian meanings in works of literature, *The Brothers Karamazov* is unmistakably a work of Christian literature, perhaps the greatest since *The Divine Comedy*. The suffering of children, the rationalism of Ivan and of the lawyers, the stench from Father Zossima's corpse, the utilitarian arguments of the Grand Inquisitor, the erroneous conviction of Dmitri—this incomparably vivid array of challenges and alternatives to the Christian faith is vanquished by Christ's silent kiss bestowed on the Grand Inquisitor, by the fates of Smerdyakov and Ivan, by the luminous teachings and personality of Father Zossima, by the parable of the onion[56] and Dmitri's dream of the babe, by the goodness and purity of Alyosha, and above all by the sense that everything will come out right in the end—that real punishment is reserved for those who choose wickedness with their eyes open, like the woman in the parable of the onion. Weisberg's suggestion that Ivan is a priestly figure and that at the end of the book Alyosha has become "garrulous," signifying the triumph of Christian ressentiment and "organic mendacity" (p. 81), is unacceptable. *The Brothers Karamazov* would fail as Christian apologetics if Dostoevsky had failed to give sin, temptation, and apostasy their due; and by not failing, he gives purchase to readers who would

---

[54] See, for example, Terras, note 52 above, at 39–40.

[55] See, for example, Cox, note 35 above, chap. 9.

[56] "Once upon a time there was a peasant woman and a very wicked woman she was. And she died and did not leave a single good deed behind. The devils caught her and plunged her into the lake of fire. So her guardian angel stood and wondered what good deed of hers he could remember to tell to God; 'she once pulled up an onion in her garden,' said he, 'and gave it to a beggar woman.' And God answered: 'You take that onion then, hold it out to her in the lake, and let her take hold and be pulled out. And if you can pull her out of the lake, let her come to Paradise, but if the onion breaks, then the woman must stay where she is.' The angel ran to the woman and held out the onion to her; 'Come,' said he, 'catch hold and I'll pull you out.' And he began cautiously pulling her out. He had just pulled her right out, when the other sinners in the lake, seeing she was being drawn out, began catching hold of her so as to be pulled out with her. But she was a very wicked woman and she began kicking them. 'I'm to be pulled out, not you. It's my onion, not yours.' As soon as she said that, the onion broke. And the woman fell into the lake and she is burning there to this day. So the angel wept and went away." Dostoevsky, note 52 above, at 330.

like to make him, as Blake and many since have tried to make Milton, of the devil's party without knowing it.

Dostoevsky realized that despite the intellectual difficulties in reconciling human suffering with divine goodness and mercy, the fact of suffering does not undermine religious belief—rather the opposite. The response to the unbeliever is not arguments and proof but commitment to a realm beyond reason, wonderfully symbolized by the kiss that Christ gives the Grand Inquisitor. One can imagine Weisberg's rejecting this approach as signifying mystification and irrationality, just as Vicinczey rejected the implied values of *Billy Budd* as authoritarian (see note 48). Equally one can imagine Weisberg's embracing Dostoevsky's central insight (minus its specifically Christian details) into the problem of religious belief in order to reconcile the suffering of the Jewish people with a continued belief in the Jewish God. Instead, Weisberg stands the novel on its head, much as when a judge or advocate contorts a precedent in a vain effort to create authority for his position.

## Literature and the Holocaust

Weisberg's culminating thesis is that the attitudes he finds in the examining magistrates in *Crime and Punishment* and *The Stranger*, the lawyers in *The Brothers Karamazov*, and Captain Vere in *Billy Budd* lead to Nazism, and in particular to the Nazis' racial policies. This thesis rests not only on the idea that punishing murderers and other criminals encourages Nazism, but also on the idea that the spiritual distance between Nietzsche and Nazism is greater than that between Christianity and Nazism; that Nietzsche, the anti-Christian, is the better anti-Nazi. One can only regard this as perverse. Granted, Nietzsche reprobated both anti-Semitism and German nationalism, and his work as a whole is perhaps better understood as a protest against conformity and repression than as an invitation to war and domination—though the temptation to whitewash Nietzsche should be resisted. And granted, the roots of European anti-Semitism are Christian; conformity and submission played an important role in Nazism; there was collaboration between organized Christianity and the fascist regimes; and many individual Nazis were consumed by ressentiment.[57] Nevertheless, the celebration

---

[57] Goebbels, for example, with his club foot, small stature, and warped intellectuality, could have been Nietzsche's archetypal resentful man. On the role of Christianity in the rise of Nazism see George L. Mosse, *Toward the Final Solution: A History of European Racism*, chap. 9 (1985).

of barbarism and the condemnation of Judeo-Christian values as worthy only of slaves were important strands in National Socialist ideology, while conversely the Judeo-Christian values have nothing in common with that ideology despite the instances of collaboration between institutional Christianity and fascism, a collaboration exaggeratedly described by Weisberg as "the participation of all Christian institutions in an unthinkable victimization of innocents" (pp. 69–70).

Perhaps because Weisberg associates ressentiment and anti-Semitism with forces neither admired by nor influential with Nazis, such as Christianity and legality, he is led to condemn French anti-Semitism more strongly than German. Not only is Weisberg's symbol of ressentiment in the Nazi era an article by a French lawyer, but Weisberg writes that "France reveled in the racial possibilities brought onto its territory by the foreign conquerors . . . Western egalitarianism and liberality embraced racial ostracism and ultimate genocide *more effusively* than had the still seemingly neobarbarous and deeply romantic Germanic states" (p. 2; emphasis added). There was indeed much anti-Semitism in France before and during World War II, but the proposition that France would have tried on its own, as it were, to exterminate the Jews, or that it embraced genocide more enthusiastically than Germany did, cannot be taken seriously. The fact that so many Frenchmen fell in with and abetted the Nazis' schemes may be unforgivable but is also understandable; France was a conquered country. Elsewhere Weisberg has presented evidence that the Vichy French racial laws were more severe, and were interpreted more strictly, than the Nazi laws,[58] but his principal source refutes his contention that France outdid Germany in viciousness toward the Jews: it shows that three-fourths of the Jews in France (many of them refugees from Nazism rather than French nationals) survived the war and that the Vichy government tried to protect at least French Jews from the Nazis and, more generally, to dissociate itself from the "Final Solution."[59] In any event, overzealous collaboration with a conqueror does not equal voluntary initiation of genocide. The behavior of the Vichy officials, although neither courageous nor admirable, was not comparable in enormity to the Germans' behavior.

Let us take a closer look at the French lawyer, Joseph Haennig, whose article "leaves us gasping" (p. 7). Entitled "What Means of Proof Can the Jew of Mixed Blood Offer to Establish His Nonaffiliation with the Jewish Race?" the article is mainly about a decision of a court in

---

[58] See Richard Weisberg, "Avoiding Central Realities: Narrative Terror and the Failure of French Culture under the Occupation," 5 *Human Rights Quarterly* 151, 161–163 (1983).
[59] See Michael R. Marrus and Robert O. Paxton, *Vichy France and the Jews* 361–362, 371 (1981).

Leipzig.[60] Haennig argues that the decision may provide guidance to interpreting Vichy's racial laws, which had been modeled on the Nuremberg laws. He obsequiously commends the Leipzig court for "a largeness and objectivity of spirit" (p. 181) in allowing a Jewish woman of mixed blood to prove nonaffiliation with the Jewish "race" without having to show affiliation with a Christian denomination. He notes that "the Court affirmed the lower court judge's view that she had only attended [Jewish] New Year's services in order to preserve family peace. The view that there was no sufficient tie to the Jewish community in the case was thus deemed correct." And he concludes that the court's "analysis indicates a possible route, without risk of distorting the statute writers' intention, and in conformity with the principles which underlie the racial statutes and cases" (p. 182).

Is this the work of a man guilty of "fatal evasiveness"—a man whose behavior raises questions described by Weisberg (p. 1) as "potentially more catastrophic in their resolution than those posed by the leaders of European repression and racism"? Without knowing anything about Haennig except what Weisberg tells us—that he was a lawyer in German-occupied Paris, that he wrote the article partially reprinted in the appendix, and (rather inconsistently in light of Weisberg's summary characterization of him) that he "was clearly not a villain" and "earlier in the Occupation . . . had defended a Jew who was facing incarceration and death for a 'political' crime" (p. 1)—I am unwilling to accept Weisberg's verdict. Although Haennig's article contains no hint of disapproval of the racial laws, it would not have been published if it had. It does not praise the laws. The only thing praised is a German decision that saved a woman who was half-Jewish from the gas chamber. The article may have saved some French half-Jews. Indeed, it may have saved more lives than if Haennig had thrown up his law practice and joined the Resistance, for which he may have been neither physically nor emotionally suited (how old was he?). Maybe he thought the racial laws grotesque but knew it would not help to let his feelings show in the article. What would Weisberg have had Haennig *do*?

It is true that if most Frenchmen had refused to collaborate with the Nazis, the Jews of France would have been made better off than they were by receiving small crumbs of assistance from the likes of Haennig. But the problem with mass defiance—a classic Prisoner's Dilemma

---

[60] There is more to the article (which may be found, in the original French, in 1943.1 *Gazette du Palais*, Doctrine 31), but that is the main part and the only one Weisberg translates. My page references are to Weisberg's book.

problem—is, who shall step forward first? Only a hero, and heroes are rare.

Weisberg's treatment of Haennig, a man who under difficult circumstances did *something* for the Jews, suggests that *The Failure of the Word* may itself exemplify the ressentiment that it denounces. Other evidence is Weisberg's belief that events like the Holocaust have primarily intellectual causes and are foretold by novelists; his propensity to euphemize barbarism—in particular the murder committed by Meursault—without Haennig's excuses; his hectoring prosecution of both Vere and Haennig in the dock of history; and his lack of sympathy for people like Vere who are called on to exercise power, and make painful choices, in defense of social order.[61] Such paradoxes asserted or implied in *The Failure of the Word* as that Nazism was the product of too much head and too little heart (p. 138), that *Mein Kampf* is in the line of descent from the Sermon on the Mount (making Nazism the culmination rather than a perversion of the Western tradition), that the Judeo-Christian ethical tradition and the Western legal tradition are stifling, and that people who investigate and punish murders are morally equivalent (even morally inferior) to murderers, bring to mind some words of George Orwell: "One has to belong to the intelligentsia to believe things like that: no ordinary man could be such a fool."[62] Yet in fairness to Weisberg I note that his outlook—not his specific views on literature or the Holocaust but his suggestion that Western values, including the tradition of rational inquiry, somehow contributed to the ugliest events of this century—is widespread among intellectuals, including literary critics.[63] And, although disagreeing with much of Weisberg's analysis, I commend his effort to mine literature for its nuggets of insight into fundamental issues that lawyers should think about more than they do—issues relating to the connection between the legal outlook and the sense of justice, between legalism and civilization,

---

[61] As Melville says in *Billy Budd* (p. 114), " 'Little ween the snug card players in the cabin of the responsibilities of the man on the bridge.' " One is put in mind of Kipling's line about "mocking the uniforms that guard us while we sleep."

[62] "Notes on Nationalism," in *Collected Essays, Journalism and Letters of George Orwell*, vol. 3, at 361, 379 (Sonia Orwell and Ian Angus eds. 1968). The "that" to which Orwell was referring was the idea being mooted about in English left-wing circles during World War II that American troops had been brought to Europe not to fight the Germans but to crush an English revolution.

[63] For an illustration see Stephen J. Greenblatt, "Improvisation and Power," in *Literature and Society* 57 (Edward W. Said ed. 1980); cf. George Steiner, "The Lost Garden," *The New Yorker*, June 3, 1974, at 100, 106 ("To know analytically . . . is to dismember"). For discussion see Gerald Graff, *Literature against Itself: Literary Ideas in Modern Society*, chap. 3 (1979).

and between law and other forms of institutionalized morality, such as organized religion. Professional training in law and the professional experiences of lawyers are narrowing. Lawyers ought to think about the great issues that law intersects, just as military officers ought to think about geopolitics and not just military strategy and tactics. The great works of literature that take law as their theme (though often just an ostensible theme) provide a convenient, though not the only, point of entry to broader thinking about law.

But Weisberg's book shows that the risks are great. He has read too much legal significance into the books he discusses and has assigned law a causal role—whether in the tragedy of Billy Budd or in the genocidal policies of Nazi Germany and its vassal states—that it will not bear. The legal details in *Billy Budd* that so preoccupy Weisberg are peripheral to the novella. That Billy is legally guilty is a given, and the author's and reader's interest is in how Captain Vere is going to meet the test of duty that Billy's guilt has placed on him.

The occupational hazard of the "literary lawyer" is putting literature to tendentious use. Weisberg wants to show that the worst features of twentieth-century life are due to the corruption of natural man, who is good, by Christianity and law. For him (in contrast to such other "literary lawyers" as Robert Ferguson and James White) law is the enemy. Weisberg is entitled to his view, but he is not entitled to enlist Melville and Dostoevsky under his banner—any more than the critical legal studies movement is entitled to enlist Kafka under its banner, as I shall discuss next.

# FOUR

## Two Legal Perspectives
## on Kafka

N O INTERDISCIPLINARY field of law has received more attention
than law and economics, which uses economic theory to
study a great variety of legal doctrines and institutions—contract law
and accident law, criminal law and family law, maritime law and
constitutional law, as well as such overtly economic fields of law as
antitrust law and public utility regulation.[1] Economics has broad
relevance to law because, contrary to popular belief, it is not just the
study of explicit economic markets, but the science of rational choice.[2]
Proceeding on the assumption that human beings are rational (in a sense
that will become clearer as this chapter unfolds), economists and
economics-minded lawyers can explain much nonmarket as well as
market behavior, including behavior of litigants, criminals, prosecutors,
judges, accident victims, and other persons involved in or affected by
such legal institutions as criminal law, property law, tort law, and
criminal procedure. The economic analyst can also make proposals for
reforming these institutions to make them operate more efficiently,
where "efficiency" means maximizing the excess of social benefits over
social costs.

The law and economics movement is controversial. It challenges
many assumptions that lawyers have held about their field. It challenges
the very autonomy of law—the idea of law as a self-contained discipline
that can be practiced without systematic study of any other field of

---

[1] For an overview of the field see my *Economic Analysis of Law* (3d ed. 1986), and for
representative criticisms see Symposium on Efficiency as a Legal Concern, 8 *Hofstra Law
Review* 485, 811 (1980).
[2] See Gary S. Becker, *The Economic Approach to Human Behavior* (1976); Jack Hirshleifer, "The
Expanding Domain of Economics," 75 *American Economic Review Special Anniversary Issue* 53
(Dec. 1985); Richard A. Posner, *The Economics of Justice*, chap. 1 (1981).

thought. It asks lawyers to learn an alien and difficult set of concepts. It rests or seems to rest on assumptions about human nature that many people, especially people trained in the humanities, find disturbing, even repulsive. It aspires to be scientific, not humanistic. And most of its practitioners are politically moderate or conservative, while most contemporary humanists are liberal or radical.

As the most humanistic field in the interdisciplinary study of law, law and literature may seem to be on a collision course with law and economics. Chapter 6 will consider the argument of some "literary lawyers" that the language of economics, when applied to law, conceals vital aspects of reality. The present chapter examines Robin West's use of Kafka's fiction to criticize the model of human behavior used in the economics of law.[3]

Much although by no means all of West's writing is in the spirit of the critical legal studies movement.[4] This current in contemporary legal thought, of which we caught a glimpse in Chapter 2, combines political radicalism with radical skepticism about the neutrality and objectivity of law, which many adherents to the movement regard as little more than a projection of capitalist ideology. They want to get rid of that ideology, of the Western liberal tradition that subtends it, and of the legal order that protects and legitimates it. The critical legal studies movement intersects the law and literature movement at two points. Some of its adherents find in literature a vivid depiction of the repressive character and effects of social, including legal, institutions. That is West's focus.

---

[3] See Robin West, "Authority, Autonomy, and Choice: The Role of Consent in the Moral and Political Visions of Franz Kafka and Richard Posner," 99 *Harvard Law Review* 384 (1985). After I replied to her article in "The Ethical Significance of Free Choice: A Reply to Professor West," 99 *Harvard Law Review* 1431 (1986), on which this chapter is based, she responded in "Submission, Choice, and Ethics: A Rejoinder to Judge Posner," 99 *Harvard Law Review* 1449 (1986). Unless otherwise indicated, page references to West in this chapter are to "Authority, Autonomy, and Choice."

[4] In addition to her two pieces on Kafka, see her "Law, Rights, and Other Totemic Illusions: Legal Liberalism and Freud's Theory of the Rule of Law," 134 *University of Pennsylvania Law Review* 817 (1986), especially pp. 859–882. On the critical legal studies movement, pro and con, see Mark Kelman, *A Guide to Critical Legal Studies* (1987); Richard Michael Fischl, "Some Realism about Critical Legal Studies," 41 *University of Miami Law Review* 505 (1987); Jane B. Baron, "self-Criticism," 60 *Temple Law Quarterly* 39 (1987) (capitalized as in original); Critical Legal Studies Symposium, 36 *Stanford Law Review* 1 (1984); *The Politics of Law: A Progressive Critique* (David Kairys ed. 1982); Lawrence B. Solum, "On the Indeterminacy Crisis: Critiquing Critical Dogma," 54 *University of Chicago Law Review* 462 (1987); John Stick, "Can Nihilism Be Pragmatic?" 100 *Harvard Law Review* 332 (1986); Roberto Mangabeira Unger, *The Critical Legal Studies Movement* (1986)—and the review by Joseph Isenbergh, "Why Law?" 54 *University of Chicago Law Review* 1117 (1987). Unger's book *Knowledge and Politics*, cited in Chapter 2, attempts to lay a philosophical foundation for the movement.

(Terry Eagleton, though he probably does not consider himself a practitioner of critical legal studies, took a similar approach in analyzing *The Merchant of Venice* and *Measure for Measure*.) Others, as we shall see in the next chapter, find in the reader-centered schools of contemporary literary criticism an interpretive skepticism which they think can be turned on legal texts to undermine the idea that law expresses impersonal norms. It was the first aspect of the movement that was touched on in Chapter 2 and is considered at greater length in this chapter, where I shall argue that whatever support political radicals can derive from the depiction of legal and social institutions in the works of other great writers, an effort to derive it from Kafka's works is bound to fail.

West's main target in discussing those works is a proposition that is basic not only to the law and economics movement but to the entire tradition of classical (not contemporary) liberalism. It is the proposition that government should as a rule not interfere with voluntary transactions that impose no uncompensated costs on third parties—"Pareto-superior" transactions, as the economists say. To avoid misunderstanding I point out that the principle is not that every consensual transaction between informed and competent adults that has no uncompensated third-party effects is beyond ethical reproach. The purpose of the Pareto concept, when conceived as a principle of political philosophy, is to define the proper role of the state, not to guide personal choice.

Other features of the political philosophy that I have defended under the rubric of "wealth maximization"[5] are more controversial than Pareto superiority, for example the proposition that transactions which raise the aggregate wealth of society are entitled to respect even if there are uncompensated losers. I shall not dwell on these matters much, since West is not much interested in the differences between Pareto-superior and merely wealth-maximizing transactions. Voluntary transactions are quite bad enough in her view even if everyone affected by them is fully compensated. This is because she believes that our choices very often, perhaps typically, make us miserable: a belief that she might try to ground in the literature of the social sciences[6] but that instead she grounds in Kafka's fiction.

---

[5] On which see Posner, note 1 above, chaps. 3–4, and also my "Wealth Maximization Revisited," 2 *Notre Dame Journal of Law, Ethics and Public Policy* 85 (1985), and "The Justice of Economics," 1987–1 *Economia delle Scelte Pubbliche* 15.

[6] Some points of entry to the relevant literature are *Rational Choice: The Contrast between Economics and Psychology* (Robin M. Hogarth and Melvin W. Reder eds. 1987), especially the articles by Simon, Tversky and Kahneman, and Arrow; Jon Elster, *Sour Grapes: Studies in the Subversion of Rationality* (1983), especially pts. 3–4; Richard B. Brandt, *A Theory of the Good and the Right*, chaps. 3–8 (1979); Hirshleifer, note 2 above, at 59–62.

## On Reading Kafka Politically

Robin West's enterprise may seem passing strange. But we have just seen how Richard Weisberg, another "literary lawyer," found prophetic significance in Dostoevsky, Melville, and Camus; and we know from Chapter 2 how enigmatic a writer Kafka was, and thus how easily— how much more easily, indeed, than the writers discussed by Weisberg—he could be thought a political writer of prophetic insight. But if my analysis of Kafka in that chapter was sound, the appearance is misleading. I am not alone in this conclusion; most students of Kafka have not thought him a topical writer like Zola or Dreiser, or a writer of political allegories like Swift or Orwell.[7] Although he was a lawyer, worked most of his adult life for an insurance institute, and borrowed scenes, symbols, and vocabulary from law and business, it does not follow that his writing is in an essential sense about these fields. Wallace Stevens was also a lawyer employed by an insurance company, and T. S. Eliot was a banker and later a publisher, but no one supposes that Stevens's or Eliot's poetry is about law or business.

As we saw in discussing *The Trial* and *In the Penal Colony*, the focus of Kafka's fiction is inward, on Kafka's mental state, rather than outward, on social institutions. Kafka was tormented by feelings of guilt, inadequacy, and self-disgust, morbidly attracted to suffering and death, and plagued by psychosomatic illnesses; he felt an extraordinary mixture of love and hate for his father; and he could not bring himself to marry. More important—for I do not want to be merely replacing one type of biographical criticism with another—his neuroses are close to the surface of his fiction. Although they do not deprive it of universality, they mark it as a literature of private feeling rather than of social commentary. Dream-like (sometimes nightmarish), often unfinished, it perplexes and disturbs the reader with its overlay of fantasy, its unexpected fondness for Christian symbols, its preoccupation with passivity in the face of suffering, cruelty, and death, and its fascination with the grotesque and macabre, of which we saw much evidence in discussing *The Trial* and *In the Penal Colony*. Politics and economics,

---

[7] Ronald Gray, *Franz Kafka* (1973), is an exemplary introduction to the literary criticism of Kafka's work. The diversity of critical responses to that work is well illustrated by the essays in *The Kafka Debate: New Perspectives for Our Time* (Angel Flores ed. 1977). Other good collections of critical essays are *Kafka: A Collection of Critical Essays* (Ronald Gray ed. 1962); *Franz Kafka Number*, 8 *Modern Fiction Studies* no. 1 (1962); *Kafka: Centenary Essays*, 26 *Literary Review* 481 (1983). The amazing volume and diversity of Kafka studies can be glimpsed in Bluma Goldstein, "You'll Laugh When I Tell You: Fifteen Books on Kafka," 73 *Monatshefte* 67 (1981).

however, have to be brought in from the outside, by the tendentious reader. Or so it seems to me—for Robin West is not alone in interpreting Kafka's fiction as a criticism of capitalism. While some Marxists consign Kafka to the "cultural dung heap of reaction," others have claimed him as one of their own.[8] But West's approach is extreme: she reads Kafka so literally that the incidents and metaphors from business and law in his fiction become its meaning. (The occupational hazard of lawyer-critics is to suppose that literature on legal themes represents law more literally than other literature represents its themes.) She might as well read *Animal Farm* as a tract on farm management, or *Moby-Dick* as an exposé of the whaling industry. Just as *Gulliver's Travels* is not really a disquisition on the problems of being a big person in a land of little people or a little person in a land of big people, or on talking horses, or on islands that float in the air, so Kafka's fiction is not really a series of disquisitions on people who starve themselves for a living, sons who commit suicide at their father's direction, traveling salesmen who are fired because they have turned into giant insects, denials of due process, judicial delay, a torturer who kills himself with his torture machine (which goes crazy in the process), singing mice, a talking ape, an introspective dog, or a horse (whom we shall meet later in this chapter) that practices law.

Of Kafka's great story *A Hunger Artist*, West writes: "Kafka's hunger artist is the ultimate Posnerian entrepreneur, and the artist's audience consists of Posnerian consumers" (p. 393). This interpretation disfigures an exquisite parable about people's indifference to the interior lives of strangers. The hunger artist is tormented by his inability to convince an indifferent world of his artistic integrity; they think he sneaks food on the side. (Inability to explain oneself is a frequent motif in Kafka's fiction; we have seen it in *In the Penal Colony*, *The Trial*, and *The Stoker*, and we shall see it again in *The Metamorphosis* and *The Judgment*.) Eventually the hunger artist's spirit is so crushed that he either pretends or comes to believe that he fasted not because of the challenge but because he was too fastidious to eat. He dies, is buried unceremoniously together with the straw in his cage, and is replaced by a panther, which has no interior life. *A Hunger Artist* may also be about the world's indifference to Kafka's own artistic scruples. It may be about many

---

[8] Compare Howard Fast, "The Metamorphosis," in *Franz Kafka: An Anthology of Marxist Criticism* 12 (Kenneth Hughes ed. 1981), from which the above quotation is taken, with Boris Suchkov, "Franz Kafka," in id. at 125, and Bluma Goldstein, "Bachelors and Work: Social and Economic Conditions in 'The Judgment,' 'The Metamorphosis,' and 'The Trial,' " in *The Kafka Debate*, note 7 above, at 147.

things. But only superficially is it about hunger, poverty, the pitfalls of entrepreneurship, and the fickleness of consumers.

West quotes a passage from *The Trial*, concerning Joseph K.'s rivalry with the Assistant Manager of the bank where he works, as evidence that "although K. suffers no physical abuse on the job, he is humiliated and dehumanized, not enriched, by his white-collar employment as Chief Clerk in a bank" (p. 396). Actually the passage merely reflects the standing rivalry between K. and the Assistant Manager[9]—in which K. gives as good as he gets. Neither here nor elsewhere is K. shown as ground down by his job. He is a big shot at work; that is one of the ironies of his situation. The passage shows not that K. is alienated from his work, but how distracted he is by the mysterious "judicial" proceeding in which he has become enmeshed. This is, after all, a novel about obsession.

A few sentences that West elides will make my point:

> He [K.] glanced up slightly, but only slightly, when the door of the Manager's room opened, [and] disclosed the Assistant Manager, a blurred figure who looked as if veiled in some kind of gauze. K. did not seek for the cause of this apparition, but merely registered its immediate effect, which was very welcome to him. For the manufacturer at once bounded from his chair and rushed over to the Assistant Manager, though K. could have wished him to be ten times quicker, since he was afraid the apparition might vanish again.[10]

Far from being "humiliated and dehumanized," K. welcomes the Assistant Manager's interruption. He wants to be rid of the manufacturer so that he can be free to think about the trial.

The reader who does not read Kafka's fiction tendentiously, seeking support for one ethical or political position or another, will not be inclined to draw inferences about the proper organization of society. As further evidence consider Kafka's greatest story, *The Metamorphosis* (not discussed by West). Gregor Samsa, who lives with his parents and sister

[9] The Muirs' translation is misleading. The "Assistant Manager" is the second in command at the bank (literally "deputy director"). Similarly, K. is an important executive, not a "clerk" in the American sense.

[10] Franz Kafka, *The Trial* 163–164 (Willa and Edwin Muir trans., definitive ed. 1960). See also id. at 165. Kafka apparently did not think his own job humiliating or dehumanizing, though he did consider it a distraction from his primary interest, which was writing. Like Stevens and Eliot (and Joseph K.!), Kafka was not a rebel or a Bohemian; despite his neuroticism, he was a successful executive—an establishment bureaucrat—diligent in his work, and not only highly regarded, but well liked, by his superiors and associates. See Ernst Pawel, *The Nightmare of Reason: A Life of Franz Kafka* 188 (1984).

(and eventually three lodgers), wakes up one morning to find that he has turned into a giant insect, something like a beetle (hard back, many legs), though the author carefully leaves it undefined. Within this grotesque and repulsive form Gregor is initially unchanged. He thinks and speaks as always, only no one can understand what he says; he sounds like an insect. The family, particularly Gregor's father—naturally—reacts to his transformation with disgust. For a while the family more or less puts up with Gregor, though at one point his mother has to intervene to prevent his father from killing him. But when Gregor's untimely appearance in the living room to hear his sister play the violin alerts the lodgers to his existence and they give notice, the family locks him up in his room. In the usual passive style of Kafka's protagonists (recall the execution of Joseph K. in the last chapter of *The Trial*), Gregor—dutiful, considerate, docile, and devoted to his parents and sister, all of whom, indeed, he had been supporting from his salesman's income before he lost his job—accepts his family's unfeeling treatment of him and dies unshaken in his love for them. Relieved by his death, they make all sorts of new plans and celebrate with a tram ride to the country. "And it was like a confirmation of their new dreams and excellent intentions that at the end of their journey their daughter sprang to her feet first and stretched her young body" (p. 139).[11]

Although money figures in the story and there is a striking scene, at once hilarious and horrifying, where Gregor, in an unsuccessful effort to save his job, crawls toward the chief clerk of his firm while delivering an intricate but completely unintelligible apology for being late to work, I do not think *The Metamorphosis* is essentially about money, the job market, or any of the other things that West thinks Kafka is about.[12]

---

[11] My page references to Kafka's stories are to Franz Kafka, *The Complete Stories* (Nahum N. Glatzer ed. 1971). The translations of the stories I discuss are all by the Muirs, with the exception of *The Refusal*, translated by Tania and James Stern.

[12] I thus am not persuaded by Goldstein's Marxist interpretation, note 8 above, at 154–159: "Gregor awakens one morning to find himself metamorphosed into a giant bug. In a sense, he actually accomplished with this event what he had long desired—he is free of work and of bosses who exploited him, he won't exhaust himself in incessant traveling, he retains his isolation and need not struggle to maintain it. He becomes a parasite, which is merely the obverse of his former situation of maintaining others as parasites." Id. at 156. "Only when he is completely divorced from the entire economic and social system, after he has been wounded several times and is incapacitated—crippled, blinded and in terrible pain—only then did Gregor rid himself of senseless clock-watching, thoughts of catching trains, worrying about family finances and his own job." Id. at 159. Another Marxist interpretation of the story is Walter H. Sokel, "From Marx to Myth: The Structure and Function of Self-Alienation in Kafka's *Metamorphosis*," 26 *Literary Review* 485 (1983). A more persuasive "economic" treatment of *The Metamorphosis* is Franz Kuna, *Franz Kafka: Literature as a Corrective Punishment*, chap. 3 (1974). And for an excellent discussion that stresses the theme of conflict

Admittedly Gregor's transformation has elements of a deliverance for him as well as for his family. They had lived parasitically on his earnings; he had been in the thrall of clock time; only after his transformation is he awakened to the beauty of music. The Marxist interpretation is a caricature, but a caricature of something that is in the story. It is Kafka's magic (we saw it in *In the Penal Colony*) to be able to give Gregor's grotesque misfortune a touch of rebirth and Gregor himself a touch of the Savior. But the deliverance is not from a social structure, let alone the specific structure of capitalist society. Nor is deliverance the dominant motif. Like *A Hunger Artist* and *In the Penal Colony*, *The Metamorphosis* dramatizes the difficulty of communicating with other people (recall the inarticulateness of the stoker in Kafka's story of that name), and, a closely related point, the gap between how we perceive ourselves and how others perceive us.[13] Gregor accepts notionally the fact that he is an embarrassment to his family, and does not resist being locked up; indeed, he expires by a kind of inanition brought on by awareness that he has become a burden to the family. But he cannot see himself through their eyes, and in his heart of hearts cannot accept his altered appearance.

We all have Gregor's problem, though in less acute forms. We can never make our aspirations fully understood or quite bring our self-conception into phase with the conception that others have of us. And looking at Gregor from the other side, his family's side, we can never completely penetrate the externals and enter the interior life of another person. Life goes on—the awakening love life of Gregor's sister, the life of the carnival managers and customers in *A Hunger Artist* and of the passersby in *The Judgment*—with remarkable, with shocking, indifference to the inner life of our fellow man. The healthy animal spirits of the sister and of the panther are set against the miserable introspection of Gregor and the hunger artist.

---

between father and son see Roy Pascal, *Kafka's Narrators: A Study of His Stories and Sketches* 51–55 (1982). Like so many of Kafka's works, *The Metamorphosis* has attracted voluminous, contentious, at times zany commentary—not all of it, of course, economic in character. For a sense of its range see Stanley Corngold, *The Commentators' Despair: The Interpretation of Kafka's Metamorphosis* (1973), and for a recent illustration see Robert F. Fleissner, "Is Gregor Samsa a Bed Bug? Kafka and Dickens Revisited," 22 *Studies in Short Fiction* 225 (1985). An example of the extremes to which *The Metamorphosis* drives commentators is this sentence by the distinguished critic George Steiner: "He who has read Kafka's *Metamorphosis* and can look into his mirror unflinching may technically be able to read print, but is illiterate in the only sense that matters." "Humane Literacy," in Steiner, *Language and Silence: Essays on Language, Literature, and the Inhuman* 3, 11 (1974).

[13] Camus's *The Stranger*, as I noted in Chapter 2, may be part of the same genre.

Gregor is not Everyman, however. The other characters in *The Metamorphosis*—Gregor's family, the charwoman, the clerk, and the lodgers—are depicted not just as ordinary people but more particularly as nonneurotic people, defined (and faintly derided) as people without an interior, like the panther in *A Hunger Artist*, and set over against the neurotic with his rich, tormented, and despairing inner life. Thus Gregor's horrible outward form symbolizes (among many other things, including loneliness and guilt) the barriers created by differences in personality.

West finds in *The Judgment* another indictment of capitalism. Georg, a young merchant who works for his father, feels guilt (only slightly tinged with *Schadenfreude*) about an unnamed friend who years ago had gone abroad in pursuit of business opportunities that have not turned out well. After finally deciding to invite the friend to his wedding (despite concern that the friend might be made envious), Georg is suddenly, gratuitously accused by his vicious, loony father of having played the friend false all these years. Here is the father talking:

> "And now that you thought you'd got him down, so far down that you could set your bottom on him and sit on him and he wouldn't move, then my fine son makes up his mind to get married!" . . .
>
> "Because she lifted up her skirts," his father began to flute, "because she lifted up her skirts like this, the nasty creature . . . because she lifted her skirts like this and this you made up to her, and in order to make free with her undisturbed you have disgraced your mother's memory, betrayed your friend, and stuck your father into bed so that he can't move. But he can move, or can't he?"
>
> And he stood up quite unsupported and kicked his legs out. His insight made him radiant. (p. 85)

Eventually father—who is still standing upright on the bed, with one hand on the ceiling to steady himself—says to son, " 'I sentence you now to death by drowning!' " And Georg, "the crash with which his father fell on the bed behind him . . . still in his ears," rushes out and drowns himself. As he leaps from the bridge, he "called in a low voice: 'Dear parents, I have always loved you, all the same,' and let himself drop. At this moment an unending stream of traffic was just going over the bridge." (Pp. 87–88.) End of story.

Because Georg's friend, a brooding omnipresence in the story, is an unsuccessful businessman, West conceives the story to be about capitalist alienation. How flat and dull her reading makes the story! If the story is not about the Oedipus complex, or Kafka's relationship with his own father, or why Kafka did not marry,[14] then it is about the sense of guilt, about the disproportion between cause and effect, about the surreal, about life's unfairness, about how people tend to accept the valuation placed on them by other people, about the dislocated feeling of modern life to highly sensitive souls, about the indifference of others to our inner turmoil—not only the passersby on the bridge but Georg's friend, who apparently knows nothing of Georg's attempts to avoid distressing him with reminders of his business failure. The story can even be regarded as a kind of sketch for *The Trial* (which was written later) and thus pulled more directly into the law and literature fold. Georg is indicted, convicted, and sentenced to death (*Das Urteil*—the title of the story— means "the judgment" in the sense of the legal decision or sentence) all by his father, and the sentence is promptly carried out (by Georg). Like Joseph K. in *The Trial*, Georg is not guilty of any crime; nor can he get the "tribunal" to listen to him. Notice, finally, the ironic twist that the story gives to the theme of the judge called upon to condemn his son.

*The Judgment* is an incredibly rich story. But in arguing that Georg kills himself because of guilt over "his own self-imposed alienation from [his friend's] suffering" (p. 410; see also p. 411), West has taken the father's side in the story, and this I find bizarre.[15]

[14] In this interpretation Kafka's worldly self, symbolized by Georg, who was engaged (as Kafka was several times to be), dies so that Georg's friend (who stands for Kafka's writing self) can be redeemed from failure and exile. See Gray, *Franz Kafka*, note 7 above, at 61–65. Another of Kafka's commentators writes, "Never before or after, it seems, has Freud ruled so supremely over a piece of literature." Erich Heller, *Kafka* 22 (1974). See also Charles Bernheimer, *Flaubert and Kafka: Studies in Psychopoetic Structure* 139–188 (1982). On the psychiatric approach to Kafka's writings generally, see (besides Bernheimer's book) Bernard McElroy, "The Art of Projective Thinking: Franz Kafka and the Paranoid Vision," 31 *Modern Fiction Studies* 217 (1985); Margot Norris, "Sadism and Masochism in Two Kafka Stories: 'In der Strafkolonie' and 'Ein Hungerkünstler,' " 93 *Modern Language Notes* 430 (1978). I am not much drawn to clinical interpretations of *The Judgment*; there has been too much emphasis in the interpretation of Kafka's fiction on his biography, as argued with specific reference to *The Judgment* by Martin Swales, "Why Read Kafka?" 76 *Modern Language Review* 357 (1981). Yet I do not deny the force of Pascal's sensitive analysis of *The Judgment* and *The Metamorphosis* as dramatic enactments of Kafka's acute conflict with his father. See Pascal, note 12 above, chaps. 3–4.

[15] Ellis and Goldstein offer a similar interpretation. See John M. Ellis, *Narration in the German Novelle: Theory and Interpretation* 188–211 (1974); Goldstein, note 8 above, at 151–152; and for criticism of Ellis's analysis see Pascal, note 12 above, at 30–32. I hesitate to register so emphatic a disagreement with so distinguished a literary theorist and student of German literature as Ellis, but I cannot understand how Georg's nutty father, in sentencing Georg to death for a nonexistent offense, can be thought to invite the reader's approval. I do not mean that Kafka could not have channeled the reader's sympathies to a man who condemns his son to death; remember *In the Penal Colony*, where Kafka makes the torturer a sympathetic figure. I just do not think the reader's sympathies are channeled to Georg's father, who, unlike the torturer, is not the central figure in the story. I also find it surprising that West should take the side of so authoritarian a figure as Georg's father.

ALTHOUGH business and therefore transactions figure in much of Kafka's fiction—which is not surprising, considering the nature of his employment—they are far from its center. What happens to Gregor in *The Metamorphosis* is neither voluntary nor transactional. The torture machine in *In the Penal Colony* is not a capitalist device; nor is the arrest of Joseph K. on unspecified charges in *The Trial*. Kafka is not a Romantic who believes that people would be happy if only they could escape the clutches of religion, the law, the market, government, and other social institutions, although one strand of Romantic thought—the alienation of the artist—is prominent in *A Hunger Artist*. Yet a mind preoccupied with politics can find political meaning in Kafka's fiction, and indeed in literature even less topical, more fantastic. A mind powerfully gripped by preconceptions of any sort can easily override the opposition of a text, especially the text of so enigmatic a writer as Kafka. Indeterminacy of meaning is a common characteristic of modern literature, and objectivity in literary interpretation seems at the moment a goal as elusive as the Holy Grail. But the wilder an interpretation, the less authority it can draw from the interpreted work. If Richard Weisberg wants to use *Billy Budd* as the jumping-off place for his attack on law, that is fine, but he should make clear that it is *his* attack, not anything to do with Melville. If Kafka reminds Robin West of how much she dislikes capitalism, and thereby stimulates her to critical reflections about it, that is fine, too, but she is not entitled to wrap her criticisms in the mantle of Kafka's immense prestige.

I do not suggest that literature can never be used as the launching pad for an attack on classical liberalism. One need look no further than *The Merchant of Venice*. When the Duke asks Shylock why he would rather have a pound of worthless flesh than a large sum of money, Shylock answers with a commonplace of liberal theory—the subjectivity of value. He explains that value is determined by willingness to pay, which is a function of the preferences and resources of each individual, rather than by some external, objective, or governmental determination of merit or desert (IV.1.42–59):

> . . . I'll not answer that,
> But, say, it is my humor. Is it answer'd?
> What if my house be troubled with a rat
> And I be pleas'd to give ten thousand ducats
> To have it ban'd? What, are you answer'd yet?
> Some men there are love not a gaping pig,
> Some that are mad if they behold a cat,
>
> . . . . .

> As there is no firm reason to be render'd
> Why he cannot abide a gaping pig,
> Why he a harmless necessary cat,
> . . . . .
> So can I give no reason, nor I will not.

Shylock further defends his position by reference to freedom of contract and the rule of law, and implies that the rejection of his claim for the pound of flesh would be redistributive, socialistic (IV.1.90–102):

> You have among you many a purchas'd slave,
> Which, like your asses and your dogs and mules,
> You use in abject and in slavish parts,
> Because you bought them. Shall I say to you,
> "Let them be free, marry them to your heirs!
> Why sweat they under burdens? Let their beds
> Be made as soft as ours, and let their palates
> Be season'd with such viands"? You will answer
> "The slaves are ours." So do I answer you.
> The pound of flesh, which I demand of him,
> Is dearly bought as mine, and I will have it.
> If you deny me, fie upon your law!
> There is no force in the decrees of Venice.

The audience is not expected to take Shylock's part in this debate! There are plenty of distinguished places in literature to find criticisms of bourgeois values, but Kafka's fiction is not one of them.

## In Defense of Classical Liberalism

Without retracting anything I have said, I shall now assume with Robin West that Kafka's works should be read literally, as tracts on entrepreneurship, suicide, and so on. When read so, what do they tell us about bourgeois values and the legal order based on them? Nothing. Kafka's works are not realistic; and read literally they provide as much insight into modern American life as *Dracula* or *The Cask of Amontillado* would. West's point may be an ironic one—that economists have so unrealistic a conception of human nature (a common view) that even the literal Kafka, the Kafka who is "Kafkaesque," is more realistic. Even Kafka's strangest characters (the officer in *In the Penal Colony*, for example) have a more recognizably human personality than a calculating machine. Indeed, such a tour de force is *In the Penal Colony* that a torturer becomes emblematic of suffering humanity.

It is true that most thieves, spouses, litigants, pedestrians, trespassers, rescuers, and other nonmarket actors increasingly encountered in economics do not consciously engage in cost-benefit analysis. But neither do most consumers consciously maximize consumer surplus or most businessmen consciously equate marginal revenue to marginal cost. Rational choice in economics does not mean self-consciously economic choice, or even conscious choice. The concern of economics is not with states of mind, but with what people—even animals, who have no minds[16]—*do*. To complain that economics does not paint a realistic picture of the conscious mind is to miss the point of economics, just as to treat Kafka as a naturalistic writer is to miss the point of Kafka.

But let us forget all this and assume that West has presented a gallery of real-life examples of people transacting. We are now far from any real engagement with Kafka's fiction; that fiction is being used as a journalistic account. This is reductionism with a vengeance, but it is West's method, and let us see where it leads.

She groups all of her illustrations together under the rubric of voluntary transactions that make people worse off. This procedure obscures the morally dissimilar ways in which an ostensibly voluntary transaction can disappoint one or both of the parties. Some of her transactions illustrate market failure, and so are not really voluntary. Others really are voluntary and increase happiness ex ante (before the fact), but turn out badly because of people's inability to predict and control the future. Others are completely unproblematic.

In the first group are West's own fictional creation—the bulimic tomato consumer[17]—and Kafka's hunger artist, who on the literal plane to which West confines Kafka is anorectic. (Dying, the hunger artist had said, " 'I have to fast, I can't help it . . . I couldn't find the food I liked.' " P. 277.) Bulimia and anorexia are mental illnesses, and a mentally ill person cannot be presumed to make choices that will maximize his satisfactions; nor can a person who would commit suicide because his father said to him, "I sentence you now to death by drowning!" But let us not be too quick to pronounce people who make weird and even self-destructive choices insane. Which of us would like to be ruled by people who thought that the administration of an insane asylum provided a model for governing the United States? We know what the

---

[16] The application of economics to the behavior of animals is illustrated by John H. Kagel et al., "Experimental Studies of Consumer Demand Behavior Using Laboratory Animals," 13 *Economic Inquiry* 22 (1975).

[17] Who "on a daily basis . . . buys twelve tomatoes, eats five plates of spaghetti, and regurgitates it all, thus destroying her digestive tract" (p. 401). The purpose of this example is to show that even the simplest consumer transaction is fraught with potential for disaster.

Soviet Union has done with an expansive definition of mental illness. I do not suggest that West wants to lock up people who have food disorders. Her article contains no policy proposals. She seems, however, insensitive to the fact that the impersonality of market transactions protects privacy and freedom; West does not have to undergo a psychiatric examination before she can buy a tomato.

The failure of the market to work well (or as well as we might like it to work) for reasons other than consumers' incompetence is illustrated by a woman's yielding to the sexual advances of a man who has power over her husband's career. Actually West appears to have misunderstood the incident in *The Trial* between K. and the woman washing clothes, from which this illustration is drawn. They are talking when the woman sees a law student who we are told may someday be a big shot. She goes over to the student, who begins kissing her. K. intervenes but the student picks the woman up bodily and makes off with her. K. then assaults the student, but the woman tells him to stop because the student is only obeying the orders of the Examining Magistrate. The student, puffing with fatigue, carries her up one of the stairways in the court's tenement. "The woman waved her hand to K. as he stood below, and shrugged her shoulders to suggest that she was not to blame for this abduction, but very little regret could be read into that dumb show . . . He was forced to the conclusion that the woman not only had betrayed him, but also had lied in saying that she was being carried to the Examining Magistrate. The Examining Magistrate surely could not be sitting waiting in a garret."[18] This is not, as West believes, a depiction of the exploitation of women; it is a mordant reverie (ending in a joke) about desire and diffidence. K. would like to believe that in yielding to the law student the woman is acting under compulsion, but he gradually realizes that this is not true, that she and the student are playing with him. (Notice also that K., not the woman's husband, is depicted as the victim in this episode.) Most of the compulsion in *The Trial* is inside K.'s head.[19]

[18] Kafka, note 10 above, at 74. This scene, which West thinks shows Kafka's sensitivity to the problem of exploitation of woman, is, curiously enough, Exhibit A in a feminist denunciation of Kafka for insensitivity to the problem. See Evelyn Torton Beck, "Kafka's Traffic in Women: Gender, Power, and Sexuality," 26 *Literary Review* 565, 569–570 (1983).

[19] See, for example, Gray, note 7 above, chap. 7; Richard Weisberg, "Avoiding Central Realities: Narrative Terror and the Failure of French Culture under the Occupation," 5 *Human Rights Quarterly* 151, 158–160 (1983). Similarly, the whipping scene in *The Trial*, which I mentioned briefly in Chapter 2 and which West interprets as a commentary on employment relations, is not that at all. Joseph K. opens the door to a storage room in his bank and there are the officers who had arrested him, being whipped for having stolen his underwear during

But suppose Kafka *were* talking about sexual harassment by supervisory employees. Such harassment (whether of a female worker or, as in *The Trial*, of a male worker's wife) is not, as West appears to believe, economically efficient and thus demonstrative of the Pareto principle's moral inadequacy. Sexual harassment by superiors is, or at least is highly likely to be, a market failure, caused by what economists call "agency costs." It reduces the output of both worker and supervisor, and also forces the employer to pay higher wages to workers to compensate them for the unpleasantness of the workplace, much as employers are forced to pay higher wages to workers to compensate them for the risk of illness or injury.[20] Could the employer offset those additional costs by paying the supervisors less, on the theory that he has given them, in lieu of some wages, a license to harass female workers? This is possible in principle, but highly unlikely. Since there are fewer supervisors than workers and not all supervisors want to harass other employees, cutting supervisors' pay is unlikely to compensate the employer fully for (1) the higher wages he must pay his female employees to compensate them for the risk of harassment and (2) the reduction in the productivity of those supervisors and workers who spend their time respectively making and fending off (or yielding to) sexual advances, rather than working. Furthermore, if sexual harassment is common, women who are less sensitive or more compliant will have a competitive advantage; they will be slower to quit and quicker to be promoted. There is no reason to think they will be the better workers, however, so there will be an inefficient sorting of workers to jobs, just as when promotions are based on nepotism rather than merit.

The fact that sexual harassment is almost certainly inefficient does not mean that competition will eliminate it without any assistance from law. The costs of detecting and proving it are high, and anyway not every

---

the arrest. See Kafka, note 10 above, at 6, 103–106. The scene reeks of sadomasochism. The employment context—the officers are being whipped on the orders of their superiors—is incidental. For good discussions see Gray, note 7 above, at 112–113; Henry Sussman, "The Court as Text: Inversion, Supplanting, and Derangement in Kafka's *Der Prozess*," 92 *Publications of the Modern Language Association* 41, 43 (1977). Cf. Norris, note 14 above. It would be reckless to make the whipping scene a part of one's empirical basis for formulating public policy toward the workplace!

[20] That workers demand and receive wage premiums for assuming risks of physical injury or death is well documented. See Richard Thaler and Sherwin Rosen, "The Value of Saving a Life: Evidence from the Labor Market," in *Household Production and Consumption* 265 (Nestor E. Terleckyj ed. 1976); Craig A. Olson, "An Analysis of Wage Differentials Received by Workers on Dangerous Jobs," 16 *Journal of Human Resources* 167 (1981); W. Kip Viscusi, *Employment Hazards: An Investigation of Market Performance*, pt. III (1979); W. Kip Viscusi, *Risk by Choice: Regulating Health and Safety in the Workplace*, chap. 3 (1983).

potential efficiency is achieved in every market. Most employers are male, and they may not evaluate issues of sexual harassment as clear-sightedly as a genderless robot would—although those who do will have lower costs than their competitors and may gradually supplant them. Probably the main reason why sexual harassment persists in the workplace, despite being doubly nonconsensual—being involuntary on the woman's part (as the word "harassment" connotes) and a source of incompletely compensated costs to the employer—is that it often is hard to tell apart from ordinary flirtations between co-workers. The costs to the employer of distinguishing between these externally similar behaviors may exceed the benefits in lower wages and greater productivity. This does not make sexual harassment either a voluntary practice (that is, consented to) or a value-maximizing one. It is still a market abuse, whether or not one worth trying to stamp out completely. Stealing from one's employer is not a voluntary or wealth-maximizing transaction even if the employer is unable to prevent it.

West says that "most of what happens to Kafka's fictional characters is fully consensual" (p. 390). This ignores not only what happens to Gregor when he is changed into a bug and Joseph K. when he is arrested, but also, as we have just seen, the fact that a decision made under the influence of a mental disease is not fully consensual; nor is extorting sexual favors. Among the "fully consensual" transactions listed in the conclusion to West's article (see p. 427) many are not consensual at all, and it is unclear whether the others are consensual, because we are not told whether there is compensation. By definition, a woman does not consent to forcible rape, but whether a worker consents to working in a dangerous environment depends on whether he is paid to do so or tricked into doing so (the dangers may be concealed). The economic analysis of fraud and duress does not treat fraudulent or coerced choices as consensual. Far from denying that fraud, duress, incapacity, and sometimes mistake should be defenses to suits to enforce contracts, economic analysis demonstrates that such defenses are necessary in order to make sure that inefficient transactions are not enforced.[21]

It might seem, however, that consenting to work in a hazardous environment and consenting to work for an employer who finds it too costly to prevent sexual harassment by supervisory employees would be the same thing—so why did I call sexual harassment a market abuse? The reason is that although the employer may be blameless in both

---

[21] See, for example, my *Economic Analysis of Law*, note 1 above, at 87–88, 90–91, 96–105.

cases, there is always a blameworthy actor in the second case. A workplace may be dangerous for reasons beyond anyone's control, or ability to prevent at reasonable cost; but sexual harassment, like murder and theft, occurs only when there is a wrongdoer. Workplace hazards may also be due to wrongdoing—to carelessness, or worse. But they need not be, and when they are not no blame attaches to anyone if a worker with adequate foreknowledge of the risks is injured. There is no market abuse in that case; there is always (or almost always) one in the case of sexual harassment.

The second type of situation that West uses to argue against the ethical significance of consensual transactions is the hard or risky choice, illustrated by my example of workplace hazards and by her example of a homosexual who continues to patronize homosexual bathhouses despite a high risk of contracting AIDS. (West abstracts, as shall I, from the most problematic aspect of the homosexual's behavior from an economic standpoint: that one who puts himself at risk of catching a communicable disease is also imposing a risk on other people and thus creating an "external cost" that may warrant regulation even under a laissez-faire theory of the state.) If homosexuality is considered to be a mental disease like bulimia or anorexia, this case can be assimilated to the first group. If not, the homosexual is merely someone put to an unhappy choice: life-style or life expectancy. West may believe that since the sex drive is instinctual, no choice that it influences can be a free one. But most human choices are determined or at least strongly influenced by preferences and aversions that have their roots in instinct—the instinct to survive, the instinct to reproduce. If any choice rooted in our "animal instincts" is on that account to invite government intervention, then West must conceive of the problem of political governance on the analogy of the governance of a zoo as well as that of an insane asylum.

The bathhouse example is in one aspect merely a sordid illustration of choice under uncertainty—choice that has the property that it may turn out badly. Here is another example. A spinal fusion operation intended to alleviate the agonizing pain of spinal disk disease carries with it a significant risk of causing paralysis. Should a patient who is fully informed of the risk and of the possible benefits of the operation be forbidden to consent to the operation, because it is a choice made under uncertainty? If, coerced by pain as it were, the patient chooses the operation and becomes paralyzed, does that show that he or she lacked freedom of choice? That such choices should be reserved to physicians, or to the state? That risky operations should be forbidden altogether, so that the occasion for choice does not arise?

Choice under uncertainty pervades our lives. The "hunger artist" (if the story is read literally) failed to predict consumer preference correctly and found himself displaced by a panther, just as a comedian might find himself displaced in popular favor by Blackie the talking cat (see the Introduction) or by an animated mouse.[22] In a figurative sense every failed entrepreneur "starves"; but if he chose entrepreneurship with his eyes open, must we feel sorry for him? It is not an unexpected change in consumer preferences that makes us feel sorry for Kafka's hunger artist.[23]

Here is another example. You have a choice between similar jobs in two different cities. You take one and years later are killed in an auto accident. The accident rate is the same in the two cities and the jobs require the same amount of driving, but of course if you had taken the other job the chances are slight that you would have been killed in an accident. Does this show that you made a bad choice? If not, does this not mean that the ex ante perspective is, normally anyway, the correct perspective in which to evaluate choices made under uncertainty?

As part of her general dislike for risk-taking, West is too hard on people who buy lottery tickets, literal or figurative. Suppose you are a farmer who does not want to assume the risk of price fluctuations, and therefore you want to sell your crop for a fixed price before it is harvested. In other words, you want to hedge. To do so, you must find someone willing to speculate—someone who likes risk-taking. And the more this someone likes risk the less he will charge you to bear it—he may even pay you to shift the risk of price fluctuations to him. Speculation thus facilitates hedging. It also reduces uncertainty about values by bringing more people into the market—speculators, on top of producers and consumers. Market price may not be a good predictor of market value when the market is very thin; speculators make it thicker.

A more important point than that risk preferrers often perform a social service is that most risk is compensated. The risk you take when

[22] This is not a ridiculous analogy, because there really were "hunger artists" on the Continent in Kafka's day, and indeed as late as 1956. See Breon Mitchell, "Kafka and the Hunger Artists," in *Kafka and the Contemporary Critical Performance: Centenary Readings* 236 (Alan Udoff ed. 1987); Meno Spann, *Franz Kafka* 191 n. 1 (1976). Their disappearance from the commercial scene both sets the stage for West's market analysis and has made Kafka's story more exotic and arresting, just as the rise of totalitarianism has made *In the Penal Colony* and *The Trial* seem prophetic. History has been as kind to Kafka as life was cruel to him.

[23] Not that Kafka meant us just to feel sorry for the hunger artist. No doubt we are meant to take the part both of the protagonist and of the other characters, and thus in *The Metamorphosis* to see Gregor from his standpoint and from his family's standpoint—to feel sorry for him and disgusted by him. We are meant to feel for the hunger artist and to laugh at him. Kafka's art is affecting but not sentimental.

you buy a lottery ticket is not compensated in pecuniary terms because the cost of the ticket exceeds the expected payoff (the prize if you win multiplied by the probability of winning). Lotteries appeal only to people who like risk; for them, the purchase of the lottery ticket is utility-maximizing. But the risk you take when you buy stock in a highly leveraged company or commit yourself to a risky career such as acting or marry someone whose qualities you are not sure about is compensated risk; you engage in the risky activity because the net expected payoff to you is positive.[24] Of course, after the fact you may be sorely disappointed. But that is the risk you assumed. If the choice was a good one ex ante, we need not listen to your bellyaching ex post, just as we need not sympathize with the losers in the lottery. And even if we sympathize with you on a personal level, your plight, being self-created, does not present a sympathetic case for using the power of government to bail you out. Government is coercion. The forced transfer of wealth from the frugal, the prudent, and the saving to a person who takes financial risks with his eyes open is morally questionable.

Another type of choice is the choice of the lesser of two evils. That may also describe some choices under uncertainty, as we saw, but now I want to abstract from uncertainty. As West notes, a job can still be a bad job even though the worker is not a slave. For a person who lacks highly marketable skills, the range of job choices is narrow; the best job the person can get may be greatly inferior to the jobs of other workers. The feasible set of choices is always limited, however; it does not follow that people should not be allowed to make choices within their feasible set, or that the choices they make lack authenticity because other people have larger feasible sets. And note that the wealthier the society is, the larger is the feasible set for most people. Wealth promotes freedom.[25] That is why, as noted in the last chapter, laws that enable people to make binding commitments and that discourage coercion increase rather than reduce human freedom.

To take another of West's examples, it is not true in our society that a wife must take abuse from her husband; she can leave him. If she stays, it will usually (though not always) be because, all things considered, the

---

[24] For evidence from the securities, job, and marriage markets, respectively, see James H. Lorie and Mary T. Hamilton, *The Stock Market: Theories and Evidence*, chaps. 11–12 (1973); John M. Aboud and Orley Ashenfelter, "Anticipated Unemployment, Temporary Layoffs, and Compensating Wage Differentials," in *Studies in Labor Markets* 141 (Sherwin Rosen ed. 1981); Gary S. Becker, *A Treatise on the Family*, chaps. 3–4 (1981).

[25] See George J. Stigler, "Wealth, and Possibly Liberty," 7 *Journal of Legal Studies* 213 (1978).

alternatives are even worse. Freedom is not Utopia and will not prevent the dietary disorders and "bad sex" (p. 390)[26] that loom so large in West's redaction of Kafka's fictional world. But a system in which government was quick to break up families in order to protect wives from themselves would be no improvement.

Between the incompetent choice of the mentally ill person and the merely hard choice lies the case of addiction. An alcoholic surrenders an important part of his freedom, and, it might seem, gets little in return. Yet to prohibit people from becoming alcoholics would infringe their freedom to choose a particular, if to the sober a revolting, mode of life. If the choice to become an alcoholic or some other sort of addict is made on incomplete information or involves uncompensated costs to third parties (for example, in the form of accidents caused by drunk driving), then it is not a "free" choice in the Pareto-superior sense; and perhaps that is the typical case of addiction.[27] But the fact that it is a choice to pursue an unfree type of life does not make the choice itself unfree.

Between the case of addiction and the merely hard choice lies the angry, impetuous, compulsive, "irrational" choice that all of us make at times. Whether such behavior should be considered "free" and entitled to respect is a profound philosophical question; but, being deeply ingrained in the

---

[26] Better described, however, by Eliot than by Kafka, in the typist passage from Part III of *The Waste Land*:

> He, the young man carbuncular, arrives,
> A small house agent's clerk, with one bold stare.
> One of the low on whom assurance sits
> As a silk hat on a Bradford millionaire.
> The time is now propitious, as he guesses,
> The meal is ended, she is bored and tired,
> Endeavours to engage her in caresses
> Which still are unreproved, if undesired.
> Flushed and decided, he assaults at once;
> Exploring hands encounter no defence;
> His vanity requires no response,
> And makes a welcome of indifference.
> . . . . .
> Bestows one final patronising kiss,
> And gropes his way, finding the stairs unlit.
>
>    She turns and looks a moment in the glass,
> Hardly aware of her departed lover;
> Her brain allows one half-formed thought to pass:
> 'Well now that's done: and I'm glad it's over.'

[27] But see Gary S. Becker and Kevin M. Murphy, "A Theory of Rational Addiction" (mimeo., University of Chicago Department of Economics, March 1986).

human animal, such behavior is not likely to be altered by changing the form of government or the nature of the social and economic organization. Moreover, by expanding the power of government to prevent individuals from making rash, angry, and crazy decisions about their own lives, we increase the likelihood of rash, angry, and crazy decisions about other people's lives: for government officials cannot be assumed to be free from the weaknesses that afflict private persons. There are different degrees of government intervention, of course. Subsidizing clinics that help people break the smoking habit is not so intrusive an intervention in the private sphere as prohibiting the sale of cigarettes. Yet the taxes required to defray the expense of such a subsidy, and of subsidies designed to wean people from their other bad choices, would reduce freedom in the functional sense noted earlier. For by reducing people's income, higher taxes reduce people's feasible choice sets. Government programs designed to reduce the number of bad choices that people make may end up reducing the number of their choices, period.

## Kafka's Quietism

Even the least problematic choices are difficult in West's version of Kafka's fictive world, because its denizens do not like to make choices; they crave submission to authority. If this were true of most Americans we would have to rethink our national commitment to relatively free markets and to popular government. But the characters in Kafka's fiction are not typical 1980s Americans.[28] Reflecting their creator's neuroticism and his historical situation as a German-speaking Czech Jew in the twilight, disintegration, and aftermath of the Austro-Hungarian Empire (Kafka died in 1924), they are marked by an extraordinary submissiveness, wonderfully illustrated not only by Georg Bendemann, Gregor Samsa, Joseph K., and the traveler in *Before the Law*, but also by the citizens in *The Refusal*, who are relieved when their petitions for exemption from onerous laws are denied.

---

[28] Anyone who doubts this should read *Amerika*, Kafka's unfinished picaresque novel about a 16-year-old German immigrant to the United States. Kafka never traveled to America—never traveled outside central Europe as a matter of fact—and the picture he gives of America is wonderfully inaccurate. Robin West's omission of this work is odd because it is the only work of Kafka's that concentrates on the working world: Karl Rossmann, its hero, seeks his fortune in America. The high points of the book—Karl's attempt to assist the stoker in his grievance against his employer and Karl's adventures as an elevator operator in the Hotel Occidental—are Kafka's most extensive explorations of the employment relation. One might also have expected West to discuss *The Castle*, which has been called a criticism of bureaucracy. See Thomas R. McDaniel, "Weber and Kafka on Bureaucracy: A Question of Perspective," 78 *South Atlantic Quarterly* 361 (1979).

*The Refusal* is set in an unimportant town in a large military empire. The town is far from either a frontier or the capital; it is a backwater. Authority is represented by the tax collector, who has the rank of colonel and in effect rules the town, and by the fierce-looking soldiers who intimidate the citizens. The public life of the town centers on the occasions when the colonel receives petitions for tax exemption, or for permission to cut timber from the imperial forests at a reduced price, or for another privilege or exemption. On these "occasions the colonel stood upright, holding in front of him two poles of bamboo in his outstretched hands. This is an ancient custom implying more or less [*etwa*—'approximately'] that he supports the law, and the law supports him" (p. 266). The petition is always refused, and when this happens "an undeniable sense of relief passe[s] through the crowd . . . Without this refusal one simply cannot get along, yet at the same time these official occasions designed to receive the refusal are by no means a formality. Time after time one goes there full of expectation and in all seriousness and then one returns, if not exactly strengthened or happy, nevertheless not disappointed or tired" (p. 267). Only the young people—those between seventeen and twenty—are not content with these refusals.

The yearning for authority, the fear of change, and the masochistic submissiveness are palpable. Perhaps in the colonel's refusal to grant exemptions from the laws one can sense an ironic commentary on the theme of "a government of laws, not men." Perhaps the colonel (described as breathing like a frog when he is listening to the petition, and collapsing into his chair after delivering his judgment) is the stunted descendant of the oracle at Delphi or the Hebrew prophets. Perhaps he is Kafka's father—or everyone's father in some obscure and disturbing sense. The citizens' relief when their requests are denied puts one in mind of the emotionally anesthetized inhabitants of *The Waste Land*, who fear life (and the epigraph of the poem reports the death wish of an oracle—the Sibyl of Cumae, mentioned in Chapter 2). *The Refusal* was written in 1920—two years before *The Waste Land*. These are distinguished works of literature but they are also period pieces, written in the aftermath of World War I by a dying man and a man recovering from a nervous breakdown, respectively. Kafka "is quite true to his time and place, but it is surely a time and place in which few of us will want to linger."[29]

West argues that in another late story, *The Problem of Our Laws*, "Kafka straightforwardly describes his vision of the nature of law and

[29] Edmund Wilson, "A Dissenting Opinion on Kafka," in *Kafka: A Collection of Critical Essays*, note 7 above, at 91, 96.

legal authority, and the mechanism of legitimation upon which it depends. The authority of law, Kafka tells us, is ultimately sustained not by force, but by the craving of the governed for judgment by lawful, 'noble' authority" (p. 422). But "straightforward" is not a word that can be used to describe *The Problem of Our Laws*. This two-page parable describes a society in which the law is kept secret by the small group of nobles (*kleine Adelsgruppe*) that rules the society. So people begin to wonder, how do we know there *are* any laws? And some decide the only law is: what the nobility does, is law. But most people reject this view, instead diligently searching the acts of the nobles for clues that those acts are manifestations of the secret laws, and hoping eventually to understand the laws—at which point, they believe, the nobility will vanish.

The secrecy of the laws, their mysteriousness, and the deference and passivity of the population link *The Problem of Our Laws* to *The Refusal* and to *The Trial*, and provide support for West's reading. However, one might read "judiciary" for "nobility," and interpret the story as a parable about legal formalism and legal realism, or about natural law and positive law, rather than interpret it in terms of political sociology. There is a sense in which law as we know it is indeed a secret of judges, for until the judges speak the law is unknown in detail. The realist or positivist regards the "law" that is behind the judges' decisions as a fake. He wants to treat the decisions themselves as the law, or, more precisely, wants to infer the law from the decisions. To him the law is a prediction, from the decisions, of what the judges will do when confronted by a particular set of facts. The formalist or natural lawyer— whose point of view, though contested, still dominates the society depicted in Kafka's parable—clings to the faith that there is some body of enduring and consistent principles underlying and determining the judges' decisions and that with enough insight we might discover that something and maybe even dispense with the judges.

Hints of such a faith can be found in other works by Kafka. In Chapter 2, I mentioned two such hints in *The Trial*; perhaps another can be found in a marvelous one-page parable, *The New Advocate*, which begins: "We have a new advocate, Dr. Bucephalus. There is little in his appearance to remind you that he was once Alexander of Macedon's battle charger," yet he "mount[s] the marble steps" to the courthouse "with a high action that made them ring beneath his feet . . . In general the Bar approves the admission of Bucephalus. With astonishing insight people tell themselves that, modern society being what it is, Bucephalus is in a difficult position . . . Nowadays—it cannot be denied—there is no Alexander the Great . . . So perhaps it is really best to do as

Bucephalus has done and absorb oneself in law books" (pp. 414–415). Is this just an ironic commentary on the disappearance of the heroic from modern life, on a par with the descent of heaven into *The Trial*'s attic court? The last sentence of the parable makes me wonder: "In the quiet lamplight, his flanks unhampered by the thighs of a rider, free and far from the clamor of battle, he reads and turns the pages of our ancient tomes" (p. 415). Bucephalus is like the people in *The Problem of Our Laws* who have faith in the existence of natural law: he thinks that if he reads the ancient tomes carefully enough he may discover something worthy of his heritage. Only he is more dignified and enterprising than they. Yet whatever else he is, Bucephalus is a horse, so that his superior dignity and enterprise reinforce the reader's impression of Kafka's dyspeptic assessment of human potential.

Misled, perhaps, by the abnormal passivity of Kafka's (human) characters, West confuses the desire to surrender the power of choice over the essential conditions of one's life (self-slavery, the pact with the devil, Antonio's bond, the abjectness of the population in *The Refusal*) with the decision to submit to partial and temporary direction or instruction by others. She considers both types of decision inconsistent with free choice, but the second is not. A person will submit to hierarchical direction by going to work for a company, rather than remaining an independent contractor, only if his expected welfare is greater as an employee than as an independent contractor. The status is freely chosen, and since the choice is not irrevocable there is no surrender of essential autonomy. Similarly, I do not surrender my freedom to choose by deciding to take piano lessons. Instruction is not coercion; the educated person is freer than the uneducated one. And a person has more rather than less freedom if he is allowed to make a legally binding contract, even though by making it he surrenders some freedom while the contract is in force. If I make a legally binding commitment to pay a builder to build a house for me, I enlarge my freedom, for without the commitment I could not get the house built unless I paid for it in advance. This is another example of the enabling function of law—a function of which West is as heedless as Weisberg.

The hardest question about freedom of contract is whether every contract between consenting and adequately informed adults should be enforced to the hilt: the suicide pact, the Faustian bargain, the penalty clause. These transactions are, or at least can be, Pareto-superior; if they ought nevertheless to be prohibited, this suggests a limitation on the Pareto principle. It is a limitation without clear bounds, since it can be expanded imperceptibly to pick up successively less risky choices—

sweeping in somewhere along the way the homosexual-bathhouse case and eventually even the purchase of tomatoes! Here is a fertile subject of inquiry, but not one on which the study of Kafka's fiction casts light or about which West has much to say. Although she is unhappy with the ethics of free choice, she has nothing to propose in its place. In our society as in every society there are many unhappy and neurotic people, many unlucky people, many stupid people, many who are prone to self-deception and wishful thinking, and many lunatics, and the existence of such people makes unflinching adherence to the principles of free choice problematic. Unfortunately, West has no suggestions for reducing the number of these unfortunates. Nor does she consider whether enough people are incompetent at coping with the challenges of life in a free society to justify making it less free, and whether we can estimate the number of such people from the fiction of Kafka, distinguished as that fiction is.

West's skepticism about choices made in market settings suggests that she may prefer a system in which more choices are made politically; she seems, after all, not averse to politicizing literature. But she does not argue the case for such a system, and the history and current practice of socialism do not make the case for her. It does not follow that because many people make some bad choices most people would be better off if they were forbidden to make choices. The choices would still be made, only by politicians rather than by the individuals who are directly concerned in them and therefore presumptively better able to make them wisely.

West underestimates the difficulty of getting from here to Utopia. She is concerned about the plight of the failed entrepreneur but does not realize that if society commits itself to bail him out it encourages risky behavior, which she does not like, by reducing the penalties for risk; it also transfers wealth from the risk-averse to the risk-preferring. Moreover, the problems of many of the people whose freedom of choice she questions, notably the promiscuous homosexual and the bulimic consumer, have nothing to do with poverty and could not be solved by a redistribution of wealth, the current socialist panacea. It is not much use saying that things are bad without being able to suggest how they could be made better.

West is worried about government's doing too much as well as too little. She is worried that because Kafka's fictional characters seem willing to surrender their freedom of political choice forever, in much the same way that a person who signs a contract constrains some of his choices for a limited time, a belief in the morality of consent could be used to legitimize authoritarianism. Put aside the fact that government in Kafka is metaphor rather than actuality and notice the pickle in which West's analysis puts her: if consent is ethically significant, authoritarian government is legitimate if consented to; if consent is not ethically significant, an authoritarian government that suppresses freedom cannot be criticized on that account. The dilemma is avoided by recognizing that most people do not want an authoritarian government; they fear the consequences of a monopoly of political power. This fear animated the original design of our government and continues strong today. World War II drove the point home for Europeans.

## The Grand Inquisitor and Other Social Theorists

If West really believes that Americans have the same desire to be ruled with an iron hand as some of Kafka's fictitious characters express—if she believes that the citizens of the freest society in the history of the world have "cravings for judgment and punishment by noble authority" (p. 422) and are "attracted to the authoritarian structure of law" and "of fate" (p. 423) and "to the power and punitive authority of the state" (p. 424), and that our world like Kafka's "is peopled by excessively authoritarian personalities" (p. 387)—then one can understand why she is troubled by a political philosophy which assumes that people are on the whole competent judges of their self-interest. But if she believes these things she lives in a world that few will think is our world. She lives in the world of the Grand Inquisitor, who tells Jesus Christ that for the great mass of mankind freedom of choice is a source of profound misery; that what people crave is to be led around like sheep, by miracle, mystery, and authority. " 'Thou didst not come down from the Cross when they shouted to Thee, mocking and reviling Thee, "Come down from the cross and we will believe that Thou art He." Thou didst not come down, for again Thou wouldst not enslave man by a miracle, and didst crave faith given freely, not based on miracle. Thou didst crave for free love and not the base raptures of the slave before the might that has overawed him forever. But Thou didst think too highly of men therein, for they are slaves, of course, though rebellious by nature.' "[30]

The Grand Inquisitor's argument can be transposed into economic terms—indeed, there is more than a hint of such a transposition in his diatribe. Some people do not want the burden of choice, such as a free market imposes on them. They want government to make their

[30] Fyodor Dostoevsky, *The Brothers Karamazov* 236 (Constance Garnett and Ralph E. Matlaw trans., Matlaw ed. 1976).

decisions, including their economic decisions, for them. " 'Dost Thou know that the ages will pass, and humanity will proclaim by the lips of their sages that there is no crime, and therefore no sin; there is only hunger? . . . In the end they will lay their freedom at our feet, and say to us, "Make us your slaves, but feed us." They will understand themselves, at last, that freedom and bread enough for all are inconceivable together' " (pp. 233–234).

The Grand Inquisitor's assessment of human nature seems not far removed from West's; and if the assessment is correct (which Dostoevsky did not believe), maybe the Grand Inquisitor's totalitarian prescription (echoed among other places in Orwell's novel *1984*) is correct too:

> "We shall allow them even sin, they are weak and helpless, and they will love us like children because we allow them to sin. We shall tell them that every sin will be expiated, if it is done with our permission, that we allow them to sin because we love them, and the punishment for these sins we take upon ourselves . . . And they will have no secrets from us. We shall allow or forbid them to live with their wives and mistresses, to have or not to have children—according to whether they have been obedient or disobedient—and they will submit to us gladly and cheerfully. The most painful secrets of their conscience, all, all they will bring to us, and we shall have an answer for all. And they will be glad to believe our answer, for it will save them from the great anxiety and terrible agony they endure at present in making a free decision for themselves. And all will be happy, all the millions of creatures except the hundred thousand who rule over them . . . There will be thousands of millions of happy babes, and a hundred thousand sufferers who have taken upon themselves the curse of the knowledge of good and evil. Peacefully they will die, peacefully they will expire in Thy name, and beyond the grave they will find nothing but death. But we shall keep the secret, and for their happiness we shall entice them with the reward of heaven and eternity." (p. 240)

West would not accept the Grand Inquisitor's program. But if (as appears) she agrees with him that mankind cannot bear freedom, she has an obligation to propose a humane and workable alternative.

The difference between the Grand Inquisitor and West is the following: he locates the human flight from freedom in the inherent and ineradicable weakness of the human creature; she, reflecting the Romanticism of Blake, Shelley, and Rousseau, believes that the institutions of bourgeois society have stunted our innate capacity for freely chosen, rewarding, nonexploitive relationships—so that if by an effort of sheer will and insight we could overthrow these institutions we might transform the human condition. When West in another article claims that individuals are "capable of empathic nurturing in the public sphere," she quickly adds that "the origin of our capacity for public, empathic nurturing is a dimly remembered feeling of life-giving solidarity with others in our world"[31]—thus echoing Wordsworth's line, "Our birth is but a sleep and a forgetting." When she says that "to the communitarian scholar, the central concern of law is the tension between our present separateness and our remembered union with the world at large, particularly with the strangers in it,"[32] she both puts one in mind of Blake's metaphor of human society as a single human body and ties it to the infant's sense, stressed by Blake and Wordsworth, of oneness with the world (that is, its mother).[33] In another article she emphasizes the esemplastic power of the imagination: "The future of community depends not just upon political or even revolutionary action. It also depends upon our imaginative, rational, spiritual, and moral freedom to break free of our present, and to conceive of other ideal worlds."[34]

The difference between a poet, such as Blake, and a law professor, such as Robin West, is that we do not require the poet to show us how to get from where we are to where in his imaginative vision he wants us to be. The urge to break free from conditions of scarcity, mortality, hierarchy, and inequality is a permanent element of human psychology, and no more is needed as a grounding for great literature. It may also be a necessary condition for social reform. But it is not a sufficient condition; indeed, in undiluted form it is a recipe for disaster. West does not have a program for achieving or even approaching the kind of apocalyptic transformation of the human condition envisaged by Blake. The record of Utopian social philosophies and social experiments is not encouraging; the record of Romantic dystopias, such as Nazi Germany, speaks for itself. Romanticism in law and politics is fraught with danger.

I have cited West's article on Freud's legal theory several times; and the reader may be wondering, in view of Kafka's tormented relationship with his father and the amenability of Kafka's fiction to Freudian interpretations, why West does not apply that theory to Kafka. Two explanations come to mind. The first is that, although paternal authority

[31] "Law, Rights, and Other Totemic Illusions," note 4 above, at 859 (footnotes omitted).
[32] Id. at 861 (footnote omitted).
[33] See Northrop Frye, "Blake's Treatment of the Archetype," in *English Romantic Poets: Modern Essays in Criticism* 55, 62 (M. H. Abrams ed., 2d ed. 1975); Frye, *Fearful Symmetry: A Study of William Blake*, chap. 1 (1947).
[34] "Jurisprudence as Narrative: An Aesthetic Analysis of Modern Legal Theory," 60 *New York University Law Review* 145, 202 (1985).

resembles legal authority and although Joseph K., the citizens in *The Refusal*, and other inhabitants of Kafka's fictional world are easily seen as seeking a missing father in their ostensible quest for law, the particulars of Freud's legal theory[35] do not fit the tone of Kafka's writings. The theory stresses human aggressiveness: Freud considered law a father substitute brought into being by the remorse felt by powerful brothers who had ganged up and killed their father; the function of law is thus to repress powerful men. The people in Kafka's fiction on whom the law bears down, or who are searching for the law, are weak. To Freud, such people would be the natural beneficiaries of law; to Kafka, they are either its victims or its hopeless suppliants.

Second, the idea that the proper as well as the actual role of law and the state is to control the excesses of individualism is not congenial to the Romantic view that these institutions have perverted man's natural goodness. West likes Freud's theory to the extent that it emphasizes the role of law in protecting the weak from the strong, for she is disturbed by the element of Social Darwinism in economic thought and believes that to make competition the preferred method of allocating resources is to favor the strong. Although she does not distinguish adequately between the role of law in preventing the use of force or fraud to reallocate resources (the Freudian, and also, with certain refinements, the economic view) and its role in equalizing the distribution of resources (the modern left-wing aspiration for law), she does realize that in emphasizing innate human aggressiveness Freud's theory casts doubt on the feasibility of reorganizing human society on the basis of empathic nurturing. As a result she declines to embrace the theory in its entirety.

This discussion should help to make clear that modern legal radicalism is not merely the continuation (or perhaps the *reductio ad absurdum*) of the legal realist movement of the 1920s and 1930s. The legal realists were meliorists. They attacked a form of conceptualism that viewed law as a closed logical system which ideas of public policy must not be allowed to penetrate.[36] In terms of the Table of Opposed Conceptions of Law in Chapter 2, they thought law had been pushed too far into the left-hand column (not left politically, of course). Some of the realists, notably Jerome Frank, were unduly hostile to "ruledness," which they associated

---

[35] Well summarized in "Law, Rights, and Other Totemic Illusions," note 4 above, at 822–844.

[36] See Martin P. Golding, "Jurisprudence and Legal Philosophy in Twentieth-Century America: Major Themes and Developments," 36 *Journal of Legal Education* 441, 452–473 (1986); William Twining, *Karl Llewellyn and the Realist Movement* (1973), especially chap. 15; George C. Christie, *Jurisprudence: Text and Readings on the Philosophy of Law*, chap. 4 (1973); "History of American Legal Thought II: The American 'Legal Realists' " (Dennis J. Hutchinson ed., mimeo., University of Chicago Law School, 1984).

(as perhaps Shakespeare did) with psychological insecurity.[37] But they were not Utopian dreamers; they did not believe in the perfectibility of human nature and society; and they had a clear idea of specific legal reforms that they wanted to and in large measure did achieve.

A book on law and literature, however, is not the place to attempt a definitive treatment of legal realism, critical legal studies, or the political, ethical, and epistemological dimensions of free choice, any more than to determine the causes of the Holocaust. The contemplation of literature by lawyers can at best open broad vistas of social significance—and only at the risk of using literature tendentiously. With this qualification I necessarily raise the issue of objectivity in interpretation. This chapter and the last have made the issue inescapable. Having seen me disagree emphatically with the literary interpretations offered by Weisberg and West, the reader is entitled to ask how such disagreements can ever be resolved (for example, what role should the author's biography play?), especially when dealing with such enigmatic literature as *Billy Budd* and the fiction of Kafka.[38] The next chapter examines this question.

[37] See Jerome Frank, *Law and the Modern Mind* (1930).

[38] *Billy Budd*, like *The Trial*, was never finished. The ambiguity of Kafka's fiction is one of the catalysts of the crisis of modern literary theory, discussed in the next chapter. See Judith Ryan, "Our Trial: Franz Kafka's Challenge to Literary Theory," 18 *Novel: A Forum on Fiction* 257 (1985); Anthony Thorlby, "The Structure of Nothing," in *Reconstructing Literature* 160 (Laurence Lerner ed. 1983); cf. Stanley Corngold, "The Hermeneutic of 'The Judgment,' " in *The Problem of "The Judgment": Eleven Approaches to Kafka's Story* 39 (Angel Flores ed. 1977).

*part ii*

# Law as a FORM of LITERATURE

# FIVE

## The Interpretation of Statutes and the Constitution

$S$O FAR I have been interpreting works of literature unself-consciously, only occasionally hinting that interpretation might be a problematic activity. However, to an increasing extent literary critics—especially those who practice deconstruction, whose premise, as wittily stated by Gerald Graff, is that "all texts are allegories of their own unreadability"[1]—and academic lawyers, especially those associated with the critical legal studies movement,[2] contend that the interpretation of literary and legal texts is deeply problematic, and

[1] *Professing Literature: An Institutional History* 241 (1987). On deconstruction as a method of literary criticism see Harold Bloom et al., *Deconstruction and Criticism* (1979); Jonathan Culler, *On Deconstruction: Theory and Criticism after Structuralism*, chap. 3 (1982); Howard Felperin, *Beyond Deconstruction: The Uses and Abuses of Literary Theory*, chap. 4 (1985); Christopher Norris, *Deconstruction: Theory and Practice* (1982); *Reconstructing Literature* (Laurence Lerner ed. 1983). On the theory of deconstruction see Henry Staten, *Wittgenstein and Derrida* (1984); translator's preface to Jacques Derrida, *Of Grammatology* (Gayatri Chakravorty Spivak trans. 1976); Culler, above, chap. 3; Richard Rorty, "Philosophy as a Kind of Writing: An Essay on Derrida," 10 *New Literary History* 141 (1978). An influential exponent of text skepticism whose views I discuss later in this chapter is Stanley Fish. See *Is There a Text in This Class? The Authority of Interpretive Communities* (1980) ("Interpreters do not decode poems; they make them," id. at 327; "Interpretation and the Pluralist Vision," 60 *Texas Law Review* 495 (1982); "Fish v. Fiss," 36 *Stanford Law Review* 1325 (1984); "Pragmatism and Literary Theory: Consequences," 11 *Critical Inquiry* 433 (1985). His position is linked indirectly to deconstruction, because it is derived (though Fish has seemed reluctant to acknowledge the derivation) from the theory of language in Wittgenstein's *Philosophical Investigations*, especially Wittgenstein's discussions of private languages and interpretive communities—on which see Saul A. Kripke, *Wittgenstein on Rules and Private Language: An Elementary Exposition* 91–92, 96–97 (1982); and that theory, in turn, as Staten shows, has strong affinities with deconstruction. See also Newton Garver, "Preface," in *Jacques Derrida, Speech and Phenomena, and Other Essays on Husserl's Theory of Signs* ix (David B. Allison trans. 1973).

[2] See, for example, Gary Peller, "The Metaphysics of American Law," 73 *California Law Review* 1151, 1160 n. 6, 1173–1174 (1985); Sanford Levinson, "Law as Literature," 60 *Texas Law Review* 373 (1982); Paul Brest, "Interpretation and Interest," 34 *Stanford Law Review* 765

maybe even impossible. If the literary skeptics are right, this may seem to have far-reaching implications for law. Like legal scholars, literary scholars deal with complex texts, many of them old; and temporal remoteness often makes one form of meaning—original meaning, arguably the most, or even the only, authentic meaning—difficult to recover: the author, the original readers, and the linguistic and cultural context will all have disappeared. If literary scholars and critics decide that meaning cannot be extracted from literary texts but can only be put into them, should not lawyers, too, give up the pretense of interpreting statutes and the Constitution and admit that what they are doing is making, not finding, law? If so, "judicial activists" no longer need apologize for reading things into the Constitution that do not seem to be there; that is simply the nature of what we naively call "interpretation." Better to say "construction"—and mean it literally.[3]

---

(1982); Jerry Frug, "Henry James, Lee Marvin and the Law," *New York Times Book Review*, Feb. 16, 1986, at 1. The application of deconstruction and other skeptical or (what amounts to the same thing) reader-centered methodologies to legal texts is criticized in Charles Fried, "Sonnet LXV and the 'Black Ink' of the Framers' Intention," 100 *Harvard Law Review* 751 (1987); Owen M. Fiss, "Objectivity and Interpretation," 34 *Stanford Law Review* 739 (1982); Thomas C. Grey, "The Constitution as Scripture," 37 *Stanford Law Review* 1 (1984); Robin L. West, "Adjudication Is Not Interpretation: Some Reservations about the Law-as-Literature Movement," 54 *Tennessee Law Review* 203 (1987). The last two pieces are particularly interesting because their authors are sympathetic to the critical legal studies movement.

Law professors typically use the word "deconstruction" imprecisely, as a synonym for destructive criticism or textual indeterminacy; these are the senses in which it is used by both the critical legal studies movement and its critics. See Clare Dalton, "An Essay in the Deconstruction of Contract Doctrine," 94 *Yale Law Journal* 997 (1985); Elizabeth Fox-Genovese, "Women's Rights, Affirmative Action, and the Myth of Individualism," 54 *George Washington Law Review* 338 (1986); Allan C. Hutchinson, "Indiana Dworkin and the Law's Empire," 96 *Yale Law Journal* 637, 658 (1987); Peller, note 2 above, at 1180; Suzanna Sherry, "Civic Virtue and the Feminine Voice in Constitutional Adjudication," 72 *Virginia Law Review* 543, 572, 578 (1986); Mark Tushnet, "Critical Legal Studies and Constitutional Law: An Essay in Deconstruction," 36 *Stanford Law Review* 623 (1984); K. C. Worden, "Overshooting the Target: A Feminist Deconstruction of Legal Education," 34 *American University Law Review* 1141 (1985); Raoul Berger, " 'Original Intention' in Historical Perspective," 54 *George Washington Law Review* 296, 303 (1986); Clark Byse, "Fifty Years of Legal Education," 71 *Iowa Law Review* 1063 (1986); Owen M. Fiss, "The Death of the Law?" 72 *Cornell Law Review* 1, 12 (1986); Frederick Schauer, "Precedent," 39 *Stanford Law Review* 571, 595 n. 49 (1987). A parallel error is to belittle literary criticism by equating it to deconstruction. See Walter Berns, "Government by Lawyers and Judges," *Commentary*, June 1987, at 17, 18; other examples appear in J. M. Balkin, "Deconstructive Practice and Legal Theory," 96 *Yale Law Journal* 743–744 nn. 2–3 (1987). Balkin's article contains a highly competent description of deconstruction (see id. at 746–761), but when he comes to apply the concept to law it turns out to be just another name for skepticism, caution about hidden premises, and other unexceptionable principles of reading that owe nothing to deconstruction.
[3] On the general question of using literary theory in the interpretation of legal texts see

This chapter seeks to evaluate the skeptical attack, mounted from literary theory, on objectivity in interpretation. My emphasis is on the many differences between the problems of literary and of legal interpretation. After introducing the reader to the principal schools of literary criticism, I explore the contrast, in both literature and law, between "New Critical" and "intentionalist" modes of interpretation. I argue that it is possible to be a New Critic when interpreting literature and an intentionalist when interpreting law; although I consider myself a legal intentionalist (with, however, significant qualifications, explored later in the chapter), I take no comfort from intentionalist literary theory, which I find unconvincing.

## Deconstruction and Other Schools of Criticism

Deconstruction is at once the most skeptical of critical methods and the one least well understood by lawyers, and it is therefore an appropriate starting point for a discussion of the methods of literary criticism. The key to a proper understanding of it is to distinguish between the theory and the literary practice of deconstruction. The theory can be understood only against the background of orthodox language theory (really theories) expounded by semiologists such as Saussure, phenomenologists such as Husserl, speech-act theorists such as Austin and Searle, and more humbly by communication theorists. Greatly simplified, the orthodox theory holds that we create from our perceptions concepts (for example, the concept of the tree that stands in front of my house) that

Kenneth S. Abraham, "Statutory Interpretation and Literary Theory: Some Common Concerns of an Unlikely Pair," 32 *Rutgers Law Review* 676 (1979); William F. Harris II, "Bonding Word and Polity: The Logic of American Constitutionalism," 76 *American Political Science Review* 34 (1982); Sanford Levinson, "Law: On Dworkin, Kennedy, and Ely: Decoding the Legal Past," 51 *Partisan Review* 248 (1984); Richard H. Weisberg, "Text into Theory: A Literary Approach to the Constitution," 20 *Georgia Law Review* 939 (1986); James Boyd White, *Heracles' Bow: Essays on the Rhetoric and Poetics of the Law*, chap. 5 (1985). For an offbeat application see Richard Craswell, "Interpreting Deceptive Advertising," 65 *Boston University Law Review* 657, 671 (1985). On interpretation generally see Josef Bleicher, *Contemporary Hermeneutics: Hermeneutics as Method, Philosophy and Critique* (1980); David Couzens Hoy, *The Critical Circle: Literature, History, and Philosophical Hermeneutics* (1978); Alexander Nehamas, "The Postulated Author: Critical Monism as a Regulative Ideal," 8 *Critical Inquiry* 133 (1981); Stein Haugom Olsen, *The End of Literary Theory* (1987); Samuel Weber, *Institution and Interpretation* (1987); Interpretation Symposium, 58 *Southern California Law Review* 1 (1985). The problematics of interpretation are sometimes attributed to the mass marketing of books, which exacerbates the "solitude of the author and the reader." Robert Escarpit, *The Book Revolution* 43 (1966). The author does not know the reader, and the reader cannot ask the author for clarification.

are outside of time and space and also distinct from the perceptions out of which they are made; the concept of the tree in front of my house exists independently of the particular angles and distances from which I have seen it. At first that concept is imprisoned in my mind. If I want to share it with another person I have to encode it in some physical form ("signifier")—a writing, a sound, a gesture, or whatever. Upon hearing or seeing the signifier, the other person will recreate the same concept in his own mind.

The orthodox theorist realizes, of course, that the process of conveying the concept in my mind to another person's mind may break down; the communication channel is not free of "noise." For one thing, the link between signifier and signified is a matter of convention, and conventions are not universal. A tree is *tree* in English, *arbor* in Latin, *Baum* in German. Sometimes a language lacks a signifier for a particular signified. English, for example, lacks words for the concepts that lie behind such Greek words as *polis*, *basileus*, and *tyrannos*; the English words by which they are usually translated, "city," "king," and "tyrant," signify other concepts in our culture. So translation is often problematic. Another source of failure in conveying concepts is that signs "overdetermine" their conceptual message; that is, there is more information in the sign than is necessary for communicating the concept. When I say "tree," my listener may be put in mind of family trees, decision trees, or shoe trees, as well as nature's trees; every word is a signifier of other concepts besides those that the speaker means to convey by a particular use of the word. Since conversation is a two-way exchange, the person to whom I am speaking can seek clarification of my utterance, but this course is unavailable if the signifiers are written rather than spoken and if the writer is dead or otherwise unavailable to be quizzed about his intentions.

Orthodox language theory regards all these impediments to perfect conceptual transfer, or "intersubjectivity," as impurities or corruptions that normally, if not always, can be overcome. And this is the point against which deconstruction mounts its theoretical assault: it insists that to regard those properties of signifiers that impede communication as secondary is arbitrary and culture-bound rather than, as the orthodox theorists suppose, logical or "natural." It is just as logical, just as natural, deconstruction insists, to subordinate the communicative function of discourse to the communication-impeding effects of the signifiers that the speaker or writer uses, and thus to attend to the "play of the signifiers," which is to say to the relations between the signifiers and other concepts besides the one intended to be signified. The practitioner of deconstruction may take an ostensibly serious prose passage and immediately get hung up on the first word, which may be an unintended pun or a homonym or a false cognate or may contain a subordinate meaning (perhaps deeply buried in its root) at war with the surface meaning. Or he may become fascinated with the shape of the letters or the visual pattern that they make on the page. Or he may juxtapose passages that are unrelated at the level of communication, in order to jar the reader out of his conventional response and into attending to the play of the signifiers. Or he may treat an earlier writing as a commentary on a later one. Moreover, consistent with his program of forcing attention to the noncommunicative aspect of language, the deconstructionist will insist on the problematic character of regarding an author as "present" in his text in the same way that we suppose a speaker to be present in his utterance. He will point out that writing, by its permanence (relative to speech), can outlive the communicative occasion that brought it forth by outliving the author, the readers whom the author intended to address, and its original linguistic and cultural context.

Much indeed is lost in clarity of communication when we move from spoken to written speech. Inflection, for example, is lost; the question of whether the commerce clause in Article I of the Constitution forbids states to burden interstate commerce unreasonably or merely empowers Congress to regulate commerce depends on whether one reads the language of the clause—"Congress shall have the power . . . to regulate [interstate and foreign] Commerce"—with the emphasis on "Congress" or on "Commerce." But to say that the properties of signifiers that make them an imperfect medium of communication are as interesting or important as communication—even to say that the "metaphysics of presence," or in other words the orthodox theory of language, is ungrounded or incoherent—is not to say that communication or "intersubjectivity" is impossible and hence that no text can be interpreted in a way that will recreate in the reader's mind the (approximate) concept that the author of the text meant to convey. Therefore it is not apparent why deconstruction should be thought to disestablish the interpretability of statutory and constitutional texts; nor have Jacques Derrida's self-appointed representatives in the American legal community given any reason why it should. But since literature is not concerned simply with conveying concepts in the most economical manner possible (in contrast, say, to an "executive summary"), one can see how deconstruction might have applications to literary criticism. The use of figurative language, rhyme, assonance, meter, fiction, parable, punning, the arrangement of words on a page (as in poetry), and other devices that call attention to the signifiers and thus decrease the transparency of the medium of communication marks literature as a mode of discourse that seems to exemplify the deconstructionists' program of placing the properties of language that impede communication on a par with the properties that enable it. It is no accident that orthodox language theorists, such as Plato, the first great theorist in the orthodox tradition, have often been impatient with literature.

But if practitioners of literary deconstruction were content merely to point out the dense and refractory character of much literary discourse they would be doing nothing new; the New Critics were pointing out the same things when Derrida was still in swaddling clothes. It just is too obvious by now that a work of literature is doing something more than conveying to the reader a paraphrasable meaning conceived in the author's mind. For most critics, however, that something more is a depiction of or commentary on some aspect of reality, such as love or war; and this makes literature "referential"—there are not just signifiers, there are things signified. So it was natural for practitioners of literary deconstruction, being interested in signifiers rather than signifieds, to train their sights on the mimetic theory of literature—the theory, propounded by (among many others) Aristotle, Samuel Johnson, and Erich Auerbach, that literature presents an imitation or representation of reality, understood as something really "out there" that people can understand. Literary deconstruction presents literature as self-referential rather than mimetic. And this textual self, in the theory of deconstruction, is necessarily the play of signifiers—disordered, contradictory, indeed incoherent.

By treating literature as self-referential, the deconstructive critics close the loop with philosophical deconstruction; if literature is self-referential, the practitioner of deconstruction can indeed regard the subject of literature as being the problematics of reading for meaning. This makes *In the Penal Colony* a work of particular resonance for deconstruction.[4] The torture machine is a writing machine, and one way of stating the officer's problem of communication is that he puts too much faith in writing as a medium of communication, while an alternative interpretation is that, in good deconstructive fashion, it is the medium, not the communication, that obsesses him. And those fearful arabesques that the machine traces out on the body of the condemned in order to protract the torture are a wonderful metaphor for overdeter-

---

[4] See Clayton Koelb, " 'In der Strafkolonie': Kafka and the Scene of Reading," 55 *German Quarterly* 511 (1982); Arnold Weinstein, "Kafka's Writing Machine: Metamorphosis in the Penal Colony," 7 *Studies in Twentieth-Century Literature* 21 (1982–1983). See also note 44 below.

mination. This sense—so central to deconstruction—that words live a life of their own, and an unruly life at that, is also precociously conveyed by T. S. Eliot in Part V of *Burnt Norton*, the first of the *Four Quartets*:

> . . . Words strain,
> Crack and sometimes break, under the burden,
> Under the tension, slip, slide, perish,
> Decay with imprecision, will not stay in place,
> Will not stay still . . .

The relevance of all this for law is obscure. Derrida does not appear to deny the possibility of communication by means of written texts, although he insists that communication has no metaphysical priority over, and therefore no necessarily superior authority to, the other uses to which texts can be put. If (as I doubt) he thinks that no writing ever conveys a concept in approximately the form intended by the author, he is, if not barmy, then simply too remote from the legal culture to be heeded. *Literary* texts may or may not be self-referential and (if the former) therefore incoherent, but it would not follow that a legal text was self-referential and therefore incoherent too; the purposes and techniques of authors of literary texts are different from those of the authors of legal texts.

What is true is that the opacity and sheer strangeness of much deconstructionist writing, notably but not only that of Derrida himself in recent years,[5] has made deconstruction a symbol of so-called post-structuralist or postmodernist literary theory to persons hostile to such theory. And since the critical legal studies movement wants to shock, it too flaunts the banner of deconstruction. Moreover, in its assault not only on the inherent authority of speaker and writer but on the inherent authority of the text itself, either as an intelligible communication (in the case of philosophical and other discursive texts) or as a coherent and intelligible artifact (in the case of literary texts), deconstruction is

---

[5] Here is Cain's mordant comment on Derrida's contribution to *Deconstruction and Criticism*, note 1 above: "for readers with a lifetime to spare, there is also a 100-page essay by Jacques Derrida, dealing with a subject yet to be determined." William E. Cain, *The Crisis in Criticism: Theory, Literature, and Reform in English Studies* 167 (1984). Or consider the translator's note at the end of Jacques Derrida, "Devant la Loi," in *Kafka and the Contemporary Critical Performance: Centenary Readings* 128, 149 (Alan Udoff ed. 1987): "Derrida's text continues; but, blind and weary, I shut the text-door here." The translator is alluding to the last sentence of *Before the Law*: "I am now going to shut it [the door]." And see John Sturrock, "The Book Is Dead, Long Live the Book!" *New York Times Book Review*, Sept. 13, 1987, at 3, reviewing Derrida's impenetrable *Glas* (1974), recently translated into English. Derrida's early works, well illustrated by *Of Grammatology* (first published in 1967), are readable, though with difficulty; see also the second interview in Jacques Derrida, *Positions* (Alan Bass trans. 1981).

Romanticism at its most rebellious. This makes it attractive to a movement that is in rebellion against the traditional sources of authority in law. But the affinities are in the atmospherics rather than the substance of these movements. And it is worth repeating that although deconstruction denies the inherent (logical or metaphysical) priority of author or concept over the medium of communication, it does not appear to deny the intelligibility of communicative discourse and hence the possibility that statutory and constitutional provisions really could communicate the commands of their authors.

Even if the particulars of deconstruction have nothing to contribute to law, the broader movement in modern thought of which deconstruction is a part—poststructuralism—might have something to contribute. The thread that connects the various schools of poststructuralism is their determination to reverse the traditional primacy of author over reader in the interpretation of texts.[6] From such a reversal the advocates of free interpretation of legal texts draw aid and comfort, while believers in the objectivity of law are discomfited. A related feature of poststructuralism is that most of its practitioners are political radicals,[7] who see their attack on objective interpretation as part of a broader campaign against bourgeois thought, one element of which is belief in the rule of law. If statutes and constitutions lack definite meanings, then judges in "interpreting" these texts must actually be exercising discretion; so the attack on interpretability is an attack on "ruledness," the law's determinacy, legal positivism, and related elements of the conception of law presented in the left-hand column of the Table of Opposed Conceptions of Law in

[6] See Culler, note 1 above, at 21, 202–206, 213–222, 273–274; Frank Kermode, *The Art of Telling: Essays on Fiction* (1983); *Reader-Response Criticism: From Formalism to Post-Structuralism* (Jane P. Tompkins ed. 1980). The case for regarding "authorship" as a cultural artifact rather than a natural or indispensable foundation of our response to a written work is forcefully argued in Michel Foucault, "What Is an Author?" in *Textual Strategies: Perspectives in Post-Structuralist Criticism* 141 (Josué V. Harari ed. 1979). Notice, however, that "interpretation" must be given a special meaning if my definition of poststructuralism is to cover deconstruction.

The restiveness of the literary critic forced, in the traditional conception of the critic's role, to play second fiddle to the literary text is the plaintive theme of Geoffrey H. Hartman, *Criticism in the Wilderness: The Study of Literature Today* (1980); and see his preface to *Deconstruction and Criticism*, note 1 above, at vii: "While teaching, criticizing, and presenting the great texts of our culture are essential tasks, to insist on the importance of literature should not entail assigning to literary criticism only a service function." The parallel to the restiveness of the judicial activist asked to play second fiddle to statutes and the Constitution is apparent. The relationship of such attitudes, in both literature and law, to the tradition of Romantic self-assertion examined in Chapter 3 should also be apparent.

[7] See Graff, *Literature against Itself: Literary Ideas in Modern Society*, chap. 3 (1979).

Chapter 2. By showing that law is essentially discretionary and there-fore, they argue, political (but could it not just be random?) the radicals hope to undermine a powerful force for maintaining the status quo. They believe, with some justification, that law's political character—which, however, they exaggerate—is masked and hence its ideological power enhanced by the claim of its votaries that law is independent of the political preferences of the judges who administer and also, to a significant but unacknowledged extent, make it.

Two things should be noted at the outset about the poststructuralist challenge to interpretability. The first is the tension it engenders between the political and the theoretical aims of poststructuralism. If objective interpretation is impossible, Robin West is wasting her time trying to show that Kafka's fiction contains a radical message; she must have put it there herself. A related point is that a posture of extreme skepticism deprives the radical critic of firm ground for advocating social change; his own proposals can be derided as culture-bound, historically contingent, subjective, unverifiable.[8] Second, poststructu-ralism has not swept literary criticism clean of rival approaches. In particular, those literary scholars who believe that their task in reading a literary work is to reconstruct the author's intentions[9] provide ammunition for the "interpretivists" of legal texts, perhaps even for the "strict constructionists." Ronald Dworkin has taken an intermediate position, a "New Critical" position, as I shall argue shortly. He contends that the way we choose between two interpretations of a work of literature is to determine which one makes the work better, more coherent, aesthetically more pleasing, and that we should do the same with statutes and the Constitution, except that the criteria of goodness would be political rather than aesthetic.[10] We should ask, for example,

---

[8] See Stanley Fish, "Anti-Professionalism," 7 *Cardozo Law Review* 645, 656–661 (1986). West, a radical but not a poststructuralist, stresses this point too. See "Adjudication Is Not Interpretation," note 2 above, especially pp. 245–254.

[9] See E. D. Hirsch, Jr., *Validity in Interpretation* (1967), *The Aims of Interpretation* (1976), and "Counterfactuals in Interpretation," 3 *Texte: Revue de critique et de théorie littéraire* 15 (1984); P. D. Juhl, *Interpretation: An Essay in the Philosophy of Literary Criticism* (1980); Frederick Crews, "Criticism without Constraint," *Commentary*, Jan. 1982, at 65; Steven Knapp and Walter Benn Michaels, "Against Theory," 8 *Critical Inquiry* 723 (1982); Knapp and Michaels, "Against Theory 2: Hermeneutics and Deconstruction," 14 *Critical Inquiry* 49 (1987); Anne Sheppard, *Aesthetics: An Introduction to the Philosophy of Art*, chap. 7 (1987).

[10] See Ronald H. Dworkin, "Law as Interpretation," 60 *Texas Law Review* 527 (1982), also published, with commentary by Stanley Fish and Dworkin's reply, in The Politics of Interpretation 249–313 (W. J. T. Mitchell ed. 1983), and in somewhat different form as chaps. 6 and 7 of Ronald Dworkin, *A Matter of Principle* (1985), and as chap. 2 of his *Law's Empire* (1986). For criticism see David Couzens Hoy, "Interpreting the Law: Hermeneutical and

what interpretation of "equal protection of the laws" makes the Fourteenth Amendment the best statement of public policy in the light of modern political theory. Reversing Shelley's dictum in *A Defence of Poetry*, Dworkin hails legislators as the unacknowledged poets of the world.

I believe, however, that there are too many differences between works of literature and enactments of legislatures to permit much fruitful analogizing of legislative to literary interpretation. Thus I do not consider myself inconsistent in being an intentionalist when it comes to reading statutes and the Constitution but a New Critic when it comes to reading works of literature. A legal intentionalist holds that what you are trying to do in reading a statute or the Constitution is to figure out from the words, the structure, the background, and any other available information how the legislators whose votes were necessary for enactment would probably have answered your question of statutory interpretation if it had occurred to them.[11] A New Critic treats a work of literature as an artifact, coherent in itself and not to be understood better by immersion in the details of the author's biography or in the other circumstances of its composition (except that some slight knowledge of those circumstances may be necessary to understand particular references in the work).[12] To complete my matrix I define an "intentionalist"

Poststructuralist Perspectives," 58 *Southern California Law Review* 135, 147–151 (1985); Stanley Fish, "Wrong Again," 62 *Texas Law Review* 299 (1983); Jessica Lane, "The Poetics of Legal Interpretation," 87 *Columbia Law Review* 197 (1987); John Stick, "Literary Imperialism: Assessing the Results of Dworkin's Interpretive Turn in *Law's Empire*," 34 *UCLA Law Review* 371 (1986). Dworkin does not use the term "New Criticism," and his discussion of literary theory is both brief and vague. But he does make clear his rejection of intentionalism, and he has no truck with the extreme skepticism of the reader-response school, so I think he is rightly classified with the New Critics as I shall define them in this chapter. But maybe all he means to argue is that all interpretation is contextual and that political principles are part of the interpretive context of constitutions and statutes—an unexceptionable position. It is odd that a text which defends the objectivity of interpretation should raise interpretive questions!

[11] See my book *The Federal Courts: Crisis and Reform*, chap. 9 (1985), and references there. On the legislative process and statutory interpretation generally see William N. Eskridge, Jr., and Philip P. Frickey, *Cases and Materials on Legislation: Statutes and the Creation of Public Policy* (1987); Henry M. Hart, Jr., and Albert Sacks, *The Legal Process: Basic Problems in the Making and Application of Law*, vol. 2, at 1144–1417 (tent. ed. 1958); Philip Shuchman, *Cohen and Cohen's Readings in Jurisprudence and Legal Philosophy*, chap. 3 (2d ed. 1979).

[12] For an early (1901) statement of this position see A. C. Bradley, "Poetry for Poetry's Sake," in Bradley, *Oxford Lectures on Poetry* 3 (1965 ed.); for a deft capsule summary see T. S. Eliot, "The Frontiers of Criticism," in his *On Poetry and Poets* 103 (1957); and for temperate criticism see Graff, note 7 above, chap. 5 (for intemperate see note 17 below). Two durable classics of the New Criticism are Cleanth Brooks, *The Well Wrought Urn* (1947), and W. K. Wimsatt, Jr., *The Verbal Icon: Studies in the Meaning of Poetry* (1954). See also Cleanth Brooks, *A Shaping Joy: Studies in the Writer's Craft* (1971). Defined as broadly as I define it,

literary critic as one who believes that the way to understand a work of literature is to try to reconstruct the author's intentions—the meaning he assigned to it, or would have assigned to it if he had reflected on his work[13]—and a "New Critic" judge as one who believes that what is important in interpreting a statute is to assign a coherent and satisfying meaning to the words.

Some members of the critical legal studies movement go beyond New Criticism and purport to deconstruct legal texts, for example by trying to show that the provision in Article II of the Constitution that one must be at least 35 years old to be President of the United States could mean merely that one must have the maturity of the average 35-year-old.[14] To read the provision so, however, is to take the words of the Constitution ("neither shall any person be eligible to that Office who shall not have attained to the age of thirty five Years") out of their context. And words

---

New Criticism includes such classics of close reading by avowed opponents of New Criticism as Wayne C. Booth, *The Rhetoric of Fiction* (2d ed. 1983). Because the term is often used more narrowly, I might be better off with a more neutral expression such as "intrinsic" or "autotelic" criticism—the tenets of which are well discussed in Stein Haugom Olsen, *The Structure of Literary Understanding* 137–155 (1978). But I shall stick with the more familiar term.

Although many New Critics would be shocked to realize it, their basic working assumption—the coherence of the literary text—is Nietzschean. As shown in Alexander Nehamas, *Nietzsche: Life as Literature*, chap. 5 (1985), Nietzsche regarded every human life as a "text" whose "author" must strive to make it coherent in every detail and moment.

[13] On the dispute between New Critics and intentionalists see Monroe C. Beardsley and William K. Wimsatt, Jr., *The Intentional Fallacy*, in Wimsatt, note 12 above, at 3; Frank Cioffi, "Intention and Interpretation in Criticism," 64 *Proceedings of the Aristotelian Society* 85 (1964) (a sharp attack on the Beardsley-Wimsatt article); A. D. Nuttall, "Did Meursault Intend to Kill the Arab?—The Intentional Fallacy Fallacy," 10 *Critical Quarterly* 95 (1968) (ditto); E. M. W. Tillyard and C. S. Lewis, *The Personal Heresy: A Controversy* (1939); and references in note 9 above. Illustrative criticisms of intentionalism are Monroe C. Beardsley, "Intentions and Interpretations," in *The Aesthetic Point of View* 188 (Michael J. Wreen and Donald M. Callen eds. 1982); John M. Ellis, *The Theory of Literary Criticism: A Logical Analysis*, chap. 5 (1974); W. K. Wimsatt, "Genesis: An Argument Resumed," in Wimsatt, *Day of the Leopards: Essays in Defense of Poems* 11 (1976); Susan J. Hekman, *Hermeneutics and the Sociology of Knowledge* 122–123 (1986); Frank Kermode, *The Classic: Literary Images of Permanence and Change* 77–78 (1975); Kermode, note 6 above, "Appendix: The Single Correct Interpretation." See generally *On Literary Intention: Critical Essays* (David Newton-De Molina ed. 1976); *Against Theory: Literary Studies and the New Pragmatism* (W. J. T. Mitchell ed. 1985). A particularly well-balanced discussion of the issue is K. K. Ruthven, *Critical Assumptions*, chaps. 9–10 (1979).

[14] See Peller, note 2 above, at 1174; Mark V. Tushnet, "A Note on the Revival of Textualism in Constitutional Theory," 58 *Southern California Law Review* 683, 686–688 (1985). I am surprised that in arguing against the literal interpretation of the age-35 provision, neither Peller nor Tushnet invokes the authority of Gilbert and Sullivan. The plot of *The Pirates of Penzance* turns on the fact that, having been born on February 29 in a leap year, Frederic, upon reaching the age of 21, is "legally" only 5 and therefore still apprenticed to the pirates.

have meaning only by virtue of context.[15] This is the least controversial precept of the interpretive tradition on which the critical legal studies movement purports to draw and is, indeed, the common ground of deconstruction and orthodox language theory. The relevant political and cultural context of the age-35 provision—a context whose cardinal features include a desire to establish orderly means of succession of officials, a practice of recording birth dates, and frequent use by lawmakers of arbitrary deadlines (as in statutes of limitations and in the age of majority)—makes it apparent that the framers of the Constitution wanted to lay down a flat rule as to age of eligibility, so that everyone would know in advance of the election whether the candidates were eligible. It would be absurd if, after the election of a 40-year-old as President of the United States, someone (the loser, perhaps) could bring suit to void the election by showing that the winner was less mature than the average 35-year-old had been in 1787, when average life spans were much shorter; or if a suit were necessary to void the election of a 25-year-old whose supporters had thought him mature enough to be President. The age-35 provision, like laws fixing the drinking age, the driving age, the marriage age, and the voting age, is designed to avoid these absurdities. If a judge can do with the provision what Peller and Tushnet think he can do, there is no way in which the framers of statutes or constitutions can communicate their will to judges. There is no more perspicuous form of words that the framers could have chosen.

## Intentionalist and New Critical Approaches to Law and to Literature

To get a better grip on these two schools of criticism, it may be helpful to note that there are four basic types of literary criticism: interpretive, methodological, classificatory, and evaluative. The first is concerned with ascertaining the meaning of works of literature, the second with the techniques that writers use to achieve their effects, the third with identifying and describing literary genres and recurrent literary symbols and motifs,[16] and the fourth with establishing the canon of literary

---

[15] "A sentence only determines a set of truth conditions relative to a set of assumptions that are not realized in the semantic context of the sentence." John R. Searle, *Expression and Meaning: Studies in the Theory of Speech Acts* 80 (1979).

[16] This, loosely speaking, is structuralism, on which see Jonathan Culler, *Structuralist Poetics: Structuralism, Linguistics and the Study of Literature* (1975); Northrop Frye, *Anatomy of Criticism: Four Essays* (1957); Frye, "Expanding Eyes," in his book *Spiritus Mundi: Essays on Literature, Myth, and Society* 99 (1983); Robert Scholes, *Structuralism in Literature: An Introduction* (1974). On genre criticism, which is closely related, see Alastair Fowler, *Kinds of Literature: An Introduction to the Theory of Genres and Modes* (1982). For an exemplary structuralist analysis of one of the works discussed in this book, see Charles Paul Segal, "The Phaeacians and the Symbolism of Odysseus's Return," 1 *Arion* 17 (winter 1962).

works. The first has affinities with epistemology, psychology, and linguistics; the second with rhetoric, semantics, and sociolinguistics; the third with anthropology, psychoanalysis, intellectual history, and social science generally; and the fourth with religion, ethics, and politics. Intentionalism and New Criticism, as I shall be using these terms (an important qualification, since the terms are protean), stake out two of three basic positions on the interpretation of literary works. In the intentionalist view, the reader's task is to open a channel to the mind of the author. The author is assumed to have had a reason for everything he put into the work; to understand the work means to discover and understand those reasons. The opposite of intentionalism is the extreme form of "reader response" criticism in which the work of literature is deemed to be the creation (not necessarily the same creation) of each reader. New Criticism occupies a middle ground— some think an uneasy middle ground: it rejects both the idea that interpretation should be cabined by the conscious mind of the author or be likened to the author's dreams and the idea that literature is a plastic medium in which each reader expresses his own creativity. The New Critic views the work of literature as an intelligible artifact, a thing almost as different from the author's mind as a pearl is different from the oyster that secretes it, but having (like the pearl) a definite structure, which is revealed on a close reading in the manner pioneered by I. A. Richards. Intentionalism assigns primacy in the creation of the meaning of the work of literature to the author, reader-response criticism to the critic or other reader, New Criticism to the work itself.

A complication is that the term "New Criticism" is often used to denote a specific body of literary criticism that was highly influential in American universities in the 1940s and 1950s—Cleanth Brooks, Robert Penn Warren, Allen Tate, and R. P. Blackmur being representative practitioners. These New Critics practiced evaluative as well as interpretive criticism. In addition to being committed to the close reading of works of literature viewed as artifacts, and hence being naturally drawn to works that best repaid such scrutiny by reason of their complex or subtle structure, these critics, taking their cue from T. E. Hulme and T. S. Eliot, expressed a preference for literature that reflects a mature, realistic attitude toward life. As a result, many of them disparaged, or at least downgraded, Romantic literature, with its cult of the child, of spontaneity, and so forth. Moralistic criticism today is more likely to reflect a Marxist or feminist than a Christian or conservative viewpoint. In retrospect it is apparent that by taking a political-ethical stance the New Critics were exposing their reputation to the winds of political fashion, which in the last thirty years have changed against them.[17]

Some American New Critics were, moreover, aggressively uninterested in biographical or historical background, and hence unwilling on principle to seek any clues to literary meaning in these things. This unwillingness reflected uncertainty about the appropriate context for interpretation. Everyone understands that a writing is intelligible only in a context, that is, only in terms of presuppositions regarding language and culture that the reader brings with him rather than finds in the text. Some New Critics, however, seem to have thought that very little in the way of context was necessary to make literature intelligible.

A more eclectic form of New Criticism flourished in England. Its outstanding practitioner was William Empson, an ingenious (sometimes too ingenious, too fanciful) close reader and a believer in the artifactual character of works of literature who also was interested, however, in the author's biography and was more catholic in his tastes than most of the American New Critics. A model current practitioner of an eclectic New Criticism is another Englishman, Frank Kermode. He accepts from the reader-response school that literature (not only modern literature) is more open-ended than was believed thirty years ago, and he is willing to assign the reader a large share in the creation of meaning.[18] But he

---

[17] Making them the butt of left-wing critics: "New Criticism's high regard for 'ambiguity', its admiration of polysemous structures, represent no real leaning towards 'total' criticism so much as a bourgeois mistrust of singlemindedness and commitment: the stances it prizes most—sophistication, wit, poise—are those of a decaying aristocracy characteristically revered by a sycophantic middle-class." Terence Hawkes, *Structuralism and Semiotics* 155 (1977). There is unintended irony here, since methodologically, as we shall see, New Criticism has significant affinities with poststructuralism, which Hawkes does not consider a product of bourgeois sycophancy. For a more temperate evaluation of the implicit political agenda of the American New Critics see Gerald Graff, "American Criticism Left and Right," in *Ideology and Classic American Literature* 91, 100–105 (Sacvan Bercovitch and Myra Jehlen eds. 1986). On American New Criticism generally, see index references to "New Criticism" in Graff, *Professing Literature*, note 1 above; also Cain, note 5 above, at 94–103.

[18] In other words, the relevant context is broadened to include readers' assumptions and beliefs that many New Critics would have thought irrelevant to understanding a work of literature. Although when pushed too far the reader-response approach makes the work of literature disappear, modest versions of the approach can illuminate. Anyone who has seen different productions of the same play realizes how much leeway the playwright leaves for competing interpretations; and when there is no performing intermediary—when the reader is alone with a novel or poem—the reader must play the mediating role himself. In addition to making general points of this sort, the reader-response school has offered some specific insights that are arresting. I am intrigued by Wolfgang Iser's point, in *The Art of Reading: A Theory of Aesthetic Response* 191–192 (1978), that serial publication (as of Dickens's novels when first published) gives the reader a more creative role than book publication. Between installments the reader will be thinking ahead and considering alternative possibilities more thoroughly than if he is reading the novel uninterruptedly or with only brief, irregular interruptions. He may therefore

refuses to go whole hog, because he believes that interpretation, and not just response, is possible. The work of literature is still an artifact, but a diamond rather than a pearl—different in different lights, corresponding to the critical intelligences of different readers in different times and places. Another model of critical eclecticism is Howard Felperin, discussing Shakespeare's sonnets in chapter 5 of *Beyond Deconstruction* (see note 1). Eclectic New Criticism means simply the close reading of a work of literature conceived of as an aesthetic rather than a didactic discourse, using whatever aids to such reading lie to hand. As such, though it no longer generates much theoretical excitement, it remains the standard method of literary criticism[19] and was the method used in Part I of this book.

Let me now give legal and literary examples of intentionalist versus New Critical interpretation. My legal text will be the provision in the Eighth Amendment that forbids "cruel and unusual punishments." The New Critic would ask, what meaning might be posited for this interesting verbal artifact? Might not one suggest that capital punishment is cruel because taking life is cruel, and unusual because with the greater tenderness that modern people feel about human life, very few people who commit capital crimes are actually executed? (Moreover, it has been abolished in most Western countries.) Capital punishment is therefore cruel and unusual, and should be forbidden.[20] The intentionalist would ask what the framers of the Bill of Rights were trying to accomplish by forbidding cruel and unusual punishments. Unfortunately, he would not get a completely clear answer. He might conclude either that they were just trying to forbid punishments that were barbaric, or that they also wanted to forbid punishments whose severity was grossly disproportionate to the crime, along with all punishments, severe or lenient, for conduct that ought not be made criminal at all.[21]

---

put up greater resistance if the novel does not come out as he has been led to expect; and this prospect may in turn restrict the novelist's freedom as he composes the novel. The reader's collaborative role in creating literary meaning is made transparent by this example. An even clearer example is an unfinished novel, like *The Mystery of Edwin Drood*, which forces every reader to write his own ending. For a fine reader-response analysis of a work discussed in this book see Stephen Booth, "On the Value of *Hamlet*," in *Reinterpretations of Elizabethan Drama* 137 (Norman Rabkin ed. 1969). And recall my analysis in Chapter 1 of the reader's unfolding emotional response to revenge dramas such as *Hecuba*.

[19] Cf. Cain, note 5 above, chap. 6.

[20] See Paul Brest, "The Misconceived Quest for the Original Understanding," 60 *Boston University Law Review* 204, 220–221 (1980).

[21] Compare Anthony F. Granucci, " 'Nor Cruel and Unusual Punishments Inflicted': The Original Meaning," 57 *California Law Review* 839, 840–842 (1969), with Ingraham v. Wright, 430 U.S. 651, 664–667 (1977).

None of the intentionalist readings, however, supports a conclusion that capital punishment is unconstitutional.

My principal literary example will be Yeats's poem *Easter 1916*. I give it in full here:

> I have met them at close of day
> Coming with vivid faces
> From counter or desk among grey
> Eighteenth-century houses.
> I have passed with a nod of the head
> Or polite meaningless words,
> Or have lingered awhile and said
> Polite meaningless words,
> And thought before I had done
> Of a mocking tale or a gibe
> To please a companion
> Around the fire at the club,
> Being certain that they and I
> But lived where motley is worn:
> All changed, changed utterly:
> A terrible beauty is born.
>
> That woman's days were spent
> In ignorant good-will,
> Her nights in argument
> Until her voice grew shrill.
> What voice more sweet than hers
> When, young and beautiful,
> She rode to harriers?
> This man had kept a school
> And rode our wingèd horse;
> This other his helper and friend
> Was coming into his force;
> He might have won fame in the end,
> So sensitive his nature seemed,
> So daring and sweet his thought.
> This other man I had dreamed
> A drunken, vainglorious lout.
> He had done most bitter wrong
> To some who are near my heart,
> Yet I number him in the song;
> He, too, has resigned his part
> In the casual comedy;
> He, too, has been changed in his turn,

Transformed utterly:
A terrible beauty is born.

Hearts with one purpose alone
Though summer and winter seem
Enchanted to a stone
To trouble the living stream.
The horse that comes from the road,
The rider, the birds that range
From cloud to tumbling cloud,
Minute by minute they change;
A shadow of cloud on the stream
Changes minute by minute;
A horse-hoof slides on the brim,
And a horse plashes within it;
The long-legged moor-hens dive,
And hens to moor-cocks call;
Minute by minute they live:
The stone's in the midst of all.

Too long a sacrifice
Can make a stone of the heart.
O when may it suffice?
That is Heaven's part, our part
To murmur name upon name,
As a mother names her child
When sleep at last has come
On limbs that had run wild.
What is it but nightfall?
No, no, not night but death;
Was it needless death after all?
For England may keep faith
For all that is done and said.
We know their dream; enough
To know they dreamed and are dead;
And what if excess of love
Bewildered them till they died?
I write it out in a verse—
MacDonagh and MacBride
And Connolly and Pearse
Now and in time to be,
Wherever green is worn,
Are changed, changed utterly:
A terrible beauty is born.

The title and some oblique references in the text reveal that the poem is in some sense about the Easter Rebellion in Ireland during World War I, which the British repressed with great firmness. A New Critic might think that you do not need to know any more about the circumstances in which the poem was composed and to which it refers to extract its full meaning. (But you must know this much!) It might help a great deal to have read other poetry by Yeats, though even this is problematic—for why are not the poet's other poems considered extrinsic to this one, just like his biography? This is another aspect of the baffling but inescapable issue of the proper context in which to read a text. No text is intelligible in a vacuum; but once contextual factors are admitted (as they must be), it is unclear what the stopping point should be. Should it be at the point where the text is no longer gibberish? Or should the reader keep going, in search of a richer, fuller meaning—maybe a private, highly personal one? There are no longer generally agreed-on answers to these questions.

An intentionalist would think it important to point out that the four people discussed in the second stanza of *Easter 1916* were real people and that three of them—the three men—were executed; that one of them, described in the poem as "a drunken, vainglorious lout," was the ex-husband of Yeats's inamorata, Maud Gonne; and that Yeats, like many of the Anglo-Irish, believed in Irish independence but did little for it and in fact lived most of his life in England.[22] From all this a personal and political meaning of the poem might be constructed.

I find the intentionalist approach to the Eighth Amendment congenial and the intentionalist approach to *Easter 1916* otiose, and I must now explain the difference in my reactions. It lies in the reasons for which the two documents were written and the reasons for which they are read. As Granucci explains (see note 21), the prohibition against cruel and unusual punishments was added to the Bill of Rights, with little debate or discussion, to mollify people worried that the strong central government ordained by the Constitution might imitate the British practice of using criminal punishment to intimidate political opponents. There was concern about methods of punishment that were barbarous and hence especially intimidating, and possibly also about the making of trivial or even completely inoffensive conduct criminal. But no effort to particularize the prohibition was made; the framers were content to appropriate the term "cruel and unusual" from the English Declaration of Rights of 1689 as a general, summary formula. Particularizing not only

[22] See James D. Boulger, "Yeats and Irish Identity," 42 *Thought* 185, 189–194 (1967); Elizabeth Cullingford, *Yeats, Ireland and Fascism* 91–98 (1981); Hugh Kenner, *A Colder Eye: The Modern Irish Writers* 227–230 (1983); C. K. Stead, "Politics as Drama," in *William Butler Yeats: A Collection of Criticism* 51 (Patrick J. Keane ed. 1973). None of these things is stated in the poem.

would have been time-consuming but might have sparked debilitating controversy, since it is easier to agree on generalities than on particulars. The courts would be there to particularize the prohibition if that became necessary. "Sufficient unto the day is the evil thereof" might be the motto of the legislative process.[23] The forging of a consensus, or even just of a majority agreement, in a diverse group may be impossible unless some disputes can be papered over with general language, leaving resolution to the courts.

The generality of constitutional language ought not, however, set a court completely at large. Courts are not supposed to act with untrammeled discretion. When a court reads the Eighth Amendment, it is (or at least should be) looking for authoritative guidance, and it would get none if it felt free to give "cruel and unusual punishments" any meaning that the words wrenched free of their historical context might yield. A New Critical and even more a poststructuralist approach would make the Eighth Amendment an uncanalized delegation to courts of the power to regulate criminal punishments. It is unlikely that the framers intended to delegate so ill-defined and sweeping a power to the courts, and it is not readily apparent how, in the absence of delegation, the exercise of such a power could be thought legitimate rather than usurpative. A New Critical approach to the Constitution would be as nondirective as the New Critical approach to interpreting specific works of literature; New Critical statutory interpretations would have no more intrinsic authoritativeness than New Critical literary interpretations.

The standards that Ronald Dworkin would use in interpreting legal enactments are not literary, but philosophical; he would read the enactment in a way that would make it the best possible statement of political philosophy.[24] But there is no agreement in political philosophy on essential issues. There are libertarian philosophers such as Robert Nozick and egalitarian philosophers such as Dworkin and John Rawls—all highly respectable—and there are many shades in between. On the specific issue of capital punishment there are philosophers who believe that justice requires capital punishment, which was Kant's view, and those who believe that justice forbids it.[25] Besides being radically

[23] Cf. Edward H. Levi, *An Introduction to Legal Reasoning* 30–31 (1949).

[24] See, for example, *Law's Empire*, note 10 above, at 379–380.

[25] See, for example, Donald Clark Hodges, "Punishment," 18 *Philosophy and Phenomenological Research* 209 (1957–1959); Ernest van den Haag and John P. Conrad, *The Death Penalty: A Debate* (1983); Richard O. Lempert, "Desert and Deterrence: An Assessment of the Moral Bases of the Case for Capital Punishment," 79 *Michigan Law Review* 1177 (1981); and references in Chapter 1, note 3, to the retributivist literature in philosophy.

indeterminate, Dworkin's approach imposes an intellectual burden on judges—that they be philosopher kings—which none is fit to bear. (Significantly, he calls his model judge "Hercules.") New Criticism has not produced convergent interpretations of the great literary texts; no more can we expect its legal counterpart to produce convergent interpretations of the great legal texts.

One alternative is an intentionalist approach to constitutional interpretation. A judge in the intentionalist tradition will want to learn what he can about what the framers intended by the words in question, even if this requires, as often it will, looking into sources outside the constitutional text. Granted, when the judge inquires into the framers' intent he will run up against the problem of intent about intent: the framers may have understood "cruel and unusual punishments" to mean something fairly precise but may also have intended that the courts should be free to depart from that understanding. This is undoubtedly true to some extent, but not when carried to the point of making the prohibition against cruel and unusual punishments a delegation of an unlimited power to formulate legal policy. For then the assumed intent of the framers of the Bill of Rights would be to write a blank check to the judges. If the framers had wanted to do this they would almost certainly have chosen a different method from the enactment of ten separate amendments, many with several, and some with several highly specific, clauses.

In acknowledging the problem of intention about intention, I am not robbing intentionalism of all meaning, as can be seen with the help of Frank Kermode, writing against the intentionalist P. D. Juhl:

> Somebody is quoted [by Juhl] as having maintained that [Swift's *Modest Proposal*] has 'something to say' about the Vietnam War, and his application is permitted as an instance of significance. The *meaning* of the pamphlet, however, is [to Juhl] entirely a matter of Irish conditions in Swift's own time. But this is surely wrong: the most that could be claimed is that Swift so *planned* it. On Juhl's own argument, what Swift intended was what he wrote, and what he wrote is compact of ironies, opacities, interpretanda of many kinds, and the hermeneutic effort required to discover what they mean (and to so determine Swift's intention) is indistinguishable from that required for the elicitation of 'significance'. Swift's work reflects upon the desirability of massacring babies as a political expedient, and so what it says is not at all entirely a matter of Irish conditions in 1729, though it applies to those conditions, as no doubt it does to the Vietnam War; it would certainly be absurd to argue that Swift meant to discuss that war, and it would be absurd to say that he did not have Ireland in mind, but these considerations are

insufficient to justify Juhl's retreat into an intentionalism far more primitive than the kind he is expounding.[26]

A primitive intentionalism in law as in literature would be to insist that the framers of a statute or a constitutional provision can intend only what they can foresee. A sophisticated legal intentionalism recognizes that the framers might intend to regulate a set of activities not all of which they could actually foresee—might intend that, within prescribed limits, the intentions of others (for example, of judges applying the legislators' handiwork in the distant future) should govern, rather than the legislators' mental pictures of the future. Hirsch, our leading intentionalist literary critic, gets this exactly right in a brief discussion of statutory interpretation.[27]

But whether the legislators' intentions are broad or narrow, the judges have to be interested in what those intentions are and not just in what is "in" the text; otherwise the center of political power will shift from legislators to judges. There is no comparable danger with literary interpretations. We can if we want use the *Modest Proposal* as a commentary about the Vietnam War without worrying about whether Swift would have wanted it used that way. His writing the piece was not an act of government.

A parallel example is this famous couplet from Yeats's poem *The Second Coming*: "The best lack all conviction, while the worst / Are full of passionate intensity." Although one tends to think of poetry as concrete and particular, Yeats here uses general language to create an aphorism of broad applicability. Many people reading it for the first time are put in mind of the behavior of the appeasing democracies in the 1930s toward the fascist powers. Since the poem was written in 1919 Yeats could not have been thinking about the political situation in the 1930s, but I see no objection to saying that the poem is "about" that situation, just as I see no objection in principle to reading Kafka

---

[26] Kermode, *The Art of Telling* (note 6 above), at 206–207, discussing Juhl, note 9 above.

[27] See *Validity in Interpretation*, note 9 above, at 124–125. Hirsch's "Counterfactuals in Interpretation," note 9 above, at 27–28, contains a good discussion of constitutional interpretation. That the framers of the Constitution indeed meant to distinguish between the "intent" of the document and the "intentions" of the authors (that is, how the authors themselves would have decided a specific case arising under the Constitution, knowing only what they knew when they wrote it), and to allow only the former to guide interpretation, is argued in H. Jefferson Powell, "The Original Understanding of Original Intent," 98 *Harvard Law Review* 885 (1985).

A curious contrast to Hirsch's intentionalist approach to statutes is another literary critic's—Kenneth Burke's—New Critical approach to the Constitution. See *A Grammar of Motives* 323–401 (1945). Someone should compare Burke's approach to Dworkin's.

"prophetically"—I merely happen not to think that Kafka's texts support the prophetic interpretations.

There is an interesting difference between the Yeats and Swift examples. Swift's satire purports to be about Ireland, so it takes a bit of a wrench to think it is also about Vietnam (maybe it would be better to say "applicable to" rather than "about"). No similar wrench is necessary with Yeats's couplet, because it is not topical. Moreover, the tone of *The Second Coming* is prophetic; if one of its prophecies happens to come true, the poem is ready at hand to "mean" it. Broadly drafted constitutional provisions have the same property of ready applicability to unforeseen situations. So I am not suggesting that the prohibition against "cruel and unusual punishments" should be limited to punishments known in 1791 when the Eighth Amendment was adopted. Given the limits of human foresight, a legislator would have to be crazy to want to confine a general law—a constitutional provision, meant to last—to the things of which he had a picture in his mind. But there is a difference between intending to limit unforeseen punishments and giving judges complete freedom to regulate criminal sanctions. The latter intention is implausible.

Swift's *Modest Proposal* is relevant in another way. Although I have been arguing against the principle of intentionalism as applied to works of literature, I have no doubt that if we knew with absolute certainty that Swift had meant the proposal in earnest we would cease to enjoy it as a work of literature. It would no longer be ironic; it would be insane. So there is a residual significance to authorial intentions in literature, but the significance is much less than in law. It may, indeed, be confined to instances, such as that of *A Modest Proposal*, where the text itself contains no clue that the work is to be read ironically, so that its irony depends on the reader's knowing, or at least being able to guess, what the author's intentions were.

In disparaging intentionalism as a literary theory I hope I will not be thought to be denying that a work of literature is a deliberate human creation, and in that sense intentional. But it does not follow that questions of literary meaning—questions of literary interpretation—are fruitfully approached as questions about the author's intentions.

Although Yeats may have had political intentions in writing *Easter 1916*, it was not written to convey authoritative commands to anyone and it has no legal or political topicality to people who read it today (except perhaps in Ireland). For us it is a beautiful and moving poem which we read for pleasure and perhaps for instruction—not about the circumstances of the Easter Rebellion, barely alluded to, but about the impact of political movements on human personality. The poem suggests that commitment to a political cause both lifts one above one's personal limitations ("He, too [the drunken, vainglorious lout], has been changed in his turn, / Transformed utterly") and destroys one's humanity ("Too long a sacrifice / Can make a stone of the heart"). That the "drunken, vainglorious lout" is that alcoholic Major MacBride (the "MacBride" of the last stanza) who had married Maud Gonne years earlier and shortly afterward left her, or that the school referred to in the second stanza was St. Enda's, or that the poem downplays Yeats's intimacy with the rebels, are interesting tidbits of historical and biographical gossip but they can add little to most readers' interest and pleasure in the poem. I, at least, would just as soon not have my mind cluttered with these and other details that patient historical research has unearthed.[28] Nor is much to be learned about the poem from reading the letters that Yeats wrote while composing it, in which he discussed the Easter Rebellion very briefly.[29]

The history of literature contains some insightful comments by creative writers on their own work (Henry James is an important though not consistent example)[30] but also many obtuse ones. These include T. S. Eliot's description of *The Waste Land* as "only the relief of a personal and wholly insignificant grouse against life; it is just a piece of rhythmical grumbling," and Kafka's pronouncement of *The Metamorphosis* as a failure because of its ending.[31] One reason for such blind spots (besides modesty, true or false) is that the creation of works of literature is not a fully self-conscious activity. Some literature is written in something close to an unconscious blur. The great fifth part of *The Waste Land* spilled out in a rush and required virtually no

---

[28] See in particular Cullingford's discussion, cited in note 22 above. This is not to say that biographical and historical data are never helpful. Another of Yeats's poems, *Upon a Dying Lady*, cannot be appreciated fully without knowing that the lady in question was Aubrey Beardsley's sister. See the superb discussion in Douglas Archibald, *Yeats* 31–38 (1983). See also Jon Stallworthy, *Between the Lines: Yeats's Poetry in the Making*, chap. 8 (1963), on the biographical background to *In Memory of Eva Gore-Booth and Con Markiewicz*. But I do not think this sort of information is essential to understanding *Easter 1916* or, indeed, most of Yeats's poems.

[29] See *Letters of W. B. Yeats* 612–614 (Allan Wade ed. 1954). In one, written to Lady Gregory a couple of weeks after the Rebellion was crushed, he said, "I am trying to write a poem on the men executed—'terrible beauty has been born again.' " Id. at 613.

[30] See Monroe C. Beardsley, "The Creation of Art," in *The Aesthetic Point of View*, note 13 above, at 239, 242.

[31] T. S. Eliot, *The Waste Land: A Facsimile and Transcript of the Original Drafts Including the Annotations of Ezra Pound* 1 (Valerie Eliot ed. 1971); Ronald Gray, *Franz Kafka* 91 (1973).

correction.[32] *The Judgment* was written uninterruptedly in one night.[33] Shakespeare did little editing of his plays (though not none,[34] as used to be believed), and, given the limitations of time under which he labored, much of the great poetry in them probably was written down as it came into his head. "Automatic" writing of this sort is unusual, and most great works of literature undergo painstaking revision before the author will authorize publication. But often the revisions seem not to be according to conscious plan. Often they are done out of some unconscious sense of feel and fitness, and when the author has completed them he may be unable to explain why he did what he did.

Another reason the author may not be his own best interpreter is that the meaning of a work of literature is often generated as a by-product of the writer's attempt to solve a technical problem, such as how to make what he has to say conform to his chosen metrical scheme or how to provide the audience with essential information (recall the discussion in Chapter 1 of the dumb show in *Hamlet*). The inspiration that sets the writer going must be distinguished from the process of selection and revision necessary to complete the work. The meaning of the work will emerge from the interaction of these activities and thus in the act of creation, rather than having been completely thought out in advance.[35] Another reason for the deficiencies of authors' self-criticism, a reason that ties in with my emphasis throughout this book on the test of time, is that the author may lack an adequate perspective for understanding his work.

If the author's conscious intentions are often banal, trying to recover them will not be a very productive endeavor. Nor will psychoanalyzing the author or his characters, as we saw in earlier chapters in discussing *Hamlet* and Kafka—always assuming that we read literature for pleasure and instruction rather than to unlock the author's secret thoughts or inner drives, or to learn about his life.

In the case of the *Iliad*—perhaps the greatest work in the Western

[32] See Eliot, note 31 above, at 82–90, 129; Peter Ackroyd, *T. S. Eliot: A Life* 116–117 (1984).
[33] See Gray, note 31 above, at 16. Another notable example of (largely) unconscious writing is the composition in three frenzied weeks in 1922 of Rilke's fifty-five *Sonnets to Orpheus*, together with about twenty other compositions—a feat that has been called "the most astonishing burst of inspiration in the history of literature." Stephen Mitchell, "Introduction," in Rainer Maria Rilke, *The Sonnets to Orpheus* 8 (Stephen Mitchell trans. 1985).
[34] See Ernest A. J. Honigmann, "Shakespeare as a Reviser," in *Textual Criticism and Literary Interpretation* 1 (Jerome J. McGann ed. 1985).
[35] See Beardsley, "The Creation of Art," note 30 above; Samuel Alexander, *Beauty and Other Forms of Value*, chap. 4 (1933); cf. Ruthven, note 13 above, chap. 4. For a brilliant case study of the emergence of poetic meaning from the process of revision see Stallworthy, note 28 above.

literary tradition—we know nothing about the author or authors and almost nothing about the society in which the work was created except what can be inferred from the work itself. Yet evidently this void in our knowledge has not diminished the prestige of the work or the pleasure and instruction it yields. For biographies of writers need not enhance the pleasure we take in their writings, and the instruction that we derive from them. This is a lesson of Kafka studies.

In suggesting that biographical and historical information should play only a minor role in the interpretation of literature, I am not succumbing to the fallacy of supposing that a work of literature, or any other text, can be read without a context. The context of *Easter 1916*, when the poem is read as literature, includes the Easter Rebellion, the political status of Ireland, and the symbolic meaning of the color green (just as the context of *Hamlet* includes the ethics and psychology of revenge). But it does not include Yeats's conscious intentions in writing the poem or the biographies of the individuals discussed in it, just as the literary context of *Billy Budd* does not include the technicalities of eighteenth-century British naval law, whether or not they were known to Melville.

Granted, in excluding these things I am just expressing an opinion, and one grounded in aesthetics rather than in epistemology. Someone steeped in Yeats's conscious intentions in writing *Easter 1916*, or in eighteenth-century British naval law, may find his knowledge of these things creeping into and altering his understanding of the works. It may be inevitable that a reader's response to a text, especially a literary text, will be affected by what he knows, including what he knows about what was in the author's mind or about any other "extraneous" matter. But the New Critics were on the right track in cutting off the background inquiry at an earlier stage than was customary when they wrote (maybe a little too early, but that is a detail). The aesthetic enjoyment that a work of literature yields is diminished rather than enhanced if the work becomes dissolved into a background of intentions and other data both remote from the textual surface and, usually, banal. It is not "wrong" to proceed so, for that may enhance the aesthetic pleasure of the work for some readers—and what else matters? Nor do I deny the importance of esoteric literature, especially in this century when the growth of the popular media has led some authors to cultivate a market limited to the highly educated. A distinguished modern novel that I have mentioned in passing, Mann's *Doctor Faustus*, will be largely incomprehensible to a reader who does not have at least some familiarity with the twelve-tone scale, the life and thought of Nietzsche, modern German history, and of course the Faust legend; all of these things are part of the context that the novel presupposes. But since in any event the decision to cut off background inquiries into a work of literature is an aesthetic decision, the issues in literary intentionalism are remote from those in legal intentionalism.

As a further example of the aesthetic irrelevance of an author's conscious intentions, consider the debate[36] over the meaning of this unnamed lyric by Wordsworth:

> A slumber did my spirit seal;
>     I had no human fears:
> She seemed a thing that could not feel
>     The touch of earthly years.
>
> No motion has she now, no force;
>     She neither hears nor sees;
> Rolled round in earth's diurnal course,
>     With rocks, and stones, and trees.

The debate is about whether Wordsworth meant the reader to feel horror at the death of Lucy (the name of the young girl, as we may infer from the surrounding poems),[37] or to feel consoled. There is extrinsic evidence, as a lawyer might say, that at the time Wordsworth wrote the poem he was a pantheist. He thought that the rocks and stones and trees were alive, and this suggests he meant the reader to be consoled rather than distressed at the prospect of Lucy's being rolled around with them.[38] But if this was his intention it was imperfectly achieved. The thought of the motionless, deaf, dumb Lucy being whirled around forever with rocks, and stones, and trees (the rhythm of the last line reinforcing the sense of circular, repetitive, perhaps dizzying motion) is a grim one. As a hymn to pantheism, the poem fails. If we want to save it as an object of aesthetic value we can impute an unconscious intention at war with and overcoming Wordsworth's conscious desire to celebrate pantheism, or we can say that he intended to write a good poem rather than to spill his guts, or we can forget intentionalism and simply say that

[36] Discussed in (among other places) Hirsch, *Validity in Interpretation*, note 9 above, at 227–230, and Walter Benn Michaels, "Against Formalism: The Autonomous Text in Legal and Literary Interpretation," 1 *Poetics Today* 23, 29–30 (1979). For a sensible comment see Charles Altieri, "The Hermeneutics of Literary Indeterminacy: A Dissent from the New Orthodoxy," 10 *New Literary History* 71, 92 (1978).

[37] Efforts to find a real-life model for Lucy have failed. See Mary Moorman, *William Wordsworth: A Biography: The Early Years, 1770–1803* 423–428 (1957).

[38] See Michaels, note 36 above, at 30.

we are interested in the poem rather than the poet's biography—not in what the poet "could possibly have meant" but in what "could possibly be meant" by the poem.[39]

If intentions are to be disregarded when they contradict what the work itself seems to be saying, maybe they should not enter into interpretation at all. Richard Baines, a contemporary of Christopher Marlowe, wrote shortly after Marlowe's death that Marlowe had boasted of being an atheist. Although Baines may have been lying, there is a fair amount of corroboration for what he reported.[40] Yet it does not follow that *Doctor Faustus* is blasphemous rather than orthodox. Even if Marlowe was an atheist, he may have wanted to write an orthodox play. He may have thought such a play would be better, more interesting, more dramatic, or more popular than an atheistic one—especially since, if believed to be atheistic, the play would have been suppressed. He may simply have wanted to stay out of trouble; atheists were still being burned at the stake in late sixteenth-century England. Knowing that Marlowe probably was an atheist may make us more alert for un-Christian undertones in *Doctor Faustus*—more sensitive to Faustus's oscillation between skepticism and faith—than we would be if we thought Marlowe had been the Archbishop of Canterbury. But we cannot determine the meaning of the play by reference to his beliefs.

Hirsch's acknowledgment that intention about intention is an intelligible concept (see note 27) threatens to make the intentionalist approach to literary meaning vacuous. Imagine asking Wordsworth when he was alive whether he insisted that 150 years hence *A Slumber Did My Spirit Seal* be firmly understood as advocating pantheism, even if, as a result, people stopped reading the poem. I expect he would have answered that he was indifferent to the precise conditions for the survival of the poem for such an immensely long time. The poet knows as well as the legislator that distant changes in culture and society cannot be foreseen. Perhaps the best statement of Wordsworth's intentions is that he wanted to create a work of literature—and we know that for a work of literature

---

[39] Olsen, note 3 above, at 37; cf. Northrop Frye, *Fearful Symmetry: A Study of William Blake* 326 (1947). Compare Wimsatt's criticism of Hirsch's intentionalist reading of Blake's poem *London*, in "Genesis," note 13 above, at 31–34; for rebuttal see Hirsch, "Counterfactuals in Intention," note 9 above. On the pitfalls of biographical criticism generally see Ruthven, note 13 above, chap. 6 and pp. 142–146.

[40] See Frederick S. Boas, *Christopher Marlowe: A Biographical and Critical Study*, chap. 15 (1940); John Bakeless, *The Tragicall History of Christopher Marlowe*, vol. 1, chap. 5 (1942); P. H. Kocher, *Christopher Marlowe: A Study of His Thought, Learning, and Character*, chaps. 2 and 3 (1946). For a judicious summary of the evidence see J. B. Steane, "Introduction," in Christopher Marlowe, *The Complete Plays* 9, 12–15 (J. B. Steane ed. 1969).

to survive, indeed to be a work of literature, it must (like a statute or a constitutional provision) be hospitable to social and cultural change.

Further, to insist[41] that the only authentic meaning of a work of art is one consistent with the understanding of the artist (or perhaps—to allow for "unconscious intention"—of his contemporaries as well) is to make the reading of literature a strictly academic activity. To think one's way into the mind of ancient Greece or Renaissance England is a prodigious scholarly feat, requiring nothing less than a lifetime of disciplined study and probably unattainable even with all that effort and devotion. One does not have to be an epigone of Hans-Georg Gadamer to agree that in reading the literature of another culture one cannot divest oneself of one's own cultural identity; understanding, like translation, is mediation, not just reconstruction.[42] This is not entirely a handicap, for the author's contemporaries may not always be able to understand a work as well as the equally intelligent members of a different or later culture. A knowledge of modern Irish, Jewish, and Negro history might conceivably help one to understand aspects of *Easter 1916*, *The Trial*, and *Othello*, respectively, that their authors and original audiences could not have understood.

And even if the "best" meaning is the one that the literary historian alone can recover, by heroic feats of research and imagination, can we be sure that it is the meaning the author intended? Would Homer and Shakespeare have wanted their work to become the exclusive preserve of scholars? Absurd as the question is, an affirmative answer would be more absurd. Although, other things being equal, the deeper the reader's understanding of the culture in which a work of literature was produced, the deeper will be his understanding of the work,[43] still an interpretation accessible to only one reader in a million has no claim to sole or even paramount authenticity. The New Critics performed a great service for literature—in the precise sense of helping it to survive

[41] As in Anthony Savile, *The Test of Time: An Essay in Philosophical Aesthetics* 64 (1982).

[42] The German hermeneutic school, which culminates in Gadamer—see Hans-Georg Gadamer, *Truth and Method* (1975), and *Philosophical Hermeneutics*, chap. 7 (David E. Linge trans. 1976) ("Aesthetics and Hermeneutics")—and which provides, together with Nietzsche, the main philosophical underpinnings for the reader-response school of literary criticism, is lucidly discussed in Richard E. Palmer, *Hermeneutics: Interpretation Theory in Schleiermacher, Dilthey, Heidegger, and Gadamer* (1969), and Georgia Warnke, *Gadamer: Hermeneutics, Tradition and Reason* (1987).

[43] As forcefully argued in Ralph Cohen, "Historical Knowledge and Literary Understanding," 14 *Papers on Language and Literature* 227 (1978). But this is subject to the qualification that we must not assume that the work uncritically endorses the dominant opinions of its age. See Richard Levin, *New Readings vs. Old Plays: Recent Trends in the Reinterpretation of English Renaissance Drama* 147–166 (1979); Ruthven, note 13 above, at 154–155.

and therefore to *be* literature—by developing and popularizing a style of interpretation that was not so freighted with historical learning as to intimidate or bore the nonspecialist reader.

The more closely one examines the concept of "intention" in literature, the more evanescent the concept becomes. A. D. Nuttall's essay on *The Stranger* (note 13) will help us see this. He distinguishes between two concepts of intentionality, what he calls the "dualist" and the "quasi-behaviorist." The dualist distinguishes between mind and action, planning and doing; he considers an act intentional only if it is pursuant to a conscious design. The quasi-behaviorist uses the word "intention" to describe particular actions irrespective of the actor's mental state. Nuttall points out that on a quasi-behaviorist view Meursault is certainly guilty of murder but that this is much less clear on a dualist view. Nuttall might have added that law, including criminal law, is generally though not consistently committed to the quasi-behaviorist view, and that Oliver Wendell Holmes, in *The Common Law* (1881), urged an extreme version of the quasi-behaviorist view.

The dualist view cannot account for literary creation, so much of which occurs at the unconscious level. The quasi-behaviorist view comes close to what Hirsch, Juhl, and other intentionalists appear to mean by intention but deprives the concept of most of its significance in the literary setting, where we are not concerned with liability or punishment, the principal concerns behind the law's ascriptions of intentionality to behavior. In the quasi-behaviorist view, the author's intention is something deduced from the work itself; so why not cut out the middleman and talk about the work and not the author?

*A Slumber Did My Spirit Seal* can be used to point up the difference—and also the continuity—between New Criticism and (literary) deconstruction. Here is an excerpt from a discussion of the poem by J. Hillis Miller:

> Lucy is both the virgin child and the missing mother, that mother earth which gave birth to the speaker and has abandoned him. Male and female, however, come together in the earth, and so Lucy and the speaker are "the same," though the poet is also the perpetually excluded difference from Lucy, an unneeded increment, like an abandoned child. The two women, mother and girl child, have jumped over the male generation in the middle. They have erased its power of mastery, its power of logical understanding, which is the male power *par excellence* . . . The poet has himself somehow caused Lucy's death by thinking about it. Thinking recapitulates in reverse

mirror image the action of the earthly years in touching, penetrating, possessing, killing, encompassing, turning the other into oneself and therefore being left only with a corpse, an empty sign . . . Lucy's name of course means light. To possess her would be a means of rejoining the lost source of light, the father sun as logos, as head power and fount of meaning . . . In spite of the diurnal rotation of the earth that earth seems to have absorbed all the light. Even the moon, reflected and mediated source of sunlight at night, and so the emblem of Lucy, has set. The consciousness of the poet has survived all these deaths of the light to subsist as a kind of black light. His awareness is the light-no-light which remains when the sun has sunk and Lucy has died, when both have gone into the earth.

This loss of the radiance of the logos, along with the experience of the consequences of that loss, is the drama of all Wordsworth's poetry, in particular of "A Slumber Did My Spirit Seal."[44]

In this kind of criticism the work of literature becomes a window into the critic's mind, just as in a narrowly intentionalist criticism the work of literature becomes a window into the author's mind. Indeed, by shifting the focus from author to critic, the critic goes into competition with the poet. Notice among other extravagances that give Miller's essay an air of free association his emphasizing the etymology of "Lucy"

---

[44] "On Edge: The Crossways of Contemporary Criticism," in *Romanticism and Contemporary Criticism* 96, 108–110 (Morris Eaves and Michael Fischer eds. 1986). For another taste of literary deconstruction try Barbara Johnson's deconstruction of *Billy Budd*, cited in Chapter 3, note 48. When deconstructed, Melville's novella turns out to be about the crisis in reading, its characters are different types of reader, and the law being "critiqued" is the law of signification. The deconstruction of Kafka has led to such *aperçus* as, "[In *In the Penal Colony*] Kafka portrays the fall of *logos* into time with the gusto of a Harpo Marx." Allen Thiher, "Kafka's Legacy," 26 *Modern Fiction Studies* 543 (1980–1981). Then there is Derrida's deconstruction of *Before the Law*, in which he finds sexual significance because "door" in French (not in German of course) is *porte*; the Latin phrase *ante portas* is a medical expression for premature ejaculation; and the man from the country never succeeds in entering the door to the law. See Derrida, "Devant la Loi," note 5 above, at 143. On the excesses of poststructuralism generally, see Graff, note 7 above; Olsen, note 3 above, at 110–118 (discussing Harold Bloom's attempt to interpret Blake's poem *London* with the aid of the Indo-European root *Bha*); Robert Alter, "The Decline and Fall of Literary Criticism," *Commentary*, March 1984, at 50; Crews, note 9 above; Cain, note 5 above, at 75. For spirited defenses of interpretive objectivity see Altieri, note 36 above; T. K. Seung, *Structuralism and Hermeneutics* 185–198 (1982). My own attitude toward the question of objectivity in literary interpretation is similar to that of Ruthven, note 13 above, at 160–161: "We are perhaps better employed in working out hierarchies of probability among the meanings we identify than in constructing elimination procedures in the hope of reaching some chimerical state of correctness in our interpretations." See also Nehamas, note 12 above, at 62–64; Sheppard, note 9 above, chap. 6. Part I of this book attempted to identify interpretations that are low in the hierarchy of probabilities, for example, Weisberg's interpretations of *Hamlet*, *Billy Budd*, and *The Brothers Karamazov*, and West's interpretations of Kafka.

even though the name does not appear in the poem itself or in its title (it has no title). This is a standard deconstructive "move"—all the more because practitioners of deconstruction are fascinated by imagery of light. Light puts them in mind of the metaphor of understanding as seeing, a metaphor that reflects the metaphysics of "presence," which deconstruction challenges.

And yet to someone who had never heard of deconstruction, Miller's essay might seem just an extreme example of New Criticism, reminding one of Ransom's rebuke to Empson for reading too much into a line from Shakespeare's Sonnet 73, "Bare ruin'd choirs, where late the sweet birds sang."[45] As should be apparent from my earlier remarks, I accept from Gadamer and the reader-response school that the meaning of a work of literature, especially one that is culturally remote, as eighteenth-century England is from late twentieth-century America, is a product of collaboration between writer and reader.[46] It is no accident that Hirsch has attacked Gadamer, or that Gadamer's theory of interpretation has been said to be compatible with New Criticism but, interestingly, not with deconstruction.[47] Miller, however, goes too far; the poem disintegrates in his hands. The close readings by the New Critics revealed unsuspected unities; but to read too closely is to pass completely through the poem.

A poem is also diminished, however, when its meaning is deemed to be circumscribed by the poet's thoughts. *A Slumber Did My Spirit Seal*

---

[45] See John Crowe Ransom, *The New Criticism* 121–130 (1941); cf. Graff, note 1 above, at 145–146; Seung, note 44 above, at 271.

[46] See Hekman, note 13 above, at 195.

[47] Hirsch, "Gadamer's Theory of Interpretation," in *Validity in Interpretation*, note 9 above, at 245; see Palmer, note 42 above, at 174–175, 246–247; Hekman, note 13 above, at 187–196. A possible difference is that some orthodox New Critics, like intentionalists and unlike Gadamer, may have thought that each work of literature had a single meaning; the artifact was unchanging—frozen, perhaps, by the meanings, in dictionaries contemporary with the authors, of the words used. My eclectic version of New Criticism rejects any such fixity. Gadamer (see *Truth and Method*, note 42 above, at 291–294, 471) has written specifically on legal, as well as literary, interpretation. He stresses the distance between a legal rule or doctrine and a specific case even if no changed circumstances have intervened. Aristotle had made this point. "Law is always a general statement, yet there are cases which it is not possible to cover in a general statement . . . Therefore . . . it is then right, where the lawgiver's pronouncement because of its absoluteness is defective and erroneous, to rectify the defect by deciding as the lawgiver would himself decide if he were present on the occasion, and would have enacted if he had been cognizant of the case in question." *Nicomachean Ethics* V.x.4–6, in Aristotle, *Works*, vol. 19, at 315, 317 (H. Rackham trans., rev. ed. 1934). Gadamer also stresses that legal interpretation is not a deductive process. These points are consistent with the broadly intentionalist approach to statutory and constitutional interpretation that I advocate in this chapter.

is more moving conceived of as an ambivalent musing on the fact that we return to nature when we die than as a pantheist tract that aims to make death a consoling union of the deceased with nature and falls short. A poet tries to create a work of art, a thing of beauty and pleasure. He either succeeds or fails. If he succeeds, we do not care how banal his intentions were, and if he fails, we do not care how elevated they were.[48] A legislature, however, is trying to give commands to its subordinates in our government system, the judges who apply legislation in specific cases. A command is designed to set up a direct channel between the issuer's mind and the recipient's; it is a communication, to be decoded in accordance with the sender's intentions.[49] If a message is garbled in transmission, you ask the sender to repeat it; that is intentionalism in practice. If you cannot reach the sender, you try to glean from everything you know about him and the circumstances of the failed message what he might have meant; again the correct analysis is an intentionalist one. One of the things that gives intentionalism its purchase in literary criticism, besides the misguided search for authoritative literary interpretations, is the Romantic fascination with the personality of the artist—the Romantic conception of the work of art as emanation rather than artifact.[50] But that a statute is an emanation is a condition of its authority.

Notice how in embracing the idea of the legislative text as command or communication I am doing just what the deconstructionists denounce: I am "privileging the spoken over the written word," that is, thinking of the written word on the model of speech. The speaker is usually successful in conveying his message to the listener with a minimum of "noise," thereby bringing the listener into his "presence." At the same time I am doing what the New Critics denounced: refusing to treat the legal text as an artifact, and instead treating it as an attempt to set up a path of clear communication between author and reader. New Criticism and deconstructionism are continuous, and both are opposed to what seems to me the right attitude toward the interpretation of statutory and constitutional texts.

Unhampered by command responsibilities, the author of a work of literature need not strive for a clear statement. Indeed, a work of

---

[48] For examples see Beardsley, "Intentions and Interpretation," note 13 above, at 201–202.
[49] See my "Legal Formalism, Legal Realism, and the Interpretation of Statutes and the Constitution," 37 *Case Western Reserve Law Review* 179, 186–190 (1986). Cf. Powell, note 27 above, at 911.
[50] See, for example, Monroe C. Beardsley, *Aesthetics from Classical Greece to the Present: A Short History* 251 (1966).

literature that is too clear, like a legal rule that is too specific, may for that reason lack adaptability—"omnisignificance"—and as a result be doomed to obsolesce rapidly and pass out of the literary realm. Nor is there much felt need (*pace* Charles Lamb) to "amend" literature to make it clearer. It is therefore no surprise that so much literature is enigmatic. Kafka's writings, many of them unfinished, have often been called the literary equivalent of the Rorschach test; they fight interpretation or, what is almost the same thing, invite multiple interpretations. Irony, a common literary device, poses obvious problems for interpretation. Often it just is not clear whether a work is ironic or "straight."[51] The suggestive, ambiguous, multifaceted or multileveled[52] character of literature is what gives literary deconstruction its purchase. (The fallacy of extreme interpretive skepticism is to suppose that a text that does not have a single, demonstrable meaning is meaningless.) Although it would be going too far to say that ambiguity is the hallmark of great works of literature, it is a frequent characteristic of them for a reason that should be obvious from the discussion of literary survival in Chapter 2. Works are called great because they transcend boundaries of period and culture; they have a certain generality and even universality— that is, they mean different things to different people.[53] They can do this

[51] See Booth, note 12 above, chap. 11, especially on Joyce's *Portrait of an Artist*; René Girard, " 'To Entrap the Wisest': A Reading of *The Merchant of Venice*," in *Literature and Society* 100 (Edward W. Said ed. 1980); Wayne Booth, *A Rhetoric of Irony* (1974); cf. Monroe C. Beardsley, *Aesthetics: Problems in the Philosophy of Criticism* 138 (1958). An excellent example from poetry is Marvell's *Horatian Ode upon Cromwell's Return from Ireland*. It seems like straightforward, even fulsome, praise, yet there are hints and more than hints of criticism. There is the magnificent picture of Charles I on the scaffold ("He nothing common did or mean / Upon that memorable scene"), about which the poet comments, "This was that memorable hour / Which first assur'd the forced power." And there is (besides much else) the somber closing couplet: "The same arts that did gain / A power must it maintain." The overall tone is, indeed, similar to that of *Easter 1916*. For good discussions of Marvell's poem see Thomas R. Edwards, *Imagination and Power: A Study of Poetry on Public Themes* 66–81 (1971); Kermode, *The Classic*, note 13 above, at 65; George deForest Lord, *Classical Presences in Seventeenth-Century English Poetry* 90–96 (1987).

[52] See Kendall L. Walton, "Degrees of Durability," *Times Literary Supplement*, Feb. 18, 1983, at 148.

[53] "It may well be that the term *classic* is significant because the works we employ it for have the power of generating classes; that is, they become prototypes of basic recurrent modes for imaginatively organizing experience." Altieri, note 36 above, at 90. "One hallmark of an authentic work of art . . . may be its ultimate irreducibility to a schema." Norman Rabkin, *Shakespeare and the Problem of Meaning* 23 (1981). Cf. Frank Kermode, *Forms of Attention* 79 (1985). A similar point has been made in explaining why general legal precedents depreciate more slowly than specific ones. See William M. Landes and Richard A. Posner, "Legal Precedent: A Theoretical and Empirical Analysis," 19 *Journal of Law and Economics* 249 (1976).

without losing their character as literature because it is not the function of literature to lay down rules of conduct.

Furthermore, meaning and message frequently diverge in literature, most dramatically but not only in works that are ironic. It usually is possible to extract a clear and definite message by paraphrasing the work. For example, the message of *Doctor Faustus* is that if you sign a pact with the devil you will be sorry in the end. At the level of message most works of literature are clear; what makes them unclear is that we are not interested in staying at that level. But the message level is the only interesting level of a statutory or constitutional text. That is why the Peller-Tushnet interpretation of the age-35 provision in the Constitution seems obtuse rather than ingenious. When we are interpreting messages we are trying to figure out what the sender was trying to tell us; and intentionalism is a natural strategy for dealing with unclear messages.

Another reason for wanting to tether the legal but not the literary interpreter to the author's intentions is the importance of minimizing inconsistent interpretations in law. Law presupposes a degree of uniformity that would be otiose in cultural affairs. For a literary critic to propose a startling new reading of a work of literature is harmless, and often healthy. But if every lawyer and judge felt free to imprint his own personal reading on any statute, chaos would threaten.[54] There is, it is true, a machinery for enforcing legal uniformity; the Supreme Court's reading would be authoritative—but only in the sense that a gun held at your head is authoritative. If interpretation is arbitrary, the Court's "interpretation" would have no intrinsic authority; it would be authoritative solely because of the Court's position in the judicial hierarchy. If statutes are invitations to the reader to supply meaning in the way that Miller supplies meaning for *A Slumber Did My Spirit Seal*, then what the Court would be doing in a case in which it interpreted the Eighth Amendment to find a prohibition against sexually segregated prisons or against denying prison inmates access to cable television would be as private and irresponsible as for a modern literary critic to read Virgil's *Fourth Eclogue*, written before the birth of Christ, as an allegory of His birth—which as a matter of fact is how it was read during the Middle Ages.[55]

---

[54] A similar point is made in Michael Hancher, "What Kind of Speech Act Is Interpretation," 10 *Poetics* 263, 276–277 (1981), and in Stanley Fish, "Fish v. Fiss," note 1 above, at 1344–1345.

[55] See, for example, T. S. Eliot, "Virgil and the Christian World," in *On Poetry and Poets*, note 12 above, at 121–123; Kermode, *The Classic*, note 13 above, at 28–29. Or *Pudd'nhead Wilson* as an allegory of the Sacco and Vanzetti case!

The example of Virgil is worth pausing over, as it illustrates so well both the differences between legal and literary interpretation and the importance of context in interpretation. For the deeply believing Christians of the Middle Ages the idea that Virgil had foreseen the birth of Christ was a natural one. We recall Virgil's role as Dante's cicerone in the *Divine Comedy*, and the association in Dante's mind (*pace* Nietzsche) between the Roman Empire and the Kingdom of God: at the bottom of Hell sits three-faced Lucifer masticating Brutus and Cassius with two sets of jaws and Judas with the third. The medieval consensus—which the authorities were fully prepared to enforce by force if necessary—provided an interpretive context that made the Christian reading of the *Fourth Eclogue* straightforward rather than, as it would appear to most of us in this skeptical and relativistic age, deeply problematic. No counterpart set of beliefs is available today that would enable us to fix the meaning of the Constitution in such a way that we could say with a straight face that the framers had (or had not) created a right to an abortion, or forbidden capital punishment or the legislative veto.

Moreover, while a literary critic may be an influential person, he or she is a private individual. The exercise of power by appointed officials with life tenure (which is the situation of all federal and, practically speaking, many state judges) is tolerated only in the belief that the power is constrained; and the principal, though not sole, constraint is authoritative texts. A judge who acknowledged being a deconstructionist or even a New Critic would be excoriated for having cut loose from moorings that are part of the fundamental design of American government. Literary texts need not be authoritative to perform their function in society.

Many contemporary critics rebel against being chained to the text. Richard Rorty has summarized the attitude of this type of critic: "He is in it for what he can get out of it, not for the satisfaction of getting something right."[56] The public would be horrified at such a conception of the judicial role. The concern of literary intentionalists with the idea of authoritative interpretation (for them, the interpretation that is faithful to the author's intent) is displaced from its proper object. The problem of legitimacy need not arise in regard to literary criticism, but it is central to law and government. The literary intentionalist is a

---

[56] *Consequences of Pragmatism (Essays: 1972–1980)* 152 (1982). These are not the only alternatives. T. S. Eliot conceived the function of literary criticism to be to enhance readers' understanding and enjoyment of literature. See "The Frontiers of Criticism," note 12 above. So defined, literary criticism is distinct from literary scholarship.

lawyer *manqué*; the legal New Critic is a critic *manqué*. The former demands a type of constraint on interpretation that law rather than literature requires;[57] the latter seeks a freedom of interpretation that literature but not law allows.

For an intentionalist like Juhl who concedes the inexhaustibility of literature, the possibility of unconscious intention, and the dangers of relying too heavily on historical and biographical materials as clues to the author's intent,[58] almost the whole significance of intentionalism is to rule out interpretations that cannot possibly be referred to the author's conscious or unconscious mind. Mainly these are interpretations that, looked at from the standpoint of the author's intentions, either imply prophetic gifts (for example, interpreting *The Trial* as an allegory of the police state, the *Fourth Eclogue* as an allegory of the birth of Christ, or *The Second Coming* as an allegory of the Munich Pact) or, what is the equivalent, contradict unequivocal biographical or historical data. Juhl illustrates with a passage from T. S. Eliot's poem *The Love Song of J. Alfred Prufrock* (lines 90–93): "Would it have been worth while . . . To have squeezed the universe into a ball." Suppose, says Juhl in *Interpretation* (pp. 58–59; see note 9), that we knew Eliot had never read Marvell's *To His Coy Mistress*, which contains the lines, "Let us roll all our strength and all / Our sweetness up into one ball." Then, Juhl argues, we could not regard the allusion to Marvell as part of *Prufrock*'s meaning. I disagree. I would say rather that in that case Eliot had made a lucky hit—had, by his choice of words, accidentally enriched the meaning of his poem for readers who remembered Marvell's *Coy Mistress* and would contrast the vigor of the lover's solicitations in that poem with Prufrock's hesitations. Why should it matter whether Eliot intended the allusion?

The legitimacy of a legal interpretation, however, requires a linkage of some sort with the plans and purposes of the framers of the statutory or constitutional provision being interpreted. I do not mean to endorse

[57] This is strikingly shown by Hirsch's discussion of "the advocacy system in [literary] interpretation as in law. The advocates have the task of bringing forward evidence favorable to their side and unfavorable to their opponents . . . But without a judge all those relevant pieces of evidence float uselessly . . . [Therefore] unless advocates sometimes serve as judges, none of this activity will actually contribute to knowledge." *Validity in Interpretation*, note 9 above, at 197. There is no mechanism for appointing authoritative judges of disputes over literary interpretation; nor would such a mechanism be welcome. And self-appointed judges with no authority are not a close analogue to official judges.

[58] See Juhl, note 9 above, at 135, 151, 225–230. And see Hirsch, *Validity in Interpretation*, note 9 above, at 22 ("it is very possible to mean what one is not conscious of meaning") and his discussion in "Counterfactuals in Interpretation," note 9 above, of the importance of distinguishing dominant from local intentions and the spirit from the letter of a work.

the kind of stupid literalism that would say that since the First
Amendment provides that "Congress shall make no law . . . abridging
the freedom of speech," a law that made it a crime to utter threats
against the President's life would be unconstitutional; or that wiretapping cannot violate the Fourth Amendment (which prohibits unreasonable searches and seizures) because a wiretap is neither a search nor a
seizure. I admit the relevance of intention about intention and hence the
propriety of treating broadly worded statutory and constitutional
phrases ("freedom of speech," for example) as delegations to the
judiciary to create and not merely determine meaning. Nor do I deny
the legitimacy of bringing pragmatic, utilitarian considerations to bear
on the interpretive process. One reason why the age-35 provision means
what it says is that the literal meaning is also the expedient meaning, just
as one reason why "I'll eat my hat" does not mean what it says is that
eating a hat is virtually impossible to do. Still, in legal interpretation the
subordination of the interpreter to the "speaker" is a condition of
legitimacy. The judge is trying to decode a communication from his
superiors in the constitutional hierarchy and must use all available
information, including whatever can be learned of the conscious intentions of those who wrote the provision that is being interpreted. The test
of a literary interpretation, in contrast, can be purely pragmatic and
utilitarian—does it make the work of literature richer, more instructive,
more beautiful?

The shortcomings of Juhl's approach to literary meaning have been
well summarized by Stein Haugom Olsen in *The End of Literary Theory*:

> Juhl fails to appreciate the logical status of emergent features like
> coherence and complexity because he believes that literary interpretation is
> aimed at revealing a meaning analogous to that revealed in the interpreta-
> tion of utterances. But a literary work has no such meaning. The aim of
> literary interpretation is to reveal those features which make the work a
> good literary work. These features, among which are coherence and
> complexity, together define a fictional universe or vision. This poetic
> vision can naturally be described by help of thematic concepts and this
> description together with the reasons for accepting it will, if it is any good,
> illuminate the work for somebody who has failed to appreciate it, but this
> description is not a paraphrase of a meaning possessed by the work. When
> an author offers a text to his audience *as a literary work of art* he commits
> himself to providing a text which repays a certain type of attention.
> Literary interpretation is governed by what one may call a principle of
> charity: one gives the work the particular type of attention which literary
> interpretation represents because one assumes that the author has honoured
> his commitment. Appreciation is an attempt to apprehend the work in a

way which will make it as good as possible as a literary work. Unity, language 'pleasurably enhanced', and 'amplitude' (to borrow three concepts from Aristotle's *Poetics*) are necessary for the aesthetic pay-off. And this is why coherence and complexity are criteria of an author's intention which override whatever the author himself may have to say about the emergent aesthetic features of a work after he has delivered the text.[59]

A statute or a constitutional provision is an instance of what Olsen calls an "utterance," or in my terms an effort to communicate a message rather than to create a work of art.

I cannot hope in this chapter, or in this book, to persuade doubters that the intentionalist or communicative view of statutory and constitutional interpretation is the correct one. That would require a book of its own. But I hope I have persuaded the reader that criticisms of an intentionalist approach to literature—criticisms I find convincing—do not undermine legal intentionalism.

I HAVE been speaking so far of statutes and the Constitution, but much that I have said applies to the interpretation of contracts as well (though not to the interpretation of judicial opinions, for reasons explained in the next chapter). It is therefore relevant to note the neglect, in a literary critic's recent discussion of the parol evidence rule, of the essential differences between law and literature.[60] The rule is that a writing intended to be the complete expression of the parties' contract may not be contradicted by oral testimony. Michaels points out that before a court can know whether oral testimony about the meaning of a contract contradicts the written contract, it must interpret the contract; and since interpretation always requires resort to extrinsic "evidence"— if only the judge's knowledge of language and life—it is arbitrary to exclude another type of extrinsic evidence that might bear on interpretation. All this is true, but it does not follow that the court should allow a party to present at trial evidence designed to change the meaning that

---

[59] Olsen, note 3 above, at 51.

[60] See Michaels, note 36 above, at 26–29. On the parol evidence rule itself see E. Allan Farnsworth, *Contracts* 447–451 (1982). (Cognoscenti no longer regard the parol evidence rule as evidentiary in purpose, see id. at 451, and what Michaels is really talking about is the distinct rule that makes extrinsic evidence inadmissible if a contract is clear "on its face," but this is a detail of no importance to my disagreement with his analysis.) On the interpretation of wills by the methods of literary criticism, a subject not discussed in this book, see Michael Hancher, "Wills and Poems," 60 *Texas Law Review* 507 (1982); Eber Carle Perrow, "The Last Will and Testament as a Form of Literature," 17 *Transactions of the Wisconsin Academy of Sciences, Arts and Letters* (pt. 1) 682 (1914).

the contract would otherwise bear. If a document states that it is the complete, integrated expression of the parties' contract for the sale and purchase of twenty pounds of frankincense, and the price stated in the document is $100 per pound, the parol evidence rule will prevent the seller (say) from later testifying that in the negotiations leading up to the contract the parties had agreed that, yes, the price would be $100 a pound but only for the first ten pounds, after which it would be $120 a pound. The parties intended the writing to control in order to prevent lying or bad memories from muddying the waters should the parties ever get into a lawsuit over the meaning of the contract.

The parol evidence rule may seem to reflect a New Critical approach, ruling out consideration of the draftsmen's intentions; this may be why Michaels, an intentionalist, is critical of it. But the rule is intentionalist *au fond*: it effectuates the intention of the parties when they signed the contract, which is the relevant intention in interpreting it. Neither party wanted the other one to be allowed to deny, if and when a dispute arose, the meaning of the contract as it would be gathered from the writing itself, interpreted in light of the general knowledge that the judge would bring to the case.

## More Objections to Reading Legal and Literary Texts the Same Way

While the authors of the Constitution, the Bill of Rights, and many of the later amendments were for the most part highly capable professionals, the relative handful of people who are the authors of the literature that hundreds or even thousands of years after it was written is still being avidly read were for the most part geniuses, and it is their best work, not necessarily all their work, that survives and is read. In dealing with work of this caliber it is natural to follow the procedure suggested by Dworkin, and well summarized by Olsen in the passage I quoted, which is to interpret the work so as to make it as good as possible.

To put Olsen's point slightly differently, a useful method of reading literature (and the most important methodological contribution of the New Criticism) is to adopt a hypothesis of total coherence—to assume that no detail of the work is an accident, that everything contributes in some way to its meaning and emotional impact.[61] It is through the study of the details and their relations that one begins to understand how great

---

[61] See, for example, Sigurd Burkhardt, *Shakespearean Meanings* 285–313 (1968). Cf. Olsen, note 12 above, at 137–155; Kermode, note 55 above, at 92. The presumption should be rebuttable; there are radically imperfect works of literature, as argued in Hershel Parker, *Flawed Texts and Verbal Icons: Literary Authority in American Fiction* (1984).

literature casts its spell and how it teaches. Thus in Yeats's great poem *The Wild Swans at Coole* we are made to feel the mystery and remoteness of nature by a surprising yet somehow "right" juxtaposition of the words "cold" and "companionable" in a description of swans on a lake:

> Unwearied still, lover by lover,
> They paddle in the cold
> Companionable streams or climb the air;
> Their hearts have not grown old;
> Passion or conquest, wander where they will,
> Attend upon them still.

The same interpretive technique—that of attributing significance to every detail—is, when used on statutes, a familiar source of absurdities. Statutes and constitutions are written in haste by busy people not always of great ability or diligence, and we are not privileged to ignore the hasty and the hackneyed provisions and reserve our attention for the greatest. Moreover, they are products of a committee (the legislature) rather than of a single mind, and of a committee whose numerous members may have divergent objectives. So a statute may well contain meaningless repetitions and inconsistencies. To suppose that its every word probably has significance, that every statute is a seamless whole, misconceives the nature of the legislative process.[62] Dworkin's claim that the interpretive task for a court is to make the statute or constitutional provision in question the best rule of law the court can imagine assumes that legislators typically strive to make the best rule of law they can, as Yeats strove to make *The Wild Swans at Coole* the best poem he could. But that is to be unrealistic about legislative intention, and the practical consequence is to substitute the judge's will for that of the legislature—which is a lot more serious than a critic's substituting his will for Wordsworth's or Yeats's. Alternatively, Dworkin may be saying that regardless of the legislature's intent the judge should make the statute the best possible rule of law; but that is to shift the responsibility for making policy from the legislature to the court—a shift of doubtful legitimacy.

Where the problems of legal and literary interpretation may seem to merge is where the legislature's intentions either are to delegate the lawmaking function to the courts or are simply inscrutable. In the first case we are in the domain of common law, that is, of avowedly and legitimately judge-made law. In the second case, where it just is not

---

[62] See the sources cited in note 11 above, and Frank H. Easterbrook, "Statutes' Domains," 50 *University of Chicago Law Review* 533 (1983).

possible to reconstruct the original intentions of the people who wrote and voted for the statute or constitutional provision but the case must be decided somehow, Dworkin's procedure may seem apt; it may seem that the judges must perforce "interpret" the provision so as to make it the best possible statement of political principle or social policy. But the parallel to literary criticism of ambiguous works is deceptive. The critic is not forcing his interpretation on anyone else, whereas the court that interprets an ambiguous provision, especially of the Constitution (so that the interpretation is very difficult to correct legislatively), is imposing its view on the rest of society, sometimes with far-reaching consequences. The critic who contends that misreading a work of literature is a liberating experience—that rebellion against the author is as refreshing as rebellion against one's father,[63] that man must learn to create his own reality in the reading of texts as well as in the governance of society—may be childish, but he is also as harmless as a child. Not so the judge who decides to rebel against the authority of the statutory and constitutional texts that he is supposed to be interpreting, not misreading. Law is coercion rather than persuasion.

There are additional reasons against interpreting legislation as freely as literature:

1. Literary critics operate in a more competitive market than judges. The extravagances of the former must pass a market test similar to that of literature itself—will they be accepted by other critics? A supreme court need convince no one of the rightness of its "interpretations"; its word is law.

2. There is a feedback loop between interpretation and legislation. If interpretation is too erratic, the making of new legislation is discouraged because legislators cannot predict the effects of the legislation they pass. There is no similar loop between critics and authors.

3. Legislators, their staffs, and lobbyists produce (in the case of all federal and some state statutes) a published "legislative history" to help guide judicial interpretation. Writers of literature sometimes offer interpretations of their own works, but for reasons discussed earlier these interpretations tend to be unreliable. Sometimes writers preserve their unpublished drafts, which are comparable to the unenacted bills that often precede an enacted statute. But though invaluable in understanding the process of creative composition, writers' rough drafts rarely dispel interpretive fogs; this is the lesson of Stallworthy's fine study of the Yeats manuscripts (see note 35). In sum, it is harder to

---

[63] This tendency in poststructuralist criticism is well described in Graff, note 7 above, at 79–82. See also note 6 above.

extract the writer's intentions than those of the legislature; often it is attempted by facile psychoanalyzing on incomplete data: the fate of Kafka, among many others.

4. The legislature has at least decided to enact the law being interpreted. But many literary works (including *The Trial* and *Billy Budd*) were left unfinished at their authors' death, leaving one uncertain whether what we have was intended to be read. Kafka left instructions to destroy all his unpublished works (including *The Trial*), though how seriously these instructions were intended to be taken is unclear. Intentionalism is deeply problematic in these instances.

5. Related to the obvious point that uniformity is more important in legal than in literary interpretation is the subtle point that multiple interpretations of the same work at the same time may be an equilibrium state for the literary marketplace, whereas they would be a source of profound disequilibrium in law. A reader's interpretation of a literary text is affected by what he knows; and different readers know different things. There is no way in which a person who has spent a lifetime studying Shakespeare can convey his entire understanding of the Shakespearean context to a nonspecialist; Shakespeare's plays will always mean different things to specialists and nonspecialists. Eliot's fourth quartet, *Little Gidding*, will mean something different to the reader who recognizes that "The dove descending breaks the air / With flame of incandescent terror" refers to a German airplane bombing London in World War II, a reference not apparent from the poem itself but assumed by every student of Eliot's poetry to have been intended. *The Wild Swans at Coole* means something different to a person who has read a lot of Yeats's poetry than to one who has read little or none of it, because the former will realize that "swan" has not just its ordinary meaning in Yeats's poetry but also a private, symbolic meaning. And, quite apart from the swan motif, *Leda and the Swan* (see Chapter 7) means something different to a reader steeped in Nietzsche, who had a big influence on Yeats, than to other readers. *The Trial* takes on additional hues of meaning if read in conjunction with Kafka's legal parables, such as *The Problem of Our Laws*, than if read in isolation. But it would be incorrect to say that you cannot understand a Yeats poem or a Kafka novel without having read extensively in, and having reflected profoundly upon, other works by these authors, and without, in addition, having immersed yourself in what *they* read. It is just that your understanding will be different. For reasons stated earlier, it would be a mistake to suppose that only the specialist possesses the authentic meaning of the great works of literature. The authors of those works

would not have wanted it so; they were not writing for a tiny coterie of professors. We must accept the existence of different but valid levels of meaning in works of literature, but not in constitutional and statutory provisions.

This and all that preceded it cannot, however, be the last word on the relative freedom of the statutory interpreter and the literary critic. If there are reasons why the statutory interpreter should feel less free than the literary critic, there are also reasons why the former should on occasion feel more free than the latter. One reason is committee authorship. A legislature is not a single mind, and the determination of collective intent is often problematic; moreover, much legislation reflects compromise rather than consensus. One way to achieve compromise is to use general language, in effect shoving off on the courts the task of completing the legislation. In such a case there may be an effective delegation of a policymaking function. Neither intentionalism nor New Criticism provides helpful analogies here. Granted, this distinction between law and literature is blurred by the undeniable element of committee authorship in literature. For example, *Hamlet* as we experience it is a collaboration of Shakespeare, the authors of the sources on which he drew, the modern editors of its various texts, and the producers, directors, and actors who put on performances of the play.

Consider now the role of *stare decisis* (decision in accordance with precedent) in statutory and constitutional interpretation. When a particular interpretation, even if unsound, has become entrenched in a long line of decisions, a court will be loath to abandon it, because of the reliance that has been engendered, because the court wants to maintain the appearance (and reality) that law is objective and impersonal, and because the court does not want to encourage legislators to be hasty and careless by leading them to think that judges will make any legislative revisions that are necessary, simply by reinterpreting legislation to keep it abreast of the times. The result of a long period of judicial interpretation, such as that undergone by the Constitution (two centuries) or the Sherman Antitrust Act (almost one century), may be a body of doctrine that bears even less relation to the intentions of the framers than a modern interpretation of an old work of literature will bear to its author's intentions. Nevertheless, courts may invoke *stare decisis* and refuse to correct even patently erroneous interpretations. (This point suggests that a modified rather than pure intentionalism is the best, or at least the most orthodox, guide to statutory and constitutional interpretation. But the modification owes nothing to literary theory.)

And while the only, though not a bad, reason for a free interpretation of a work of literature—an interpretation that makes it mean something different from what it meant to its original audience—is to get greater pleasure and insight from the work, a free interpretation of a statute or the Constitution may be necessary to avert a catastrophe. The limitations that the Constitution appears to place on the powers of the President and the Congress have been considerably relaxed in judicial interpretations of the Constitution in order to accommodate the perceived exigencies of modern government. For example, the Second Amendment provides that "a well regulated Militia, being necessary to the security of a free State, the right of the people to keep and bear Arms, shall not be infringed." These words seem to say without equivocation that the federal government shall not forbid law-abiding citizens to keep military weapons, but the government has felt compelled to forbid this and the Supreme Court has not interfered. Comparing the wording of the Second Amendment (or of the provision requiring that the President be at least 35 years old) with that of the lines I quoted earlier from *The Second Coming*, we have an example of legislative wording that is more particular and confining than poetic wording. Lacking generality and hence adaptability, the Second Amendment, like a too-topical work of (attempted) literature, has become obsolete and, rightly or wrongly, has been ignored. With the rise of Marxist and feminist literary criticism it is no longer possible to say that there is no political pressure in this country to interpret literature freely (unconventionally, unexpectedly)— and perhaps the American New Critics illustrate the ubiquity of "political" criticism—but there is less such pressure than in the case of legislation.

To make the point more dramatically, there is a morality of rebellion as well as of obedience. Like Captain Vere in *Billy Budd*, I have stressed the latter, appropriately in a civilized democratic society such as ours. In a wicked society, the proper course for a judge might be to defy the law. With power to deprive citizens of their property, liberty, or even lives comes responsibility for the wise exercise of this power as well as duty to obey the legal limitations on its exercise.[64] Even in a civilized legal system the circumstances of an individual case may rightly cause the judge to decide in a way that cannot easily be squared with the text of the statutory or constitutional provision being interpreted. This is another example of the force of discretionary, equitable, or political considerations in judicial decisionmaking, an issue discussed in Chapter

[64] Cf. West, note 2 above; Robert M. Cover, "Violence and the Word," 95 *Yale Law Journal* 1601 (1986).

2. Such considerations are elements of the law, just as rules handed down by higher authority are. Aristotle introduced the idea of equity (*epieikeia*) to justify judicial departures from literal interpretation of statutes (see the quotation in note 47).

Consider by way of analogy the problem of a platoon commander in an attack who comes up against an unexpected obstacle and radios his company commander for orders. The company commander replies, but on the wrong frequency, and as a result no order is received. It would not be responsive for the platoon commander to take the view that he should do nothing because of the failure of communication. He must decide what the commander would have wanted him to do, and act accordingly. In other words, he must do what he thinks will best advance the common enterprise. This is intentionalism even though the actual command is unknown. The situation with regard to statutory and constitutional interpretation is often similar: the legislative intention not having been intelligibly expressed in the enacted text, the judge's job is to pick the interpretation that is most likely to advance the common enterprise of governance.[65] The literary critic does not have such a responsibility.

Another reason why legislative interpretation can sometimes be freer than literary interpretation—a reason that requires qualification of my earlier endorsement of New Criticism as a proper technique for interpreting literature—is that ignoring historical context may sometimes do more damage to the understanding and enjoyment of works of literature than to the understanding of statutes and constitutions. The cultural distance between a work of literature and its reader usually is greater than that between a statute and the judge concerned with its meaning. The legal texts that are authoritative in the American legal system are texts written by American lawyers no earlier than 1787 and usually much later. Works of literature are often much older, often foreign, often written by individuals from a radically different cultural milieu than that of the modern American reader. To read literature composed in a different culture without being aware of the difference can be a reckless undertaking. Imagine trying to read *Hamlet* without

---

[65] The military analogy and the conception of statutory and constitutional interpretation that it supports are elaborated in Posner, note 51 above, at 189–190, 199–201. I take it that no one would suggest that the platoon commander's proper response would be to deconstruct his orders; and I infer from this example that the practitioners of deconstruction would not argue that a communicative model of speech or writing is never appropriate. For a good summary of communication or information theory see Louis T. Milic, "Information Theory and the Style of *Tristram Shandy*," in *The Winged Skull: Papers from the Laurence Sterne Bicentenary Conference* 237 (Arthur H. Cash and John M. Stedmond eds. 1971).

knowing how such words as "brave" and "fat" have changed meaning (Gertrude's statement during Hamlet's duel with Laertes that Hamlet "is fat and scant of breath" does not mean that Hamlet is overweight but either that he is sweaty or that he is out of condition), or that the English thought Danes given to excessive drinking (that is the "custom / More honour'd in the breach than the observance," that is, more honorably rejected than followed, to which Hamlet refers), or that marriage to a brother-in-law was deemed incestuous. Imagine trying to read *The Merchant of Venice* thinking that Jews had the same position in Elizabethan society as they do in ours. Imagine reading works of literature written half a century ago and thinking that when they used the word "gay" (as in the following line from Yeats's poem *Lapis Lazuli*: "They know that Hamlet and Lear are gay") they meant homosexual.

It is possible that some readings based on ignorance and error can be considered better, in the sense of imparting a greater resonance to the work of literature, than readings scrupulously confined by historical knowledge. The Christian interpretation of Virgil's *Fourth Eclogue* may be a case in point, and there are a number of famous mistranslations in the King James version of the Bible that seem superior on literary grounds to the originals, though maybe it is only habit and tradition that make us think so. Mark Twain's careless revising of *Pudd'nhead Wilson* may be an example of serendipitous error.[66] The Duke's admonition to Claudio in *Measure for Measure*, "Be absolute for death," is more impressive if "absolute" is taken in its modern sense rather than in its Elizabethan senses of resolute or (as in Hamlet's outburst at the literalistic gravedigger, "How absolute the knave is") single-minded. But such serendipity is rare. The introduction of a random element is unlikely to improve a work of literature; and except in the rare instance where the reader is as talented as the author, the reader is unlikely to improve the work by using it as a mirror for his own insights. If, however, as in the case of *Easter 1916*, the circumstances in which the work of literature was created are not culturally remote from our own, the task of historical reconstruction may be a light one.

Judges read statutes and the Constitution not for enjoyment but for assistance in deciding a lawsuit and in devising or refining a rule of

[66] Parker, note 61 above, chap. 5, thinks not. But he is, I respectfully suggest, a prisoner of the view that the only authentic literary meanings are those intended by the author. He asks, how can the chapters that Mark Twain wrote before he decided to make the false "Tom" a black, and included without change after making him black, be taken seriously as meditations on race, or genetics, or slavery? See id. at 135–145. The answer is that context shapes meaning. Mark Twain may have retained these chapters because, relocated in a work about blacks and whites, they acquired a new meaning.

conduct that may have a significant impact on the welfare of the community. The community is not always willing to allow its choices to be controlled by what people who lived two centuries ago wrote into the Constitution, talented as those people were; and the procedure for amending the Constitution is so cumbersome that the judges are under great pressure to use the interpretive process to keep the original document flexible. The framers themselves may not have wanted to control tightly a future they knew they could not foresee, even if the result of flexible interpretation would be to impair the symmetry and elegance of what they wrote. Works of literature are not written to provide rules of conduct that may chafe hundreds of years later. The sources of interpretive legitimacy in the law are various. They are not just the words, and not just the words plus the intentions, of the framers of the text being interpreted.

Finally, while the law strives to fix a single authoritative meaning for each enactment, the literary "equilibrium," as I noted earlier, allows for a plurality of meanings, and the original meaning is an important one, not only for scholarly but for educational reasons. A basic goal of education is to give students a sense of other cultures; this is an argument (having no close counterpart in law) for continuing to stress the original meaning of works of literature, though not to the exclusion of other meanings.

LET ME try to anchor some of these observations in two cases of statutory interpretation. The first, *United States v. Locke*,[67] involved a federal statute that requires any firm with an unpatented mining claim on federal public lands to reregister it annually, "prior to December 31." Claims not reregistered on time are forfeited. Mines are abandoned frequently, and the requirement of annual registration provides an easy means of determining whether abandonment has occurred. The plaintiffs in *Locke* filed the required form on December 31. The government declared the plaintiffs' mine forfeited, and the Supreme Court upheld this determination.

The Court's decision is impeccable as a matter of lexicography; "prior to" December 31 means no later than December 30. However, it is highly probable that the statute contains a drafting error and that what Congress meant was that you must file before the end of the year—that is, on or before December 31. The same section of the statute distin-

[67] 471 U.S. 84 (1985), interpreting section 314(a) of the Federal Land Policy and Management Act of 1976, 43 U.S.C. § 1744(a).

guishes between claims "located prior to October 21, 1976," and claims "located after October 21, 1976," thus leaving a gap for claims located on October 21, 1976—if "prior to" is read literally. No one has ever given a reason why Congress might have wanted the filing made *before* December 31 (which is not a holiday). It is not enough to say that all deadlines are arbitrary and that, if the plaintiffs in *Locke* had won, the next plaintiff would file on January 1 and call it timely. The end of the year is a common deadline and almost certainly what Congress intended, so a claim filed on January 1 would be too late.

Anyone familiar with the legislative process knows how easily drafting errors are made and escape notice. The statute as drafted, and as enforced by the Supreme Court, became a trap, destroying valuable property rights (and thereby precipitating a constitutional controversy which the plaintiffs also lost) because of a natural and harmless inadvertence.[68] What makes the Supreme Court's decision questionable rather than plainly incorrect is that the plaintiff was not asking the Supreme Court to interpret an ambiguity or plug a gap but to rewrite clear statutory language; yet I can see no harm and much good in the Court's doing just that, given the unusual circumstance. Aristotle would have approved; his notion of equitable interpretation (note 47) seems tailor-made for the *Locke* case.

My suggested disposition of *Locke* is not inconsistent with refusing to read the age-35 provision in Article II of the Constitution flexibly. The selection of a fixed age for eligibility, like the selection of a fixed age to determine the assumption of adult rights and responsibilities or a fixed period of years in a statute of limitations, reflects a preference for a definite rule over a standard uncertain in application. To interpret 35 years old to mean as mature as the average 35-year-old would thus undo a choice deliberately made by the framers. The Federal Land Policy and Management Act also reflects a preference for a fixed deadline, but not necessarily for one of December 30. Congress probably thought it was setting December 31 as the deadline, even though it said December 30.

Notice what I am doing: I am using the statutory text as evidence for legislative intention—almost like using the words as a window into the legislators' minds, subject to my earlier point that statutory interpretation is not limited to discovering the applications actually foreseen by

---

[68] That a statement made in ignorance of its full context (here, the legislature's setting of a deadline in ignorance of how it would actually be applied) can boomerang against the maker of the statement is best illustrated in literature by Oedipus's cursing the murderer of his father without realizing the full context of the remark, which made the curse a curse of himself. See Staten, note 1 above, at 127–128.

the legislators. I thus am using a form of intentionalism less primitive than the one attacked by Frank Kermode in the passage I quoted earlier yet more primitive than I would consider proper in dealing with a work of literature. And I am using it in effect to rewrite a statute, something that would be considered vandalism if attempted on a work of literature (Hamlet "is sweating and panting")—though there are, of course, respectable textual emendations (a polite word for rewriting), as we shall see.

Rule 35(b) of the Federal Rules of Criminal Procedure provided, before a recent amendment, that a federal district court "may reduce a sentence within 120 days after the sentence is imposed" or becomes final on appeal. A number of courts read this to require that the *motion* for reduction of sentence be filed, rather than the *reduction* made, within 120 days; if the motion was filed within that period, the judge could act on it within a reasonable time, even if the result was that he would be acting after the 120 days were up (as it often would be if the motion had been filed late in the period).[69] This interpretation, flatly contrary to the language of the rule, was motivated by an understandable concern that if the rule were read literally many defendants would lose their chance for a reduction in sentence merely because the district judge had not gotten around to acting on their motion within the 120-day period. There was, however, an argument of policy for the literal reading: it served to enforce the division of responsibilities between the sentencing judge and the parole authorities.[70] If the judge waited to see how the defendant was adjusting to prison before he decided the Rule 35(b) motion (which was in fact a common reason for missing the 120-day deadline), he would be encroaching on the authority of the Parole Commission to fix, in part on the basis of the defendant's behavior in prison, the actual length of the defendant's imprisonment. Maybe as an original matter this reason for a 120-day deadline on reductions of sentence is overborne by other considerations, but it was a sufficient reason to enforce the rule as written, until it was amended. For suppose the draftsmen of the original rule really and truly wanted to impose a 120-day deadline on the judge; how could they have done it more clearly? And maybe they did want to impose such a deadline; with this a real possibility, the prudent judicial course was to defer to the language of the rule and let those responsible for promulgating and amending the rules of procedure change it if they wanted (as they did with no great fuss).

[69] See Note of Advisory Committee on 1985 Amendment to Criminal Rule 35(b).
[70] See United States v. Kajevic, 711 F.2d 767 (7th Cir. 1983).

My preferred method of judicial interpretation depends on considerations that have no counterpart in interpreting literature. The judge, whose function is ultimately a political one, must be concerned not to exceed the boundaries set by the legislature (which had authorized the Supreme Court to promulgate rules of criminal procedure for the federal courts); and in determining those boundaries he must consider both the language used by the legislature and the intentions behind that language. The literary critic labors under no such constraint. If he strays too far from the text the result is likely to be a new and rather banal work of attempted literature, which is how I would describe Hillis Miller's reading of *A Slumber Did My Spirit Seal*, rather than an interpretation that illuminates and ennobles the text; but if this is a form of cultural usurpation, it does not have the political resonance of judicial usurpation.

## Other Approaches

I close this chapter with a brief discussion of efforts by four scholars to think about legal interpretation on the model of literary interpretation. The first is a suggestion by Ronald Dworkin that is distinct from his New Critical stance on statutory interpretation.

Scholars who believe that legal texts can be analogized to literary texts usually do not specify which literary genre provides the best analogy to law. Drama may seem the obvious choice (it is the implicit choice of Sanford Levinson, as we shall see), since it involves not just authors and readers but a professional corps of interpreters—producers, directors, and actors, corresponding to lawyers and judges. Dworkin has a more offbeat suggestion: that we conceive of constitutional (and, presumably, statutory) interpretation on the analogy of a chain novel.[71] One author writes Chapter 1, and this sets a certain direction, for the next author must write Chapter 2 in such a way that it seems to grow out of Chapter 1 (so the two will seem like work of the same hand), and likewise with subsequent chapters. Each author thus has less freedom than the one before him. Dworkin suggests that the judge who must first interpret a constitutional text is like the author of Chapter 2, while a judge asked to interpret a constitutional text on which additional meaning has been placed by judicial interpretations is like the author of one of the subsequent chapters. The problem with this ingenious analogy is that it places the judges who interpret the Constitution on the same plane as the

---

[71] See, for example, *Law's Empire*, note 10 above, at 228–250, 313. For criticism see the articles by Lane and Stick cited in note 10 above.

framers of the Constitution: the framers just get the ball rolling. Except for the fact that the author of the first chapter of the chain novel may by his choice of genre exclude some possible sequels, all the chapters are equally authoritative. But decisions interpreting an authoritative legal text, such as the Constitution or a statute, inherently stand on a different, and lower, level than the text. Only the text is fully authentic; all the interpretive decisions must return, Antaeus-like, to the text for their life-giving strength. Dworkin's analogy equates the judges who interpret the Constitution with the framers of the Constitution: a frequent modern view.

Even as a description of common law rather than statutory or constitutional law, the chain-novel analogy is misleading. First, "Chapter 1" in the evolution of common law doctrine is likely to be highly tentative—more like a preface or introduction. Second, the "authors" of the subsequent chapters are not bound to adhere to the directions set by the author of Chapter 1. If accumulating experience shows that Chapter 1 took the wrong direction, the judges can discard it. Third, a related point, common law doctrines tend to evolve over a long period of time, during which the background conditions are changing, and the changes will and should influence the later "chapters" even if the result is to make them discordant with the early ones.

The final oddity about Dworkin's analogy is that there are no good chain novels.[72] There might be no good constitutional law if it were constructed on the chain-novel analogy.

COMMON law differs from statute law in a way highly pertinent to the subject of this chapter. Common law is the set of legal concepts created by judicial decisions, and as with any concept the precise articulation is mutable, can be refined, reformulated. The concept is inferred from the decision (more often from a sequence of decisions) but exists apart from it. The common law judge thus is not engaged in the exegesis of fixed, authoritative texts.[73] The literary critic, the biblical exegete, and the judge engaged in statutory and constitutional interpretation all have the difficult task of interpreting a fixed text. The skeptical

[72] He would have been better advised to discuss the serial publication of Victorian novels. Cf. note 18 above.

[73] This frees him to seek overarching unities in a way that would be artificial in dealing with a series of texts created at different times for different purposes. So a kind of New Critical approach might be usable, though for reasons different from Dworkin's, on the materials of the common law. Notice how, in distinguishing concepts and texts, I am once again resisting the deconstructive turn.

vein in contemporary literary criticism, and the hermeneutic theories that inform it, help to show how difficult the interpretation of texts can be, and by doing so should make lawyers, judges, and legal scholars more cautious, more self-conscious, more tentative about the process of interpreting legal texts; but no specific techniques or discoveries of literary criticism seem transferable to the law. Like law, literary criticism lacks a formalizable method or theory—a lack that all the theoretical endeavors of the last thirty years show no signs of closing.[74] A good literary critic is a careful, thorough, scrupulous, informed, logical, and practical reader of literary texts and a good lawyer is a careful, thorough, scrupulous, informed, logical, and practical reader of legal texts. They are both close readers, but of different materials. Their strength as close readers comes from immersion in a voluminous, diverse, but particular body of texts rather than from mastery of a theory.

Consider some of the tricks of the critic's trade. One that is particularly helpful with Shakespeare's plays is to pay especially close attention to the opening remarks of a character when he first appears onstage, for often they offer a thumbnail sketch of the character. Think of Shylock ("Three thousand ducats, well"), or Angelo ("Always obedient to your grace's will, / I come to know your pleasure"—both an ironic foretaste of his lawlessness and a clue to his character as a natural underling), or Hamlet ("A little more than kin, and less than kind"—a play on words, a remark addressed to the audience rather than Claudius, and a query about Hamlet's place in the scheme of things). Another trick is to ask, why did the writer start the story where he did, rather than at its natural chronological beginning? Why does the *Iliad* open in the tenth year of the Trojan War rather than the first? Why does the *Odyssey* start on Ogygia, rather than with Odysseus's adventures, later narrated in flashback form to the Phaeacians? Why does *Oedipus Tyrannus* open with the plague sent on Thebes rather than with the decision of Oedipus's parents to expose him as an infant? Why does *Hamlet* begin after Hamlet's father is killed? Another technique is, using the postulate of total coherence that I mentioned earlier, to ask what dramatic function a seemingly incongruous incident or scene might play, such as Laertes' warning Ophelia against Hamlet's importunings. (Answer: to show how the members of Polonius's family—Polonius, Ophelia, and Laertes—always get things wrong. Although Hamlet will

---

[74] "Criticism is not an art; it is not a science; it has no method and no theory. It is a craft with varying maxims and devices." Jacques Barzun, "A Little Matter of Sense," *New York Times Book Review*, June 21, 1987, at 1, 28.

indeed be the death of Ophelia, this will not be because of his overmastering attentions to her but for the opposite reason—his neglect of her.)

What is true is that literary theory is more highly developed than legal theory, both because the study of literature is a somewhat more rigorous discipline than academic law (more on this in the Conclusion), and because literary theorists and critics have been aware of the problematic nature of interpretation for a longer time than theorists and practitioners of law. Literary critics are therefore less likely to fall into obvious interpretive traps than lawyers are. Few literary critics would be so obtuse as to say that in interpreting a work of literature they start with its words (not genre or other contextual elements)—though applied to constitutional and statutory texts this is a commonplace.[75] But lawyers could learn to be more sophisticated about interpretation from philosophers as well as from literary theorists. And at the level of criticism rather than theory, both critics and lawyers are practitioners rather than theorists of interpretation (another group of interpretive practitioners are the theologians); while literary and legal texts are so different that the interpretive practices in the two fields do not overlap.

At a sufficiently high level of abstraction, the interpretive tasks in the two fields may seem to merge. A problem in textual interpretation can always be cast in the form of hypothesis and verification: the proposed interpretation is the hypothesis, and the criterion of its soundness is the goodness of the "fit" it makes with the "data" furnished by the text. Goodness of fit is indeed one way to interpret Ronald Dworkin's rather elusive "New Critical" approach (as I have called it) to interpreting statutes and the Constitution. But as soon as one gets down to cases the commonality of the legal and the literary inquiries disintegrates. I will illustrate with the famous question of whether the Macbeths (in Shakespeare's play) had children. This may seem an absurd pseudo-question, treating as real people what are (for Shakespeare's purposes anyway) fictitious entities. But it is not absurd. A careful reader or viewer of the play is perfectly entitled to wonder why Macbeth would be upset (as he plainly is) when he learns from the weird sisters

[75] "It is axiomatic that 'the starting point in every case involving construction of a statute is the language itself.' " Landreth Timber Co. v. Landreth, 471 U.S. 681, 685 (1985). "In determining whether the Board was empowered to make such a change, we begin, of course, with the language of the statute." Board of Governors of Federal Reserve System v. Dimension Financial Corp., 106 S. Ct. 681, 686 (1986). For other examples see Aloha Airlines, Inc. v. Director of Taxation, 464 U.S. 7, 12 (1983); Funbus Systems, Inc. v. California Public Utilities Commission, 801 F.2d 1120, 1126 (9th Cir. 1986); Wronke v. Marsh, 787 F.2d 1569, 1574 (Fed. Cir. 1986).

that Banquo's descendants will be kings of Scotland, if Macbeth had no children of his own; for then his own descendants could not be kings of Scotland; and Macbeth feels no enmity toward Banquo apart from the question of whose descendants will rule. The reader may therefore conclude that the hypothesis that the Macbeths did have children, or at least were planning to have children, makes the best "fit" with the "data" provided by the playwright. And perhaps the same sort of reasoning would enable us to determine whether *Brown v. Board of Education* and *Roe v. Wade* were correctly decided.

But the analogy is unsatisfactory because the question about the Macbeths' children is unanswerable after all. Macbeth's concern about Banquo's descendants is one datum, but against it is the complete silence of all the characters about the Macbeth children. If Macbeth had had children the question of what to do with them—and specifically how to make sure that none of them succeeded him on the throne of Scotland— would be bound to arise and to be discussed in the world created by the play. And it is impossible to picture the Macbeths as a young couple planning to have a family sometime in the future. The hypothesis of Macbeth progeny may appeal to a literal-minded person but is incongruous with the atmosphere of the play; one just cannot imagine the Macbeths as parents. So in one sense they must have children for the play to parse, but in another and equally compelling sense they must *not* have children. This is completely illogical—except from the aesthetic standpoint, which is after all the relevant one for literary interpretation. It is unclear what any of this can have to do with law.

So, to say as Sanford Levinson does that "there are as many plausible readings of the United States Constitution as there are versions of *Hamlet*, even though each interpreter, like each director, might genuinely believe that he or she has stumbled onto the one best answer to the conundrums of the texts,"[76] implies a relation between interpretive problems that actually are unrelated. Among the things that open *Hamlet* to different interpretations are that it was written almost 400 years ago (and is thus almost 200 years older than the original U.S. Constitution and the Bill of Rights) and in another country, that it was written in haste, that the text is corrupt, that there is no evidence of the author's intentions beyond what is in the text, that it was written to be performed rather than read, that great literature is, almost by definition, pitched at a level of generality that invites divergent interpretations, that part of the fascination of *Hamlet* is the number of interpretive puzzles it

[76] Levinson, note 2 above, at 391 (footnote omitted); Levinson, note 3 above, at 259.

poses, and that we do not care much about what Shakespeare thought he was trying to accomplish—partly because we do not know, partly because we doubt that he fully knew. The things that make the Constitution open to different interpretations include multiple authorship, the apparent decision of the framers to leave certain issues open through the use of general language, the social, economic, legal, political, and institutional changes that have occurred since the Constitution was drafted, and the lack of agreement on how free a judge should feel in interpreting a constitutional provision and what weight he should give to previous interpretations of it. Although there are many genuine puzzles about the Constitution, as there are about *Hamlet*, the two sets of puzzles are so different from each other that it is unlikely that a *Hamlet* scholar will have anything useful to say about the Constitution or a constitutional scholar anything useful to say about *Hamlet*.

This is not to deny the competence of literary theorists to participate in the debates over statutory and constitutional interpretation that are so prominent a part of legal theory today. When a law professor such as Dworkin or Levinson or Owen Fiss uses literary theory in these debates, he invites ripostes from literary theorists such as Stanley Fish (see notes 1, 8, and 10). But Fish's own contributions suggest the limitations of literary theory in relation to legal interpretation. It is not Fish the Milton scholar who enters the lists; it is Fish the interpretive skeptic, deploying an analytical apparatus that he got from Wittgenstein. He makes three main points. The first is that meaning does not reside in a text but is imposed by the reader. The second is that such interpretive agreement as is found is due to the existence (in both law and literature) of authoritative interpreters, whether judges or prestigious critics, who compel agreement with their interpretations by pulling rank in various ways. His third point is that interpretive theories do not affect interpretive practices—a proposition that, unless understood as merely a corollary of the general truth that extreme skepticism does not affect behavior, is contradicted by the positions that rival theorists have taken in the debate over the meaning of *A Slumber Did My Spirit Seal*. Fish's second point is an attempt to reconcile his interpretive skepticism with the undeniable fact that in literature as in law there is considerable consensus with regard to the meaning of particular works, or at least considerable consensus with regard to the range of possible meanings.

Whatever the ultimate merits of Fish's position, it does not, as he is the first to admit (it is his third point), light the way to particular interpretations of legal texts. Skepticism is an interesting and perhaps irrefutable philosophical stance, but, when pushed as far as Fish pushes it, one incapable of guiding action or interpretation. It might seem, however, that in the concept of interpretive communities (one way in which Fish states his second point) we might have a clue to a mode of interpretation that would cross the law-literature divide. We might, for example, try using the concept to explain why the age-35 provision in the Constitution is easy to interpret: because it is addressed to an interpretive community (the people of the United States) that has not changed significantly in any relevant particulars since 1787; we still record birthdates, we measure years the same way, speak the same language, and so forth. But this tack would owe little or nothing to literary theory as such, for "interpretive communities" was Wittgenstein's concept (and, before him, Nietzsche's and Peirce's) before it was Fish's.

Moreover, unlike James White for example, Fish uses the concept of interpretive communities not to interpret legal or literary texts but merely to state what is obvious—that there is, as a matter of empirical fact, some agreement about the meaning of each legal as of each literary text. Consistent with his thoroughgoing skepticism Fish finds the source of this agreement not in the text itself but in the training, experience, and political power (broadly defined) of the interpreters. (Notice the parallel to John Ellis's definition of literature: to Ellis, literature is whatever the community of readers treats as literature.) If because of selection, or training, or hierarchy whether professional or official, people can be made to think alike or like-thinking people come to control the interpretive process, then interpretations of the same text will converge. But the resulting consensus will not reflect any objective or determinate properties of the text. No text has any, according to Fish. "Interpretive community" is a misnomer; there is no interpretation in the usual sense, but rather an imparting of meaning to the text by its readers. This position does not help either the judge or the literary critic in "interpreting" a particular text.[77]

So skeptical is Fish that he considers skepticism just another dogma of interpretation. Arguing against Levinson, he remarks that "there is nothing in principle to prevent the emergence of a unified legal interpretive community. All that is required is that a number of

---

[77] What Rorty has said about Wittgenstein and Derrida on language can equally be said about Fish (whose links with those two I mentioned in the first note of this chapter) on interpretation: "It is never very clear whether we are getting a new philosophy of language (one in which 'social practice' plays the role once played by 'picturing the world') or instead getting a protest against the very idea of 'philosophy of language.' " Richard Rorty, "Derrida on Language, Being, and Abnormal Philosophy," 74 *Journal of Philosophy* 673, 674 (1977). I think Fish is best understood as protesting against theories of interpretation rather than as proposing a substitute theory of interpretation. For penetrating criticism of Fish's position see David Luban, "*Fish V. Fish* or, Some Realism about Idealism," 7 *Cardozo Law Review* 693 (1986).

assumptions be so firmly held that they are no longer regarded as assumptions, but as truths so unchallengeable that the determinations (of fact, constitutionality, etc.) they entail would be universally recognized and acknowledged. As an institution the law would then be in the happy state (if it is happy) enjoyed by certain branches of the physical sciences."[78] But since this "happy state" neither exists nor is foreseeable in American legal culture, Fish leaves us stranded on the skeptical shoals.

With Fish, a literary critic and theorist, gliding effortlessly between skepticism about the possibility (at least as things are, and can be expected to remain) of objective literary interpretations and skepticism about the possibility (subject to the same qualification) of objective legal interpretations, it is no wonder that Levinson should connect the multiplying interpretations of *Hamlet* with the multiplying interpretations of the Constitution. And, though different, the two phenomena do have a common cause. The 1950s were a period of relative calm and consensus in both English departments and law schools; and literary critics who share similar values, and lawyers who share similar values, are apt to generate in their respective fields interpretations that command wide agreement and therefore seem authoritative. Since the fifties, both fields have experienced a decline in political and methodological consensus and a resulting increase in interpretive divergence. English and other literature departments today are riven by interpretive disputes among New Critics, Marxists, feminists, structuralists, "new historicists," deconstructionists, "reader response" critics, intentionalists, and psychoanalytic critics, and law schools by interpretive disputes among "process" theorists, interpretivists and anti-interpretivists, intentionalists, conventionalists, Realists, formalists, textualists, libertarians, natural lawyers, Marxists, and feminists. (In neither list are all positions mutually exclusive.) In both fields a school of antitheorists has arisen[79]—

---

[78] "Interpretation and the Pluralist Vision," note 1 above, at 498. Compare A. W. B. Simpson, "The Common Law and Legal Theory," in *Oxford Essays in Jurisprudence* 77, 95 (2d ser., A. W. B. Simpson ed. 1973), arguing that the determinacy of the English common law in its heyday was due to the extraordinary degree of social and educational uniformity among the judges.

[79] In literature, see, for example, Walter Benn Michaels and Steven Knapp, "Against Theory," note 9 above, at 742 (pretending to be antitheoretical, but actually advocating intentionalism); in law see Charles Fried, "The Artificial Reason of the Law or: What Lawyers Know," 60 *Texas Law Review* 35 (1981); Owen M. Fiss, "The Death of the Law?" 72 *Cornell Law Review* 1 (1986). Oddly, White aligns himself with the antitheorists. See James Boyd White, "Judicial Criticism," 20 *Georgia Law Review* 835, 843–845 (1986). On the fissures in contemporary literary scholarship see Stanley Fish, "Profession Despise Thyself: Fear and Self-Loathing in Literary Studies," 10 *Critical Inquiry* 349 (1983).

but this is another theory. With such political and methodological diversity, divergent interpretations whether of literary or of legal texts are inevitable and are difficult to iron out or paper over. In law as in literature, if the readership of a text is culturally diverse the plausible readings of the text will be diverse; if there is no interpretive community, there will not be even the appearance of determinate meaning.

Not too much should be made of this point, however. The abyss of complete subjectivity can be skirted by noting, first, that it does not follow that just because a text has no single determinate meaning it has no meaning, period; and, second, it does not follow that just because two people disagree about the meaning of the same text and there is no way to resolve their disagreement by logic or scientific experimentation or some other method of exact inquiry, neither can be shown to be more probably correct than the other. I hope that Part I of this book showed that some interpretations of complex and ambiguous texts can be shown to be probably right or probably wrong, though no doubt its persuasive power depends on a degree of cultural homogeneity among its readers.

Nevertheless, there has been a great decline in interpretive consensus in law. But since literary theory is neither the cause nor the cure, I take exception to Charles Fried's effort (see note 2) to infer the intelligibility of the Constitution from the intelligibility of Shakespeare's Sonnet 65:

> Since brass, nor stone, nor earth, nor boundless sea,
> But sad mortality o'ersways their power,
> How with this rage shall beauty hold a plea,
> Whose action is no stronger than a flower?
> O! how shall summer's honey breath hold out
> Against the wrackful siege of batt'ring days,
> When rocks impregnable are not so stout,
> Nor gates of steel so strong, but Time decays?
> O fearful meditation! where alack,
> Shall Time's best jewel from Time's chest lie hid?
> Or what strong hand can hold his swift foot back?
> Or who his spoil of beauty can forbid?
>    O! none, unless this miracle have might,
>    That in black ink my love may still shine bright.

Fried argues that the poem's premise is the intelligibility of writing, and that the premise has been triumphantly vindicated by time, for the poem is 400 years old, yet (he implies) it poses no interpretive problems for the contemporary reader.

He has overlooked those problems. First and least, he has *sub silentio* modernized the spelling and punctuation.[80] Second, in writing "spoil of beauty" he has (again without comment) used an emended version of Shakespeare's original text, which reads "spoil or beauty."[81] Third, Fried has misinterpreted the poem slightly by overlooking the note of dubiety sounded by "unless" and "may" in the concluding couplet and by the possible pun in "might." Shakespeare is not so confident as Fried supposes that "black ink" can survive time's ravages.[82]

There may be a graver misinterpretation. It has been suggested that the reference to "black ink" is somewhat contemptuous and that Shakespeare, careless of publication as we know, saw the "miracle" elsewhere: "The truth is, that there is indeed a poetic 'miracle', but it is not just a matter of publication and perpetuity. Rather the poet knows that through his poetry, or the poetic consciousness, he establishes, or focusses, a supernal reality, or truth, what we may call a 'poetic dimension', that cannot otherwise be attained; and of this the written poetry ('black ink'), though it be necessary, is really subsidiary, the carrot to the donkey, but not the journey's purpose."[83]

I will put these quibbles aside and concede that Fried has shown that a work of literature—a great work, I might add, as Sonnet 65 is—can be universal because of the timelessness of its theme without being ambiguous. Still, the implications of this point for the interpretation of the Constitution are obscure. Granted that some of Shakespeare's works may not pose acute interpretive difficulties, others do, as do considerably more recent works of literature. If we are to pursue what I contend is the misguided quest for literary analogies to problems of legal interpretation, then we must ask in every case whether the particular statutory or

---

[80] On the uncertainties of meaning created by the erratic punctuation of Shakespeare's sonnets as originally published, see Theodore Redpath, "The Punctuation of Shakespeare's Sonnets," in *New Essays on Shakespeare's Sonnets* 217 (Hilton Landry ed. 1976). To compare the original with the modern spelling and punctuation of Sonnet 65, see Shakespeare's *Sonnets* 58–59 (Stephen Booth ed. 1977), where the original and modern versions are printed side by side. I have quoted the version of the sonnet published in Fried's article.

[81] Booth, note 80 above, at 247, argues against the emendation. On the inescapability of literary theory in textual emendation see G. Thomas Tanselle, "Recent Editorial Discussion and the Central Questions of Editing," 34 *Studies in Bibliography* 23 (1981).

[82] Compare Fried, note 2 above, at 756, with Booth, note 80 above, at 247; Felperin, note 1 above, at 165–172; Murray Krieger, *A Window to Criticism: Shakespeare's Sonnets and Modern Poetics* 170–172 (1964); Philip Martin, *Shakespeare's Sonnets: Self, Love and Art* 153–155 (1972); Kenneth Muir, *Shakespeare's Sonnets* 66 (1979); Rodney Poisson, "Unequal Friendship: Shakespeare's Sonnets 18–126," in *New Essays on Shakespeare's Sonnets*, note 80 above, at 1, ll.

[83] G. Wilson Knight, *The Mutual Flame: On Shakespeare's Sonnets and The Phoenix and the Turtle* 86 (2d ed. 1962).

constitutional provision under discussion is, in point of interpretive difficulty, more like Sonnet 65 (or what Fried thinks Sonnet 65 is like) or more like other and more ambiguous literary works such as *Billy Budd*, written in this country a mere century ago. On such questions Fried is silent. Literary theory provides no more comfort for the legal Right than for the legal Left: one can no more argue the interpretability of the Constitution from Sonnet 65 than one can argue the inscrutability of the Constitution from *Hamlet*.

# SIX

# Judicial Opinions
as Literature

C AN THE study of literature help us understand the judicial opinion-writing process better, and perhaps even lead to better judicial opinions? Note that I do not ask whether it can assist the interpretation of judicial opinions. The interpretation of a judicial opinion may be difficult but is rarely problematic, as the interpretation of a statute or a constitutional provision often is. An opinion is an effort to formulate, refine, or apply a concept, and whether that concept is a common law doctrine or a meaning drawn from a statute, the judges in a subsequent case can always revise the formulation to make it approximate the concept better. It is only because judges are not supposed to have this freedom with statutes and constitutions that the interpretation of these texts raises such difficult questions—although, if the preceding chapter is right, not questions that literary theory or practice can answer. The interpretive problem just is not very important in the case of opinions. Yet I think the literary analysis of opinions is highly promising.

To explain this paradox I shall have to distinguish between style and meaning, while granting that the distinction is artificial in the case of rhetorical writing, as both literary writing and judicial writing are. Literary meaning is not exhausted in paraphrasable content—often the least interesting thing in a work of literature, especially a short one (a paraphrase of *Easter 1916* or *The Wild Swans at Coole* would be trite). It is inseparable from style. The meaning of *The Wild Swans at Coole* is something the reader picks up as much from surprising juxtapositions such as "cold / Companionable," a kind of oxymoron and thus a stylistic device (and notice how the juxtaposition is reinforced by alliteration and enjambment), as from what the poem overtly "says" to the reader. Yet, as this example shows, style can be separated from meaning for purposes of analysis. And most prose, including prose that can have no hope of ever counting as literature, has a style. We might or might not want to call Orwell's essays, Lincoln's speeches, and Holmes's judicial opinions literature,[1] but we could hardly deny that they use stylistic devices of a sort found in what indisputably is literature and that their style can be studied separately from the political or legal meanings of their work. The example of Holmes, a writer of judicial opinions, suggests a potential application of literary criticism to law.

The main topics of this chapter are the relationships between literary and judicial style and between literary and judicial meaning. Because style and meaning merge in literature, the distinction between the two topics is not as clear as I am pretending. But, in broad terms, the first emphasizes the emotive side of literary method, and the second the craft values that give a work of literature integrity as well as power.

## Style as Persuasion

I do not expect the reader to take for granted that the literary study of judicial style is a worthwhile endeavor. Students of language and argument study style without sole reference to literary values and sometimes without any explicit reference to them.[2] Brutus's and Antony's funeral orations can be detached from their dramatic context in *Julius Caesar* and their effectiveness as persuasive utterances studied, as I shall do later.[3] It is an open question whether the style of judicial opinions is better studied from the standpoint of linguistics and rhetoric[4]

---

[1] See *Collected Essays, Journalism and Letters of George Orwell* (Sonia Orwell and Ian Angus 1968) (4 vols.), and the chapters on Lincoln and on Holmes (chaps. 3 and 16) in Edmund Wilson, *Patriotic Gore: Studies in the Literature of the American Civil War* (1962). For the text of Lincoln's two greatest addresses—the Gettysburg Address and the Second Inaugural—see *Collected Works of Abraham Lincoln*, vol. 7, at 22 (Roy P. Basler ed. 1953); id., vol. 8, at 332. For a literary analysis of the Gettysburg Address see Monroe C. Beardsley, *Aesthetics: Problems in the Philosophy of Criticism* 264 (1958); on Lincoln's rhetoric generally see Richard M. Weaver, *The Ethics of Rhetoric*, chap. 4 (1953). There is a good selection of Holmes's opinions in *Justice Holmes Ex Cathedra* (Edward J. Bander ed. 1966). For an interesting discussion of literary style in discursive prose generally, see Ronald Weber, *The Literature of Fact: Literary Nonfiction in American Writing* (1980).

[2] Examples are George Orwell, "Politics and the English Language," in *Collected Essays, Journalism and Letters of George Orwell*, note 1 above, vol. 4, at 127; Gunther Kress and Robert Hodge, *Language as Ideology* (1979); F. R. Palmer, *Semantics* (2d ed. 1981); Herbert Spencer, *Philosophy of Style: An Essay* (1873).

[3] See also Allan Bloom (with Harry V. Jaffa), *Shakespeare's Politics* 82–83 (1964).

[4] As in George C. Christie, "Vagueness and Legal Language," 48 *Minnesota Law Review* 885 (1964); Brenda Danet, "Language in the Legal Process," 14 *Law and Society Review* 445 (1980); May L. Dudziak, "Oliver Wendell Holmes as a Eugenic Reformer: Rhetoric in the Writing of

or from that of literary criticism—or perhaps from both standpoints, especially since they are merging.[5]

As used by Aristotle and his successors, "rhetoric" ran the gamut of persuasive devices in communication, excluding formal logic. It thus embraced not only style but much of reasoning. Since the Middle Ages the word has come more and more to mean just the eloquent or effective use of language, and that is the approximate sense in which I shall use the word "style." The broader signification of "rhetoric" has its adherents, though.[6] And much of the current writing on the rhetoric of judicial opinions reflects a still broader usage[7] in which rhetoric assumes ethical overtones (absent from Aristotle), so that to praise or criticize the rhetoric of a judicial opinion is virtually synonymous with praising or criticizing the opinion, period.[8]

---

Constitutional Law," 71 *Iowa Law Review* 833, 859–867 (1986); Peter Goodrich, "Rhetoric as Jurisprudence: An Introduction to the Politics of Legal Language," 4 *Oxford Journal of Legal Studies* 88 (1984); David Mellinkoff, *The Language of the Law* (1963); Frederick A. Philbrick, *Language and the Law: The Semantics of Forensic English* (1949); Teresa Godwin Phelps, "The New Legal Rhetoric," 40 *Southwestern Law Journal* 1089 (1986); Pierre Schlag and David Skover, *Tactics of Legal Reasoning* (1986).

[5] See Jonathan Culler, "Literature and Linguistics," in *Interrelations of Literature* 1 (Jean-Pierre Barricelli and Joseph Gibaldi eds. 1982); E. L. Epstein, *Language and Style* (1978); Graham Hough, *Style and Stylistics* (1969); Richard A. Lanham, *Style: An Anti-Textbook* (1974); Brian Vickers, *Classical Rhetoric in English Poetry* (1970).

[6] See, for example, Chaim Perelman, *The Realm of Rhetoric* (1982); Cleanth Brooks and Robert Penn Warren, *Modern Rhetoric* (4th ed. 1979); Edward P. J. Corbett, *Classical Rhetoric for the Modern Student* (2d ed. 1971); *Essays on Classical Rhetoric and Modern Discourse* (Robert J. Connors, Lisa S. Ede, and Andrea A. Lunsford eds. 1984). The last two works reflect a long American tradition of rhetorical analysis in the Aristotelian manner. See, for example, John Franklin Genung, *The Working Principles of Rhetoric* (1900). For a most serviceable introduction to the field of rhetoric broadly conceived, see James L. Kinneavy, *A Theory of Discourse: The Aims of Discourse* (1971); also very good are Weaver's book, cited in note 1 above, and *The Rhetoric of the Human Sciences: Language and Argument in Scholarship and Public Affairs* (John S. Nelson, Allan Megill, and Donald N. McCloskey eds. 1987). On classical rhetoric, George Kennedy, *The Art of Persuasion in Greece* (1963), is particularly good; also Ernst Robert Curtius, *European Literature and the Latin Middle Ages* 62–105 (1953).

[7] See, for example, Bruce McLeod, "Rules and Rhetoric," 23 *Osgoode Hall Law Journal* 305 (1985); Robert A. Prentice, "Supreme Court Rhetoric," 25 *Arizona Law Review* 85 (1983).

[8] In Prentice's hands (see note 7 above), rhetoric becomes a synonym for the entire judicial process. Could literary criticism similarly be used to illuminate the judicial process in the large, as distinct from particular judicial opinions? David Cole, in "Agon at Agora: Creative Misreadings in the First Amendment Tradition," 95 *Yale Law Journal* 857 (1986), uses Harold Bloom's theory of poetic influence—in which poets, in an effort to get out from under the shadow of their illustrious predecessors, misread those predecessors' work; see Harold Bloom, *The Anxiety of Influence: A Theory of Poetry* (1973)—to frame a discussion of how the Supreme Court often misreads precedents when changing the direction of the law. The objection to Cole's analogy is the same as that to using the methods of literary criticism on the interpretation of legal texts: the problems being compared are too dissimilar. The reasons poets

Whatever its utility in other settings, the broad usage (or usages) of rhetoric is out of place in a discussion of the overlap between law and literature. Literature is not concerned with establishing the truth of propositions, at least by the patient marshaling of rational arguments and rationally probative evidence; it is not (not generally, at any rate) didactic, as works of scholarship or of political advocacy are. With so much of rhetoric in its broader senses being irrelevant to the study of literature, "style" and "rhetoric" really do coalesce in that study. That is why Wayne Booth's *Rhetoric of Fiction*—the apogee of neo-Aristotelian "rhetorical" criticism—can be regarded as a masterpiece of the New Criticism despite the New Critics' hostility to assigning a didactic function to literature.

The disadvantage of the word "style" is that it sounds too much like ornamentation, when what is particularly interesting about the style both of a work of literature and of a forensic utterance such as a judicial opinion is its contribution to making the reader believe, and not merely enjoy, the writer. My interest is in style as a rhetorical (in the sense of persuasive) device, though not in rhetoric in the broader sense that equates it with practical reasoning or, broader still, with right reason.

Might one argue that style should have no role in legal writing? That it can only be an impediment to understanding? I doubt this, even in regard to comparatively humble specimens of legal writing such as wills, deeds, indentures, and contracts; there, repetition, and even archaism, may serve to remind the signatories of the gravity of their commitment and to impart emphases that assist interpretation. Clearly, as we shall see, judicial opinions (and briefs, but I shall confine my attention in this chapter to opinions) are unavoidably rhetorical, and in much the same way as literature is.

There are kinds of writing in which style does not matter much. When a scientist (including the practitioner of a "hard" social science such as economics or linguistics) proposes a hypothesis, and then reports in a paper the design and results of an experiment, natural or controlled, designed to test it, the style of the paper is of little interest except that an extremely badly written paper might confuse the reader. Of even less stylistic interest is a work of deductive logic, where the author states his premises and derives conclusions by logical operations, so that in

---

might have for misreading their predecessors have nothing to do with why a court misreads precedents. The court does so to conceal the extent to which it is changing course, and thus to emphasize continuity. These were not concerns of Romantic and modern poets (the poets Bloom is primarily concerned with), with their emphasis on originality. Anyway, Cole makes no use of Bloom's analysis when it comes to discussing specific judicial opinions; nor does he convey the sheer strangeness of Bloom's book (to which I alluded in Chapter 5, note 40).

principle and often in practice the entire demonstration is mathematical.[9] Somewhere in between literature and science (or mathematics), but closer to science and perhaps in a broad sense scientific or "referential" (objective, truth-seeking), would be a work of historiography, or anthropology, or nonevaluative literary criticism, or nonpolemical legal scholarship. In such works rhetoric as style is relatively unimportant, though rhetoric in its broader sense of rational but not logically or scientifically compelled persuasion is highly important. For example, in Chapter 4 I defended my interpretations of Kafka in part by reference to authority—a type of argument that would be out of place in an exact science.

In areas of exact inquiry, Orwell's stated goal of writing prose as clear as a windowpane seems, if properly understood, an attainable ideal.[10] This observation helps show why survival works differently in science than in literature. Newton will survive as long as Homer, but the essential Newton—the Newton that will survive—is not the language in which he described his theories and findings but the theories and findings themselves, while the essential Homer cannot be detached from the language in which he wrote or chanted. Much of Homer is lost even in the most skillful translation.

Outside of the areas of inquiry in which logic and experimentation (or other exact observation) are the dominant sources of knowledge,

[9] In this example, even rhetoric in its broadest Aristotelian sense is absent. Kinneavy, note 6 above, chap. 3, has an interesting discussion of scientific "style." See also Weaver, note 1 above, chap. 1, on "neuter" rhetoric.

[10] See "Why I Write," in *Collected Essays, Journalism and Letters of George Orwell*, note 1 above, vol. 1, at 1, 7. Not everyone agrees. See, for example, Philip J. Davis and Reuben Hersh, "Rhetoric and Mathematics," in *Rhetoric and the Human Sciences*, note 6 above, at 53. And in literature the plain style is just another artifice. See the excellent discussions in Hugh Kenner, "The Politics of the Plain Style," *New York Times Book Review*, Sept. 15, 1985, at 1; Richard A. Lanham, *Literacy and the Survival of Humanism* (1983); Lanham, note 5 above, at 52–53; K. K. Ruthven, *Critical Assumptions* 46 (1979). (We shall see this point dramatically illustrated in Antony's funeral oration in *Julius Caesar*.) A feminist critic has even associated Orwell's plain style with his (alleged) male chauvinism. See Daphne Patai, *The Orwell Mystique: A Study in Male Ideology* 266–267 (1984). This seems off-base but does show that the "windowpane" is not transparent; notice also the tension between Orwell's advocacy of plain style and his parodying of Basic English (as "Newspeak") in *1984*. Cf. Howard Fink, "Newspeak: The Epitome of Parody Techniques in Nineteen Eighty-Four," 5 *Critical Survey* 155 (1971). The use of the plain style in what is incontestably literature (Swift, for example, or Hemingway's, Camus's, or Orwell's novels) shows that there is no such thing as a "literary" style which by its nature could not appear in a legal setting. Any style can be put to literary use; recall John Ellis's point that a work of literature is a text used in a certain way, not a text written in a particular way or with particular intentions. And see the interesting discussion of the "plain style" of the U.S. Constitution in Robert A. Ferguson, " 'We Do Ordain and Establish': The Constitution as Literary Text," 29 *William and Mary Law Review* 3 (1987).

imaginative literature is a source of knowledge or at least belief. When science was not very advanced there were poets of science, such as Democritus, Lucretius, the metaphysical poets, and Erasmus Darwin— a point both consistent with the fact that poetry and other forms of literature usually deal with subjects not yet annexed by mathematics and science, and suggestive of an informing as well as an emotive function for literature. We can still learn something about ambition from *Macbeth*, about justice, revenge, maturity, conflict, and individualism from the works discussed in Part I of this book, about social class from the Victorian novelists, about religion from Dante, Milton, and Dostoevsky, about terrorism from *The Possessed*, about despair from the early poetry of T. S. Eliot, and about guilt and obsession from Kafka. These are areas in which scientific thought is still not advanced. The creative writer can hold his own with the sociologist, the anthropologist, the political—or the legal—philosopher, the historian, and the psychologist, in broad areas of their fields. Swift's satire on the referential theory of language, in the story of the Laputians in *Gulliver's Travels*, has not lost its point.

Thus I disagree with the idea that literature is concerned not with knowledge or belief but only with emotion,[11] that what you learn when you read *Macbeth* is merely how it feels to have the attainment of a great ambition almost within your grasp only to see it slip away because you have let imagination outrun reality. Creating emotion is an important thing that literature does, but it also persuades—though obliquely. It does not, not characteristically anyway, preach to the reader (though *Pilgrim's Progress* is a famous exception); and when it uses the syllogism the purpose is more likely to be ironical, as in Marvell's *To His Coy Mistress*, than logical. It is because literature is not (or not mainly) didactic that paraphrases of works of literature tend to be trite and that so many works of literature are destroyed by translation. The cognitive, informing, or persuading part of literature operates by presenting the reader with a dramatic scene that stirs imagination and emotion and leaves a residue of insight (into love, ambition, revenge, the human condition, or whatever) about which the literary critic can talk but which he cannot reproduce in the way that one economist can restate the contribution of another in different words with no loss of meaning or impact.

If you paraphrased Keats's *Ode to a Nightingale* you might come up with the very same trite summary as you would if you paraphrased *The*

[11] For a classic statement of this position see T. S. Eliot, "Shakespeare and the Stoicism of Seneca," in Eliot, *Selected Essays* 107, 115–118 (new ed. 1950).

*Wild Swans at Coole*: the narrator, contemplating avian beauty, is moved to the reflection that although people die, and individual birds too, of course, nature as symbolized by the swan or the nightingale is immortal. But the force of the two poems lies elsewhere, and their effects on the reader are dissimilar. The beauty of the nightingale's song is for the narrator of the *Ode to a Nightingale* both justification and consolation for wanting to die (something so much lovelier and happier will live on forever), while the point of *The Wild Swans at Coole* lies in presenting nature as composing the cool, formal, aesthetic—and silent—pattern of a work of art. The imagery and tone of the poems are different, and as a result their meanings are different despite the similarity of their overt themes.

To show how literature persuades and to build a bridge to the rhetoric of judicial opinions I want to consider again one of the supreme moments of modern poetry, the concluding couplet of the first stanza of Yeats's *The Second Coming*. Here is the poem in full:

> Turning and turning in the widening gyre
> The falcon cannot hear the falconer;
> Things fall apart; the centre cannot hold;
> Mere anarchy is loosed upon the world,
> The blood-dimmed tide is loosed, and everywhere
> The ceremony of innocence is drowned;
> The best lack all conviction, while the worst
> Are full of passionate intensity.
>
> Surely some revelation is at hand;
> Surely the Second Coming is at hand.
> The Second Coming! Hardly are those words out
> When a vast image out of *Spiritus Mundi*
> Troubles my sight: somewhere in sands of the desert
> A shape with lion body and the head of a man
> A gaze blank and pitiless as the sun,
> Is moving its slow thighs, while all about it
> Reel shadows of the indignant desert birds.
> The darkness drops again; but now I know
> That twenty centuries of stony sleep
> Were vexed to nightmare by a rocking cradle,
> And what rough beast, its hour come round at last,
> Slouches toward Bethlehem to be born?

The poem was written in 1919, partly, it appears, with reference to the civil war in Ireland and partly with reference to the Russian

Revolution.[12] Yet, as I noted in the last chapter, the couplet that concludes the first stanza has seemed an uncanny prophecy of the relationship in the 1930s between the fascists and the appeasing democracies—all the more uncanny because the poem is overtly prophetic. The couplet in question could just as well describe the situation in American universities during the student uprisings of the late 1960s. Other readers will supply other referents. But historical confirmation aside, it strikes the reader with a self-evident sense of rightness. It seems true; yet no effort to demonstrate its truth is made.

How can a writer persuade, without an effort at logical or empirical proof? The answer is that in areas of uncertainty, areas not yet conquered by logic or science, we are open to persuasion by all sorts of methods, some remote from logic and science. It is not that people are irrational; it is that when unable to obtain direct confirmation of an assertion they do not just suspend judgment—they seek indirect confirmation or refutation. The clearest example and perhaps the commonest of all rhetorical devices (called the "ethical appeal" by rhetoricians) is the speaker's attempt to convey a sense that he is a certain kind of person, namely one you ought to believe. An audience that cannot verify the truth of what the speaker says will grant or withhold belief insofar as it seems probable or improbable that what the speaker says is true; and one thing that makes it more probable is if he seems the sort of person who is likely to tell the truth.[13]

The ethical appeal is not found in *The Second Coming,* but plenty of

[12] See Conor Cruise O'Brien, "Passion and Cunning: An Essay on the Politics of W. B. Yeats," in *In Excited Reverie: A Centenary Tribute to William Butler Yeats 1865–1939,* at 207, 276–278 (A. Norman Jeffares and K. G. W. Cross eds. 1965); Edward A. Bloom, Charles H. Philbrick, and Elmer M. Blistein, *The Order of Poetry* 51 (1961); Jon Stallworthy, *Between the Lines: Yeats's Poetry in the Making* 17–21 (1963). George Bornstein, *Transformations of Romanticism in Yeats, Eliot, and Stevens* 61–64 (1976), is a good general discussion of the poem's meaning.

[13] See Corbett, note 6 above, at 35, 73, and my book *The Economics of Justice* 173 (1981), which discusses the importance of rhetoric in primitive societies, where "hard" information is difficult to come by. The point in text illustrates the difficulty of separating the methods of rhetoric from those of literary criticism, even in a discussion of literature. Much literary criticism is the study of the rhetorical devices employed in works of literature—this is particularly true of criticism of short poems—and often the only difference between rhetorical and literary criticism is terminological. Specifically, the rhetorician's "ethical appeal" corresponds to the creation by the fiction writer of an "implied author" with whom the reader is asked to identify. See Wayne C. Booth, *The Rhetoric of Fiction* 71, 211–221 (2d ed. 1983). One of the objections to biographical or intentionalist literary criticism not mentioned in Chapter 5 is that it makes it harder for the reader of the work of literature to keep (in his own mind) the implied author separate from the actual author, thereby blunting one of the effects that the writer was trying to convey by creating an implied author different from himself.

other rhetorical tricks are. One is the placement of the couplet in question at the end of a stanza. It is thus in the normal position for a conclusion, suggesting that the writer has set forth premises that lead up to it. Yet the preceding lines do nothing of the sort; instead they present an incantatory series of images. Nevertheless the "conclusion" gains authority from being offered as the culmination of a cascade of emotionally powerful although not logically consecutive images.

The persuasiveness of the "conclusion" is further enhanced by the absence of qualification. Yeats does not say that some of the best people are perhaps this and many of the worst doubtless that; he does not hedge. Very few people have the courage of plain speaking, so when we hear it we tend to give the speaker a measure of credit. Only a big man, we might say, would put it so bluntly, without equivocations that he could retreat behind if attacked.

Another rhetorical device is the absence of "poetic" diction in these two lines, in contrast to the preceding ones. It is as if the poet, overwhelmed with sudden insight, had been moved to drop all poetic craft in order to announce the simple truth that had been revealed to him. There is finally the contrast between the multisyllabic, sibilant richness of "passionate intensity" and the clipped matter-of-factness of "lack all conviction." We are made to feel the stronger emotions of the "worst" people, and this somehow makes us more convinced of the opposition asserted by the poet.

Well, you may say, a child might be taken in by such tricks—but an adult? Surely an adult reader would not be persuaded of the truth of the proposition asserted by Yeats unless the reader believed it anyway, on other, more rationally probative evidence. I am not so sure. People who are open to the appeal of poetry feel the force of genius in this poem and are willing to grant the poet a presumption of insight. This is not to say that they can be persuaded by all the things poets tell them, many of which are false and even absurd, such as the eloquent denunciations of usury in Pound's *Cantos*; on the other hand, if what a poet tells us is absurd we are not likely to rate the poem so highly. If what the poet tells us is at least plausible, the way in which it is told may make it persuasive.

The rhetoric of *The Second Coming* is not forensic; but the forensic tradition in literature is very old, and rich in techniques that lawyers and judges use. The tradition may be said to begin with line 17 in Book I of the *Iliad*, in Chryses' plea to Agamemnon to return Chryseis, a wonderfully compressed example of lawyer-type pleading. I translate the passage literally, to preserve the word order, which is important:

> Sons of Atreus, and other well-greaved Greeks, may the
> gods who have their homes in Olympus grant you
> the sacking of Troy and an auspicious return home,
> but let my dear child go and, on the other hand, accept ransom,
> reverencing the son of Zeus, far-shooting Apollo.

The carrot and stick are neatly tendered—carrot first, which is subtler and more polite. Chryses, a priest of Apollo, asks the gods to bestow victory and a good return home on the Greeks in general and Agamemnon and his brother Menelaus in particular; and since Chryses is a priest, the invocation of divine assistance is more than perfunctory. But to make assurance doubly sure, Chryses also offers a more tangible and immediate benefit, requiring no divine intervention—a ransom. The offer of the ransom comes immediately after the request to free Chryseis, thus underscoring the element of quid pro quo. Chryses ends his plea by pointedly, though as before courteously, suggesting that by accepting his offer the Greeks will be conciliating a powerful god, Zeus's son who shoots from afar, Apollo—who, not incidentally, is Chryses' patron. The Greek words for far-shooter Apollo, which are given emphasis by their place at the end of a line and the end of Chryses' plea, have the ominous sound of a roll of thunder (*hekēbolon Āpollōna*).

A more elaborate literary example of forensic oratory is the pair of speeches given by Brutus and Antony at Caesar's funeral, in Act III of *Julius Caesar*. Brutus's speech is short, and in prose. Although it is elaborately wrought, with careful use of repetition and antithesis—"Not that I lov'd Caesar less, but that I lov'd Rome more" (III.2.21–22), and so forth—the rhetorical structure is so conspicuous that the listener is made immediately aware that he is hearing an oration, and this awareness opens an emotional gap between audience and speaker. By the overtly rhetorical character, the brevity, the balance, and the prose form of the oration, Brutus—very much in character—forbears to stir the passions of the mob. He also fails to elaborate the charge of Caesar's ambition, saying merely, "but, as he was ambitious, I slew him" (III.2.26–27). (And notice how he buries the charge in a subordinate clause.) This omission will make it easy for Antony to "refute" the charge. We are meant to understand, I think, that Brutus's speech, while elegant, is maladroit. One clue is that someone in the crowd shouts in response to the speech, "Let him be Caesar" (III.2.50)—showing that the crowd has missed the point.

Antony's speech—much longer than Brutus's, and in verse rather than prose—is far more effective. It starts, characteristically, with a falsehood: "I come to bury Caesar, not to praise him" (III.2.76). Both parts are false: Antony has come to praise Caesar, and also, in effect, to resurrect him, by loosing Caesar's revenging spirit on the conspirators. Antony's rhetorical problem is that as he starts speaking the crowd is still with Brutus. His initial task must be to win their confidence and undermine Brutus's standing with them. So while first saying that he will not praise Caesar he immediately follows this up by complaining (ever so gently) about the unfairness of a funeral at which only the faults of the dead man can be spoken of (III.2.77–79):

> The evil that men do lives after them;
> The good is oft interred with their bones.
> So let it be with Caesar . . .

Antony continues to emphasize his own good faith by assuring the audience that "Brutus is an honorable man." But the incessant repetition of this formula, mingled with reminders of Caesar's great deeds, causes the refrain to become increasingly, and eventually savagely, ironical (III.2.123–129):

> O masters! If I were dispos'd to stir
> Your hearts and minds to mutiny and rage,
> I should do Brutus wrong, and Cassius wrong,
> Who, you all know, are honorable men.
> I will not do them wrong; I rather choose
> To wrong the dead, to wrong myself and you,
> Than I will wrong such honorable men.

—by which point "honorable men" has become redefined for the listener; it now means "ungrateful traitors."

To raise the crowd's emotional temperature even higher, Antony resorts to suspense. He refuses, at first, to read Caesar's will and instead invites the crowd to gaze on Caesar's wounds. And still using suspense to good rhetorical effect, before exhibiting the wounds he describes them in loving detail. He emphasizes Brutus's ingratitude to Caesar, and makes it seem as if Caesar had died of a broken heart (III.2.180–185):

> For Brutus, as you know, was Caesar's angel.
> Judge, O you gods, how dearly Caesar lov'd him!
> This was the most unkindest cut of all;
> For when the noble Caesar saw him stab,
> Ingratitude, more strong than traitors' arms,
> Quite vanquish'd him. Then burst his mighty heart.

Lest the crowd tumble to the fact that Antony is playing on its emotions, he becomes ever more emphatic in denying any inflammatory design on them or breach of faith with those who gave him leave to speak (III.2.209–229):

> Good friends, sweet friends, let me not stir you up
> To such a sudden flood of mutiny.
> They that have done this deed are honorable.
> What private griefs they have, alas, I know not,
> That made them do it. They are wise and honorable,
> And will no doubt with reasons answer you.
> I come not, friends, to steal away your hearts.
> I am no orator, as Brutus is,
> But, as you know me all, a plain blunt man,
> That love my friends; and that they know full well
> That gave me public leave to speak of him.
> For I have neither wit, nor words, nor worth,
> Action, nor utterance, nor the power of speech
> To stir men's blood. I only speak right on.
> I tell you that which you yourselves do know,
> Show you sweet Caesar's wounds, poor poor dumb mouths,
> And bid them speak for me. But were I Brutus,
> And Brutus Antony, there were an Antony
> Would ruffle up your spirit, and put a tongue
> In every wound of Caesar that should move
> The stones of Rome to rise and mutiny.

Almost everything in this passage is false. Brutus and the other conspirators will not be able to answer Antony with reasons because, as Antony well knows, by the time he finishes his speech the mob will be in a frenzy—and anyway Brutus had left before Antony began to speak. Antony is not a plain (in the sense of artless) speaker, and if Brutus were Antony he would not stir the mob on Caesar's behalf any more than he had done on the rebels' behalf. Antony did come to stir the hearts of his listeners and does not think the rebels are honorable.

At last Antony lets the other shoe drop and tells the crowd (by now inflamed) what Caesar has left them in his will, and he ends his oration with the great line, "Here was a Caesar! When comes such another?" (III.2.250). The crowd, on cue, rushes off to burn down the conspirators' houses. Yet Antony has not tried to refute the charge of ambition that Brutus had laid against Caesar, except by misleadingly reminding the audience that Caesar had three times refused the crown that Antony had offered him the day before the assassination; Antony neglects to add that Caesar was lured to the Capitol on the morning of the assassination by a representation that the Senate would offer him a crown that day.

Not for nothing has Antony's speech been called "an exhibition of the destruction of reason by rhetoric."[14] It is not that he is insincere, or that he does not have a case; the irony of the conspirators' honorableness is genuine. It is that he uses emotion rather than reason to make his case. Because he is addressing the Roman mob, while the narrator of *The Second Coming* is addressing us, there is a difference in the authors' implied evaluations of these two rhetorical masterpieces. Yet while Shakespeare probably meant us to be critical of the Roman mob for being so easily swayed by such an emotional appeal, he must also have meant us to admire Antony's consummate rhetorical skill.

## *The Style of Judicial Opinions*

I begin my exploration of judicial style with the most famous opinion of our most famous judge: Holmes's dissent in *Lochner v. New York*.[15] The decision invalidated, as a deprivation of liberty without due process of law, a state statute limiting the hours of work in bakeries. The most famous sentence in Holmes's dissent—one of the most famous in law and as precious to those of us who think the majority opinion was sound public policy though unsound law as to advocates of regulating the employment relation—is: "The Fourteenth Amendment does not enact Mr. Herbert Spencer's *Social Statics*." This proposition is offered without proof; and it is also possible to agree with it yet think the case correctly decided. Somehow these points seem not to detract from the authority of the dissent, now more than eighty years old. The number of opinions that survive from that period is minuscule, and a disproportionate number of them were written by Holmes. Yet as David Currie has shown, Holmes's opinions often (and, as we shall see, in this instance) are not closely reasoned.[16] What then is the source of their power?

---

[14] Nicholas Brooke, *Shakespeare's Early Tragedies* 157 (1968). For good discussions of the funeral speeches see Gayle Greene, " 'The Power of Speech / To Stir Men's Blood': The Language of Tragedy in Shakespeare's *Julius Caesar*," 11 *Renaissance Drama* 67 (1980); David Daiches, *Shakespeare: Julius Caesar* 36–41 (1976). On the amorality of rhetoric generally, see Kenneth Burke, "The Rhetoric of Hitler's 'Battle,' " in *The Philosophy of Literary Form: Studies in Symbolic Action* 191 (1941); D. J. Conacher, "Euripides' *Hecuba*," 82 *American Journal of Philology* 1, 16–18 (1961) (arguing that *Hecuba* is an implied criticism of rhetoric as deployed for example by Odysseus).

[15] 198 U.S. 45, 75 (1905). Compare Dudziak, note 4 above, at 859–867, analyzing Holmes's controversial opinion in Buck v. Bell, 274 U.S. 200 (1927), which I discussed briefly in Chapter 3 and will discuss again after *Lochner*.

[16] See David P. Currie, "The Constitution in the Supreme Court: Full Faith and the Bill of Rights, 1889–1910," 52 *University of Chicago Law Review* 867, 900 (1985); Currie, "The Constitution in the Supreme Court: 1910–1921," 1985 *Duke Law Journal* 1111, 1145–1155, 1161.

Here is the full text of Holmes's dissent in *Lochner*:

I regret sincerely that I am unable to agree with the judgment in this case, and that I think it my duty to express my dissent.

This case is decided upon an economic theory which a large part of the country does not entertain. If it were a question whether I agreed with that theory, I should desire to study it further and long before making up my mind. But I do not conceive that to be my duty, because I strongly believe that my agreement or disagreement has nothing to do with the right of a majority to embody their opinions in law. It is settled by various decisions of this court that state constitutions and state laws may regulate life in many ways which we as legislators might think as injudicious or if you like as tyrannical as this, and which equally with this interfere with the liberty to contract. Sunday laws and usury laws are ancient examples. A more modern one is the prohibition of lotteries. The liberty of the citizen to do as he likes so long as he does not interfere with the liberty of others to do the same, which has been a shibboleth for some well-known writers, is interfered with by school laws, by the Post Office, by every state or municipal institution which takes his money for purposes thought desirable, whether he likes it or not. The Fourteenth Amendment does not enact Mr. Herbert Spencer's Social Statics. The other day we sustained the Massachusetts vaccination law. *Jacobson v. Massachusetts*, 197 U.S. 11. United States and state statutes and decisions cutting down the liberty to contract by way of combination are familiar to this court. *Northern Securities Co. v. United States*, 193 U.S. 197. Two years ago we upheld the prohibition of sales of stock on margins or for future delivery in the constitution of California. *Otis v. Parker*, 187 U.S. 606. The decision sustaining an eight hour law for miners is still recent. *Holden v. Hardy*, 169 U.S. 366. Some of these laws embody convictions or prejudices which judges are likely to share. Some may not. But a constitution is not intended to embody a particular economic theory, whether of paternalism and the organic relation of the citizen to the State or of *laissez faire*. It is made for people of fundamental differing views, and the accident of our finding certain opinions natural and familiar or novel and even shocking ought not to conclude our judgment upon the question whether statutes embodying them conflict with the Constitution of the United States.

General propositions do not decide concrete cases. The decision will depend on a judgment or intuition more subtle than any articulate major premise. But I think that the proposition just stated, if it is accepted, will carry us far toward the end. Every opinion tends to become a law. I think that the word liberty in the Fourteenth Amendment is perverted when it is held to prevent the natural outcome of a dominant opinion, unless it can be said that a rational and fair man necessarily would admit that the statute proposed would infringe fundamental principles as they have been understood by the traditions of our people and our law. It does not need research to show that no such sweeping condemnation can be passed upon the statute before us. A reasonable man might think it a proper measure on the score of health. Men whom I certainly could not pronounce unreasonable would uphold it as a first instalment of a general regulation of the hours of work. Whether in the latter aspect it would be open to the charge of inequality I think it unnecessary to discuss.

After setting a properly serious and deferential tone in the first sentence, Holmes begins the body of his dissent with an arresting proposition— "This case is decided upon an economic theory which a large part of the country does not entertain"—that is not elaborated. The reader is told neither what the economic theory is, nor the relevance of the fact (which is not elaborated either) that a large part of the country does not entertain it. The serious charge that the majority is deciding the case on economic rather than legal grounds is not defended. Instead of explaining and supporting what he has just said, Holmes changes the subject, to remark that, "If it were a question whether I agreed with that theory, I should desire to study it further and long before making up my mind."

The force of Holmes's opening sally lies in the assurance with which it is made. It puts the reader on the defensive; dare he question a statement made with a conviction so confident and serene? We know how an ordinary judge would express the same thought. Many have, and a fair composite would be: "I respectfully but earnestly dissent from the majority's unwarranted substitution of its own views of public policy for the more flexible mandate of the Constitution." And he will then devote pages of argument and citation to supporting the assertion. Holmes's method is more effective because in areas where our own knowledge is shaky we tend to take people at their own apparent self-evaluation and thus to give more credence to the confident than to the defensive.

The next sentence in the dissent (beginning "If it were a question") is the ethical appeal. An ordinary judge would say something like, "My personal views on the truth of the majority's economic theory are irrelevant." That is the essential paraphrasable content of Holmes's sentence, but by putting it as he does he slips in the additional suggestion, which makes the sentence more credible, that he is slow to jump to conclusions. It is a masterful touch; it happens also, as is often the case with the ethical appeal (Antony's, for example), to be false. Holmes was not slow to jump to conclusions, and as a matter of fact he had years earlier made laissez-faire his economic philosophy.[17] He probably thought the statute invalidated in *Lochner* nonsense. Many judges when voting to uphold statutes that they dislike will say so to

[17] See Robert W. Gordon, "Holmes' *Common Law* as Legal and Social Science," 10 *Hofstra Law Review* 719, 740 (1982); Joseph Frazier Wall, "Social Darwinism and Constitutional Law with Special Reference to *Lochner v. New York*," 33 *Annals of Science* 465, 475–476 (1976).

make themselves sound impartial. That is a type of ethical appeal, but of a crass and self-congratulatory sort. Holmes's is subtle, disarming. It is a version of the "simple man" style that George Orwell used so effectively. The "I" in Orwell's essays and journalism is not Eric Blair (Orwell's real name); it is the very model of a plain-speaking, decent, honest Englishman. The plain style is often, and in these examples, an artifice of sophisticated intellectuals; and the idea that if Holmes had thought that a case turned on an economic theory he would have conducted a patient study of the theory is a fantasy. The implied author of the *Lochner* dissent is not the real Oliver Wendell Holmes.

Meanwhile in the dissent the reader's suspense is building to find out what Holmes thinks the "economic theory" of the majority is, since the majority opinion does not use any such term. (Notice how Holmes, like Antony, uses suspense to rhetorical effect.) We discover at last that it is indeed the theory of laissez-faire, "which has been a shibboleth for some well-known writers, [and which] is interfered with by school laws, by the Post Office, by every state or municipal institution which takes [the citizen's] money." Observe the nicely understated derision in "shibboleth," and how it is reinforced by portraying the advocates of laissez-faire, with some exaggeration, as people who would abolish the Post Office. (Notice that Holmes does not say, who would privatize the Post Office.) This portrayal provides the lead-in to the climactic sentence of the opinion, the one about Herbert Spencer—one of the "well-known writers"—which gains its force from its concreteness. How much weaker the sentence would have been if for "Mr. Herbert Spencer's Social Statics" Holmes had written "laissez-faire," or even if for "enacts" he had written "adopts"! The absurdity of the idea that the Constitution would enact a book with a weird title, written by an Englishman, lends emotional force to the sentence and—my essential point—operates as a substitute for proof. Holmes has made Spencer's book the metaphor (broadly defined; technically the figure of speech employed is not metaphor but metonymy) for the philosophy of laissez-faire. And metaphors, because of their concreteness, vividness, and, when they are good, unexpectedness, are more memorable than their literal equivalents. This is one reason why the dissent in *Lochner* not only contributed to the shift of opinion that culminated many years later in the repudiation of "Lochnerism" but also became the symbol of opposition to the judicial philosophy reflected in the majority opinion.

After dispatching Herbert Spencer, Holmes does at last give some evidence for his position. For example, he cites the case in which the Supreme Court had recently sustained a compulsory-vaccination law

(*Jacobson*). But the case is inapposite. Vaccination confers what economists call an external benefit (a term explained in the next chapter),
because it protects not only the person vaccinated but persons who
might otherwise catch the disease from him. Compulsory vaccination is
therefore consistent with most versions of laissez-faire, while a law
fixing maximum hours of work is paternalistic and therefore inconsistent with it.[18] Holmes moves quickly again to the general, remarking
that a constitution "is made for people of fundamentally differing views,
and the accident of our finding certain opinions natural and familiar, or
novel, and even shocking, ought not to conclude our judgment upon the
question whether statutes embodying them conflict with the Constitution of the United States." But the majority had never said it should. It
said the statute was an unreasonable interference with freedom of
contract. About this virtually all Holmes says is, "A reasonable man
might think it a proper measure on the score of health."

Would the dissent in *Lochner* have received a high grade in a law
school examination in 1905? I think not. It is not logically organized,
does not join issue sharply with the majority, is not scrupulous in its
treatment of the majority opinion or of precedent, is not thoroughly
researched,[19] does not exploit the factual record, and is highly unfair to
poor old Herbert Spencer, of whom most people nowadays know no
more than what Holmes told them in the *Lochner* dissent. The dissent
also misses an opportunity to take issue with the fundamental premise of
the majority opinion, which is that unreasonable statutes violate the due
process clause of the Fourteenth Amendment; the dissent is silent on the
origins or purposes of the amendment. Indeed, at the end Holmes seems
to concede the majority's fundamental (and contestable) premise that the
due process clause outlaws unreasonable legislation, and to disagree
merely with the majority's conclusion that New York's maximum-
hours statute is unreasonable. The sweeping assertions at the beginning
of the dissent are thus discordant with its conclusion. Read as a whole,
the opinion does not clearly challenge Lochnerism but just the abuses of
Lochnerism. It is not, in short, a good judicial opinion. It is merely the
greatest judicial opinion of the last hundred years. To judge it by
"scientific" standards is to miss the point. It is a rhetorical masterpiece,

[18] Holmes's citations to *Holden* and *Otis*—cases in which the Supreme Court had upheld an
eight-hour maximum workday for miners, and a prohibition of sales on margin, respectively—
are more pertinent. See David P. Currie, "The Constitution in the Supreme Court: The
Protection of Economic Interests, 1889–1910," 52 *University of Chicago Law Review* 324, 380 n.
332 (1985).
[19] Currie mentions two important cases that Holmes failed to cite. See id. at 380 n. 332.

and evidently rhetoric counts in law; otherwise the dissent in *Lochner* would be forgotten.[20]

The reason why rhetoric or style is important in law is that many legal questions cannot be resolved by logical or empirical demonstration. After eighty-two years it is impossible to *prove* that *Lochner* was decided wrongly.[21] The statute struck down in *Lochner* was paternalistic, and by striking down such statutes (though fitfully) until finally overwhelmed by political pressures in the late 1930s the Supreme Court probably made the United States marginally more prosperous than it would otherwise have been. Although there is great doubt whether the Fourteenth Amendment was intended to authorize the kind of free-wheeling federal judicial intervention in the public policy of the states that *Lochner* has come to symbolize (thanks to Holmes's dissent), it is no greater than the doubt about the free-wheeling federal judicial intervention of recent decades in the public policy of the states in such areas as abortion, capital punishment, and obscenity. Some think both forms of intervention improper, although that is a minority view among judges and other lawyers, including law professors. In any event, those who think "Lochnerism" (a word whose currency is due to Holmes's dissent) bad law continue to draw comfort and support from the enchanting rhetoric of the *Lochner* dissent. And maybe the dissent was one of the things that persuaded them—and even after they have bared all its tricks continues to persuade them—to that view.

The dissent in *Lochner* is more than a symbol, however, and more than a tour de force. The second sentence—"This case is decided upon an economic theory which a large part of the country does not entertain"—was one of the opening salvos in the legal-realist movement, whose essential teaching was as we know that many cases are decided on the basis of the judges' own policy preferences rather than of legal principles imposed on the judges from without.[22] Holmes had said such

---

[20] With the dissent in *Lochner* compare the subdued, almost perfunctory, opinions of the dissenting Justices in the abortion case—the modern *Lochner*. Roe v. Wade, 410 U.S. 113, 171 (1973); Doe v. Bolton, 410 U.S. 179, 221 (1973).

[21] A growing scholarly movement regards it as having been decided correctly. See, for example, Richard A. Epstein, *Takings: Private Property and the Power of Eminent Domain* 108–109, 128, 280–281 (1985), and references in my *Economic Analysis of Law* 589 n. 3 (3d ed. 1986). It has been argued that the Supreme Court's decisions bringing commercial advertising under the umbrella of the First Amendment are a revival of the jurisprudence of *Lochner*. See Thomas H. Jackson and John Calvin Jeffries, Jr., "Commercial Speech: Economic Due Process and the First Amendment," 65 *Virginia Law Review* 1 (1979).

[22] See the excellent brief summary of legal realism in Andrew Altman, "Legal Realism, Critical Legal Studies, and Dworkin," 15 *Philosophy and Public Affairs* 205–214 (1986); and recall the brief discussion of legal realism in Chapter 4.

things before he was appointed to the Supreme Court,[23] but for a Supreme Court Justice to say them carried greater weight.

The dissent in *Lochner* is a document of legal realism in a deeper sense. Holmes's implicit view of judicial decisionmaking, it has been argued, is that the decision of a hard case is a policy judgment, rather than a deduction from authoritative premises.[24] (This was his "realism.") The characteristic abruptness of Holmes's opinions is consistent with a belief that an effort to demonstrate the correctness of his result, even to the extent of exploring the intentions of the framers of the Fourteenth Amendment, would be a fake. Evidently there is something to this conception of law. The dissent in *Lochner* does not make its points by carefully marshaling the facts and authorities, yet we do not miss these things; maybe reason really cannot decide the hard cases (a possible implication of the discussion of interpretation in Chapter 5). Thus does the style of the dissent in *Lochner* invite reflection on the profoundest issues of legal process.

In comparing Holmes to Marc Antony and to the narrator of *The Second Coming* I may seem to be suggesting a view of legal reasoning that is not only "realistic" but cynical. I may seem to be saying that there are only two forms of persuasion: on the one hand logic—which cannot be used to decide the difficult and important cases[25]—and on the other hand the tricks of rhetoric, as illustrated by my examples. To forestall such cynicism, however, it is necessary only to recall that between the extremes of logical, or scientific, persuasion and emotive persuasion lie a variety of methods for inducing justified true belief that are rational though not rigorous or exact. This is the domain of practical reason;[26] it includes, among many other methods of persuasion available within the legal culture, appeals to common sense, to custom, to precedents and other authorities, to intuition and recognition (through which we grasp the meaning of a statutory or constitutional text), to history, to consequences, and to the "test of time" stressed throughout this book. Resolving disagreement in difficult legal cases need no more be a pure

[23] See, for example, "The Path of the Law," 10 *Harvard Law Review* 457 (1897).

[24] See G. Edward White, "The Integrity of Holmes' Jurisprudence," 10 *Hofstra Law Review* 633, 650–652, 664, 668–671 (1982).

[25] See, for example, Neil MacCormick, *Legal Reasoning and Legal Theory*, chap. 3 (1978).

[26] "Legal reasoning is thus a very elaborated individual case of practical reasoning." Chaim Perelman, *Justice, Law, and Argument: Essays on Moral and Legal Reasoning* 129 (1980). That rational inquiry is not exhausted by the methods of the exact sciences is the theme of Hilary Putnam, *Reason, Truth and History*, chaps. 5–9 (1981). See also Martha C. Nussbaum, *The Fragility of Goodness: Luck and Ethics in Greek Tragedy and Philosophy*, chap. 10 (1986); Anthony T. Kronman, "Living in the Law," 54 *University of Chicago Law Review* 835 (1987); Kronman, "Practical Wisdom and Professional Character," 4 *Social Philosophy and Policy* 203 (1986).

matter of taste than the resolution of literary disputes over the merit of Kafka's fiction. (I have deliberately chosen an example of evaluative criticism; much literary scholarship is quasi-scientific.) A patient exposition of the text and history of the constitutional provision on which the majority in *Lochner* relied would have been an alternative strategy for Holmes (alternative because by lengthening the opinion it would have diminished its rhetorical force). But because the rational arguments of judges, like those of literary critics, fall short of being conclusive when the dispute is a difficult one to resolve by the methods of reason, a "rhetorical" strategy in a perhaps not wholly creditable sense may have great persuasive force. It is no accident that the most influential judges and literary critics have been effective stylists.

I anticipate the objection that Holmes's rhetorical tricks in *Lochner* are tolerable only because we think his legal position either correct (the dominant view) or defensible, and that if he performed such tricks in support of an outrageous result the rhetoric would only make us more indignant. Yet is not *Buck v. Bell* (see Chapter 3) an eloquent and moving opinion even if one is revolted by the author's evident enthusiasm for the eugenic breeding of human beings? I quote the heart of the opinion (206 U.S. at 207; citation omitted):

> We have seen more than once that the public welfare may call upon the best citizens for their lives. It would be strange if it could not call upon those who already sap the strength of the State for these lesser sacrifices, often not felt to be such by those concerned, in order to prevent our being swamped with incompetence. It is better for all the world, if instead of waiting to execute degenerate offspring for crime, or to let them starve for imbecility, society can prevent those who are manifestly unfit from continuing their kind. The principle that sustains compulsory vaccination is broad enough to cover cutting the Fallopian tubes. Three generations of imbeciles are enough.

This is beautiful prose—vivid, passionate, topped off by a brilliant aphorism—but it is dubious legal reasoning. The comparison to conscription is incomplete; the sacrifice demanded of draftees may be greater but so is the need for their sacrifice. The analogy to compulsory vaccination depends on the unexamined assumption that "feeble-mindedness" begets crime. Holmes does not try to show that compulsory sterilization is the only alternative to either executing degenerate offspring or letting them starve to death. In *Buck v. Bell* Holmes drops the mask of judicial detachment and makes clear his personal approval of the Virginia statute—though on his view of the Fourteenth Amendment his opinion of the merits of the statute is irrelevant to the judicial function. *Buck v. Bell* would be a poorly reasoned, brutal, and even vicious opinion even if Carrie Buck really had been an imbecile; but it is a first-class piece of rhetoric—thus demonstrating, like Antony's speech, that there is no inherent moral or truth value in rhetoric. Scholarly analysis of the "rhetoric" of judicial decisions would be more fruitful, and certainly clearer, if scholars stopped trying to equate good rhetoric with goodness.

INVESTIGATING the literary properties of judicial opinions is not a new undertaking. Cardozo did it in his essay *Law and Literature*; and an English professor, Walker Gibson, in an unjustly neglected essay, did a fine job on a Learned Hand opinion.[27] More recently, Richard Weisberg has performed a literary analysis on several of Cardozo's opinions and one by Justice (now Chief Justice) Rehnquist,[28] while James Boyd White has done the same for Chief Justice Marshall's opinion in *McCulloch v. Maryland* and for two of the opinions in *Olmstead v. United States*.[29] Weisberg's analysis of the Rehnquist opinion advances, though with redeeming urbanity and good humor, the alarming thesis that Rehnquist was as unfair to the losing party in that case as Weisberg believes Captain Vere was to Billy Budd. Weisberg's encomiums for Cardozo and criticisms of Rehnquist are more political than literary, reflecting the tendency in discussions of judicial opinions to use rhetoric in its broadest sense, while White's discussion of *McCulloch* is at times vague, as when he says that in Marshall's conception of constitutional interpretation "the activity of interpreting [the Constitution] cannot be limited to

[27] See Benjamin N. Cardozo, "Law and Literature," in *Selected Writings of Benjamin Nathan Cardozo* 339 (Margaret E. Hall ed. 1947 [1925]); Walker Gibson, "Literary Minds and Judicial Style," 36 *New York University Law Review* 915, 928–930 (1961). For a nice selection of Hand's opinions see *The Art and Craft of Judging: The Decisions of Judge Learned Hand* (Hershel Shanks ed. 1968). It is a small selection: Hand wrote some 3,000 opinions in his fifty-year career as a federal district and court of appeals judge.

[28] See Richard H. Weisberg, "Law, Literature and Cardozo's Judicial Poetics," 1 *Cardozo Law Review* 283 (1979); Weisberg, "How Judges Speak: Some Lessons on Adjudication in *Billy Budd, Sailor* with an Application to Justice Rehnquist," 57 *New York University Law Review* 1, 42–58 (1982). The Rehnquist opinion is Paul v. Davis, 424 U.S. 693 (1976).

[29] McCulloch v. Maryland, 17 U.S. (4 Wheat.) 316 (1819), is discussed in James Boyd White, *When Words Lose Their Meaning: Constitutions and Reconstitutions of Language, Character, and Community*, chap. 9 (1984). The Taft and Brandeis opinions in Olmstead v. United States, 277 U.S. 438 (1928), are discussed in White, "Judicial Criticism," 20 *Georgia Law Review* 835 (1986). Taft wrote the majority opinion in *Olmstead*, Holmes and Brandeis wrote dissenting opinions. See text at note 34 below.

Ferguson, note 10 above, is a *bravura* interpretation of the Constitution as a work of literature.

looking to see what is there or to an obedience to plain commands; it becomes instead a literary and constructive art, a way of making sense *of* living speech *in* living speech," and that the Constitution "must be regarded not as a mere legal instrument, resting on some abstract authority, but as a true *constitution*: of language, of community, and of culture."[30] The italics are faintly alarming.

Judges like Marshall, Cardozo, Brandeis, Learned Hand, and Robert Jackson—and above all Holmes—have extremely interesting styles, but the tendency in legal writing about judicial rhetoric to think of rhetoric as something grander than style has retarded the application of specifically literary insights to the study of judicial opinions. I am trying in this chapter to make amends.

Marshall's style alone of the judges I have mentioned is magisterial, but it is never pompous. Patient, systematic, unadorned, unemotional, unpretentious, it is the calm and confident voice of reason—the quintessential Enlightenment style. A related characteristic of Marshall's opinions, remarkable in our legal culture, is the absence of citations to previous decisions, American or English (and there were plenty he could have cited); also related, and also remarkable, is Marshall's avoidance of legal jargon. Whether such a style remains possible in a mature legal system is a matter of doubt; in any event Marshall has had no successful imitators. He had, of course, the advantage of interpreting the Constitution while it was still fresh. Although he required (and fortunately possessed) great political wisdom, he did not face as severe an interpretive problem as his successors did; nor did he have the modern judge's burden of negotiating a minefield of authoritative precedents.

The main issue in *McCulloch v. Maryland* (1819) was whether Congress had the power to create a bank as something "necessary and proper" to carry out the legislative powers enumerated in Article I of the Constitution. The Court held that it did. This conclusion required that a flexible approach be taken to constitutional interpretation, and Marshall's formulation of that approach remains canonical:

> A constitution, to contain an accurate detail of all the subdivisions of which its great powers will admit, and of all the means by which they may be carried into execution, would partake of a prolixity of a human code, and could scarcely be embraced by the human mind. It would probably never be understood by the public. Its nature, therefore, requires, that only its great outlines should be marked, its important objects designated, and the minor ingredients which compose those objects be deduced from the

[30] *When Words Lose Their Meaning*, note 29 above, at 260.

nature of the objects themselves. That this idea was entertained by the framers of the American constitution, is not only to be inferred from the nature of the instrument, but from the language. Why else were some of the limitations, found in the ninth section of the 1st article, introduced? It is also, in some degree, warranted by their having omitted to use any restrictive term which might prevent its receiving a fair and just interpretation. In considering this question, then, we must never forget that it is *a constitution* we are expounding.[31]

This is not flashy prose, but it is simple and logical, and builds nicely to the famous aphorism of the last sentence.

Here is how Holmes made a similar point about the need for flexibility in constitutional interpretation:

When we are dealing with words that also are a constituent act, like the Constitution of the United States, we must realize that they have called into life a being the development of which could not have been foreseen completely by the most gifted of its begetters. It was enough for them to realize or to hope that they had created an organism; it has taken a century and has cost their successors much sweat and blood to prove that they created a nation. The case before us must be considered in the light of our whole experience and not merely in that of what was said a hundred years ago.[32]

Compared with Marshall, Holmes is racy. But Holmes was not chief justice, was not writing when the constitutional convention was a living memory, and, most important, did not have Marshall's eighteenth-century faith in the power of reason to resolve difficult legal questions— though the Holmes passage calls to mind another great eighteenth-century mind, that of Edmund Burke, who set definite limits on that power.

One might suppose from my comparison of Marshall to Holmes that Marshall would have escaped the kind of academic censure that opinions like the *Lochner* dissent and *Buck v. Bell* invite. But this is not the case. Here are the comments of David Currie, a distinguished professor of constitutional law, on the characteristics of Marshall's constitutional opinions:

. . . great rhetorical power, invocation of the constitutional text less as the basis of decision than as a peg on which to hang a result evidently reached

---

[31] 17 U.S. at 407. Marshall's famous italicization in the last sentence shows that rules of style (for example, one should not italicize for emphasis)—like rules of grammar and, in a sense that should be familiar from Chapter 2, rules of law—are made to be broken, though selectively.

[32] Missouri v. Holland, 252 U.S. 416, 433 (1920).

on other grounds, a marked disdain for reliance on precedent, extensive borrowing of the ideas of others without attribution, an inclination to reach out for constitutional issues that did not have to be decided, a tendency to resolve difficult questions by aggressive assertion of one side of the case, and an absolute certainty in the correctness of his conclusions.[33]

It seems, then, that despite his more sedate style Marshall displays the same lack of judicial craftsmanship as Holmes does. Since these are probably the two greatest judges in our history, I am moved to ask whether it is the conception of craftsmanship that is deficient rather than the judges. Maybe the art of judging is inescapably rhetorical, and a failure to appreciate this fact is a shortcoming of the school of legal formalism, of which Currie is one of the most illustrious members. Maybe some cases cannot be resolved otherwise than by "aggressive assertion of one side"—perhaps a balanced analysis would leave the court and reader in equipoise. Currie criticizes Marshall for what are undoubtedly faults in academic writing, but are we to understand from this that the best judicial opinion is the one that most closely resembles a good law review article? That the best law professor would be the best judge? That, perhaps, the best law-school exam-taker would be the best Supreme Court Justice? Currie does not discuss these questions.

Brandeis wrote well by judicial standards, but one may say of him with more justice than T. S. Eliot said of Milton that his style was a bad influence on that of his successors. It is the style of the sledgehammer. Here is the central passage from one of his most famous opinions, the dissent in *Olmstead*, the case (later overruled) which held that wiretapping was not a search or seizure within the meaning of the Fourth Amendment:

> The makers of our Constitution undertook to secure conditions favorable to the pursuit of happiness. They recognized the significance of man's spiritual nature, of his feelings and of his intellect. They knew that only a part of the pain, pleasure and satisfactions of life are to be found in material things. They sought to protect Americans in their beliefs, their thoughts, their emotions and their sensations. They conferred, as against the government, the right to be let alone—the most comprehensive of rights and the right most valued by civilized men.[34]

---

[33] David P. Currie, *The Constitution in the Supreme Court: The First Hundred Years: 1789–1888* 74 (1985).

[34] Olmstead v. United States, note 29 above, at 478–479. In Katz v. United States, 389 U.S. 347 (1967), the Court overruled *Olmstead*, thus vindicating Brandeis's position. For criticisms of Brandeis's logic in his dissent in *Olmstead* that parallel my criticisms of Holmes's logic in *Lochner* see Aviam Soifer, "Reviewing Legal Fictions," 20 *Georgia Law Review* 871, 898–909

This is less adroit than the best of Marshall or Holmes, and I am a little surprised that White, in his recent discussion of the opinion (see note 29), does not point out its rhetorical flaws; but, like Weisberg, his primary interest is in a broader sense of rhetoric, in which style does not much matter. The staccato style of Brandeis's dissent (sentences of roughly equal length, starting the same way, and full of lists—"their beliefs, their thoughts, their emotions," and so on—and repetition, notably of "they" and of "their") conveys a distracting sense of Brandeis's own excitement, making the reader wonder whether Brandeis may not have been projecting onto the long-dead framers his own vision of a just society. It is also a hectoring style; it grabs you by the lapel and shouts in your face, demanding your assent rather than engaging you in a discussion. This and its emotionality make it a discordant style in which to celebrate the classical liberal ideal of personal autonomy. It is also easily imitable and is the model for the windy jeremiads found in so many modern judicial dissents. Compare with it the style, at once more rational (less "rhetorical") and more pungent, of this passage from an opinion by Justice Jackson, protesting his colleagues' greater willingness than his to sit in judgment on state supreme court decisions involving the rights of criminal defendants:

> Whenever decisions of one court are reviewed by another, a percentage of them are reversed. That reflects a difference in outlook normally found between personnel comprising different courts. However, reversal by a higher court is not proof that justice is thereby better done. There is no doubt that if there were a super-Supreme Court, a substantial proportion of our reversals of state courts would also be reversed. We are not final because we are infallible, but we are infallible only because we are final.[35]

As with Marshall and Holmes, the aphorism gains force from the relaxed manner in which it is introduced. These judges are masters of prose rhythm, of timing.

I will leave Learned Hand to Walker Gibson and move finally to Cardozo, the most mannered of the great judicial stylists. Cardozo's best writing is found in his marvelously compact and vivacious summaries of the facts of cases; the weakness of his style is an ornateness that at times lends an unserious quality to his prose and to his thought. I will

---

(1986). With Brandeis's dissent compare Holmes's characteristically terse and eloquent dissent, 277 U.S. at 469–471, describing the government's illegal wiretapping as "dirty business," and stating, "We have to choose, and for my part I think it a less evil that some criminals should escape than that the government should play an ignoble part."

[35] Brown v. Allen, 344 U.S. 443, 540 (1953) (concurring opinion).

illustrate with the climactic passage of his opinion in *Palko v. Connecticut.* The issue was whether carrying out Palko's sentence of death would be a denial of due process of law because the sentence had been imposed upon retrial after the state had appealed from Palko's original conviction, which was for second-degree murder, a crime that did not carry the death penalty. Cardozo assumed that, in a federal prosecution, to allow the prosecution to appeal in these circumstances would place the defendant in double jeopardy, and would therefore be forbidden by the Fifth Amendment. Even so, he concluded that Connecticut's decision to allow such an appeal was not so basic a deprivation of human rights that it violated the looser restraints imposed on the states by the due process clause of the Fourteenth Amendment. (Years later the Supreme Court was to hold that the Fourteenth Amendment gives state criminal defendants the same rights under the double-jeopardy clause as federal defendants have.) In support of this conclusion Cardozo stated:

> If the trial had been infected with error adverse to the accused, there might have been [appellate] review at his instance, and as often as necessary to purge the vicious taint. A reciprocal privilege, subject at all times to the discretion of the presiding judge, has now been granted to the state. There is here no seismic innovation. The edifice of justice stands, its symmetry, to many, greater than before.[36]

This is an ingenious use of metaphor. As long as the innovation is not "seismic"—that is, as long as there is no earthquake—the "edifice" of justice will not be shaken. Indeed, the edifice will be more symmetrical, since now the state can appeal if it loses, as well as the defendant if he loses. The ingenuity of the figure, however, bordering as it does on cuteness, strikes a sour note in a death case. And the appeal to "symmetry"—to an aesthetic rather than a political or juridical concept—made, as it is, without any elaboration, is as irrelevant as it is frivolous in a discussion of criminal procedure. Such procedure is deliberately asymmetrical. The prosecution must prove guilt beyond a reasonable doubt; would the edifice of justice be grander or straighter if the burden of persuasion were reduced, so that, perhaps, if the evidence was in equipoise, the defendant's guilt would be determined by tossing a coin? Rabelais's Justice Bridlegoose might have thought so (see Introduction, note 14), but not Justice Cardozo. Rather than completing a thought, the geological metaphor is a substitute for thought—and so obvious is this that the figure fails as effective rhetoric. Cardozo has Brutus's problem: his rhetoric draws attention to itself.

[36] 302 U.S. 319, 328 (1937).

I do not suggest that only a plain style is effective in legal or other discursive prose. *Lochner* shows that metaphor can be a powerful tool of legal persuasion.[37] Here is another example, this one by James Boyd White. White is in favor of affirmative action, that is, of discrimination in favor of (rather than against) members of minority groups and women. But he is dissatisfied with the rhetoric by which this result is defended, and proposes:

> We must change our statement of what we are doing, and why. The idea is not that he [the white victim of affirmative action] must pay for what someone of his race did a hundred years ago, or more . . . There is, after all, another possibility. Think for a moment of the relationship between the ideal Union soldier and the slave he fought to free: he was not paying a debt for his past transgressions, but risking, perhaps losing, his life and wealth, in order to live in a national community in which no people would be slaves, and in which the effects of slavery would be destroyed. He was not the competitor but the friend of the slave. What we say to the modern white applicant is that he too is a member of a community that is seeking to rid itself of the residual and terrible evils of slavery, and that he should look upon what it costs him as a burden of that improvement, a burden like the soldier's burden which is in some sense a privilege to bear, even when imposed upon a draftee, then or now. This argument rests upon his imagined identity not with the white slave owner, but with the white liberator.[38]

One can quarrel with the analogy. The union soldiers were fighting not to free the slaves but to preserve the union, and the current disadvantages under which black people labor and which affirmative action seeks to alleviate are neither comparable to, nor demonstrably a residuum of, the evils of slavery. But all that is beside my point, which is that White has found a brilliant metaphorical formulation of the case for affirmative action, one that judicial supporters of affirmative action could employ with profit in their opinions.

One has only to read Lincoln's speeches to appreciate the possibility of placing the cadences of Renaissance English (as found in the King James Bible) in the service of political and legal oratory; Lincoln was a lawyer, and many of his speeches discuss the legality of slavery. Indeed, the American ear may be more attuned to the rhetoric of the Bible than to metaphysical wit, well illustrated by the *Palko* opinion, which echoes

[37] For an interesting example from Thomas More, see Stephen J. Greenblatt, "Improvisation and Power," in *Literature and Society* 57, 65–66 (Edward W. Said ed. 1980).
[38] James B. White, "A Response to 'The Rhetoric of Powell's *Bakke*,' " 38 *Washington and Lee Law Review* 73, 75 (1981).

the metaphoric reference to earthquakes in Donne's *A Valediction: forbidding Mourning*:

> Moving of the earth brings harms and fears,
>   Men reckon what it did and meant;
> But trepidation of the spheres,
>   Though greater far, is innocent.[39]

The subject of judicial rhetoric is both rich and comparatively unexplored. Yet in their recent books Weisberg and White devote much more attention to writers than to judges—I would guess in the ratio of 9 to 1.[40] It is true that if you appreciate great writing you are not likely to dwell too long on judicial opinions. But this makes the neglect of Holmes by the law and literature movement all the more surprising. Of all the judges in the Anglo-American tradition he is the only one who belongs in the very first rank of prose writers, just as Lincoln is the only American politician who belongs there. Holmes was a grandmaster of metaphor. Here is an example from a speech he gave in 1886 to students at the Harvard Law School: "The Professors of this School have said to themselves more definitely than ever before, We will not be contented to send forth students with nothing but a rag-bag full of general principles—a throng of glittering generalities, like a swarm of little bodiless cherubs fluttering at the top of one of Corregio's pictures."[41]

Holmes makes his point memorable first by casting his thought in a dramatic mode ("the Professors of this School have said to themselves . . . We will" rather than "the Professors of this School are not content to . . . "), and then by piling on a crescendo of images. Two metaphors ("a rag-bag full of general principles" and "a throng of glittering generalities"), the second employing consonance, precede the climactic simile ("like a swarm of little bodiless cherubs fluttering"). The "swarm of little bodiless cherubs" is a master stroke. Cherubs are in fact (if one

---

[39] See Monroe C. Beardsley and W. K. Wimsatt, Jr., "The Intentional Fallacy," in Wimsatt, *The Verbal Icon: Studies in the Meaning of Poetry* 3, 12–14 (1954). Notice how Donne "deconstructs" Cardozo, by belittling earthquakes!

[40] Here an interesting aspect of White's work should be noted. Like practitioners of deconstruction (whom he in no other respect resembles—whom he in fact deplores, see "Judicial Criticism," note 29 above, at 843–845), White applies his interpretive technique to literary and nonliterary works interchangeably—discussing a novel of Jane Austen in one chapter, Samuel Johnson's *Rambler* essays in another, a dialogue of Plato or Thucydides' history in the third, and eventually a legal text such as the opinion in *McCulloch v. Maryland*. In a sense his work is about how to read complex texts; indeed, the tone is strongly pedagogical throughout. Moreover, he is more interested in the ethical integrity of the texts than in their effectiveness as rhetoric. Stated differently, his primary interest is in rhetoric in its very broadest sense. For a good discussion of White's overall enterprise see Geoffrey P. Miller, "A Rhetoric of Law," 52 *University of Chicago Law Review* 247 (1985).

[41] Oliver Wendell Holmes, "The Use of Law Schools," in Holmes, *Collected Legal Papers* 35, 42 (1920).

can speak of them thus) little and bodiless; but describing them so makes them the very quintessence of ineffectuality. That they are in a picture, and, even more, that they are fluttering at the top of the picture and thus at the edge of the viewer's focus, makes the image even sharper. Notice also how the progression—general principles, glittering generalities, bodiless cherubs—enables the reader to accept a simile that, without any preparation, might have seemed grotesque. An abstraction ("general principles") is made perfectly visualizable. Never has law been more securely a form of literature.

But of what value is it to know that some great judges are distinguished rhetoricians? The rhetorical methods of the masters cannot be reduced to a set of rules that, if faithfully obeyed, will raise a writer above the pedestrian. Consider the question, much discussed in textbooks on rhetoric, whether you should put your strongest arguments first or last, or some first and some last. If you lead off with your weak arguments the audience may tune out, but if you end with them the audience will be left with a bad impression; so the third approach (the "Nestorian") is usually recommended. (This reasoning fits a speech better than a writing, since the listener, unlike the reader, cannot skip ahead or go back; but it is meant to apply to persuasive writings too.) The *Lochner* dissent manages to avoid all three approaches. It starts on a logically weak foot by questioning the majority's decision merely because the majority by striking down a statute is being antimajoritarian (that is, going against a political majority)—an essential, and some would say the defining, characteristic of a judicially enforceable constitution. And the dissent ends very weakly—it just peters out. Yet rather than weakening the opinion, this structure strengthens it by making it seem artless.

It is not possible to learn to write greatly, but it is possible to learn not to write poorly. If it were generally accepted that rhetoric is an important part of the judicial opinion—that the importance, one might even say the meaning, of the *Lochner* dissent lies in how it says rather than in what it says—judges and law clerks might pay more attention to the style of their opinions. Many of the stylistic shortcomings of judicial opinions, and of legal writing generally,[42] could be ameliorated if it

---

[42] On which see my discussions in *The Federal Courts: Crisis and Reform* 107–109, 230–236 (1985); "Goodbye to the Bluebook," 53 *University of Chicago Law Review* 1343, 1349–1351 (1986); "The Constitution as Mirror: Tribe's Constitutional Choices," 84 *Michigan Law Review* 551, 564–567 (1986). For excellent guides to good legal writing see Richard H. Weisberg, *When Lawyers Write* (1987); Richard C. Wydick, *Plain English for Lawyers* (2d ed. 1985); Bryan A. Garner, *A Dictionary of Modern Legal Usage* (1987). See also Terence Collins and Darryl Hattenhauer, "Law and Language: A Selected, Annotated Bibliography on Legal Writing," 33 *Journal of Legal Education* 141 (1983).

A recent and conspicuous example of rhetorical ineptitude is the use of ellipses in the

were more generally realized that style is organic to judicial writing, as it is to literature but not to science; and that in the areas of law that matter—the areas of disagreement—to divorce style and content is not an attainable ideal.

Against the importance of judicial style it can be argued that only a small minority of opinions survive beyond a few years, because in most the content and not the style really is the meaning, and so the content is taken over in subsequent cases and the husk discarded. Actually, the depreciation rate of judicial opinions (especially those of the Supreme Court) is rather low,[43] while most writings that aspire to be literature do not survive for even a few years after publication. Because most judicial opinions deal with subjects of narrower, more transient interest than most works of literature, they may have on average less survival value even when written by someone as able as a great poet or novelist, which anyway is rare—perhaps unknown. But that would not make them less rhetorical. It would just be a consequence of the fact that literary survivorship is a function of generality.

A more serious objection to trying to improve the style of judicial opinions is that style, and more broadly rhetoric, are amoral in point of both means and ends. The purpose of rhetoric is to persuade, and we have seen that emotive, nonrational—even false and misleading— rhetorical devices abound for persuading. And rhetoric can induce false as well as true beliefs; one interpretation of Weisberg's criticism of Justice Rehnquist is that Weisberg thinks Rehnquist too good a rhetorician. But it would be wrong to think that *The Second Coming* or the *Lochner* dissent or even *Buck v. Bell* is basically false—even that Antony's funeral oration is basically false. All four of these rhetorical masterpieces make the reader take seriously and think hard about important though not fully argued propositions: in Yeats's poem, the disjunction between

---

majority opinion in Farmworker Justice Fund, Inc. v. Brock, 811 F.2d 613 (D.C. Cir. 1987), a case that holds that the Occupational Safety and Health Administration had failed to require adequate sanitation facilities for farmworkers. Judge Stephen Williams, dissenting, has much fun at the expense of the majority in discussing the "verbal surgery by which the majority has travestied [OSHA's] reasoning" and the "orphaned clause" that the majority opinion creates by stripping the "critical, qualifying words" from OSHA's stated reasons for leaving the matter of sanitation to the states. Id. at 638 and n. 3. The majority could easily have pulled the sting from this part of Williams's dissent by restoring the deleted words to its quotations. Instead it dropped a footnote (id. at 625 n. 12) in which it said that "Judge Williams faults us for inserting ellipses in quoting two of [OSHA's] sentences," and then tried to defend the ellipses. Such a procedure just draws attention to the dissent, producing the unedifying back-and-forth so characteristic of contemporary judicial opinions.

[43] See William M. Landes and Richard A. Posner, "Legal Precedent: A Theoretical and Empirical Analysis," 19 *Journal of Law and Economics* 249, 280–284 (1976).

power and morality; in Antony's speech, the ties of natural loyalty, gratitude, and compassion set against the claims of an abstract political principle ("necessary murder," as Auden put it in his communist phase);[44] in Holmes's two opinions, the inappropriateness of forcing a particular economic system on the states in the name of the Constitution, and the right of the state to demand sacrifices, respectively. All four works are serious contributions to reflective thought despite, maybe even because of, their emotive character. The conditions of judicial as of literary production may prevent the scholarly demonstration of a thesis. Neither judges nor poets are scholars, and neither work under auspicious conditions for scholarship. Still, there is tension between honest and dishonest rhetoric, as we shall see in the next section.

## The Integrity of Judicial Opinions

Judges can obtain insights from literature that have nothing to do with effective presentation or persuasion but have rather to do with the spirit, meaning, or values found in literature, and so in a rough sense with content rather than just form. The relevant content, however, is not necessarily or even primarily paraphrasable content, which is the focus of the moralizing tradition in criticism, whose adherents range from Plato, Horace, Augustine, Samuel Johnson, Bentham, and Tolstoy to F. R. Leavis and Yvor Winters, to Marxist critics such as Terry Eagleton, and to feminist critics. Moralistic or didactic critics hold with varying degrees of emphasis that the function of literature is to edify and that the canon should be confined to those works (if any—Plato thought there were few, and Bentham thought there were none) that do edify. So one can imagine these critics preparing a reading list for judges. If poets are the unacknowledged legislators of the world, should not judges, above all others, pay attention to the poets' preachments? More mundanely, should not judges look to literature for instruction in the moral principles that guide or should guide judicial decisionmaking in that large open area where text and precedent and other conventional sources of legal authority run out? Might *Buck v. Bell* have been decided differently if Holmes had been steeped in William Blake and Jane Austen?

Wigmore's list of great books for lawyers (see Introduction, note 25) was compiled in the spirit of these questions at a time (1913) when the moralizing tradition was more influential than it is today. Living in an

---

[44] In his poem *Spain*. See George Orwell, "Inside the Whale," in *Collected Essays, Journalism and Letters of George Orwell*, note 1 above, vol. 1, at 493, 516.

age of relativism, most of us hesitate to impose our own moral values on the great writers of the past. And ever since the most cultured nation in Europe took its recent plunge into barbarism it has been hard to argue that immersion in the monuments of Western civilization makes one a better person.[45] Actually a fair amount of literature is immoral by current standards. This reflects not only the political extremes to which many creative people are drawn[46] and the personal irresponsibility that some creative people consider their badge of office, but also the cultural remoteness of so much great literature. Anyone who today took seriously the implied moral values of literature otherwise as various as the *Iliad, Tamburlaine,* the novels of D. H. Lawrence, the later poems of Yeats, and parts of the Old Testament would be a public menace.

The fact that these are great works of literature is, to one who finds survivorship arguments persuasive, a powerful refutation of the didactic school. Edifying works seem to have no advantage in the struggle for literary distinction. Since only the most disciplined, self-denying reader deliberately ignores the moral dimensions of what he reads, the reason must be that great literature can make the reader suspend moral judgments. And it can do this because the moralizing aspects of a work of literature are part of its paraphrasable content, which usually is not at the center of the reader's attention.[47] I have said that it does not matter

---

[45] In my experience, a certain type of person, nowadays rare, continues reading literature after graduating from college, but reading literature does not make one a certain type of person. "Despite their familiarity with the classics, professors of literature do not appear to lead better lives than other people, and frequently display unbecoming virulence on the subject of one another's shortcomings." Ruthven, note 10 above, at 184. See also George Steiner, "To Civilize Our Gentlemen," in *Language and Silence: Essays on Language, Literature, and the Inhuman* 55, 61 (1974); Richard Poirier, *The Renewal of Literature: Emersonian Reflections* (1987).

[46] See William M. Chace, *The Political Identities of Ezra Pound and T. S. Eliot* (1973); John R. Harrison, *The Reactionaries* (1966); Renée Winegarten, *Writers and Revolution: The Fatal Lure of Action* (1974).

[47] A similar point is made in John Crowe Ransom's criticism of Yvor Winters. See *The New Criticism,* chap. 3 (1941). On the didactic tradition see also Beardsley, note 1 above, at 564–567, and Anne Sheppard, *Aesthetics: An Introduction to the Philosophy of Art,* chap. 9 (1987), and the sensible statement in T. S. Eliot, "Goethe as the Sage," in Eliot, *On Poetry and Poets* 207, 222–226 (1957); also "The Social Function of Poetry," in id. at 15. Orwell, though himself a moralistic critic, made incisive criticisms of moralistic criticism. See "Benefit of Clergy: Some Notes on Salvador Dali," in *Collected Essays, Journalism and Letters of George Orwell,* note 1 above, vol. 3, at 156; "Politics vs. Literature: An Examination of *Gulliver's Travels,*" in id., vol. 4, at 205; "Lear, Tolstoy, and the Fool," in id., vol. 4, at 287. Speaking of the "reactionary" moderns such as Yeats, Eliot, and D. H. Lawrence, Calinescu remarks: "What strikes me when I see the reactionary pronouncements of these authors, besides their irrelevance to the artistic substance of their authors' work, is that they do not carry the weight (ineffable but recognizable) of true commitment," and he quotes Spender's remark that "often their politics only shows that they care less for politics than for literature." Matei Calinescu,

whether that content is banal; no more will it matter, ordinarily, whether it is immoral. The *Iliad* presents human and animal sacrifice, slavery, concubinage, treachery, and rape as usual, and usually ethical, practices; anti-Semitism is similarly depicted in *The Merchant of Venice* and indeed throughout Western literature from the Middle Ages to T. S. Eliot and Ezra Pound. But the reader, unless an anthropologist or a historian, will be no more interested in obsolete ethics in literature than in obsolete building materials, or obsolete military technology, in literature. Against Shelley's conception of the poet as the unacknowledged legislator of the world, I set Auden's "poetry makes nothing happen" (*In Memory of W. B. Yeats*). The reader's interest in a work of literature lies in aesthetic qualities that are severable from local, time-bound elements, including beliefs and prejudices that are outmoded or at least widely believed to be vicious or absurd. Otherwise these works would not survive into our day; they would no longer be literature. The irrelevance of the overt moral content of literature is thus another implication of the "test of time" theory of literature.

The didactic strain in literary criticism is increasingly assuming a political form. This is no surprise; the massive growth of the state has made our age one of politics. By the left we are told that "the ideology which saturates [Shakespeare's] texts, and their location in history, are the most interesting things about them," and by the right "that Jane Austen is a greater novelist than Proust or Joyce" and "T.S. Eliot's later, Christian poetry is much superior to his earlier."[48] I find the first statement bizarre, but I disagree with the second also, because I do not like the idea of letting politics shape my cultural life. It is true that neither statement attempts to truncate the literary canon for political reasons—we are not told to take *no* interest in the aesthetic dimensions of Shakespeare or in the Dionysian strain in literature (if, as I greatly doubt, that is the correct way to contrast Proust, Joyce, and early Eliot

---

"Literature and Politics," in *Interrelations of Literature*, note 5 above, at 123, 138–139. However, Ezra Pound and Louis-Ferdinand Céline are important exceptions. See Chace, note 46 above, at 225–232 (reprinting the transcript of one of Pound's radio addresses from Rome in World War II); Ian Noble, *Language and Narration in Céline's Writings: The Challenge of Disorder*, chap. 5 (1987).

[48] Jonathan Dollimore and Alan Sinfield, "History and Ideology: The Instance of *Henry V*," in *Alternative Shakespeares* 208, 227 (John Drakakis ed. 1985); Irving Kristol, "Reflections of a Neoconservative," 51 *Partisan Review* 856, 859 (1984). Kristol is quite right to identify Jane Austen with a literature of mature values. See Darrel Mansell, *The Novels of Jane Austen: An Interpretation* (1973), especially chap. 6. But such values are present in Proust, Joyce, and early Eliot, though only Austen is serenely Apollonian—and a distinguished moralist, besides. See Alasdair MacIntyre, *After Virtue: A Study in Moral Theory* 239–243 (2d ed.1984).

with Austen and late Eliot). But we are told to apply political criteria in evaluating literature; and to carry one's politics into the reading of literature, while to some extent inevitable, should not be encouraged. The literary should be a sphere apart. Conservatives in the classical liberal tradition—conservatives who believe in a minimal state—should be especially wary about embracing a test of political orthodoxy for literature. As we shall see in the next chapter, the proper role of government in regulating literature, art, and entertainment is a narrow one, and does not extend to the political, social, or ethical opinions expressed or implied in works of literature. The separation of literature and the state is menaced by the didactic strain in criticism, which, by assigning to literature the function of promoting sound moral (including political) values, associates literature with such public functions as the inculcation of civic virtue and thereby makes literature a potential subject for public regulation.

If the overt moral content of literature does not provide reliable guidance for judges, there is still the possibility that immersion in literature might make a person a better judge by enlarging his knowledge of the human condition, and by doing so might make him not only a wiser judge but maybe also a juster judge. In putting this suggestion on the table I am reflecting (not endorsing) an opinion widely held by educated people and well articulated in the following passage by the philosopher Hilary Putnam, commenting on Bentham's statement that there is no difference in value between poetry and the child's game of pushpin:

> We find it virtually impossible to imagine that someone who really appreciates poetry, someone who is capable of distinguishing real poetry from mere verse, capable of responding to great poetry, *should* prefer a childish game to arts which enrich our lives as poetry and music do. We *have* a reason for preferring poetry to pushpin, and that reason lies in the felt experience of great poetry, and of the after effects of great poetry—the enlargement of our repertoire of images and metaphors, and the integration of poetic images with mundane perceptions and attitudes that takes place when a poem has lived in us for a number of years. These experiences too are *prima facie* good—and not just good, but enobling [*sic*], to use an old fashioned word.[49]

Two separate ideas are merged. The first, which seems unquestionably correct, is that people steeped in literature tend to compare their day-to-day experiences with the literary counterparts of those experiences, to derive some of their expectations concerning other people's

---

[49] Putnam, note 26 above, at 155.

behavior from the behavior of characters in literature, and, in short, to view experience through literary lenses. I, for example, might be tempted to characterize a career spent working for a legal-aid or public defender's office in the following lines from *Easter 1916*: "Too long a sacrifice / Can make a stone of the heart." And sometimes, when my judicial colleagues and I become restive as a long-winded lawyer talks through our lunch hour, I think of the following lines from *The Rape of the Lock* (III.19–22):

> Mean while declining from the Noon of Day,
> The Sun obliquely shoots his burning Ray;
> The hungry Judges soon the Sentence sign,
> And Wretches hang that Jury-men may Dine.

Putnam's second idea, which seems dubious to me, is that the result of making the sorts of connections that come naturally to persons of literary bent is ennobling. As I said before, people who read literature do not appear to have higher ethical standards than people who do not. The remaining possibility, not directly addressed by Putnam, is that literature provides a surer source of knowledge about human nature, social interactions, and other background information important to judges than other sources of such knowledge, including reading in other fields, professional experiences, and contact with people. I doubt that. People to whom literature is important may prefer to obtain their knowledge of human nature from books rather than from living people, but whether books are superior to life as a source of such knowledge is an undemonstrated and not especially plausible proposition. In addition, there are many documentary sources of knowledge about life besides works of literature. I do not deny that literature has great social value, but merely question whether it is an essential source of either the psychological or the moral knowledge that judges need.

The benefits of literature for judges must be sought elsewhere than in the moral or information content of literature; specifically, they must be sought in the craft values displayed in works of literature, notably *impartiality*[50] (detachment, empathy, balance, perspective, a complex awareness of the possibility of other perspectives than the writer's own), *scrupulousness*, and *concreteness*. These values, which can be summarized in the term "aesthetic integrity," affect the moral as well as the aesthetic valuation of a work of literature.

---

[50] See James Boyd White, *Heracles' Bow: Essays on the Rhetoric and Poetics of the Law*, chap. 6 (1985); Gibson, note 27 above, at 925–930; cf. T. S. Eliot, "Andrew Marvell," in *Selected Prose of T. S. Eliot* 161, 170 (Frank Kermode ed. 1975).

If you read *The Merchant of Venice* without preconceptions (as if such a thing were really possible!) you can have no doubt that Shylock is a villain; likewise Satan in *Paradise Lost*.[51] And if you read the *Iliad* carefully you can have no doubt that you are meant to think it a fine thing that the Trojans are going to be slaughtered. But in all of these cases the poet has refused to load the dice by depriving the villains of their essential humanity (in the case of Satan, his "angelicity"). Forgoing the facile triumph, the poet makes the reader see the situation from the villain's point of view too, thereby internalizing the actor's adage that no man is a villain in his own eyes. To visualize a Jew as fully if wickedly human was something few Elizabethans could have done; Shakespeare's great contemporary, Christopher Marlowe, could not do it. To portray Satan as a heroic figure, Milton was bordering on blasphemy.[52] And the *Iliad* is the oldest surviving expression of awareness that foreigners who are your mortal enemies might nevertheless have the same feelings as you. What strikes the modern reader about these works is not the detritus of obsolete beliefs (as they may seem to him) but the writer's detached perspective on them. Shakespeare's depiction of women (notably of both Portias—in *The Merchant of Venice* and in *Julius Caesar*) is another case in point.

There is a lesson here for law. Trial lawyers have trouble developing empathy with their opponents or even their clients, and judges characteristically score short-lived rhetorical triumphs by suppressing the facts and law favorable to the losing side.[53] There is no better advice to a legal advocate than to empathize[54]—with the client (what would the client

---

[51] The contrary view has long been argued, of course. See, for example, William Empson, *Milton's God* (2d ed. 1981). The orthodox view has been forcefully restated in Jeffrey Burton Russell, *Mephistopheles: The Devil in the Modern World* 95–127 (1986).

[52] Notice how, in the following description of Satan (*Paradise Lost* I.594–598)—

> . . . As when the Sun new ris'n
> Looks through the Horizontal misty Air
> Shorn of his Beams, or from behind the Moon
> In dim Eclipse disastrous twilight sheds
> On half the Nations . . .

—the power, the glory, the gloom, and the diminution of Satan are all beautifully conveyed. See Cleanth Brooks, *A Shaping Joy: Studies in the Writer's Craft* 337–338 (1971). On the famous impartiality of Homer's representation of reality, see the classic treatment by Erich Auerbach, *Mimesis: The Representation of Reality in Western Literature*, chap. 1 (1957).

[53] This is Weisberg's essential criticism of Justice Rehnquist's opinion in *Paul v. Davis* (see note 29 above) and is also a point stressed both by Gibson (see note 27 above) and by White, *When Words Lose Their Meaning*, note 29 above, at 269–270.

[54] The relation between empathy and effective lawyering is noted in Greenblatt, note 37 above, at 65. A plea for greater empathy by judges is made in Lynne N. Henderson, "Legality and Empathy," 85 *Michigan Law Review* 1574 (1987).

say on his own behalf if he knew the content and methods of law?), with the client's adversary (what can he say in reply to my points?), and with the judge (what will appeal to him in my position, what will trouble him, and how can I limit my submission so that its acceptance would not require an unsettling change in doctrine or have untoward practical consequences?). The adversary system gives each disputant a chance to speak his part, and he can learn how to do so from the example of the great dramatists and other great writers of imaginative literature.

Here is an example of the judicial tendency toward one-sided, hyperbolic utterance against which I am speaking. The question in *Eisenstadt v. Baird* was whether a state could forbid the sale of contraceptives to unmarried persons. The Supreme Court had held earlier that the state could not forbid the sale of contraceptives to married persons, but now it refused to consider this a significant distinction: "The married couple is not an independent entity with a mind and heart of its own, but an association of two individuals each with a separate intellectual and emotional makeup. If the right of privacy means anything, it is the right of the *individual*, married or single, to be free from unwarranted governmental intrusion into matters so fundamentally affecting a person as the decision whether to bear or beget a child."[55]

The dice are loaded here. No one is likely to describe a married couple as "an independent entity with a mind and heart of its own," or to defend "unwarranted" government intrusion into the decision whether to have children. The Court is knocking down straw men, with the clumsy aid of italics. If it had stated the issue as whether a state is constitutionally obligated to allow the sale of goods that facilitate fornication and adultery by making these practices less costly, its refutations would not have sounded so convincing. The most remarkable assertion in the passage is that if the right of privacy means "anything," it means that unmarried people are entitled to buy contraceptives. This is to say that until 1972, when the Supreme Court decided the case (or maybe 1970, when the court of appeals rendered its decision, which the Supreme Court affirmed), there had been no right of privacy. One might have thought the right of privacy peripheral to, rather than centrally engaged by, the issue in *Eisenstadt*. Although stylistically gentler than the passage I quoted earlier from Brandeis's dissent in the wiretapping case, the passage from *Eisenstadt* comes across as more strident because its content is so hyperbolic.

[55] 405 U.S. 438, 453 (1972).

Although judges might learn rhetorical restraint from the example set by the great imaginative writers, there is a counter-lesson— Antony's funeral speech and its judicial counterpart, the dissent in *Lochner*, which gives short shrift to the arguments of the majority and the authorities marshaled by it. And consider the suppression of complexity in the *Ode to a Nightingale*. To heighten the contrast between the happy world of the nightingale and the miserable world of human suffering, Keats describes the latter as a place "where men sit and hear each other groan; / Where palsy shakes a few, sad, last gray hairs"—and on in this vein for several more lines. It is beautiful poetry, but it conveys a one-sided picture, bordering on the hysterical, of the human condition. So does the line "I fall upon the thorns of life! I bleed!" in Shelley's magnificent *Ode to the West Wind*, even after one recognizes the Christian allusion in "thorns." I confess to a preference for literature that expresses a realistic awareness (it need not be "realistic" literature) of the tensions and ironies of the human condition to literature that reflects an immature or incomplete conception of that condition.[56] Does this make me a "closet" moralist, restating as a literary taste the political-ethical strictures I offered in Chapter 3 on the Romantic movement?[57] I think not. The essential distinction is between the moral values and the craft values in literature. The tendency to lose perspective that is illustrated by the passages I quoted from Keats and Shelley is just that, a tendency; in the two great poems from which I quoted, the consequence is a minor blemish. Much poetry that is Romantic to its fingertips so far as its overt moral tenor is concerned, or "modernist" in a way that Irving Kristol deprecates, is free from that tendency—*A Slumber Did My Spirit Seal*, for example, or *Tamburlaine*, or *The Waste Land*, or *Ulysses*.

[56] For classic statements of this position see T. E. Hulme, "Romanticism and Classicism," in *Criticism: The Major Texts* 564 (Walter Jackson Bate ed., enlarged ed. 1970); T. S. Eliot, "The Metaphysical Poets," in *Selected Essays*, note 11 above, at 241; Ransom, note 47 above, at 219–220, 280–281; Robert Penn Warren, "Pure and Impure Poetry," in Warren, *Selected Essays* 3, 27 (1958); cf. Denis Donoghue, *The Ordinary Universe: Soundings in Modern Literature* (1968). For criticism see Terry Eagleton, *Literary Theory: An Introduction* 46–53 (1983). I of course am not suggesting that Antony's speech is flawed by being one-sided. He is just one character in a play, and it is the interplay among the different characters that gives the audience the full range of the work's implied values.

[57] Compare Ransom, note 47 above, who, after blasting Yvor Winters in chapter 3 for indulging in moralistic criticism, promptly turns around and denounces Shelley for having a shallow outlook. See id. at 249–250. Eliot was on both sides of this fence, too; and compare Wimsatt's brilliant defense of the Romantic nature lyric against New Critical attack, in *The Verbal Icon*, note 39 above, at 103–116, with his apparent endorsement of Eliot's criticisms of Shelley, in id. at 85, 99.

Thomas Edwards gives an interesting example of the Romantic tendency toward one-sidedness. He points out that when Shelley in *The Mask of Anarchy* urges the common people of England to "shake your chains to earth like dew" and promises that "tyrants would flee / Like a dream's dim imagery," he is inadvertently belittling the struggle for liberty by making the enemies of liberty appear insubstantial, negligible.[58] But I hasten to add that it would be equally one-sided to disregard the Romantic impulse—that sense of infinite human potential that is not only a permanent part of human nature but a source historically of much good as well as ill. Had it not been for the "aspiring minds" saluted in *Tamburlaine* there might have been no Renaissance, no scientific revolution, no Enlightenment—maybe little progress on any front. Yet in such scenes in *Tamburlaine* as the slaughter of the virgins on the walls of Damascus and Bajazeth's braining himself on the wall of his cage, we are shown the dark side of the Romantic vision in a way that eluded Shelley in *The Mask of Anarchy*.

Although finding ethical content between the lines of poetry is a controversial undertaking today, and the criticisms that the New Critics offered of the Romantic vision fall largely on deaf ears, even people captivated by the methods of Romantic poetry at its most extreme might be horrified to discover those methods being used to compose judicial opinions. Is not the judicial process quintessentially Apollonian? Holmes's dissent in *Lochner* shows that one can achieve judicial greatness, as Shelley achieved poetic greatness, without doing full justice to the complexity of the phenomena under consideration. But it is an even rarer achievement in law than in literature; and if we do not have the gifts of Holmes we had best cultivate all the more carefully the literary traits that are within our reach.

I have spoken at length about the set of literary craft values that I have called impartiality. About scrupulousness—the search for the exact word and phrase—I shall be brief, and merely refer the reader to Ronald Gray's fine book on Kafka. In his opening chapter, contrasting Kafka with one of his imitators, Gray shows how Kafka's power derives in part from his refusal to strive for the sensational effects that his frequently fantastic subject matter seems to invite—from the sobriety, the restraint, and in short the integrity of Kafka's writing.[59] This quality

[58] See Thomas R. Edwards, *Imagination and Power: A Study of Poetry on Public Themes* 167 (1971).
[59] Ronald Gray, *Franz Kafka* 10–28 (1973). See also Joseph Strelka, "Kafkaesque Elements in Kafka's Novels and in Contemporary Narrative Prose," 21 *Comparative Literature Studies* 434–435 (1984).

is missing from many modern judicial opinions, which as we have seen traffic in exaggeration.

Concerning concreteness, let us look at the second stanza of *The Second Coming*, which begins:

> Surely some revelation is at hand;
> Surely the Second Coming is at hand.
> The Second Coming! Hardly are those words out
> When a vast image out of *Spiritus Mundi*
> Troubles my sight . . .

Don't worry about what all this might mean or what *Spiritus Mundi* is[60] or how these lines are going to modulate into the great closing lines of the poem. The word I want to direct attention to is "sight" in the fifth line. In recollection one is likely to think of it as "mind"; a vision is something in the mind. Only to a poet it is something one sees, because what one sees is real but what one imagines is often imaginary, and the poet wants to make the reader believe in the reality of the vision. It is a small touch, and there is of course an air of unreality in talking about the concreteness of a fantasy. It is, however, a characteristic literary touch, this use of visual or tactile imagery to drive home a point. Touches like these give literature its artifactual quality—a quality that Holmes's writings have (remember the fluttering cherubs, or the Fallopian tubes in *Buck v. Bell*) and that modern judicial opinions could use more of. The degree to which the euphemism has displaced the concrete word in judicial opinions, and, more generally, the degree to which judges shy away from concrete description, is remarkable. An able Supreme Court Justice who died recently may be remembered in no small part for having said of pornography that he could not define it but "I know it when I see it, and the motion picture involved in this case is not that."[61] The candor (in acknowledging the limits of legal reasoning) and bluntness of this statement make a refreshing contrast to the characteristic evasions of the modern judicial opinion. The statement had the effect of opening a window in a stuffy room. It did for the legal discussion of pornography what Orwell had done for the literary discussion of revolutionary violence (see note 44).

Illustrative of the modern judge's attitude toward concreteness is the first sentence in the statement of facts in *Cox Broadcasting Corp. v. Cohn*, a case which holds that the First Amendment forbids a state to allow the

---

[60] See Richard P. Blackmur, "Yeats: The Second Coming," in *Master Poems of the English Language* 847 (Oscar Williams ed. 1966).
[61] Jacobellis v. Ohio, 378 U.S. 184, 197 (1964) (Stewart, J., concurring).

family of a rape victim (killed by the rapists) to get damages for the invasion of privacy caused by broadcasting the victim's name. The sentence reads, "In August 1971, appellee's 17-year-old daughter was the victim of a rape and did not survive the incident."[62] The words "did not survive the incident" are an unconscious borrowing of the standard phraseology for describing a medical procedure in the course of which the patient dies: "X was operated on for a tumor but did not survive the operation." No normal person says, "X was shot, and did not survive the incident"; he says, "X was killed." The Court shied away from stating the blunt truth. It euphemized in order to smooth the way for the startling conclusion of the opinion, which is that the First Amendment immunizes from legal liability the public dissemination of the macabre and irrelevant detail of the victim's name.

The avoidance of the concrete is ubiquitous in legal prose. To a judge or legislator, a 14-year-old pregnant girl is a "minor pregnant woman," a 12-year-old murderer a "delinquent minor."[63] More than euphemizing is involved; the legal mind is insensitive to the imagery of language. This point is illustrated by the standard legal cliché for the abortion cases: "*Roe* and its progeny."[64] A person who writes such things is "not seeing a mental image of the objects he is naming."[65] A judge (or judge's law clerk) who is comfortable using the word "progeny" to describe the "descendants" of the case that legalized abortion is, in all likelihood, a person who thinks of abortion in abstract rather than concrete terms. There are obvious dangers if judges lose sight of the consequences of their decisions and fool themselves into thinking that they inhabit a purely conceptual realm.

## Economic Rhetoric in Law

In emphasizing the importance of an approach to judicial composition that shows an awareness of the texture and complexity of the human condition and of perspectives other than the writer's own, I may seem to be arming the critics of the application of economics to law, of whom

[62] 420 U.S. 469, 471 (1975). On the right of privacy see the brief discussion in the Introduction.
[63] Akron Center for Reproductive Health, Inc. v. City of Akron, 651 F.2d 1198, 1205 and n. 4 (6th Cir. 1981), affirmed in part and reversed in part, on other grounds, 462 U.S. 416 (1983); In re Hester, 3 Ohio App. 3d 458, 459, 446 N.E.2d 202, 204 (1982).
[64] For example, City of Akron v. Akron Center for Reproductive Health, Inc., 462 U.S. 416, 420 n. 1 (1983); Harris v. McRae, 448 U.S. 297, 312 (1980). The reference of course is to Roe v. Wade, note 20 above.
[65] "Politics and the English Language," in *Collected Essays, Journalism and Letters of George Orwell*, note 1 above, vol. 4, at 127, 134.

Robin West is but one. The focus of her criticism is the economic model of human behavior. Peter Teachout, in an admiring review of James Boyd White's book *When Words Lose Their Meaning*, argues that the language of economics, in its coldness, colorlessness, and striving for scientific precision, distorts human reality and smothers alternative perspectives. Teachout attacks the economic approach to law as "tak[ing] an inherited cultural rhetoric that to a certain extent is already ethically integrated and subject[ing] it to the disintegrative pressures of radical market theory."[66] He uses as an example an article I once wrote on *Bird v. Holbrook*,[67] a suit for damages brought by a young man who had been seriously wounded by a spring gun. The owner of a garden had experienced a theft of valuable tulips and expected the thief to come back for more. So he set a spring gun, and because he hoped to wound the thief on the latter's return to the garden, he posted no warning signs. The young man, however, was not a thief; he had entered the garden merely to rescue a peahen that had strayed into it. He sued the owner of the garden and won. Commenting on my statement that "the case involved two legitimate activities, raising tulips and keeping peahens, that happened to conflict,"[68] Teachout states, "In his utter preoccupation with the efficiency question—a preoccupation required by the deepest structures of the language he has chosen to employ—[Posner] virtually steps over the body of the seriously maimed young man."[69] There are two objections to this statement (besides the redundancy—maybe intended for rhetorical effect—of "seriously maimed"), although only the second concerns the use of economic analysis in judicial opinions as distinct from scholarly papers. The first objection is that respect for the division of labor implies that a scholar should be permitted a choice of approaches to his subject rather than being forced to use every possible approach. If, as applied to a particular problem in law, the economic approach falls short because it fails to take account of all relevant considerations, let those scholars who are knowledgeable about the omitted considerations bring them to the attention of the scholarly community by their own writings.

More important, the argument that an economic approach to tort law dulls sensitivity to human suffering is unsound both in general and with

[66] Peter Read Teachout, "Worlds beyond Theory: Toward the Expression of an Integrative Ethic for Self and Culture," 83 *Michigan Law Review 849, 881 (1985)*. See also James Boyd White, "Economics and Law: Two Cultures in Tension," 54 *Tennessee Law Review* 161 (1987).
[67] 4 Bing. 628, 130 Eng. Rep. 911 (C.P. 1828).
[68] "Killing or Wounding to Protect a Property Interest," 14 *Journal of Law and Economics* 201, 209 (1971).
[69] Teachout, note 66 above, at 882.

regard to the problem of spring guns. The article that Teachout criticizes approves the result in *Bird v. Holbrook*, rejects the old common-law rule that permitted the police to kill a fleeing felon, and warns against the danger of relying entirely on tort law to control the use of spring guns and other traps in preventing crime. Elsewhere economic analysts of law have advanced the proposition, which Teachout should find congenial, that in some circumstances the value of a human life is infinite.[70] Nothing in either the theory or the vocabulary of economics should blind an economist or economically minded lawyer to issues of life and death, which in fact bulk large in the economic analysis of law.[71] A work of economic analysis will not have the rich texture of a poem by Donne or a play by Shakespeare, but it is a fallacy to think that a mode of analysis that does not wear its emotions on its sleeve is therefore callous. Would Teachout think a medical paper insensitive or "disintegrative" if its author did not express sympathy for the people whose disease he was writing about?

I agree with Teachout (and with Orwell, Swift, Pope, Cicero, and many others before him) that language shapes thought, that choice of words can therefore have political and social consequences, that an impoverished vocabulary can impoverish thought.[72] But these insights should caution one not only against deforming reality to make it fit into a professional jargon, but also against launching political attacks on allegedly "insensitive" or "reductionist" modes of expression. As Margaret Radin acknowledges in what is otherwise a reprise of Teachout's attack on the description of human behavior in economic terms, if we abolish the line between speech and action by reconceiving speech as a form of action we open the door to censorship.[73] For example, the attempt by some feminists to coerce the adoption of a "gender-neutral" vocabulary is an attempt at censorship defended by reference to the effect of language in shaping thought.

The lesson to be drawn from the study of the effect of language on thought and therefore on action is the desirability of enriching the resources of human communication—not of rejecting whole classes of discourse because they allegedly are callous or incomplete. The political objection to "Newspeak" (Orwell's parody of Basic English, in *1984*) is

[70] See Posner, note 21 above, at 182, 184–185, 204.
[71] See id. at 182–185 (damages in wrongful-death cases), 210–211 (murder), 221–222 (reckless driving), 344–345 (regulation of safety and health).
[72] See Posner, note 13 above, at 44–47.
[73] See Margaret Jane Radin, "Market-Inalienability," 100 *Harvard Law Review* 1849, 1882–1887 (1987).

not that it is false and reductive, and thereby distorts and constricts thought, but that it is the only language that the rulers of "Oceania" allow its people to use.

In supposing that the language of economics is a kind of Newspeak, Teachout reveals a misunderstanding of the nature of a scientific vocabulary, such as that of economics. The aim of such a vocabulary is not to conceal unpleasant realities but to achieve analytical precision. It is a mistake to confuse these two things, and to suppose, for example, that the reason that mathematicians talk about numbers rather than things is to conceal the social or political consequences of mathematical theorizing. The distinctive language of economics consists of precise definitions that enable economic phenomena to be modeled in mathematically exact terms. The layman's "cost" is too vague for this purpose; the economist's "opportunity cost," "long-run marginal cost," and "average total cost" are precise. The bureaucratic impersonality of legal prose, as illustrated by the *Cohn* case, may give an impression of precision to the unschooled, but the real purpose is to obfuscate and euphemize, a goal foreign to economic and other scientific discourse. Conceptualizing does involve abstraction from the world of tangible, observed objects. (Mathematics makes this transparent: its subject is numbers—abstract identities—not things.) The economic concept of "marginal cost," for example, is not an entry on any company's books of account; it is something economists have invented to improve their understanding of human behavior. The purpose of abstraction, however, is not to avoid confronting reality but to frame scientific hypotheses and identify underlying regularities, all in the hope of learning more about reality and maybe improving the human situation.

There is irony in denouncing the economic vocabulary as a flight from reality, when the economic approach to human behavior insists on just the sort of gritty realism that the New Criticism taxed some Romantic poetry with trying to evade. In its insistence on the centrality of self-interest (and hence of incentives) in motivating human action, in its insistence that everything has a cost—that there is no such thing as a free lunch—and in its consequent skepticism about Utopian projects, economics is revealed as a bastion of Enlightenment values. The absence of Romantic uplift is precisely what makes economics—the rejection of Romanticism in the sphere of government—so repugnant to the heirs of Romanticism.[74]

---

[74] The link between Romantic thought ("unconstrained vision") and economic thought ("constrained vision") is made explicit in Thomas Sowell, *A Conflict of Visions: Ideological Origins of Political Struggles* (1987).

I am speaking of economic theory, not of the writing of economics; but the words and (increasingly) the mathematical and statistical formulas in which that theory is expressed are designed to make the theory as perspicuous as possible. A principal value of expressing economic theories in mathematical models is to force the theorist to make all his assumptions explicit.[75]

It is true that by furnishing a scientific vocabulary and a conceptual scheme in which any social practice can be analyzed, economics facilitates thinking about the unthinkable. Newspeak shrinks the possible range of thought; economics expands it. But to object to a form of discourse because it broadens the intellectual horizons and brings dangerous ideas within range of the human mind is to invite the worst kind of censorship. Nevertheless, there is no doubt that one of the reasons for the hostility of many law professors, philosophers, and other humanists to economics is that it provides an intellectual framework for assessing the efficiency of repulsive practices, such as torture and slavery.[76] And it invites such deflating observations as that "slavery" is merely the name given to those forms of involuntary servitude whose costs exceed their benefits. Conscription, employment compelled by threat of monetary sanction for breach of contract, and school attendance pursuant to compulsory school laws are examples of involuntary servitude that we do not call slavery; and maybe this is because their benefits are thought to exceed their costs.

A frequently expressed concern is that if every social practice were tested by the exclusive criterion of efficiency, some monstrous practices might pass; that we need stronger bulwarks against them than efficiency can provide, even if it is true that most of the abhorred practices are inefficient—and maybe that is ultimately why they are abhorred. I have discussed this issue elsewhere[77] and will content myself here with

---

[75] Of course much of the actual writing done by economists is very bad, but that is true of every profession, notably law, as we have seen. See Donald N. McCloskey, *The Writing of Economics* (1987). For examples of sparkling prose by distinguished economists, pick up any book or article by Milton Friedman, Robert Solow, or George Stigler.

[76] See Robert William Fogel and Stanley L. Engerman, *Time on the Cross: The Economics of American Negro Slavery* (1974); Ronald Findlay, "Slavery, Incentives, and Manumission: A Theoretical Model," 83 *Journal of Political Economy* 923 (1975); Yoram Barzel, "An Economic Analysis of Slavery," 20 *Journal of Law and Economics* 87 (1977); David W. Galenson, "The Market Evaluation of Human Capital: The Case of Indentured Servitude," 89 *Journal of Political Economy* 446 (1981).

[77] See, for example, Posner, note 72 above, chaps. 3–4, and my "Wealth Maximization Revisited," 2 *Notre Dame Journal of Law, Ethics and Public Policy* 85 (1985), and "The Justice of Economics," 1987–1 *Economia delle Scelte Pubbliche* 15.

pointing out that judges in our system are not allowed to use efficiency as the exclusive criterion of law and justice. The Constitution rules many abhorrent social practices such as slavery and torture out of bounds; and however personally committed he may be to the economic approach to law and society, a judge is required by his oath of office and the informal rules of the judicial process to subordinate his personal values, often to those of his predecessors and always to those of the framers of (constitutional) statutes and of the Constitution, insofar as those values can be discerned through the interpretive process. There is a broad area in which judges can properly bring economics to bear on law, but they cannot make it the sole guide to their job; more important, the language of economics will not conceal from them what they are doing when they use economics to make or change the law.

Teachout did not invent the idea that literature is the last bulwark against the social-science perspective on law; he is faithfully reflecting White's view. But the view, at least as developed thus far, lacks bite; it is feeling rather than program. Although highly critical of discussing spring guns in economic terms, Teachout makes no suggestion for how better to discuss them; and if you read White's extensive writings about the relation of law to literature you will find much on literature but rather little on law[78] beyond exhortation to the judge and the lawyer to be more sensitive, candid, empathetic, imaginative, and humane. The reminder is timely, and in its emphasis on the need for the judge to be sensitive to alternative perspectives it anticipates one of the main points of the present chapter. But exactly what White envisages by law as a humanity is unclear. His recent effort to explain is pitched at so high a level of generality that I have trouble holding onto the thread of his discourse. I get little out of being told that "the language that the lawyer uses and remakes is a language of meaning in the fullest sense," or that the judicial opinion "might be far more accurately and richly understood if it were seen not as a bureaucratic expression of ends-means rationality [that is, in economic terms] but as a statement by an individual mind or a group of individual minds exercising their responsibility to decide a case as well as they can and to determine what it shall mean in the

[78] For example, in chapter 6 of *Heracles' Bow*, note 50 above, suggestively entitled "The Judicial Opinion and the Poem: Ways of Reading, Ways of Life," there is a fine discussion of literature; but of the thirteen texts referred to in the chapter only two are judicial opinions, and the discussion of them is perfunctory. White's discussion of the *Olmstead* case (see note 29 above) may mark the beginning of a new phase of his work, shifting the emphasis from literary to legal texts—or perhaps the return to an earlier phase, for his first venture in law and literature, *The Legal Imagination: Studies in the Nature of Legal Thought and Expression* (1973), gave much greater play to law than *When Words Lose Their Meaning* or *Heracles' Bow* does.

language of the culture."[79] The promise of the richer understanding (note the buried economic allusion!) has yet to be redeemed. In setting a richly textured, humane "linguisticality" in opposition to an arid scientism, White displays an affinity (I believe unconscious) with the German hermeneutical school, and like the members of that school he has difficulty getting beyond the manifesto stage and showing what difference it makes whether we agree with him or not.

Obviously White is unhappy with where he thinks economic analysis is leading the law, and this unhappiness is shared by many other legal scholars.[80] But to say that instead of guiding by the light of economics judges should "decide a case as well as they can" is to beg the question. White's dislike of theory[81] is not much of a theory. By what signs shall we recognize a judicial job well done? Maybe the best way to decide cases is to view judicial decisions as instruments for promoting social goals such as prosperity and equality. Although the law and literature movement can contribute to the understanding and improvement of judicial opinions by close attention to the style and craft of particular judges and particular opinions, broad appeals to the humane values in literature, a Manichaean conception of the relationship between the humanities and the social sciences, and a blanket rejection of all theories are unlikely to be productive.

If White is too hard on the language of "ends-means rationality," he is, perhaps, too soft on traditional legal rhetoric. This can be seen in his interesting essay on Plato's dialogue *Gorgias*.[82] Like Aristophanes' play *Clouds*, *Gorgias* is about the rhetoric used by litigants (and their advocates—the forerunners of the modern litigator) in the extraordinarily litigious society of ancient Athens.[83] Plato, acutely conscious of the amoral character of persuasive speech, was exceedingly critical of this rhetoric, but White tries to defend the lawyers from Plato's criticisms:

> The task of the lawyer is not simply to persuade, using whatever cultural devices lie at hand, but to persuade a judge or jury that one result or another is the best way to act in the cultural situation defined by these facts or this evidence and by this set of statutes and opinions and understandings . . .

[79] White, note 50 above, at 36, 41. See also White, note 66 above.
[80] See, for example, Joseph Vining, *The Authoritative and the Authoritarian* (1986), a book written by a colleague of White's.
[81] See "Judicial Criticism," note 29 above, at 843–845.
[82] See James Boyd White, "The Ethics of Argument: Plato's *Gorgias* and the Modern Lawyer," 50 *University of Chicago Law Review* 849 (1983), which appears in abridged form as chapter 4 of *When Words Lose Their Meaning*.
[83] See Robert J. Bonner, *Lawyers and Litigants in Ancient Athens: The Genesis of the Legal Profession* (1927), especially chaps. 8–10; Kennedy, note 6 above, at 126–152.

> [The lawyer] speaks to the judge or jury not as they are defined by their individual interests, passions, and biases but as they are defined by their role, which is to do justice.[84]

The forensic orators whom Plato attacked were addressing a "tribunal" (a jury, often of hundreds) not much, if at all, superior in understanding and emotions to the Roman mob in *Julius Caesar*; the audience for a modern oral argument or judicial opinion is more reflective. But so ill-defined a concept is "justice" that much room is left for appeals to "individual interests, passions, and biases," especially, of course, in jury trials; thus modern legal rhetoric is emotive too. White overlooks, as we saw, the emotive element in Brandeis's judicial prose, and he has not told us what he thinks of the dissent in *Lochner*. His suggestion that conventional legal rhetoric is a more rational mode of discourse than the language and concepts of economics is not highly plausible, remains to be demonstrated, and may well rest on an idealized conception of legal rhetoric. The strength of White's approach may have little to do with its power, if any, to change our understanding of law. It may have everything to do with the potential of literary sensitivity to make legal advocacy more persuasive, well demonstrated by White's attempt to find a new metaphor with which to defend affirmative action.[85]

---

[84] *When Words Lose Their Meaning*, note 29 above, at 270. For a fuller discussion see White, "The Ethics of Argument," note 82 above, at 871–895. For a contrary view see Anthony T. Kronman, "Foreword: Legal Scholarship and Moral Education," 90 *Yale Law Journal* 955, 959 (1981). To give a more balanced picture of White's contributions, let me mention here his very interesting analysis of the lawyerlike rhetoric employed by the characters in Sophocles' play *Philoctetes*. See White, note 50 above, chap. 2, discussed in Richard H. Weisberg, "Law and Rhetoric," 85 *Michigan Law Review* 920 (1987), especially pp. 923–928.

[85] See text at note 38 above.

# part iii

# The Regulation of Literature by Law

# SEVEN

## Defamation, Obscenity, and Copyright

*T*HE LEGAL regulation of literature has a long and fascinating history. Mainly it is a history of censorship—the political expression of the moralistic tradition in criticism. I shall glance at that history, but my main focus will be on three problems in the contemporary American regulation of literature. The first is the portrayal in fiction of living persons, who may be able to obtain damages from author or publisher for defamation or invasion of privacy. The second is the use in literature of obscene language or subject matter, which can make author or publisher criminally liable or result in the destruction of the work.[1] The third is the copying of other authors' works, which can violate copyright law and result in a damage award, an injunction, or even a criminal sanction against the copier. The question I shall examine is whether the study of literature can improve the law's performance in any of these areas.[2]

The areas can be connected through the concept of "externalities." A cost or benefit is said to be external if it is not taken into account by the person (or enterprise) imposing it when deciding whether or how extensively to engage in an activity. The result will be too much of the

[1] Governments frequently suppress literature as seditious or immoral even though not obscene. See, for example, Elizabeth Turner, "The Artist in the Amphitheatre," 43 *Law and Contemporary Problems* 308 (spring 1979). And public libraries in this country sometimes refuse to buy books to which members of the school board, or influential individuals or groups in the community, object (not necessarily on grounds of obscenity). See, for example, Robert M. O'Neil, *Classrooms in the Crossfire: The Rights and Interests of Students, Parents, Teachers, Administrators, Librarians, and the Community* (1981). There is also much private censorship by editors and publishers unrelated to concerns with obscenity. Incidentally, I ignore pictorial obscenity, even though literature sometimes has a pictorial component: witness William Blake.
[2] I have found only four articles in which the study of literature is used to gain a purchase on any of these issues. See Richard H. Weisberg, "Costs, Contexts, Reader Response and the

activity from a social standpoint if it creates an external cost, too little if it creates an external benefit. For in the first case the activity will be cheaper to the actor than to society as a whole, while in the second it will be more costly to the former because he is not receiving all its benefits. Pollution and charity illustrate external costs and external benefits, respectively—charity because one person's donation will benefit everybody who wants that charity to prosper.[3]

An important function of law is to internalize costs and benefits. Laws against pollution illustrate this function on the cost side, and the charitable exemption from income taxation illustrates it on the benefit side (by making it cheaper to give to charity, the exemption lowers the cost of producing an external benefit). The laws examined in this chapter can be viewed in similar terms. Defamation and obscenity laws illustrate the law's effort to internalize the external costs imposed by literature, copyright the law's effort to internalize the external benefits created by literature.

## Defamation by Fiction

The main application of the law of defamation to the printed word concerns reportage, in newspapers, books, or magazines, that makes statements about a living person which are intended to be believed yet are false. Such statements tend to harm the person named by injuring his reputation and consequently making other persons less willing to transact with him, whether personally or commercially or both. The harm imposes a social as distinct from a merely private cost when the statement is false. A true statement about a person's character or

---

Absolute Protection of Fiction from Libel Suits: Reputation Neutral Contexts and Defamation by Fiction" (Cardozo Law School, mimeo., 1987); Comment, " 'Clear and Convincing' Libel: Fiction and the Law of Defamation," 92 *Yale Law Journal* 520 (1983); Vivian Deborah Wilson, "The Law of Libel and the Art of Fiction," 44 *Law and Contemporary Problems* 27 (autumn 1981); Rochelle Cooper Dreyfuss, "The Creative Employee and the Copyright Act of 1976," 54 *University of Chicago Law Review* 590 (1987). The first three articles deal with defamation by fiction, a topic that is the subject of a vast legal literature. Other examples of this literature include Marc A. Franklin and Robert Trager, "Literature and Libel," 4 *Comm/Ent* 205 (winter 1981–82); Frederick Schauer, "Liars, Novelists, and the Law of Defamation," 51 *Brooklyn Law Review* 233 (1985); Paul A. LeBel, "The Infliction of Harm through the Publication of Fiction: Fashioning a Theory of Liability," 51 id. at 281 (1985); Comment, "Defamation by Fiction," 42 *Maryland Law Review* 387 (1983); Isidore Silver, "Libel, the 'Higher Truths' of Art, and the First Amendment," 126 *University of Pennsylvania Law Review* 1065 (1978). A nineteenth-century antecedent to conceiving the legal regulation of literature as a distinct field of law is James Appleton Morgan, *The Law of Literature* (1875) (2 vols.).
[3] See my *Economic Analysis of Law* 62 (3d ed. 1986).

competence promotes the efficient functioning of the market in reputations; a false statement distorts that market, just as fraud distorts markets in goods and services.[4] The costs of such distortion are external because the author or publisher will not bear them unless forced to do so.

The importance of truth and falsity in the law of defamation makes the use of that law against producers of fiction problematic. If the work is indeed one of fiction and is so represented to its readers, it is not intended to be believed; but, by the same token, if it is believed there can be no defense of truth.

Although the dilemma is real, this formulation of it is infected by the fallacy stressed throughout this book of imposing arbitrary definitions on literature. A play, novel, or short story—to name the literary genres most likely to give rise to claims of defamation under modern law—cannot be put into a box labeled "fiction—not intended to be believed." Some works of "fiction" are didactic (think of Swift, Orwell, and C. S. Lewis) and convey a meaning—political, religious, or ethical—that the author desperately wants the reader to accept. Some are *romans à clef*—thinly disguised descriptions of real people and real events. Some add real persons to the *dramatis personae* to lend verisimilitude or for other reasons; one thinks of Napoleon in *War and Peace*, Martin Luther in *Michael Kohlhaas*, Booker T. Washington in *Ragtime*, and (one of the most curious examples) Machiavelli in Marlowe's *Jew of Malta*. Many use real persons with different names—often living persons, often unflatteringly characterized. Among many examples[5] is the portrayal of the Romantic poet Leigh Hunt in *Bleak House* under the name Harold Skimpole, that epitome of childish selfishness and irresponsibility who sponges off Mr. Jarndyce. Leigh Hunt's feelings were badly hurt by this portrayal, and Dickens wrote him a letter of apology.[6] Another example is Casaubon, the most riveting character in *Middlemarch*: a pathetic, dusty pedant, transparently modeled on a former patron of George Eliot, Dr. Brabant.[7] An example relevant to an earlier chapter in this book is the modeling of Polonius in *Hamlet* on Lord Burghley.[8]

---

[4] This view is elaborated in my book *The Economics of Justice*, pt. 3 (1981), and in William M. Landes and Richard A. Posner, *The Economic Structure of Tort Law* 163–166 (1987).

[5] See William Amos, *The Originals: Who's Really Who in Fiction* (1985); H. M. Paull, *Literary Ethics: A Study in the Growth of the Literary Conscience*, chap. 22 (1928); Thomas Mann, *The Story of a Novel: The Genesis of Doctor Faustus* (1961), especially pp. 87–88, 199, 216, 218; Randy F. Nelson, *The Almanac of American Letters* 181–204 (1981).

[6] See Paull, note 5 above, at 246–247; but cf. *Oxford Companion to English Literature* 485 (5th ed., Margaret Drabble ed. 1985).

[7] See Ruby V. Redinger, *George Eliot: The Emergent Self* 134–135, 470–471 (1975).

[8] See A. L. Rowse, *William Shakespeare: A Biography* 323 (1963).

Much fiction is heavily peopled by acquaintances and relatives, often thinly disguised, of the author; often the author's depiction of these people is unflattering, and sometimes it is in the poorest possible taste and deeply offensive. Much literature was originally written as nonfiction, and thus is "about" real people: such works as Boswell's *Life of Johnson*, Gibbon's *Decline and Fall*, much of Orwell's journalism. And how is one to classify Shakespeare's history plays or Roman plays, or for that matter *Macbeth*? Most of Shakespeare's plays are quasi-historical and are peopled with historical personages. Indeed, some works of literature *intend* to defame. Dante populated Hell with his personal enemies (with their proper names), albeit only those who had died before 1300, the date of the events depicted in the *Divine Comedy*. (The great, but damned, lovers, Paolo and Francesca, were real Florentines of those names.) Shakespeare relentlessly libeled the House of York in his history plays. Pope's *Dunciad* is an extended libel of his literary antagonists, Dryden's *Mac Flecknoe* a savage libel of Dryden's rival Shadwell. Joyce's *Ulysses* contains a fair amount of settling of scores, *Gulliver's Travels* more. Some of these works defamed persons already dead when the work was written; and the heirs of a defamed person cannot (with immaterial exceptions) sue for defamation. But others defamed living persons.

It is true that literature is a mode of expression that does not make truth claims[9]—that one of the adjustments we make in reading a work as literature rather than as history or sociology is to ignore issues of factuality, such as whether Shakespeare fairly portrayed Macbeth or Julius Caesar, or whether Kleist depicted Martin Luther accurately. But this observation does not negate the possibility of defamation by fiction. The same work may be read by some as literature and by others as something else—history, biography, journalism, or gossip. Or the author may, despite all his efforts, fail to create a pure work of literature, that is, a work that is read as making no truth claims whatever. (The publisher may have a lot to do with this.) Or a work destined to become literature may, when first created, be offered to the public—and accepted—as history or journalism rather than, or as well as, literature. So the problem of defamation by fiction is a real, though not necessarily a serious, problem; let us consider whether the law's efforts to prevent it are likely to inhibit literary enterprise unduly.

[9] See Stein Haugom Olsen, *The End of Literary Theory* 156–175 (1987), and references cited there; K. K. Ruthven, *Critical Assumptions*, chap. 11 (1979); cf. John R. Searle, *Expression and Meaning: Studies in the Theory of Speech Acts*, chap. 3 (1979).

THE GENERAL issue in a case of defamation by fiction (or what is not clearly distinct and need not be discussed separately, invasion of privacy by fiction)[10] is how to reconcile two competing interests: the interest of the members of the general public in not being falsely defamed; the interest of authors (and hence of their public) in being allowed both to work real people into their books and to make their fictional characters realistic. If an author does either of these things, a real person who resembles the fictional character may suffer a harm to reputation when readers confuse the two. The law's usual solution to such conflicts is to weigh the competing interests, either categorically by a system of rules or on a case-by-case basis, and give judgment to the injured party if his is the weightier interest. The difficulty with this approach in a case of defamation by fiction is that although harm to reputation can be measured, or at least approximated, by the methods of litigation, literary merit cannot be. Literary merit is determined by a process of survival that can take many years. By the time the process is complete (if it can ever be said to be complete), it will be too late to redress an injury to reputation if the defamatory work turns out to have little merit. Moreover, the issue is not the merit of the work *tout court* but its merit if revised to delete or modify the offending character so that the work ceases to defame the character's model in real life.

The testimony of literary critics can be solicited, of course; but the use of expert witnesses on matters of literary merit is likely to be an even sourer joke than in other areas where expert witnesses are used, such as antitrust law and medical malpractice.[11] Since there are no agreed-upon

---

[10] A writer or publisher may commit the tort of invasion of privacy by describing a person in a "false light" or by revealing intimate or embarrassing details of the person's life. See discussion of *Melvin v. Reid* in the Introduction; and Posner, note 4 above, at 254–266. On the law of defamation and invasion of privacy generally see Bruce W. Sanford, *Libel and Privacy: The Prevention and Defense of Litigation* (1985), and, for a briefer treatment, W. Page Keeton et al., *Prosser and Keeton on the Law of Torts*, chaps. 19–20 (5th ed. 1984). Sanford has a good brief discussion of defamation by fiction on pp. 50–56 and 470–473. See also the articles cited in note 2 above.

[11] See the analysis of expert testimony in the obscenity trials of *Tropic of Cancer* in Al Katz, "Free Discussion v. Final Decision: Moral and Artistic Controversy and the *Tropic of Cancer* Trials," 79 *Yale Law Journal* 209 (1969); the transcript of the expert witness's testimony in the obscenity trial of Allen Ginsberg's poem *Howl*, in J. W. Erlich, *The Lost Art of Cross-Examination* 151–169 (1970); and, above all, Frank Kermode, " 'Obscenity' and the 'Public Interest,' " 3 *New American Review* 229 (1968), a mordant description of a distinguished critic's experience as an expert witness in an obscenity case. The problem of expert witnesses' objectivity is both a general and an old one. Judges have long remarked the problem of expert witnesses who are "often the mere paid advocates or partisans of those who employ and pay

standards of literary merit, there is no difficulty in finding critics of equal plausibility and credentials to testify on opposite sides of a dispute over literary merit. And there is no way, even in principle, to decide which of the contending experts is right. Only time determines literary merit, and time is not a device that the legal system can use to decide cases.

A further complication is that it is not enough to know whether an equally or at least a nearly as good work could have been produced without libeling anyone; the burden of revision on the author must also be considered, and might outweigh the injury to the person libeled. If so, the work might be published without revision even if the author (or publisher) were liable for the consequences; the damages would be less than the cost of avoiding having to pay them. But by reducing the incomes of authors, liability in such cases might in the long run cause a reduction in the amount of literature produced. A possible solution to this problem, as we shall see, would be to confine liability to cases of intentional defamation.

There is yet another complication. The method that the Supreme Court, acting in the name of the First Amendment, has used to limit the liability of authors and publishers for defamation of public figures—namely, requiring proof that the author or publisher knew that the offensive characteristic that the work attributes to the public figure is false, or did not care whether it was false or not[12]—cannot be used in a case of defamation by fiction. First, the people defamed by a work of fiction are more likely to be private figures (the family and acquaintances of the author) than public figures. And with regard to private figures a lesser standard, requiring only proof of negligent falsehood, has been held constitutionally adequate.[13]

Second and more basic, the falsity of the ascription may be essential to the author's purposes. Authors of fiction aim at realism (broadly defined: even Kafka's fiction is realistic in the sense of being "about," in some substantial sense, real human problems—otherwise it would not be read) rather than descriptive accuracy, and a character may be more

---

them, as much so as the attorneys who conduct the suit. There is hardly anything, not palpably absurd on its face, that cannot now be proved by some so-called 'experts.'" Keegan v. Minneapolis and St. Louis R.R., 76 Minn. 90, 95, 78 N.W. 965, 966 (1899). For recent judicial commentary in the same vein see In re Air Crash Disaster at New Orleans, 795 F.2d 1230, 1233–1234 (5th Cir. 1986).

[12] See New York Times Co. v. Sullivan, 376 U.S. 254 (1964).

[13] See Gertz v. Robert Welch, Inc., 418 U.S. 323 (1974). On the distinction between public and private figures see Geoffrey R. Stone, Louis M. Seidman, Cass R. Sunstein, and Mark V. Tushnet, *Constitutional Law* 1076–1078 (1986).

realistic after being doctored up by the author than his real-life prototype was. Real people are confusing mixtures. Part of the appeal of literature is that, by taking liberties with "reality," it isolates aspects of human nature with greater clarity than is possible in the observation of real people. Consider the liberties that Shakespeare took in *Julius Caesar* and *Antony and Cleopatra* with the historical figures of Julius and Octavius Caesar, Brutus, Antony, and Cleopatra as they were depicted in Shakespeare's source, Thomas North's translation of Plutarch's *Lives*. Literature creates types rather than individuals; this is one of the reasons why Aristotle thought literature more instructive than history, and is one of the conditions of literary survival. The broader point is that theories of literary creativity and attitudes toward liability for defamation by fiction are linked. The Romantics taught us to value originality, but that is not the only and may not be the highest form of creativity in the arts. Shakespeare took many of his plots and characters from real, though not contemporary, life; for example, only one character in *Julius Caesar* (Lucius) does not appear in Plutarch's lives of Caesar or Brutus. If writers must spend time concealing the origins of, or whitewashing, their fictional characters, the cost in literary quality could be considerable.

Finally, many novelists say that real people are too complicated to be put into a novel without change—and anyway that no one knows anyone else well enough to effect a perfect transference from life to the written page.[14]

These considerations not only reinforce my earlier point that liability for defamation by fiction is apt to reduce the quality and increase the cost of producing literature, but may also seem to tell against the possibility that defamation by fiction could ever harm anyone's reputation. But the particular trait of a person that the writer attaches to a fictional character may so identify the person to those who know (or know of) him that readers will assume that the fictional character is he, and discrepancies between the fictional character and the real person will be ascribed to the novelist's having had to make changes for the sake of his art or having wanted to ward off a libel suit. Nevertheless, the likelihood of serious damage to reputation is less than in a work ostensibly factual and the danger of impeding literary creativity is, as we have seen, significant. A mundane but important consideration is that it is difficult for a publisher to do a "libel check" on a fictional manuscript

---

[14] See, for example, *Writers on Writing* 203–204 (Walter Allen ed. 1948); cf. E. M. Forster, *Aspects of the Novel*, chap. 3 (1927). The best biographers must come close, but novelists are not biographers.

submitted for publication. Since he is unlikely to know who the real people are from whom the fictional characters are drawn (or even whether the characters *are* based on real people), he will be unable to estimate the probability of defamation. And if, as is usually the case, the person libeled is a private figure, the publisher will be legally liable if deemed not to have used due care in checking the manuscript for potential defamation.

The distinction in constitutional law between public and private figures, to which I have just alluded, points to another reason why defamatory fiction is unlikely to cause great harm to the reputation of those who are defamed by it. A public figure—say, the President who finds himself a minor character in a spy novel, or the religious leader, movie star, or media mogul lampooned in a novel—usually has access to the media to rebut defamatory charges. A private figure does not, but unlike the public figure he can sometimes, perhaps often, protect himself in advance: if you do not want to be a character in someone's play, novel, or short story, do not marry or befriend an author. Almost by definition, a private figure is in little danger of being defamed by a writer whom he does not know personally. Lawyers will recognize the parallel to the tort doctrine of assumption of risk. The parallel is not exact: people do not always choose their intimates (they do not choose their parents, for example).

There are objections to abolishing liability for defamation by fiction. The first and least is that it would place fiction on a pedestal that it is not entitled to occupy; one might just as well propose that writers of fiction be exempted from the income tax. (Oddly, at this moment writers are in a tussle with the Internal Revenue Service over the proper tax treatment of their expenses.) This objection can be met by emphasizing how little harm defamation by fiction has ever been shown to do and how hard it is for publishers to prevent such defamation. These are reasons for abolishing or curtailing liability regardless of the social value of literature, especially when one considers how much legal services cost and how crowded the courts are. The second objection to abolition is that the line between fiction and nonfiction is arbitrary. Much great literature is not fictitious, and some fiction contains real people under their proper names. Should not real people portrayed under their real names have an action for defamation if they are libeled? Probably so; defamation that names names, whether or not in an otherwise fictional work, is both more harmful to the victim and easier for the publisher to prevent. Third, abolishing liability for defamation by fiction would encourage defamers to place a thin fictional gloss on their work—

enough to fool the law but not enough to fool the reader. Journalists would become novelists and short-story writers. To prevent the use of fiction as a shield for defamation the law would somehow have to distinguish thin from adequate glosses, as if it were appraising a paint job.

The fourth objection to abolishing liability for defamation by fiction is rather Utopian in character: if the legal system worked perfectly, the case for abolition would be greatly weakened. Persons not seriously harmed by such defamation would not recover substantial damages, and authors and publishers who could not have avoided the defamation at reasonable cost would not be found negligent, and so would escape liability altogether. Maybe, therefore, the focus of reform should be on improving procedures and remedies, for example by outlawing punitive damages in cases of defamation by fiction or refusing to award even compensatory damages unless the victim could prove an actual pecuniary loss.

How powerful are these objections? Powerful enough to persuade me that if liability for defamation by fiction were abolished, there would probably have to be an exception (*pace* Dante) for cases where the author named (and defamed) a real person and for cases where the author wanted to defame someone and, without naming him, used deliberate falsehoods to accomplish his purpose—that is, where the author attached to a character drawn from life a repugnant trait that he knew the real-life person on whom the character was modeled did not possess, and he did this intending readers to identify the fictional character with the real person and to infer that the latter possessed the trait. Maybe there should also be an exception for defamation by fiction published in a magazine or newspaper rather than in a book. For consider the reasons why the harm to reputation is likely to be less, on average, from defamation by fiction than from defamation by writings that invite literal belief. Many readers will not pierce even a thin fictional disguise; or they will think the coincidence between the real and fictional person accidental; or they will discount the defamatory aspects of the portrayal on the ground that after all the author is not an expert in truth-telling. These reasons have more force for books than for magazines, and not only because the book-reading public probably is, on average, somewhat more critical than the magazine-reading or newspaper-reading public. Since most magazines (and all newspapers) publish nonfiction as well as fiction, magazine or newspaper fiction that alluded to real people might be thought by many readers an extension of the publication's nonfiction section.[15] On the other hand, the great Victorian novels were first published as serials in magazines, and even today distinguished fiction is often published first in magazines, some not noted for good taste.

I HAVE left for last a theoretically interesting though inconclusive argument against liability for defamation by fiction, one based on the external benefits of literature. Much of the benefit in pleasure and instruction that literature confers cannot be captured by the author in royalties or other income. This is not because literature humanizes or ennobles (a doubtful proposition, as I noted in the last chapter), but because copyright protection is limited both in time and in scope. Literary genres such as the sonnet, the novel, and the tragedy, and literary techniques such as blank verse or the obtuse narrator or the *deus ex machina*, cannot be copyrighted; nor can most plots, characters, themes, or images. Even if there had been a copyright law in Shakespeare's time, Shakespeare could not have captured for his own (or his descendants') use and enjoyment more than a trivial fraction of the benefits that his literary output has conferred on society; nor could the playwrights and historians from whom he borrowed so liberally, and sometimes literally.

Of course only a minute fraction of the literary output of any age confers benefits above what the author can capture in royalties or other forms (including a variety of nonpecuniary satisfactions), and, as I have stressed throughout this book, we cannot know in advance which works they will be. But reflection on the cultural impoverishment that would ensue if we lost even a small part of what today is accounted great literature provides some reason for concluding that literature has produced benefits in excess of the pecuniary and nonpecuniary income of the authors who created it, and hence for wanting to lighten the legal liability of contemporary authors. The common law has long used the granting of immunity from tort liability as a method of encouraging the creation of external benefits.[16]

The argument concerning external benefits cannot be decisive, for a

---

[15] A variant of this problem is presented by the famous English case of Jones v. E. Hulton & Co., 2 K. B. 444 (1909), affirmed, A. C. 20 (H.L.) (1910). A newspaper published malicious gossip about "Artemus Jones," whom the publisher believed to be a fictitious character. There was a real Artemus Jones, though, and readers took him to be the subject of the column. He sued the publisher successfully for libel.

[16] For examples see Posner, note 3 above, at 175–176, 235–236, 642.

variety of reasons. One is its speculative premise. Another is the arbitrariness of singling out one source of external benefits—literature— for exceptional privilege. (I repeat my rhetorical question: why not just exempt authors from the income tax?) A third reason is that the Supreme Court, in implicit recognition of the external benefits of information (broadly defined), has already, in the name of the First Amendment, curtailed the common-law liability of authors and publishers for defamation and related torts. Maybe it has done enough to reduce the liability costs of authors and publishers.

## Obscenity, the First Amendment, and the Moralistic Tradition in Criticism

Although the suppression of obscene literature is an issue of great theoretical and historical interest, it may appear to have little practical significance in America today because so little nonpictorial obscenity is being prosecuted.[17] However, this appraisal may be shortsighted. First, the legal position could change (perhaps is changing). Obscenity is not deemed to be protected by the First Amendment, and the operative legal tests for obscenity are spongy and leave much to the vagaries of juries asked to evaluate expert testimony on literary merit, offensiveness, and other unmeasurables.[18] The judiciary is growing more conservative, though this may be a temporary trend. And the AIDS crisis, at this writing acute, may alter current mores concerning sex, including its literary depiction. The United States has more than a trace of its Puritan founding, and Comstockery could break out anew at any time, for, historically, censorship of the obscene has come in cycles (early Chris-

[17] It was not always so, of course. See Leo M. Alpert, "Judicial Censorship of Obscene Literature," 52 *Harvard Law Review* 40 (1938); Paul S. Boyer, *Purity in Print: The Vice-Society Movement and Book Censorship in America* (1968); Anne Lyon Haight, *Banned Books: Informal Notes on Some Books Banned for Various Reasons at Various Times and in Various Places* (3d ed. 1970); Harry Kalven, Jr., "The Metaphysics of the Law of Obscenity," 1960 *Supreme Court Review* 1 (Philip B. Kurland ed.); Felice Flanery Lewis, *Literature, Obscenity, and Law* (1976); William B. Lockhart and Robert C. McClure, "Literature, the Law of Obscenity, and the Constitution," 38 *Minnesota Law Review* 295 (1954); Richard Sieburth, "Poetry and Obscenity: Baudelaire and Swinburne," 36 *Comparative Literature* 343 (1984). For a compendious list of books that have been suppressed at various times and places in this country as immoral or obscene—not only the usual suspects but works by Tolstoy, Flaubert, Faulkner, and Mark Twain—see Nelson, note 5 above, at 140–144.

[18] A work is obscene in the eyes of the law if it is found both to be extremely offensive by community standards in its depiction of sexual activities and to lack serious social value. See Miller v. California, 413 U.S. 15, 24–26 (1973); Pinkus v. United States, 436 U.S. 293 (1978); Pope v. Illinois, 107 S. Ct. 1918 (1987); Robert E. Riggs, "*Miller v. California* Revisited: An Empirical Note," 1981 *Brigham Young University Law Review* 247.

tian, Puritan, Victorian). Second, prosecutions for obscenity are not the only method by which government censors literature. Public libraries, and especially the libraries of public schools, respond to community pressures in deciding what books to stock; this official though informal censorship shows no signs of abating. Third, the intellectual opposition to censorship has been weakened by the speech-is-action school, mentioned in the last chapter and reinforced by the feminist arguments for censorship, which I shall discuss shortly. Fourth, the methods of literary theory and literary criticism can be, have been, and are being applied to the visual media, another area where censorship continues unabated.

So there is ample practical reason to take up the issue of obscenity in a book on law and literature. Despite my fourth point, I shall limit my attention to literary obscenity, and within the category of literature to nonpictorial obscenity. Although drama is pictorial as well as literary (I once saw a performance of *Measure for Measure* in Stratford, England, in which Barnardine was nude), books and drama on the one hand, and movies and television on the other, differ in that the latter generally have a greater immediate emotional impact and their audiences generally are less well educated.

The legal suppression of obscenity in works of literature is an offshoot of the tradition of moralistic criticism. The obscene is a category of the immoral, and the task that moralistic critics from Plato to the present have set themselves is that of distinguishing moral from immoral literature.[19] Depending on how "literature" is defined, the task may be quixotic. "Immoral literature" is an oxymoron if the word "literature" is used to denote works that have been received into the canon of literature—that have passed the test of time; for as explained in the last chapter, the obsolete morality (or immorality) of such works will have ceased to move the reader. Moreover, only a minority of Americans (the best educated) continue to read literature after graduating from college, so that only a minority of a minority could conceivably be affected by obscene *literature*.

Granted, to defend literature against censorship on the grounds that literature is harmless or is little read nowadays is to wield a two-edged sword. If literature is marginal, the case for granting it constitutional protection may be little stronger than the case for not trying to suppress

[19] Of course the category of the immoral extends far beyond the obscene, to take in all sorts of blasphemous, violent, and politically obnoxious literature that is not offensive sexually. See note 1 above; and Donald Thomas, *A Long Time Burning: The History of Literary Censorship in England* (1969).

obscenity or immorality in it. For reasons explained in the last chapter, the proposition that works of literature are morally uplifting is unproved and not especially plausible—but of course it does not follow that literature has no social value. Apart from the pleasure and information that it conveys to the minority of Americans who read it for love rather than out of duty, literature continues to be an essential component of high-school and college education because of its effects in enlarging the student's imagination, expanding his cultural perspectives, and assisting him to read difficult texts and express complex thoughts. The widespread suppression of literature, in the name of morality, would be a national calamity.

In so arguing, I raise inescapably the question of a hierarchy of First Amendment values. It has sometimes been thought that discursive, especially political, expression is closer to the "core" of the First Amendment than artistic expression. Frederick Schauer puts the point bluntly: "Fiction is parasitic on nonfiction, if by nonfiction we mean simply telling the whole truth as accurately as possible."[20] He argues that if there were no concept of truth, there would be no benchmark against which to assess a work as fictional. This argument is unpersuasive. It locates the heart of imaginative literature in its departure from descriptive accuracy rather than in its use of the power of imagination to enrich the reader's understanding. Schauer's argument is also irrelevant to any practical issue in the regulation of speech and writing. If the issue were whether it would be worst to abolish all political expression, all scientific expression, all religious expression, or all literary and artistic expression, an argument could be made that we should sacrifice literary and other artistic expression first. But that is not the practical issue; the practical issue is whether a *particular* political, artistic, scientific, or religious work should be suppressed. And it is not at all clear that, evaluated at the margin in this way, literary expression is characteristically less valuable to society than political, scientific, or religious expression. I add that as literary criticism becomes increasingly politicized, the very possibility of distinguishing between political and artistic expression becomes increasingly problematic.[21]

[20] Schauer, note 2 above, at 266. The idea of a hierarchy of First Amendment values is defended in id. at 254–258.

[21] The politicization of literary studies is particularly evident in articles discussing pedagogy in English departments. See, for example, Daniel L. Zins, "Teaching English in a Nuclear Age," 47 *College English* 387 (1985); Jay L. Robinson, "Literacy in the Department of English," 47 *College English* 482 (1985); Kenneth Johnston, Book Review, 47 *College English* 407 (1985).

These points do not, however, resolve the question of whether to regulate obscenity in *contemporary* "literature"—the body of works that aspire to literary status and may fit in some crude way the recognized genres of literature (may, for example, be fictional), though most of these works will never achieve literary status and it is too early to say whether any will, or which ones. We cannot be confident that the moral content of these works is irrelevant, or even secondary, to the qualities for which they are being read. Still, the difficulty, in a relativistic age and a pluralistic society, of achieving a consensus on what is immoral expression, coupled with the untrustworthiness of those persons likely to seek appointment as public censors, the associated risk of destroying much literature in its incipience—not just by suppressing particular works but, more important, by inducing self-censorship by authors and publishers through threat of suppression—and the lack of convincing evidence that immoral works of fiction cause immoral conduct, argues compellingly against authorizing government to suppress nonpictorial writings of any kind on grounds of immorality. Moreover, a desire to forbid adults to read immoral works of literature reflects—in the absence of any persuasive reason to believe that such works cause harm to others besides the readers themselves—a paternalistic rather than a cost-internalization perspective, and is thus in tension with the tenets of classical liberalism, which are still influential. An adult reader can protect himself from being corrupted by literature simply by not buying; self-protection would be harder if the danger came from air or water pollution. The reply that the danger of corruption is insidious—undiscoverable until too late—is condescending and, given the level of education and information in our society, implausible.

Public schools and public libraries must decide which books to buy and keep, and they are responsive, as I have said, to complaints about immoral literature. Should they be? This is a legal question because the First Amendment has been held (by interpretation of the Fourteenth Amendment) to apply to actions by state and local government, as well as by the federal government, that infringe freedom of speech and of the press. The study of literature may help to answer the question. A work that is securely a part of the canon (a work by Rabelais, Dickens, or Shakespeare, for example) is, for reasons explained already, unlikely to have immoral effects on mature readers. Nor is there much reason for fearing the impact of such works on young children—who cannot understand them—or on immature adult readers, few of whom have any interest in the classics. The modern audience for the classics is limited essentially to two groups: a small subset of the highly educated, interested in literature as literature and therefore (if I am correct in my analysis of literary survival) unmoved by the obsolete beliefs found in many works of literature; and students in high school and college, who read literature under the guidance of their teachers and who in any event are likely to be immunized from any immoral effects of literature by cultural distance from author and work.

Moreover, an obscene work is merely one that is sexually graphic beyond the limits deemed tolerable by society, and so wide are those limits today that very little, perhaps no, canonical literature exceeds them; the closest to doing so may be Aristophanes' *Lysistrata* and the novels of Henry Miller. Remember that literature, as I am using the word, is by definition work composed in the past, often the remote past. The barriers of time and culture do not prevent us (or all of us) from enjoying literature, but they greatly diminish whatever aphrodisiacal quality it may once have had. Moreover, we live in one of the most licentious cultures in the history of the world, so we are hard to shock by the works of the past, composed in more inhibited times. However, since sexually graphic literature may upset children and embarrass their teachers, public schools and public libraries should not be required to make it accessible to children.

As with defamation by fiction, so with obscene literature, the idea of balancing the harms of the obscene against literary merit is fatuous because literary merit cannot be measured but must be allowed to emerge through a competitive process that can take decades or even centuries to do its work. Efforts to define the obscene through defining literature in a particular way are also misguided, and for related reasons. The usual approach taken by opponents of the obscene is to define obscenity as material intended to arouse sexually, in contrast to literature, which is intended to induce a more reflective response.[22] There are three flaws in this approach. First, the obscene includes material intended to disgust rather than to arouse, and some literature was written with the intention, or an intention, of disgusting its readers; Céline's *Voyage to the End of the Night* and Miller's *Tropics* novels may be examples. Second, literature is intended to excite the emotions, and sometimes they are sexual ones. Third and most important, the effect of a work of literature on the reader may be different from the intention

[22] See, for example, Frederick Schauer, "Speech and 'Speech'—Obscenity and 'Obscenity': An Exercise in the Interpretation of Constitutional Language," 67 *Georgetown Law Journal* 899 (1979). On obscenity in general see Walter Kendrick, *The Secret Museum: Pornography in Modern Culture* (1987); David Foxon, *Libertine Literature in England 1660–1745* (1964).

with which it was written, "literature" being the body of texts that are read outside of their original context.

Moreover, merely establishing a category of the obscene and disgusting, if that is possible to do, does not make the case for suppression. Again there is the objection that such suppression is paternalistic—which is fine if we are dealing with children, but problematic otherwise. The evidence that *nonpictorial* obscene literature has external effects, as by inciting its readers to commit sex crimes, is nil.

A group of radical feminists, opportunistically supported by social and religious conservatives, invites us to consider the obscene less as a matter of excessive frankness in the portrayal of sex than as a point of view harmful to women, and to suppress as obscene some works that would not flunk the *Miller* test of obscenity.[23] This movement defines the obscene as sexually explicit material that depicts women as enjoying rape or mutilation or, in general, forcible submission to men. The danger to literary values comes from the fact that much of the world's great literature, though not sexually explicit by modern American standards, portrays with approval the subordination, often by force, of women to men (though this is not the same thing as depicting women enjoying that subordination—the particular concern of the feminist opponents of pornography). A notable example is the treatment of Briseis and Chryseis in the *Iliad*. The Bible contains many instances of what by contemporary standards is misogyny; so do *Paradise Lost* and *The Taming of the Shrew*, not to mention *Eumenides*—the list is endless. Because literature is by definition the writing that survives a protracted competitive process, most literature is old and much of it therefore reflects, and some of it approves, values that modern readers find offensive—such as anti-Semitism or belief in the racial inferiority of blacks or in the natural subordination of women. Maybe the values in some works of literature will become so repulsive that the works themselves disappear from the body of literature. But this process

[23] See note 18 above. The feminist attack on pornography is sketched in K. K. Ruthven, *Feminist Literary Studies: An Introduction* 87–90 (1984). For fuller statements see Andrea Dworkin, *Pornography: Men Possessing Women* (1981); Andrea Dworkin, "Against The Male Flood: Censorship, Pornography, and Equality," 8 *Harvard Women's Law Journal* 1 (1985); Catharine A. MacKinnon, *Feminism Unmodified: Discourses on Life and Law*, pt. 3 (1987); *Take Back the Night: Women on Pornography* (Laura Lederer ed. 1980). For the law's (as yet negative) response see American Booksellers Association, Inc. v. Hudnut, 771 F.2d 323 (7th Cir. 1985), affirmed without opinion, 475 U.S. 1001 (1986); Eric Hoffman, "Feminism, Pornography, and Law," 133 *University of Pennsylvania Law Review* 497 (1985); Stone et al., note 12 above, at 1136–1141. And for a cautionary note sounded by a feminist see Robin West, "The Feminist-Conservative Anti-Pornography Alliance and the 1986 Attorney General's Commission on Pornography Report," 1987 *American Bar Foundation Research Journal* 681.

should be left to the competition of the literary marketplace rather than hurried along by politicians, prosecutors, judges, and jurors. And in that competition it is more likely that the values will become even more irrelevant (if that is possible) to the reasons why these works continue to be read than that the works themselves will disappear.

A feminist might reply that as long as the only works suppressed are sexually graphic, the threat to literature is small, for how much literature is sexually graphic? The problem with this reply is twofold. First, we shall see in a moment that the requirement that works be sexually graphic before they may be suppressed is not organic to the feminist case against pornography. Second, the "sexually graphic" is a culturally relative and ever-shifting category, like poverty. "Male chauvinist" authors of works that were sexually graphic in their times include Aristophanes, Boccaccio, Rabelais, and D. H. Lawrence. *Ulysses* was sexually graphic by the standards of its time, and so, remarkably, was Synge's *The Playboy of the Western World* (1907) because it used the word "shift" to describe a woman's slip.[24] Some works that are sexually graphic by today's standards may someday be recognized as great literature—unless their creation is deterred by a broad definition of pornography. Conversely, standards may become more conservative, in which event literature that is not sexually graphic by today's liberal standards may come to be thought so, and may therefore be suppressed if the principle is accepted that sexually graphic literature which presents women in a demeaning light can be suppressed on that account.

The trade-offs would be complex if the evidence for the external effects of sexually graphic literature that portrays women in positions of subordination to men were more persuasive than it is. But so far the main evidence consists of reasonably well documented reports of coercion and sexual abuse of pornographic models and actresses—but this evidence has no relevance to nonpictorial pornography—and of laboratory studies finding that violent pornography (again, pictorial) can arouse aggressive feelings toward women in male college students.[25]

[24] See Hugh Kenner, *A Colder Eye: The Modern Irish Writers* 37–38 (1983). On trends in the presentation of sex in literature see Charles I. Glicksberg, *The Sexual Revolution in Modern American Literature* (1971); Charles I. Glicksberg, *The Sexual Revolution in Modern English Literature* (1973).

[25] See Note, "Violent Pornography and the Obscenity Doctrine: The Road Not Taken," 75 *Georgetown Law Journal* 1475, 1490–1492 (1987), for a brief summary of the evidence; for much fuller summaries see Edward Donnerstein, Daniel Linz, and Steven Penrod, *The Question of Pornography: Research Findings and Policy Implications* (1987); Attorney General's Commission on Pornography, *Final Report* 901–1033 (1986). Some members of the Attorney General's Commission thought there should be no governmental suppression of purely verbal obscenity.

The absence of evidence that nonpictorial pornography causes sex crimes is not decisive, since one of the feminist concerns is with the tendency of pornographic materials to foster sexual stereotypes. One person's stereotype, however, is another's truth; and if the real objection to pornography is that it induces false or pernicious beliefs (which can of course have consequences in action), then the sexually graphic angle is a red herring and we are in the presence of a massive and deeply problematic challenge to the liberal tradition of freedom of speech and of the press. Since that challenge is the logical terminus of the speech-is-action school of thought, examined briefly at the end of the preceding chapter, it casts a retrospective doubt over the program of that school.

To make my concern about the implications for literature of the feminist attack on pornography more concrete, I quote in its entirety one of Yeats's masterpieces, *Leda and the Swan*:

> A sudden blow: the great wings beating still
> Above the staggering girl, her thighs caressed
> By the dark webs, her nape caught in his bill,
> He holds her helpless breast upon his breast.
>
> How can those terrified vague fingers push
> The feathered glory from her loosening thighs?
> And how can body, laid in that white rush,
> But feel the strange heart beating where it lies?
>
> A shudder in the loins engenders there
> The broken wall, the burning roof and tower
> And Agamemnon dead.
>
>                         Being so caught up,
> So mastered by the brute blood of the air,
> Did she put on his knowledge with his power
> Before the indifferent beak could let her drop?

This is pretty graphic; and it presents rape (albeit by Zeus) in rather a favorable light. (It also invites interpretation as a blasphemous parody of the Annunciation, and thus as a companion piece to the blasphemous Nativity in *The Second Coming*.) I doubt that any feminist would want the government to suppress this great poem; but the challenge to

---

See id. at 381–385. As far as I can tell, none of the pornographic works on which the Commission based its finding that pornography may cause crime was purely verbal, the vast majority being movies.

feminist jurisprudence is to furnish a principled, reasonably definite, and readily applicable standard for deciding when literature that is not obscene in the modern legal sense may be suppressed because of its antisocial, and specifically its antifemale, tendencies.

I want to close my discussion of obscene literature with an example of censorship in action: the decision by a well-respected federal court of appeals in 1953 upholding an order to destroy copies of Henry Miller's novels *Tropic of Cancer* and *Tropic of Capricorn* under a federal statute forbidding the importation of obscene books.[26] In its prudery, incoherence, and absurdity, the opinion is a cautionary lesson for anyone who believes that nonpictorial obscenity should be suppressed. Miller's two novels are, in the court's view, a "sticky slime" of filth and degradation; however, the erotic episodes are not of that "stark ugliness [which] might repel many," but rather "lure on with the cleverness of scene, skilfulness of recital, and the use of worse than gutter words" (p. 145). (The words are not specified, no doubt because they are too awful to be published in the *Federal Reporter*, with its sensitive readership.) Continuing on this theme, the opinion elsewhere states: "Of course, language can be so nasty as to repel and of course to seduce as well" (pp. 146-147).

Although the novels are "heavily larded" with "disgraceful scenes" (p. 145), Miller's real offense seems to be his vocabulary, to which the opinion recurs again and again: "Dirty word description of the sweet and sublime, especially of the mystery of sex and procreation, is the ultimate of obscenity" (p. 146). Bawdy classical authors are enigmatically distinguished on grounds of cultural relativity; there are ominous suggestions that if Aristophanes, Chaucer, Boccaccio, and the authors of the Bible were writing today, they would be in deep trouble: "We are not well acquainted with Aristophanes or his times, but we know they were different from ours. We have chanced upon Chaucer and we know his times were different from ours. Boccaccio is lurid. The Bible is not free from the recounting of immoral practices. But the translators, from the languages in which The Bible was originally written, did not word-paint such practices in the lurid-Miller-morally-corrupt manner" (p. 146). Later the court seems to retract the suggestion that classical authors might be forgiven for having written in ruder times: "We risk the assertion that there is an underlying, perhaps universal, accord that there is a phase of respectable delicacy related to sex, and that those compositions which purposefully flaunt [*sic*] such delicacy in language

---

[26] Besig v. United States, 208 F.2d 142 (9th Cir. 1953).

generally regarded as indecent come under the ban of the statute" (p. 147).

In some places the court appears to be suggesting that certain aspects of human experience (for example, excretion) and even dirty words are out of bounds even to the moral artist, and in other places that if only Miller had depicted his sordid subject matter with remorse or disapproval, or lightened the erotic episodes with an occasional touch of "the grace of purity or goodness" (p. 145), he might have succeeded in avoiding the morally corrupt *manner* that marks the books as obscene; apparently the offense lies in the message, not just in the manner of expression. In some places the court appears to concede that Miller's novels have literary merit, though not enough to redeem them from the charge of obscenity; in other places to assert that their literary merit makes them more dangerous; in others to assert that their only literary merit lies in a kind of sleekness, itself pornographic, in the depiction of sex; in others to concede literary merit only to the nonerotic scenes, which however are not frequent enough to save the work; and in still others to suggest that a single offensive incident, no matter how integral to a work's literary structure, might condemn the work as obscene. Writers have only themselves to blame for censorship: "Congress has chosen to enact a censorship which would not have been possible except for the self-styled prophets of truth who offend so grievously" (p. 145). And we are invited to consider the prospect of elderly men incited by Henry Miller's novels to commit serious sex crimes: "Salacious print in the hands of adults, even in the hands of those whose sun is near the western horizon, may well incite to disgusting practices and to hideous crime" (p. 146).

It is easy to laugh at the court, but only because courts have gotten out of the business of censoring books on grounds of obscenity. They are being invited to get back in. May they resist the invitation.

## Copyright and Creativity

The classic example of an external benefit is agriculture in a society without property rights. If I sow a crop, but anyone can reap it, then I bear the cost and others will obtain the benefit. This pattern will create incentives to shift investment from agriculture to activities that do not require as much preparatory investment, such as hunting. It has long been thought that a similar problem would arise if authors had no property rights in what they wrote. Then anyone could copy their writings; the author would not be able to secure royalties; and the amount of writing would drop, maybe to zero, as authors reallocated their time to other pursuits.

The situation is more complex than this.[27] Copyright is relatively recent. The first copyright law in England, for example, dates only from 1710, and it was far narrower than modern copyright laws—for instance, translations from a foreign language were not considered to infringe the author's copyright. Yet almost as much of the world's great literature was written before 1710 as since (some would say more), though this conclusion owes much to how the literary canon is determined. Three reasons why literature could thrive before there were copyright laws come to mind. First and least, since the cost of writing has always been low—it is mainly the time cost to the author—authors can afford to do some writing even if they have little or no hope of royalties. This would not be true if writing were a full-time occupation, but most writers write only part-time even if they are well paid for writing. Second, many writers receive nonmonetary rewards from writing—fame, prestige, the hope of immortality, therapy, inner satisfaction. These rewards reduce the net cost of writing; and some of them, notably fame, can be translated into money. Third, until modern times the cost of copying was high—books were very expensive to make, relative to peoples' incomes. The higher the cost of a copy relative to the cost of the original, the smaller the advantage to the copier of not having borne all the costs of creating the original, in particular the cost of the author's royalty. Moreover, since cost is often inverse to time, if copying is very expensive it may take a long time to make copies economically, and the lag will give author and publisher time to make money from the sale of the book even without legal protection against copying. Fourth (and a point I will come back to), the absence of copyright protection reduces the cost of writing, by enabling an author to copy freely from his predecessors.

Even today, copyright protection is limited both in time—the

---

[27] For good introductions to the economics of copyright see Robert M. Hurt and Robert M. Schuchman, "The Economic Rationale of Copyright," 56 *American Economic Review Papers and Proceedings* 421 (May 1966); S. J. Liebowitz, "Copyright Law, Photocopying, and Price Discrimination," 8 *Research in Law and Economics* 181 (1986); Michael O'Hare, "Copyright: When Is Monopoly Efficient?" 4 *Journal of Policy Analysis and Management* 407 (1985); Arnold Plant, "The Economic Aspects of Copyright in Books," 1 *Economica* (n.s.) 167 (1934), and his "The New Commerce in Ideas and Intellectual Property" (University of London 1953). On the history of copyright law—which appears to have emerged first in fifteenth-century Venice—see Bruce W. Bugbee, *The Genesis of American Patent and Copyright Law*, chap. 2 (1967); Brander Matthews, *Books and Play-Books: Essays on Literature and the Drama*, chap. 1 (1895); Comment, "Copyright: History and Development," 28 *California Law Review* 620 (1940); and references in note 39 below.

author's lifetime plus fifty years—and in the aspects of the copied work that are protected. In general, only the exact verbal form is fully protected; a subsequent author is free to copy genre, technique, style, and even—to a significant though not unlimited extent—plot and characters.[28] Moreover (though this may be a corollary, as we shall see), if a subsequent author duplicates the first author's work by coincidence rather than by copying there is no infringement. Thus the property right in literary creativity that the copyright system creates is highly limited; that is why much of the social gain from such creativity is external to the author. The system also discriminates among types of literary work, and in principle could distort writers' choices among genres. A lyric poem, unless it employs a new meter (such as dactylic hexameter) or a new form (such as the sonnet), receives maximum protection under copyright law, because the verbal pattern is almost everything in poetry and it is verbal pattern that copyright law protects most securely. Novels and plays, in which plot and character often are more important than the specific words, receive only limited protection.

One might suppose that since the property right is incomplete, literature is being underproduced and therefore copyright protection should be expanded. But the matter is not so simple. Consider first the difficulty of distinguishing between copying and independent inspiration when one is dealing with structural resemblances, such as similar plots. Those works of literature that last do so in part because, as Samuel Johnson and before him Aristotle stressed, they depict general features of human nature and the human condition. It is not to be believed that if Homer had not lived no one would have written a poem about revenge, or about gods, or about a war over a beautiful woman. On the other hand, once the *Iliad* is in existence, it will be hard to determine whether subsequent authors of works on these themes are copying the *Iliad* or copying life. The analytic problem could be solved by extending protection to all original features of a work regardless of whether the infringer was copying (it might be a case of independent discovery). That is the approach used in patent law. It is not used in copyright law precisely because copyright protection is confined to the specific form of

[28] See Stephen Clark, "Of Mice, Men, and Supermen: The Copyrightability of Graphic and Literary Characters," 28 *St. Louis University Law Journal* 959 (1984); Michael V. P. Marks, "The Legal Rights of Fictional Characters," 25 *Copyright Law Symposium (ASCAP)* 35 (1980); Leslie A. Kurtz, "The Independent Legal Lives of Fictional Characters," 1986 *Wisconsin Law Review* 429, 451–467. On copyright law generally see Alan Latman, Robert Gorman, and Jane C. Ginsburg, *Copyright for the Eighties: Cases and Materials* (2d ed. 1985); William F. Patry, *Latman's The Copyright Law* (6th ed. 1986); Zechariah Chafee, Jr., "Reflections on the Law of Copyright I, II," 45 *Columbia Law Review* 503, 719 (1945).

the work, so that independent discovery is unlikely. This makes proof of copying easy in most cases, but only because copyright protection is narrowly defined. We are left with the question of whether that protection should be broader.

An objection to broad copyright protection that is of theoretical interest only is that it would have yielded windfalls to the earliest authors and their heirs. To have given Homer (putting aside the question of *his* predecessors) and his heirs the complete, perpetual stream of earnings generated by an invention that his genius may merely have accelerated—to have awarded copyright for absolutely fundamental literary discoveries bound to be made sooner or later, and probably sooner—might have overcompensated the discoverer. But this notion is vague; "overcompensation" implies a benchmark, and what is it? The objection is further weakened when we turn from the copying of broad literary themes to the copying of specific literary devices—the sonnet, or *terza rima*, or the obtuse narrator, or the specific revenge plot that Shakespeare in *Hamlet* borrowed from *The Spanish Tragedy* or perhaps from some earlier and now lost *Hamlet*, or the plot of the *Odyssey*, which James Joyce borrowed for his novel *Ulysses*. Most of these copyings would not be actionable even if the original were copyrighted, and even though the thing copied was not as basic as the theme of the *Iliad*. Finally, the handful of basic themes, basic methods, basic meters, and so forth has long since entered the public domain. New forms of literary originality are unlikely to exercise so commanding a sway over future writers as the discoveries (or inventions) of a Homer or a Milton.

A better argument against broad copyright in literature proceeds from the distinction that copyright lawyers make between "idea" and "expression"; only the latter is protected by copyright law. It may seem odd to deny legal protection to what at first blush must seem the more important form of originality, but the legal treatment makes sense once the nature of the "ideas" found in literature is understood. Most literature is written for a mass audience—regardless of the author's intentions. This proposition is inherent in the definition of literature employed in this book; even the most esoteric literature, to count as "literature" under the test of time, must accrue over time a substantial audience. To be able to do this a work must be relatively impervious to temporal and cultural change, which means it must deal with the elementary, the timeless, the recurrent problems of the human condition—with the commonplaces of life, with stock situations, stock characters, stock narratives. That is why paraphrasing literature tends to yield bromides and banalities. The "ideas" in literature are not like the ideas of science or philosophy; they are more like painters' subjects. Since the ideas are not the creative element, to recognize property rights in them would overreward the earliest writers and deplete the stock of literary raw material for later writers.

Literary technique—for instance, the sonnet form, the flashback, the beginning of a work *in medias res* (as in the *Iliad*, the *Odyssey*, or *Oedipus Tyrannus*), stream of consciousness, the realistic depiction of sex—is intermediate between idea and expression. It involves genuine creativity; but to give the creator a property right could shut out subsequent writers, or at least burden them excessively, by requiring them, before beginning work, to negotiate for a license from an earlier writer or the writer's heir. The implicit social judgment in denying copyright protection to techniques is that the benefits from such protection in encouraging the creation of new (and often, when introduced, controversial and unremunerative) literary techniques would be offset by the burden to subsequent writers. But again this point has more force when we imagine broad copyright protection as having been in effect in the early days of literature than when we imagine it being in effect today, when the scope for originality is limited by the existing and by now extensive repertoire of themes and techniques, reflecting almost three millennia of literary development.

Another argument against broad copyright protection is the costs of enforcement. All property rights are costly to enforce and copyrights particularly so, because the infringed and infringing works lack the ready observability of conflicting uses of tangible propery. You can more easily see the trespasser standing on your land than you can spot and prove a plagiarism.

Still another cost of a broad copyright law stems from what economists call "rent seeking."[29] This term refers to the incentive to overproduce goods that promise a return greater than the cost of production (that is, an economic "rent"), and to the resulting waste when rents are transformed, through competition to obtain them, into costs. Suppose that the cost of creating a new genre, meter, style, plot, or character type were very low yet whoever was first to create it would, by virtue of copyright law, have a monopoly of exploiting it. There would be a tremendous race to be first, and the costs consumed in the race might exceed the social benefits of accelerated production. Literary creativity does not require as heavy an investment in training, equipment, and testing as technological creativity—the domain of

[29] See Posner, note 3 above, at 35–36; *Toward a Theory of the Rent-Seeking Society* (James M. Buchanan, Robert D. Tollison, and Gordon Tullock eds. 1980).

patent and trade secrets law—does. The principal investment required is the author's time, which he could be using to make a surer income either from some other, economically more secure occupation or from some secure, more conventional form of literary endeavor. Is this cost in opportunities forgone great enough to warrant a costly expansion in the existing copyright protection for literature? The information necessary to answer this question has never been gathered. One is not even sure that *any* copyright protection is necessary to generate the socially optimal amount of book production, given the advantages that accrue to the first publisher (it takes a while to copy) and the fact that royalties are usually only a small fraction of the overall cost of producing and selling a book.[30]

Economists emphasize another cost of copyright protection. By increasing the cost and hence the price of each copy sold of a book, copyright reduces the number of copies sold, thereby deflecting potential readers to substitute products that may cost society more to produce. This problem can exist even if the author's total royalty income is just equal to his costs of writing the book. For it might be that one extra copy could be made and sold at a cost less than that of a substitute product, if only the royalty were eliminated; then the author would not be harmed, but a potential buyer would be benefited. Unfortunately, costs of information and of preventing resale (arbitrage) make it infeasible to vary the price of a book continuously over all copies and all buyers so that the royalty component does not result in the loss of a single sale that would cover the costs of making and selling one more copy.

From a literary standpoint, the most serious objection to an expansion of copyright protection is that the expansion might reduce the output of literature by increasing the royalty expense of writers. If every author of an epic poem had had to pay royalties to Homer's heirs,[31] then Virgil, Dante, Milton, Pope, and others would have had to incur an additional

---

[30] Compare Stephen Breyer, "The Uneasy Case for Copyright: A Study of Copyright in Books, Photocopies, and Computer Programs," 84 *Harvard Law Review* 281 (1970), with Barry W. Tyerman, "The Economic Rationale for Copyright Protection for Published Books: A Reply to Professor Breyer," 18 *UCLA Law Review* 1100 (1971). There is an especially powerful argument for copyright protection of plays, since without it the author will have an incentive not to publish, in order to prevent copying.

[31] On the influence of Homer on subsequent epic writers, see the interesting discussion in Martin Mueller, *The Iliad*, chap. 7 (1984). The topic of literary influence is vast. For a painstaking examination of one great writer's influence see Raymond Dexter Havens, *The Influence of Milton on English Poetry* (1922), and for an excellent study of the entire subject of artistic influence see Göran Hermerén, *Influence in Art and Literature* (1975). See also Ruthven, note 9 above, chap. 8; *Influx: Essays in Literary Influence* (Ronald Primeau ed. 1977).

expense to write their epics. The expense might have deflected some of them to a different literary form, or caused them to write less, resulting in a social loss unless the prospect of additional royalties for their great predecessor would have encouraged him to write an offsetting amount more. In principle, Homer's heirs would want to negotiate with each prospective writer of an epic a royalty schedule that would not deter the writer from writing it, since if he were deterred there would be no royalty. But this would be impossible in practice, and even if possible costly. The case of Dante suggests another problem—the definition of the property right when copyright is conceived broadly. He never read Homer, but he did read and in part imitate Virgil, and Virgil's *Aeneid* is modeled on the Homeric epics.

Examples like this, and the other arguments I have discussed, suggest that greater copyright protection for works of literature would be undesirable; but what about the desirability of less protection? The methods of Shakespeare suggest that copyright law even in its present modest scope—perhaps any copyright law, however narrow—inhibits literary creativity, at least of the type that his work displays. Shakespeare's characteristic mode of dramatic composition was to borrow the plot and most of the characters—and sometimes actual language—from an existing work of history or fiction but then to improve the plot, add some minor characters, alter the major ones, and write all or most of the dialogue. Alexander Lindey gives a good example of Shakespeare's "plagiarism" in *The Tempest*; notes (with considerable exaggeration, however) that "some of the most impressive passages in the Bard's Roman plays are Sir Thomas North's prose strung into blank verse";[32] and, most surprisingly, reports that of the 6,033 lines in the first three parts of *Henry VI*, 1,771 were copied intact (presumably from Holinshed) and 2,373 were paraphrased from the same source.[33]

[32] *Plagiarism and Originality* 75 (1952). Actually the poetic genius of Shakespeare is nowhere more evident than in his transformation of North-Plutarch's prose into the magnificent poetry of the Roman plays, for example Enobarbus's description of Cleopatra's barge—in turn brilliantly "plagiarized" by T. S. Eliot in Part II of *The Waste Land*.

[33] See Lindey, note 32 above, at 74–75. Lindey's book contains many other examples of plagiarism from various periods. See also Horace G. Ball, *The Law of Copyright and Literary Property* 1–6 (1944); Augustine Birrell, *Seven Lectures on the Law and History of Copyright in Books*, chap. 6 (1899); Paull, note 5 above, at chap. 9. On Dostoevsky's heavy borrowings from life and literature in *The Brothers Karamazov* see Victor Terras, *A Karamazov Companion: Commentary on the Genesis, Language, and Style of Dostoevsky's Novel* 11–24, 27–31 (1981). I shall not get into the tangled question of what Shakespeare's competitor Robert Greene meant when he called Shakespeare "an upstart Crow, beautified with our feathers." The view that this is an accusation of plagiarism is spiritedly argued in J. Dover Wilson, "Malone and the Upstart Crow," 4 *Shakespeare Survey* 56 (1951). See also Peter Berek, "The 'Upstart Crow,' Aesop's

*Measure for Measure* provides an excellent example of the trouble in which Shakespeare would have found himself in an age of copyright. Its main source, a play called *Promos and Cassandra*, had been written by George Whetstone in 1578, and thus was recent enough to have been protected by copyright when *Measure for Measure* was written, had there been copyright; I ignore the complication that Whetstone himself had done some heavy borrowing from his predecessors. The play is set in a Hungarian city where the law against fornication has for a long time not been enforced. Promos, the king's deputy, sentences Andrugio to death for fornication. Andrugio's sister, Cassandra, pleads with Promos for his life. Promos at first refuses but then relents on condition that she yield her body to him. She does so, but he reneges and orders the jailer to send him Andrugio's severed head. The jailer substitutes the head of another, recently executed felon. (The literary device of substituting someone else for the condemned goes back at least as far as Ovid's rendition of the legend of Jason and Medea. Ovid's heirs would have been among the greatest all-time beneficiaries of a system of perpetual royalties.) Cassandra complains to the king, who orders that Promos shall first marry Cassandra, then be beheaded. As soon as the marriage is solemnized, Cassandra discovers that she loves Promos, or at least that she owes him the duties of a wife; in any event she pleads movingly for his life. The king refuses till Andrugio—until then thought to be dead—steps forward; then the king pardons both Andrugio and Promos.

Shakespeare made the plot more ingenious and rewrote the dialogue completely, but he retained the theme of justice perverted by a corrupt judge. And even though he used none of Whetstone's dialogue he used enough nonobvious details of the plot to be guilty under modern law of copyright infringement (in all likelihood—the standards for infringement by paraphrase, that is, copying that is not verbatim, are notably vague, as perhaps in the nature of the problem they must be).[34] And

---

Crow, and Shakespeare as a Reviser," 35 *Shakespeare Quarterly* 205 (1984). Other scholars dispute this. See, for example, Leo Kirschbaum, "The Authorship of *1 Henry VI*," 67 *Publications of the Modern Language Association* 809, 814–815 (1952); Harold Ogden White, *Plagiarism and Imitation During the English Renaissance: A Study in Critical Distinctions* 100–106 (1933). The whole issue of the authorship of *Henry VI* is incredibly tangled. See Judith Hinchcliffe, *King Henry VI, Parts 1, 2 and 3: An Annotated Bibliography* 167–185 (1984).

[34] Judge Learned Hand drew the line between permissible and impermissible borrowing as follows: "If *Twelfth Night* were copyrighted, it is quite possible that a second comer might so closely imitate Sir Toby Belch or Malvolio as to infringe, but it would not be enough that for one of his characters he cast a riotous knight who kept wassail to the discomfort of the household, or a vain and foppish steward who became amorous of his mistress." *Nichols v. Universal Pictures Corp.*, 45 F.2d 119, 121 (2d Cir. 1930). A leading scholar, applying the test

since the plot of Whetstone's play was fictitious, Shakespeare could not have argued that he was plagiarizing history rather than Whetstone.

There was a notion of plagiarism in the Renaissance,[35] but it was more limited than the modern notion. The dominant theory of literary creativity, as it had been in classical and medieval times, was creative imitation: the imitator was free to borrow as long as he added to what he borrowed.[36] The modern equation of creativity to originality is a legacy of the Romantic era, with its cult of individual expression.[37] The older conception of creativity is illustrated by what Shakespeare did with North's translation of Plutarch in the barge scene in *Antony and Cleopatra*. Here is North:

> She disdained to set forward otherwise, but to take her barge in the river of Cydnus; the poop whereof was of gold, the sails of purple, and the oars of silver, which kept stroke in rowing after the sound of the music of flutes, hautboys, citterns, viols, and such other instruments as they played upon in the barge. And now for the person of her self, she was laid under a

of "substantial similarity" that many courts use, concludes that *West Side Story* would infringe *Romeo and Juliet* if the latter were copyrighted. *Nimmer on Copyright*, vol. 3, §13.03[A], pp. 13–26 to 13–27 (1986). By the same token, *Measure for Measure* would infringe *Promos and Cassandra*, and *Ragtime* would infringe *Michael Kohlhaas*, while *Romeo and Juliet* itself might infringe Ovid's story of Pyramus and Thisbe, the inspiration for Shakespeare's play. For illustrative cases (besides *Nichols*) in which courts are struggling to determine when paraphrase should be deemed copyright infringement, see Sheldon v. Metro-Goldwyn Pictures Corp., 81 F.2d 49 (2d Cir. 1936) (Judge Learned Hand again); Dymow v. Bolton, 11 F.2d 690 (2d Cir. 1926); MacDonald v. Du Maurier, 144 F.2d 696 (2d Cir. 1944); Reyher v. Children's Television Workshop, 533 F.2d 87 (2d Cir. 1976); Burroughs v. Metro-Goldwyn-Mayer, Inc., 683 F.2d 610 (2d Cir. 1982); Fendler v. Morosco, 253 N.Y. 281, 171 N.E. 56 (1930); Frankel v. Irwin, 34 F.2d 142 (S.D.N.Y. 1918); Echevarria v. Warner Bros. Pictures, Inc., 12 F. Supp. 632 (S.D. Cal. 1935); McConnor v. Kaufman, 49 F. Supp. 738 (S.D.N.Y.), affirmed, 139 F.2d 116 (2d Cir. 1943); Schwarz v. Universal Pictures Co., 85 F. Supp. 270 (S.D. Cal. 1945); Greenbie v. Noble, 151 F. Supp. 45 (S.D.N.Y. 1957); Burnett v. Lambino, 204 F. Supp. 327 (S.D.N.Y. 1962); Davis v. E. I. DuPont de Nemours & Co., 240 F. Supp. 612 (S.D.N.Y. 1965); Leeds Music, Ltd. v. Robin, 358 F. Supp. 650 (S.D. Ohio 1973); Universal City Studios, Inc. v. Film Ventures Int'l, Inc., 543 F. Supp. 1134 (C.D. Cal. 1982); Davis v. United Artists, Inc., 547 F. Supp. 722 (S.D.N.Y. 1982). On the copying and "paraphrasing" of paintings see the fascinating discussion in Hermerén, note 31 above, at 62–74.

[35] See the sources cited in note 33 above, and Thomas M. Greene, *The Light in Troy: Imitation and Discovery in Renaissance Poetry* (1982).

[36] As emphasized in White, note 33 above. See also Richard McKeon, "Literary Criticism and the Concept of Imitation in Antiquity," in *Critics and Criticism: Ancient and Modern* (R. S. Crane ed. 1952); Ruthven, note 9 above, chap. 7 and pp. 123–124. A particularly good treatment of both plagiarism and imitation in the Renaissance is Stephen Orgel, "The Renaissance Artist as Plagiarist," 48 *ELH* 476 (1981). Modern instances of literary plagiarism are discussed in Peter Shaw, "Plagiary," 51 *American Scholar* 325 (1982).

[37] See, for example, Ruthven, note 9 above, chap. 7; Hermerén, note 31 above, at 129–144; Edward Young, *Conjectures on Original Composition* (1759).

pavilion of cloth of gold of tissue, apparelled and attired like the goddess
Venus, commonly drawn in picture: and hard by her, on either hand of her,
pretty fair boys apparelled as painters do set forth god Cupid, with little
fans in their hands, with the which they fanned wind upon her.[38]

There is much more, but I will stop here and quote the corresponding
passage in Shakespeare:

> The barge she sat in, like a burnish'd throne,
> Burnt on the water. The poop was beaten gold;
> Purple the sails, and so perfumed that
> The winds were love-sick with them; the oars were silver,
> Which to the tune of flutes kept stroke, and made
> The water which they beat to follow faster,
> As amorous of their strokes. For her own person,
> It beggar'd all description: she did lie
> In her pavilion—cloth-of-gold of tissue—
> O'er-picturing that Venus where we see
> The fancy outwork nature. On each side her
> Stood pretty dimpled boys, like smiling Cupids,
> With divers-color'd fans, whose wind did seem
> To glow the delicate cheeks which they did cool,
> And what they undid did. (II.2.201-215)

And here for good measure is T. S. Eliot's version, in Part II of *The
Waste Land*:

> The Chair she sat in, like a burnished throne,
> Glowed on the marble, where the glass
> Held up by standards wrought with fruited vines
> From which a golden Cupidon peeped out
> (Another hid his eyes behind his wing)
> Doubled the flames of sevenbranched candelabra
> Reflecting light upon the table as
> The glitter of her jewels rose to meet it.

In both cases there is unmistakable copying. In Shakespeare's the
beautifying effect is astonishingly vivid, while Eliot's pastiche of
Shakespeare achieves an ironic reduction. In an age of copyright,
Shakespeare, to be able to write the plays in the form in which we have
them, would have had to get licenses from the owners of copyrights on

---

[38] Plutarch, "The Life of Marcus Antonius" (translated by Sir Thomas North, 1579), in
*Shakespeare and His Sources* 575, 577 (Joseph Satin ed. 1966). For more on Shakespeare's sources
see Kenneth Muir, *The Sources of Shakespeare's Plays* (1978); cf. *Shakespeare's Plutarch* (T. J. B.
Spencer ed. 1964).

works from which he took plot details or actual language.[39] The costs of finding and negotiating with each copyright owner might have reduced Shakespeare's output, or changed (for the worse—else presumably he would have made the change on his own) his method of composition. The expense of the royalties themselves might also have had these effects, but there might have been offsetting effects as a result of the encouragement that greater copyright protection would have given Shakespeare's predecessors.

Thus, although an expansion of copyright protection might—as in the example of copyrighting an entire genre, such as epic—be devastating for literary creativity, even the existing scope of copyright protection may be damaging to it. Much literature, not only by Shakespeare, builds on previous works in a way that would be copyright infringement if the works borrowed from were copyrighted. The best theory of the composition of the Homeric epics is that the genius (or geniuses) whom we call Homer reorganized, and added extensive finishing touches to, existing epic works.[40] *The Waste Land* is a tissue of quotations, though all from long-dead authors. The literary imagination is not a volcano of pure inspiration but a weaving of the author's experience of life into an existing literary tradition.[41] The more extensive copyright protection is, the more inhibited is the literary imagination. This is not a good reason for abolishing copyright altogether, as we shall see; but it is a reason possibly for narrowing it, and more clearly for not broadening it.

In the extraordinary allusiveness of Eliot's poetry we find a concrete reason for his hostility to the Romantic movement. To the Romantic idea of creativity as originality Eliot opposes, and in his

---

[39] Although there was no copyright law in Shakespeare's day, the Stationers' Company had a monopoly of printing, and this gave the company the equivalent of copyright protection. With the decline of the company a need for a copyright law was felt, and the first general copyright law (in England) was passed at the beginning of the eighteenth century. See Benjamin Kaplan, *An Unhurried View of Copyright*, chap. 1 (1967); Philip Wittenberg, *The Protection of Literary Property*, chap. 1 (1968).

[40] See, for example, Seth L. Schein, *The Mortal Hero: An Introduction to Homer's Iliad*, chap. 1 (1984), and references there. Or as Rudyard Kipling put it:

> When 'Omer smote 'is bloomin' lyre,
>     He'd 'eard men sing by land and sea;
> An' what he thought 'e might require,
>     'E went an' took—the same as me!

[41] See, for example, Anatole France, *On Life and Letters* 149 (Bernard Miall trans. 1924); T. S. Eliot, "Tradition and the Individual Talent," in *Selected Prose of T. S. Eliot* 37 (Frank Kermode ed. 1975).

poems exemplifies, the older idea of creativity as imitation with enrichment.

      PARODY and burlesque are ancient and important literary genres[42] (*The Battle of Frogs and Mice*, for example, is an ancient Greek parody of the *Iliad*) that have given rise to extensive copyright litigation.[43] Parodies often depend for their effect on copying distinctive features of the original, as in this parody, from Part II of *The Sweeniad* by the pseudonymous "Myra Buttle," of the opening stanza of *The Waste Land* (footnote omitted):

> Sunday is the dullest day, treating
> Laughter as profane sound, mixing
> Worship and despair, killing
> New thought with dead forms.
> Weekdays give us hope, tempering

[42] See *Parodies: An Anthology from Chaucer to Beerbohm—And After* (Dwight Macdonald ed. 1960); *The Faber Book of Parodies* (Simon Brett ed. 1984); *American Literature in Parody: A Collection of Parody, Satire, and Literary Burlesque of American Writers Past and Present* (Robert P. Falk ed. 1955); Walter Hamilton, *Parodies of the Works of English and American Authors* (6 vols., 1884–1889). Scholarly treatments include Linda Hutcheon, *A Theory of Parody: The Teachings of Twentieth-Century Art Forms* (1985); Gilbert Highet, *The Anatomy of Satire*, pt. 3 (1962); G. D. Kiremidjian, "The Aesthetics of Parody," 28 *Journal of Aesthetics and Art Criticism* 231 (1969). Literary critics frequently use the term "parody" quite broadly, to refer to any imitative literary composition—an immense category even when limited to modern times. See, for example, Hutcheon, above; John Barth, "The Literature of Exhaustion," 220 *Atlantic* 29 (1967); David Bennett, "Parody, Postmodernism, and the Politics of Reading," 27 *Critical Quarterly* 27 (winter 1985).

[43] See, for example, Note, "The Parody Defense to Copyright Infringement: Productive Fair Use after *Betamax*," 97 *Harvard Law Review* 1395 (1984); Leon R. Yankwich, "Parody and Burlesque in the Law of Copyright," 33 *Canadian Bar Review* 1130 (1955); Sheldon N. Light, "Parody, Burlesque, and the Economic Rationale for Copyright," 11 *Connecticut Law Review* 615 (1979); Richard A. Bernstein, "Parody and Fair Use in Copyright Law," 31 *Copyright Law Symposium (ASCAP)* 1 (1984); Michael C. Albin, "Beyond Fair Use: Putting Satire in Its Proper Place," 33 *UCLA Law Review* 518 (1985); Harriette K. Dorsen, "Satiric Appropriation and the Law of Libel, Trademark, and Copyright: Remedies without Wrongs," 65 *Boston University Law Review* 923 (1985). I omit the issue of *droit moral* (moral right), a European doctrine which gives authors and artists a right to prevent mutilations or other alterations in their work that might impair their artistic reputation. The doctrine has been rejected in all but a handful of our states, though similar protection is sometimes available under copyright, contract, or unfair competition law. For a sample of the extensive literature on the subject see Martin A. Roeder, "The Doctrine of Moral Right: A Study in the Law of Artists, Authors and Creators," 53 *Harvard Law Review* 554 (1940); Note, "Authors' and Artists' Rights in the United States: A Legal Fiction," 10 *Hofstra Law Review* 557 (1982); Phyllis Amarnick, "American Recognition of the Moral Right: Issues and Options," 29 *Copyright Law Symposium (ASCAP)* 31 (1983).

Work with reviving play, promising
A future life within this one.
Thirst overtook us, conjured up by Budweisserbrau
On a neon sign: we counted our dollar bills.
Then out into the night air, into Maloney's Bar,
And drank whiskey, and yarned by the hour.
*Das Herz ist gestorben*, swell dame, echt Bronx.
And when we were out on bail, staying with the Dalai Lama,
My uncle, he gave me a ride on a yak,
And I was speechless. He said, Mamie,
Mamie, grasp his ears. And off we went
Beyond Yonkers, then I felt safe.
I drink most of the year and then I have a Vichy.

Direct though the copying so often is, parody is rarely held to infringe copyright, the main reasons being (I conjecture) two. First, many parodies are intended as criticisms of the original,[44] and for the author to be able to suppress criticism would interfere with the literary marketplace and distort the test of time. Second (and closely related), a parody is not intended to be a substitute for the original, in the way that *Measure for Measure* was a substitute for *Promos and Cassandra*; therefore, except insofar as it is effective criticism, the parody should not diminish the sales of the original author's work and indeed may increase them.

The difficult case is that of the noncritical parody, perhaps better described as "burlesque." It is best illustrated by Jack Benny's burlesque of *Gas Light*.[45] Benny was not making fun of *Gas Light* the way "Myra Buttle" was making fun of *The Waste Land*, any more than Abbott and Costello were making fun of *Frankenstein* or *Dracula* in *Abbott and Costello Meet Frankenstein*. Humorous but not ridiculing versions of the original, these burlesques are derivative works in a pure form, and modern copyright law gives the copyright holder the exclusive right to make such works. A derivative work is a substitute, though an imperfect one, for the original; it may therefore siphon revenues from the original work not by disparaging that work but by satisfying part of the demand for it. So maybe the law should try to distinguish between parody and burlesque and treat the latter but not the former as infringing. The difficulty of doing this should be obvious. Yet the law may already be doing it implicitly by the emphasis it places on whether

---

[44] An excellent discussion with many examples is Joe Lee Davis, "Criticism and Parody," 26 *Thought* 180 (1951). See also J. G. Riewald, "Parody as Criticism," 50 *Neophilologus* 125 (1966).
[45] See Benny v. Loew's Inc., 239 F.2d 532 (9th Cir. 1956), affirming a judgment against Benny.

the allegedly infringing work is fulfilling the demand for the original work (which a parody does not do); if so it is a derivative work, and infringing.[46]


     ALTHOUGH the modern emphasis on originality is Romantic, copyright law is not purely a Romantic legacy. The first copyright law in England was passed at the beginning of the eighteenth century and might have been passed earlier if books had not been so expensive—as I noted earlier, when copying is costly the gains from copyright protection are reduced—and if printing had not been licensed. Even when the theory of literary creativity is one of creative imitation rather than original expression, the imitator will want protection for the details he adds; otherwise he may not be able to recoup the cost of his investment in making them. Although a strong copyright law might have inhibited Shakespeare's creativity, the absence of any copyright law may be one reason why neither he nor his theatrical company (which owned the manuscripts) took any steps to get his plays published, and why, therefore, many of the texts we possess are so corrupt.[47]

But no doubt the law we have today is stronger than it would be if the theory of literary creativity had remained one of creative imitation. So if the theory of literary creativity ever swings back toward creative imitation, the copyright law, which in its present form reflects the Romantic conception of creativity, will inhibit the swing. The law would have to be changed before the new theory of creativity could be fully applied. The change would no doubt focus on the defense of fair use,[48] whereby (in its simplest form) a book reviewer or a subsequent author is allowed to quote a brief snippet from a copyrighted work without the owner's permission—more in the case of parody, for reasons already indicated. This defense could be expanded to allow more extensive literary borrowings. But not only would the scope of the expanded defense be hard to define with precision; any expansion would burden literary creativity at the same time that it benefited it, by reducing the copyright protection of the author whose work was being made use of. If through fair use a subsequent author is able to convey the

---

[46] See, for example, Berlin v. E.C. Publications, Inc., 329 F.2d 541, 545 (2d Cir. 1964); Fisher v. Dees, 794 F.2d 432, 437–438 (9th Cir. 1986); Note, note 43 above, at 1398–1400.

[47] See generally Horace Davis, "Shakespeare and Copyright," 71 *Atlantic Monthly* 256 (1893).

[48] See 17 U.S.C. §107; William Fisher, "The Trouble with the Fair Use Doctrine" (forthcoming in *Harvard Law Review*); Posner, note 3 above, at 38; Thomas R. Leavens, "In Defense of the Unauthorized Use: Recent Developments in Defending Copyright Infringement," 44 *Law and Contemporary Problems* 3 (autumn 1981).

essence of the first author, only improved, why buy the first author's books? Who would have gone to see the *Ur-Hamlet* (see Chapter 1) after Shakespeare wrote *Hamlet*?

To answer these questions would require a more comprehensive study, not only of literature but of the conditions of writing and publishing today, than I can provide in this book. Although I believe that the law and literature movement can help to improve the legal regulation of literature in the areas of defamation and invasion of privacy, obscenity, and copyright, more work must be done to vindicate this faith, and two cautionary notes must be sounded. The first is that despite my earlier suggestion that books can be distinguished from the visual media, many of the legal problems cut right across the distinction, as we saw in discussing burlesque. And since today so much more of the "action" in copyright, defamation, and obscenity law is in the visual media, a focus on the application of these bodies of law to literature may miss important precedents and analogies. Moreover, even within the category of books, the problems (especially of copyright and defamation) encountered by authors and publishers of "nonliterary" books are similar to those encountered by "literary" authors and publishers.

Second, a related point, the fact that at any moment most literature is, almost by definition, old makes the legal regulation of literature almost a misnomer. What is regulated is fictional or imaginative writing some fraction of which will someday be recognized as literature, plus nonfiction some (presumably smaller) fraction of which may someday be recognized as literature, too. Since the study of literature is for the most part the study of the past, while only works currently being written encounter problems of defamation, copyright, or obscenity, the student of literature may have only a modest contribution to make to these branches of law after all. But modest is not zero.

# Conclusion

*T* IS TIME to summarize the results of this inquiry into law and literature and to consider its institutional implications. In a book devoted so heavily to the close reading of specific texts and the examination of specific issues in the theory and practice of interpretation, pithy summarization is difficult; this chapter can only recapitulate the major themes and conclusions of the book.

The book has registered a warm though qualified enthusiasm for the field of law and literature. I have been critical of several of its practitioners and have rejected the grandest claims that have been made on its behalf, such as that it can illuminate the Holocaust or debunk the economic approach to law. The interdisciplinary study of law and literature will not transform either the study of law or the study of literature. For some students and teachers in each field, however, and, in law, for some judges and practicing lawyers, it can provide a valuable supplementary perspective, stimulating new insights and inquiries. It can do this as much by stressing the differences as the similarities between law and literature; the ability to make distinctions is as important to knowledge as the ability to make connections.

In general, the lawyer's training and experience do not equip him to read imaginative literature—even that nominally "about" law—with greater insight than specialists in literary criticism, or indeed ordinary cultivated readers; that was a principal theme of Part I. The legal element in literature is for the most part metaphoric, and the lawyer has no greater comparative advantage in studying literature that is about law in a metaphoric sense than a military historian or tactician has in studying literature that is about war in the same sense. But this is in general, not in every case. Shakespeare, with his remarkable range and penetration, worked law in more than merely its metaphoric sense into the fabric of

*The Merchant of Venice* and *Measure for Measure*, and maybe a lawyer can say something new about these works and correct some misunderstandings about them.[1] *Bleak House* and *Doctor Faustus*, and Kafka's parable *The Problem of Our Laws*, may be other instances where the lawyer's perspective can assist the reader to a greater understanding and enjoyment of works of literature. A lawyer can also help the American reader understand features of the Continental system of criminal justice that figure in such novels as *Crime and Punishment, The Trial,* and *The Stranger* (this is one of Richard Weisberg's contributions), and no doubt could perform a parallel service for Continental readers of English and American literature that contains legal material.

The lawyer-critic can also contribute to the study of literature by identifying recurrent features of the literary treatment of law. Recall how in works as otherwise diverse as *Eumenides, The Brothers Karamazov, Pudd'nhead Wilson,* and *The Stranger* a trial is used to provide a dramatic confrontation between rational methods of inquiry and the nonrational side of human nature. (*Billy Budd* may be another example.) Recall the preference shown by writers of imaginative literature for legal arguments based on technicalities, their fondness for strict liability and for miscarriages of justice, and how the choice between adversary and inquisitorial procedure in the literary depiction of the legal process seems correlated with tonal or thematic differences between works of literature. Recall the liberties that authors so often take with the law, not to misrepresent or to criticize the law but for dramatic effect. Recall the intricate structure of revenge tragedy, and its implied commentary on the rule of law. Literature on legal themes composes a coherent though varied order of literary works; it can, despite its diversity, be studied profitably as a unity.

Turning to how the study of literature might enrich law, rather than vice versa, I do not expect it to bring about *fundamental* changes in our understanding of legal institutions—but the qualification should be noted. Revenge literature can supply insights into the nature and origins of law by depicting the system of justice that precedes an organized legal system, provides a template for the legal system when law first emerges, reasserts itself when the legal system breaks down, and, because of its personalistic and emotional character, offers an illuminating contrast to the ideals of impersonality, neutrality, and objectivity that inform the law

---

[1] Just as a political theorist has been able to make interesting observations about Shakespeare's plays. See Allan Bloom (with Harry V. Jaffa), *Shakespeare's Politics* (1964). See also *Shakespeare as Political Thinker* (John Alvis and Thomas G. West eds. 1981), a collection of essays by literary critics and political scientists.

and, as we saw, disturb writers of literature (for example, Shakespeare in *Measure for Measure*). The reason why revenge literature has not heretofore engaged the interest of the law and literature movement may be that the social practice of revenge, despite its importance for legal theory, falls outside the narrow limits of professional training in law. The "literary lawyer" may therefore fail to recognize revenge literature as a body of texts potentially within his ken. This is an argument for broadening legal education along other dimensions as well as the literary.

The body of literature more directly "about" law—such as *Antigone*, *Bleak House*, *Billy Budd*, and *The Trial*, as well as Shakespeare's "legal plays"—contains some very great works indeed, and although they have rather little to say about law that will strike a lawyer as relevant to his professional concerns, this is partly due to the narrowness of legal training and the resulting narrowness of the lawyer's idea of law. Mainly the law as it appears in these works of literature is, as I have said, metaphorical; the authors have other fish to fry. Yet these works can stimulate the lawyer who reads them with the proper receptivity to fruitful reflections on the tension between formal legal concepts and broader ethical notions of justice, and within law itself between the various polarities of "ruledness" and discretion summarized in the Table of Opposed Conceptions of Law in Chapter 2. I hope the trade-school characteristics of much legal training will not dash this hope. Law must become more theoretical in ways superficially unrelated to literature before the law and literature movement can come fully into its own.

I argued against Ronald Dworkin and others that literary theory and literary criticism have little relevance to the interpretation of statutory and constitutional texts—so different are literary and legal texts in character, origins, and (above all) use or social function—despite the attempts made recently to apply New Critical, intentionalist, and even deconstructive techniques to legal texts. But since many scholars disagree with me on this point, the well-educated lawyer should have some acquaintance with current controversies in literary theory and their potential bearing on legal interpretation. Moreover, an understanding of the differences between legal and literary interpretation may improve our understanding of the former indirectly. The lawyer who understands the limitations of reader-centered literary criticism may be less eager to attempt a parallel approach to legal texts, while the lawyer who understands the importance of allusion and other aspects of context in the interpretation of literary works (recall the discussion of *Easter 1916*) may be less likely to embrace the opposite fallacy of interpreting legal texts literal-mindedly.

I pointed out in Chapter 6 that judicial opinions often employ literary devices, and not merely as ornaments. A student of literature may be quicker to spot these than a lawyer would be. The literary critic can also help us to understand the staying power of an opinion like Justice Holmes's dissent in *Lochner,* can criticize opinions that lack the literary artist's respect for language and reality, and can differentiate among judicial styles and stylists. Such a critic can help us see what I believe may be a warp in the scholarly evaluation of judicial opinions, illustrated by David Currie's strictures on the opinions of Chief Justice Marshall and Justice Holmes. It should be recognized, however, that an alternative approach which may be equally fruitful is through the study of semantics, sociolinguistics, rhetoric, the philosophy of mind and language, and other branches of (or related to) communication and language theory.

Finally, the literary critic, or the lawyer knowledgeable about literature, should be able to cast some light on the legal regulation of literature under the rubrics of defamation, obscenity, and copyright. (The general point has broad application to legal education and scholarship: intelligent legal reform requires a deeper knowledge of the practices regulated by the law than lawyers qua lawyers have.) A practical impediment is that literature is only a corner of the expressive and communicative domain that is the subject of the law of defamation, obscenity, and copyright—and the main legal "action" lies elsewhere within it. Indeed, the character of literature as writing that survives after the original cause for its creation has disappeared makes it an inherently elusive subject for a study of current legal regulation. Yet the law and literature perspective does provide arguments for curtailing liability for defamation by fiction, for resisting the feminist attack on pornography, and, perhaps, for somewhat curtailing copyright protection in the interest (paradoxical as this may seem) of promoting literary creativity.

I am a little concerned lest law and literature be oversold as a field of interdisciplinary study. I do not think the field will expose the roots of fascism, overthrow conventional understandings—if there are any—of such classics as *Hamlet* and *Billy Budd,* humanize law, reveal the deepest flaws of capitalism, socialism, or Christianity, solve the age-old problem of objectivity in law, or bring on (or forestall) the universal reign of text skepticism. Those who state or imply that it will do any of these things are either taking undue liberties with literary texts or exaggerating the implications of literary theory for law. Moreover, it damages literature to press it into the service of political debate. Some people think that the way to preserve literature in the twentieth century is to make it speak to twentieth-century problems. But what literature speaks to are the eternal problems of the human condition, not the specific manifestations of those problems in the politics of our century. We are apt to miss what is distinctive in works of literature if we turn them into propaganda tracts, even or perhaps especially on such urgent questions as genocide, totalitarianism, racial discrimination, and the politics of law. By insisting on the separateness of law and literature, even while exploring their interactions, we help preserve both fields.

Granted, my conception of the limitations of the law and literature field may reflect the limitations of my own approach—one aspect of which is a reluctance, not universally shared these days, to make literary texts the launching pads for flights of critical fancy. I reject the most free-wheeling methods of interpretation (or noninterpretation). This rejection, combined with my personal—and again contestable—unease with Romantic values, prevents me from accepting the approaches of Richard Weisberg and Robin West to the specific works of literature that they discuss. Those scholars view these works as screeds rejecting conventional norms of legality and justice, and I am not convinced that the works will bear such an interpretation. I am also unconvinced by the arguments of White and Teachout that a humanistic approach to law, even perhaps one lacking in distinctive substantive content, is a necessary and proper antidote to an instrumental conception of law. But I hope I have explained, and not merely asserted, my grounds for disagreement with these scholars.

Another reason for my doubting some of the larger claims made on behalf of the law and literature movement is my belief, stated at a number of critical points in my analysis of the relation between law and literature, in a "survival" theory of literature.[2] This theory supports my claims that the frequency of legal subject matter in literature is accidental, that the interpretive problems of literary texts are fundamentally different from those of legal texts, and that to speak of the legal regulation of "literature" as a distinct category of law is problematic. To round out my list of negatives I remind the reader that in discussing the

---

[2] A theory that itself reflects an economic outlook, for economics and evolutionary biology are closely related. See Armen A. Alchian, "Uncertainty, Evolution, and Economic Theory," 58 *Journal of Political Economy* 211 (1950); Gary S. Becker, "Altruism, Egoism, and Genetic Fitness: Economics and Sociobiology," 14 *Journal of Economic Literature* 817 (1976); J. Hirshleifer, "Economics from a Biological Viewpoint," 20 *Journal of Law and Economics* 1, 9–16 (1977); and his "Natural Economy versus Political Economy," 1 *Journal of Social and Biological Structures* 319 (1978), and "The Expanding Domain of Economics," 75 *American Economic Review Special Anniversary Issue* 53, 64–66 (Dec. 1985).

moralistic or didactic tradition in literary criticism I argued that literature does not make us better (or worse) people.


MAYBE I underestimate the potential of the law and literature enterprise. But a more important point is that even if I do not, the field deserves a place in legal teaching and research. Law schools should offer courses in law and literature; some are doing so already. Most of the issues that would be covered in such a course could, it is true, be covered in a course on jurisprudence or legal process stressing the rhetoric, ethical underpinnings and dilemmas, interpretive problems, and epistemology of law. But such a course is not likely to be so vivid, memorable, and entertaining as a well-taught course in law and literature. There are grand legal cases and a fine secondary literature dealing with such issues as the choice between law and equity, the balance between rules and standards, positive law versus natural law, the transformation of revenge into law, the discretionary enforcement of obsolete law, provocation and forgiveness, the rhetoric of judicial opinions, and the ambiguity of language and consequent difficulty of interpretation. But law students who are open to the appeal that literature makes to a select few in an electronic age may find it most rewarding to address these and other jurisprudential topics in a perspective shaped by works of literature.[3] A course in law and literature can also provide an introduction to legal history, legal anthropology, and comparative law (recall the discussion of *The Stranger*). It may even provide a solution to the age-old problem of teaching legal writing. In addition, law and literature provides a way into feminist legal theory (touched on in Chapters 2 and 7), the law-as-a-humanity movement (see Chapter 6), and the critical legal studies movement (see Chapters 2, 4, and 5), some of whose practitioners are attempting to use literary theories (including, I have argued, an inaccurate conception of deconstruction) to undermine conventional understandings of legal texts and institutions. Although many law professors find the critical legal studies movement appalling in its political radicalism and childish incivilities,[4] it looms too large on the contemporary horizon of academic law to be ignored. And the major works of Continental philosophy that provide the movement with such intellectual steam as it has—works by Nietz-

---

[3] Saul Touster, "Parables for Judges," 27 *Boston Bar Journal*, Nov. 1983, at 4, describes an interesting continuing legal education course in law and literature for judges.
[4] Well illustrated by Allen David Freeman and John Henry Schlegel, "Sex, Power and Silliness: An Essay on Ackerman's *Reconstructing American Law*," 6 *Cardozo Law Review* 847 (1985).

sche, the German hermeneuticists, Wittgenstein, Derrida, and others—do bear on modern problems of American jurisprudence and are more easily approached through literature than by other routes. Finally, professors who teach courses dealing with the legal regulation of literature, such as tort law (defamation), constitutional law (obscenity), and copyright law, would do well to bring the literary perspective into the classroom.

I want to amplify my remark about the teaching of legal writing. Legal education involves imparting skills of analysis but also skills of presentation, of advocacy broadly understood. Rather little effort, however, is made in leading law schools (an important qualification) to impart the latter skills. The main vehicle is moot court programs, in which students practice briefing and arguing appellate cases. Mainly this is learning by doing; there is little instruction. The instructional component is slight because instruction in advocacy is thought to lack intellectual content and because such instruction is labor-intensive and therefore expensive. The possibility of teaching advocacy from the great literary examples of eloquence and persuasion, such as the funeral orations in *Julius Caesar*, has been overlooked. Yet what better way to impart a feeling for the essentials of advocacy than by careful study and comparison of Brutus's and Antony's speeches?[5] Among the weaknesses in Brutus's speech, which are equally weaknesses when found in an oral argument to an appellate court or a closing argument to a jury, are its overtly rhetorical character (which puts the audience—equivalent to the tribunal in a law case—on its guard), its failure to engage the audience in dialogue, its abstractness and lack of detail or anecdote, its failure to appeal to the concrete self-interest of the audience (equivalent to the concerns, which also are often quite parochial, of a legal tribunal), its failure to present evidence to support the crucial charge (Caesar's ambition), and the decision to waive rebuttal by departing before Antony begins to speak. Antony makes no such mistake. After neatly and "unrhetorically" (that is, with studied casualness) ingratiating himself with an audience predisposed to be hostile, he plunges directly into Brutus's only charge against Caesar (ambition) and offers three arguments against it. They are far from airtight, but since Antony has the last word he need not worry about rebuttal. He then displays emotion; brandishes Caesar's will (his first use of a prop); tells an

---

[5] "There can be no better introduction to the study of English law than the speeches of the Attic orators." F. A. Paley and J. E. Sandys, *Select Private Orations of Demosthenes* viii (3d ed. 1898). See George Kennedy, *The Art of Persuasion in Greece* 126–152 (1963), on Attic legal oratory.

anecdote about Caesar; displays Caesar's body (second use of a prop); shows the gashes and bloodstains in Caesar's toga, and then dramatically unveils the maimed body itself (the third prop, all of these props corresponding to physical evidence and visual aids in a trial or appeal); disclaims oratorical ability in a successful attempt to disarm the audience; uses the terms of the will to appeal to the audience's concrete interests and sense of gratitude; invites frequent interruption to create the impression of conversation rather than monologue; and moves about on the stage. He thus "proves" his points with a variety of demonstrative, kinetic, emotional devices (including meter, sarcasm, repetition, and suspense). It is a veritable catalogue of rhetorical tricks and turns. Concrete, vivid, personal, conversational, versatile, dramatic, empathetic with his audience, Antony is supremely effective at persuasion.

The optimal tactics for persuading the Roman mob are not the same as those for persuading a panel of professional judges; but Antony's speech shows that the problem is indeed a tactical one or at least has an important tactical dimension. One must know one's audience, one's case, and one's opponent, and one must fashion a strategy and tactics of persuasion from that knowledge, drawing on a rich repertoire of rhetorical devices vividly displayed in literature.

To all this it may be replied that the law student can be assumed to have learned all that can be learned from *Julius Caesar* or equivalent masterpieces of rhetoric from his or her undergraduate education. There was a time in this country when undergraduates studied rhetoric by declaiming the funeral orations from *Julius Caesar*,[6] but that time is long gone. Most law students today, even at the best law schools, have little acquaintance with the classics of Western literature. This is partly because new academic fields such as computer science, and old fields of increasing prestige and sophistication such as mathematics and economics, have crowded out curricular space formerly devoted to literature; partly because television and the movies have drained considerable interest away from literature; and partly because professors of literature have lost confidence in their authority to prescribe a fixed canon of classical works in the face of demands by women and members of minority groups for admission of works by the members of their groups to the canon. And many students are entering law school from "prelaw" programs in college, which take college time away from courses in the humanities and may produce a stunted race of legal specialists. A law teacher cannot assume that his students have any literary background at

---

[6] See Gerald Graff, *Professing Literature: An Institutional History* 41 (1987).

all. Yet the insights as well as the rhetorical devices of literature can be professional assets for lawyers. One function of a course on law and literature is to provide remedial education in literature—a remedial education not wasted even from the narrow perspective of purely professional goals.

Another overlooked method of instruction in legal advocacy is the study of the great fictional trials, such as the trial of Dmitri Karamazov, in which the elements of trial advocacy are displayed in a form at once more economical and more arresting than in the transcript of any actual trial. The performance of Dmitri's lawyer, Fetyukovitch, demonstrates not only cross-examination at its best but also two fundamental requirements of effective trial practice: meticulous preparation; and a theory of the case, which a trial lawyer creates by organizing, selecting, and recasting the raw events to make an intelligible, coherent, and appealing story. The analogy between what Fetyukovitch and his adversary do in their closing arguments and Dostoevsky's own activity as a novelist has not escaped notice.[7]

I am not suggesting that a course in law and literature should be placed at the center of the law school curriculum. The field lacks the theoretical coherence, convergent thrust, parallelism to legal doctrine, and practical application to lucrative fields of practice that have given the law and economics movement so important a place in the curriculum of leading law schools. Moreover, insofar as immersion in the field of law and literature may impart an excessively detached or skeptical view of legal doctrine, law students may be led to reject legal doctrine before they have learned it—a grave mistake for anyone planning to practice (or teach, or administer) law. I am not proposing a curricular revolution.

Teaching without research is not likely to appeal to many law professors at leading schools, so the next question is, what is the agenda of research on law and literature? If my analysis is correct, the application of literary methods to the analysis of judicial opinions and the legal regulation of literature are more promising subjects than the application either of legal methods and insights to literature or of literary methods to statutory and constitutional interpretation, though I certainly do not rule out the possibility of interesting work on the jurisprudential questions explored in Chapters 1 through 5 of this book; indeed, I hope those chapters have illustrated the possibility. There has

---

[7] See Victor Terras, *A Karamazov Companion: Commentary on the Genesis, Language, and Style of Dostoevsky's Novel* 108–109 (1981). Much of James White's rhetorical analysis can be understood in this light—that is, as instruction, with the aid of literature, in the higher forms of legal advocacy.

been relatively little work, however, on judicial opinions as literature and on legal regulation of literature—Chapters 6 and 7 just scratch the surface—so here are particularly good research opportunities.

What of legal studies in departments of literature? The research opportunities are limited, though hardly negligible; in any event a course in law and literature might be a worthwhile addition to the offerings in such departments. This would be particularly true if the course were open to undergraduates. Although young people's interest in law as a career may have declined some in recent years, it is still substantial, and a course in law and literature could provide undergraduates with a first glimpse of the law, in a setting made familiar to them by their other studies. Such a course could be made the core of prelaw programs, thus helping to overcome the tendency of such programs to narrow the cultural range of students who go on to law school. Of course it should be made clear to students that the literary depiction of law will give few clues to the actual conditions of a contemporary law practice.

One potentially troublesome feature of the law and literature movement is that it seems to draw some of its law-trained practitioners away from law. This may be because the field has relatively few applications to concrete practitioner problems in law as distinct from broader issues of jurisprudence and legal process. But the most important reason is that full participation in the movement requires immersion in a large and demanding body of materials—a reasonable cross-section of canonical works of literature, many written in foreign languages imperfectly translatable into English, plus satellite bodies of historical, critical, and literary-theoretical writing about literature—and all this for a relatively modest payoff in understanding law better. The field is thus likely to attract people more interested in literature than in law, yet law is itself a demanding field which demands immersion and not merely occasional visits.

But the important question is not whether law and literature should have a big place in the activities of universities but whether it should have a place at all, and I hope I have convinced the reader that it should. And if it should, this is one more piece of evidence that the study of law is undergoing fundamental change.[8] Until about twenty-five years ago the study of law was pretty universally considered a subject for lawyers only, using what they had learned in law school only, which was law (rather narrowly conceived) only. Today it is widely accepted that the study of law is inescapably interdisciplinary and that unless the academic

[8] See my article "The Decline of Law as an Autonomous Discipline: 1962–1987," 100 *Harvard Law Review* 761 (1987).

lawyer borrows the methods and insights of other fields, he will lose his right to dominate legal studies. Recognition of this point has progressed furthest with regard to the use of economics in the study of law, but philosophy is also making great strides, as are statistics, game theory, and other subjects. And now there is this new form of interdisciplinary legal studies, law and literature, making rapid strides though perhaps on short legs. Some of the "literary lawyers," as we saw in Chapter 6, see themselves as plugging the humanistic dikes against the inrush of economists and other technocrats. That is rubbish. There is no incompatibility among the interdisciplinary approaches. When they turn their minds to law, the economist and the literary critic have more in common with each other than with the "black letter" lawyer.

The biggest danger in any interdisciplinary field is amateurism. The lawyer who writes about literature may dazzle other lawyers, and the literary critic who writes about law may dazzle other literary critics, and in neither case may the dazzled be able to evaluate the quality of the contribution. The danger is particularly acute in the case of the lawyer who writes about literature, or the literary critic about law, for publication in law journals. The editors, who usually are law students and rarely use referees to evaluate work submitted for publication, are often unable to evaluate interdisciplinary work. The norms of scholarship in law are contested and ill defined to begin with, and they are in danger of breaking when stretched to take in interdisciplinary legal studies. A partial answer is the refereed, faculty-edited journal; one would like to see such a journal emerge in the law and literature field.

The situation in law and literature reflects the general problems of interdisciplinary legal scholarship, about which I have written elsewhere.[9] It is a melancholy reflection on law as a scholarly discipline that virtually all the creative thinking about interpretation has come in recent years from philosophy and literature, not from law. Although both law and literature have moved from a largely atheoretical stance in the 1950s to a position where theoretical concerns are prominent in both fields today, departments of literature have made the transition more successfully than law schools have. The former are organized in conventional academic fashion, with Ph.D. programs and refereed journals and faculty workshops and the other accoutrements of modern scholarly research. Law schools continue to provide what is essentially an undergraduate education in law (though to college graduates), administered by professors who have not undergone the rigors of a

---

[9] See my book *The Federal Courts: Crisis and Reform*, chap. 10 (1985).

Ph.D. program, who publish most of their scholarship in student-edited journals, who have no (or very few) graduate students, who are not schooled in the methodology of scholarly research, and who often place more emphasis on teaching and consulting than on research and writing.[10] As a result, much legal writing on topics in legal theory, such as interpretation, is naive or superficial, and legal theorists tend to be importers of ideas generated elsewhere in the university rather than exporters of ideas to other departments. This need not be so; and I hope this book will both promote the cause of interdisciplinary legal studies and encourage fresh thinking about the structure of academic law. But if it merely reawakens a delight in literature in some lawyers, or stimulates some fresh thinking on the eternal problems of law and justice, I shall be content.

[10] See George C. Christie, "The Recruitment of Law Faculty," 1987 *Duke Law Journal* 306.

# Index